ROOT OF BITTERNESS

ROOT of BITTERNESS

DOCUMENTS OF THE
SOCIAL HISTORY
OF AMERICAN WOMEN

SECOND EDITION

Edited, with an introduction, by

NANCY F. COTT
JEANNE BOYDSTON
ANN BRAUDE
LORI D. GINZBERG
MOLLY LADD-TAYLOR

NORTHEASTERN UNIVERSITY PRESS
BOSTON

Northeastern University Press

Library of Congress Cataloging-in-Publication Data
Root of bitterness : documents of the social history of American women
/ [edited by] Nancy F. Cott . . . [et al.]. — 2nd ed.
p. cm.
Includes bibliographical references.
ISBN 1-55553-255-1 (cloth : alk. paper). —ISBN 1-55553-256-X
(pbk. : alk. paper)
1. Women—United States—History—Sources. 2. Women—United
States—Social conditions—Sources. I. Cott, Nancy F.
HQ1410.R65   1996
305.4'0973—dc20   95-44965

Designed by Amy Bernstein

Composed in Berkeley by Coghill Composition, Richmond, Virginia.
Printed and bound by Edwards Brothers, Inc., Ann Arbor, Michigan.
The paper is Glatfelter Offset, an acid-free stock.

MANUFACTURED IN THE UNITED STATES OF AMERICA
00 99 98 97 96   5 4 3 2 1

That there is a root of bitterness continually springing up in families and troubling the repose of both men and women, must be manifest to even a superficial observer, and I believe it is the mistaken notion of the inequality of the sexes.

—Sarah Moore Grimké

Letters on the Equality of the Sexes and the Condition of Women, 1838

CONTENTS

VII. WOMEN'S WORK IN AN INDUSTRIAL AGE

VIII. NEW WOMEN, NEW WORLDS

ACKNOWLEDGMENTS

The collaboration that produced this anthology extended beyond its five editors to a wider network of historians, including students and former students, whose help we gratefully acknowledge. First, Holly Allen, Rachel Devlin, Ellen DuBois, Jacqueline Jones, Jane Levey, and Elizabeth Varon, who have used the first edition of *Root of Bitterness* in teaching undergraduates, very helpfully commented on the strengths and weaknesses of that collection. Second, a number of individuals responded generously to our requests for advice about the shape of the new book and about possible documents. To all of them—Holly Allen, Juliana Barr, Jon Butler, George Chauncey, Michael Denning, Ileen DeVault, Michael Edmonds, Sarah Fatherly, Drew Faust, Glenda Gilmore, Michael Goldberg, Sarah Barringer Gordon, William Hart, Hendrick Hartog, Susan Johnson, Jacqueline Jones, Jane Kamensky, Jean Lee, Jill Lepore, Teresita Martinez-Vergne, Stephanie McCurry, Sally McMurry, Anne Lewis Osler, Nell Painter, Peggy Pascoe, Leslie Schwalm, Christine Stansell, Michael Stevens, Brenda Stevenson, Rebecca Tannenbaum, and Elizabeth Varon—we are very grateful, whether or not we finally included documents they pointed out. Third, to those who located or provided us with copies of documents we published in this volume, we owe a special debt. Their names are noted on the first pages of the appropriate documents but they deserve additional acknowledgment here: Kathy Borkowski, Joan Cashin, George Chauncey, Mary Churchill, Ileen DeVault, Carolyn De Swarte Gifford, Glenda Gilmore, Michael Goldberg, Charlotte Haller, Clare Lyons, Colleen McDannell, Peter Nabakov, Dana Lee Robert, Bethel Saler, Christine Stansell, Brenda Stevenson, Rachel Seidman, Judith Tick, Elizabeth Varon—thank you for making our collection richer! Last, but certainly not least, we would like to express thanks to Juliana Barr, Monica Najar, Elaine Naylor, Joanne Passet, Jessica Steigerwald and Nancy Van Der Schee for excellent assistance in research; and also to Lee Cott and Bruner/Cott Associates, Joy P. Newmann, Joel Steiker and the folks at Praxis, Barbara Ruth Wells-Howe, Macalester College, and the History Department and the Institute for Research in Humanities of the University of Wisconsin-Madison, for personal and material support.

INTRODUCTION

This volume is an invitation to examine the range and depth of American women's past experiences. The documents collected here, written or spoken by or addressed to women, present particular instances and individuals in order to illustrate both the common and the disparate circumstances of women's lives. We hope that the documents will both inspire a host of questions—about women's family roles and their part in the transmission of culture, about the relation of women's work to the economy, about distinctions of age, marital status, class, region, religion, and race among women, for example—and provide evidence that helps to answer them.

The very existence of a volume such as this testifies to the tremendous growth in attention to women's history over the past twenty-five years. The women's movement of the 1960s and 1970s provoked new interest in the historical meanings of "woman's place," bringing to life a flourishing field of scholarly and popular endeavor. Now, in schools and colleges, community organizations and women's centers, museums and historical societies, many individuals delve into women's past and analyze the meanings of gender in history. New models of inquiry, in which women's lives and roles are central, have challenged traditional assumptions about which historical actors and issues are worth investigating.

The effort to rethink what is important in history and to retrieve women from their relative historical obscurity makes documents from the past essential. Mary Ritter Beard, a pathbreaker in women's history, captured this basic truth in 1940 when she wrote to Dorothy Porter, the librarian at Howard University: "Without documents; no history. Without history; no memory. Without memory; no greatness. Without greatness; no development among women."* We cannot hope (nor would we even aim) to document the lives of women in the United States over three centuries comprehensively in this anthology, but we can hope that our selection will be demonstrative and illustrative. That was the intent when Nancy Cott compiled the first edition of *Root of Bitterness* in 1972. At that time the feminist movement's concentration on sex roles, female socialization, and women's political consciousness of themselves informed the choice of documents. The newly emerging field of American women's history was then struggling to ascertain the historical relationship be-

*Mary Ritter Beard to Mrs. Dorothy Porter, Mar. 31, 1940, folder 1, box 1, series 4, National Council of Negro Women records, National Archives for Black Women's History, Bethune Museum-Archives, Washington, D.C.

tween mostly white, urban, elite, northeastern women's self-definitions and their culture's prescriptions for them as women. The first edition asked, consequently, what roles have women been compelled to take, and which ones have they chosen? How have they seen their circumstances and opportunities? How have they operated within the constraints placed upon them?

These questions still drive much scholarship and reflection. Twenty-five years later, however, new historical knowledge leads us to question whether there is "a complex unity that is American women's condition" as posited in the introduction to the 1972 edition. Each of the questions that book asked about American women as a group would now have to be clarified by the further question "which women?" Decades of research have produced an enormously diversified field of women's history, a growing acknowledgment of conflict among women, more understanding of the complex ways in which women have produced as well as con-fronted the dominant culture—and a staggeringly enlarged awareness of primary source materials. The present volume retains twenty-some docu-ments from the original *Root of Bitterness* but adds almost three times as many new ones. This greatly revised edition results from a collaboration among Cott and four co-editors—Jeanne Boydston, Ann Braude, Lori D. Ginzberg, and Molly Ladd-Taylor—all of whom were once graduate stu-dents under her direction. Thus, this edition marks the passage of several generations of women's historians into the academy and a spirit of com-radeship that has continued since the first (often nonacademic) endeav-ors in this field.

The collaborative nature of this collection makes it an arena of de-bate—a lively conversation among five historians deciding which histori-cal experiences to ferret out, study, represent, and interpret, and why and how they matter. In the process of selection and even in the overall emphases, each of us has adapted her own vision to some extent in order to reach consensus. The result is a volume that goes beyond individual inclinations and creates a richer mix than any one of us alone would have selected. Our collaborative process required not only locating and agreeing upon sources but also rethinking the appropriate framework for an overview of women's history in the United States from 1600 to 1900. We have focused on social history, making the lives and social relations of ordinary people of central interest. While some well-known names are included, the great majority of the documents originated with women who lived in relative anonymity. We present them less as representatives of distinct types than as individuals whose experiences allude to larger, recurring themes in the social history of women.

Six dominant themes emerge from the documents we have selected. Women's work—inside and outside the household—forms a major one. The documents reflect the fact that most women have spent most of their time working, whether to earn their sustenance, to support and nurture others in their families, or to benefit their communities. The indentured servant, the factory worker, the seamstress, the housewife, the slave, the midwife, the prostitute, the teacher, the missionary—these are some of the working women who appear in these pages.

Another prevalent theme—hard to name exactly—might be called the power of gender. Conceptions of masculinity and femininity have played a fundamental role in the ordering of American life. Documents in our collection convey some of the many ways in which women expressed or were affected by this societal ordering, which both differentiates between the sexes and creates inequality and hierarchy. The power of gender registers not only in the sexual division of labor apparent in these documents but also in the consciousnesses of the women and men speaking and writing, from Governor John Winthrop chastising Anne Hutchinson in the Massachusetts Bay Colony in 1637 ("We do not mean to discourse with those of your sex"), to tailoresses on strike in the 1830s analyzing urban workingwomen's oppression, to an African American educator addressing the condition of women in black sharecropping families in rural Alabama in 1901. The epigraph to our book (the source of its title) is a quotation from the early nineteenth-century theorist and reformer Sarah Moore Grimké, in which she acknowledges and rebels against the power of gender: "That there is a root of bitterness continually springing up in families and troubling the repose of both men and women, must be manifest to even a superficial observer, and I believe it is the mistaken notion of the inequality of the sexes." (Grimké took the phrase from the apostle Paul's biblical warning to the Hebrews to take care "lest any root of bitterness springing up trouble you" [Heb. 12:15]). Our collection tracks neither the organized women's rights movement nor the suffrage movement because it focuses on social history; nonetheless, it insistently reveals women's awareness of gender and shows resistance as well as accommodation to its power.

A related theme has to do with the body—specifically, the ways in which women's social relations react and refer to the physical body. Part 6, "Health, Medicine, and Sexuality," comes closest to making this theme explicit. It documents women's different experiences of their bodies, explores variations among cultures in the meanings borne by the female body, and suggests how a single culture may hold inconsistent views of the female body: for example, many nineteenth-century Americans believed that bourgeois women were physically frail while working-class women were strong and vigorous. Historically a powerful emblem of gender, the female body reappears as an issue far beyond part 6, too—from the "remarkable signes" of abuse on Sarah Taylor's body, to the designation of slave status through the body of the mother, to Murray Hall's success in disguising her female body as that of a man. Documents in several sections depict women's physical capacities, tolerances, and sufferings in instances such as childbirth, rape, physical punishment, overwork, disease, and surgery. The pleasures of the body are less prominently displayed. Many women were denied the comfort of adequate food, clothing, housing, and rest, and the enjoyment of recreation or sensuality. Still, from Sally Wister's adventuresome flirting, to Martha Wright's doting on her toddler, to Sadie Frowne's determination to "put on plenty of style," the documents do suggest women's desires for intimacy, beauty, and bodily satisfactions.

Fourth, women's collective efforts outside the family circle recur through the documents, though more frequently in the nineteenth-century selections than the earlier ones (as the history warrants). Women associated and allied with like-minded men as well as with other women. The colonial documents show women as vital and not always compliant members of face-to-face communities. In the nineteenth-century materials, a broader spectrum of local and voluntary organizations emerges (including religious and reform groups and political and professional associations), and the women involved are more diverse culturally and ethnically. Associational activities were so common among American women in the nineteenth century and such an important element in the social order that they might be even better represented here, but minutes of meetings rarely make interesting reading.

A fifth theme in the documents is the potency of diversity in religion, region, race, nationality, age, class, and social status among women. Although we know we cannot be comprehensive in this volume, we have tried to suggest the range among American women, and some of the relations and conflicts between different groups. The prostitute and the moral reformer, the slaveholder and the slave, the dispossessed Native American and the migrant or immigrant settler moving in, the domestic servant and her employer, the white supremacist and the victim of racism, the teacher and the student, the midwife and the professional doctor appear in these documents. Our selection is not exhaustive. Yet all women exist in social relation—to women and men—and any woman's life may prompt inquiries that can usefully be extended to the lives of others.

A sixth theme concerns women's relation to state authority. From the examination of Anne Hutchinson, to an African American woman's anonymous appeal to President McKinley, these documents show women operating within a framework established by government. The nation-state sets expectations for women's behavior in all sorts of interactions, from the national crises of wars to the most mundane aspects of rearing the next generation. A Native American women's petition additionally raises the issue of cultural distinctiveness in relations between gender and political systems. The force of law as the principal arm of the state in daily life looms in women's documents in examples from stealing to rape, to marriage, to slavery, to Indian "removal." Before 1900, women (few of whom could vote) played little direct role in state authority—yet their lives were shaped by the state and at least some women exerted a shaping influence on political institutions. Women also exercised political agency in private and public ways. They wrote petitions and propaganda; they lobbied relatives and legislative bodies, and even posed as men to win political power.

Our choice of a roughly chronological order for our anthology accommodates the standard organization of United States history around turning-points of state authority, from colonial settlements of the British empire in North America through the American Revolution, Civil War and Reconstruction. The first two sections, "Colonial Encounters and Communities" and "Transitions to a New Republic," take the reader from the earliest English settlement in what would become the United States, to the 1820s. The remaining six sections delve into the nineteenth century in depth. These documents overall suggest that the history of women cannot be separated from the national history and leave either of them whole.

Part 1 (1630s to 1720s) shows us women in a preindustrial society primarily English in its customs yet affected in vital ways by transplantation to North America, where existing settlements of Native Americans presented stark cultural contrasts. The documents here highlight women's central roles within the close circle of colonial communities, the operation of church and state authorities, the development of labor systems based on race and class as well as gender categories, the kinds of work ordinary women did, and challenges to English assumptions about gender raised by Native American societies. This section, more than any other, is dominated by legal materials—a result of our effort to represent women's social history in documents about ordinary lives. In this era, only a small minority of women in North America could read and write, and therefore personal accounts are few and far between (and usually limited to the elite).

Part 2, "Transitions to a New Republic" (1730s to 1820s) contains a greater diversity of documents, from legal materials to memoirs, letters, diaries, pamphlets, petitions, and newspaper advertisements. This selection reflects the spread of basic education and consequent literacy for women in the middle to late eighteenth century. The publication revolution, of which literacy was a part, was only one of the revolutions that rocked this era. The religious revivals later summarily called "the Great Awakening," the explosion of political and social theorizing of the trans-Atlantic Enlightenment, the turmoil of the American Revolution, the shift to a market economy—all reshaped the worlds of the women documented here. The documents provide food for thought about women's contributions and adaptations to an emerging emphasis on personal liberty, property, and market relations, and to changing notions of deference and piety, all of which reordered daily lives and broad social practices of gender.

Part 3, "Woman's Sphere and Women's Employments," moves into the antebellum period of industrial and commercial development, juxtaposing the ideology of domesticity of that era to the actual work and social relations of women of different classes. Numerous voices, including those of immigrants, factory workers, housewives, didactic authors, and reform activists, offer a sampling of colloquy and contention over the nature and appropriate role of women. This and subsequent sections go beyond the types of documents in part 2 to include recorded narratives, fiction, music, speeches, institutional reports, scientific papers, and propaganda for many causes. Here readers can compare prescriptions offered for "true womanhood" with the everyday outlooks and occupations of some native-born and immigrant, black and white, middle-class and working class, northern and southern women.

Part 4, "Women and the National Mission," investigates the participation of women in establishing a continent-wide nation identified with Protestantism and English cultural traditions. Broadly spanning the nineteenth century, this section shows women settling new territories and contributing by means of religious, secular, and moral education to the "rising American empire," as it was called at the time. The documents suggest that in addition to Anglo-American Protestants, Americans who were Catholics, Mormons, and immigrants from outside the British Isles had their own ideas about building a nation. They promoted territorial expansion and advanced the national mission from their distinctive perspectives. Indigenous women, for their part, both resisted and engaged with European and American soldiers, missionaries, and settlers. Since our collection uses the territorial framework of standard treatments of United States history and reflects the ascendancy of Anglo-American culture, it only hints at the history of women living under other European colonial empires in North America, such as Eulalia Pérez. She was born in California when it belonged to Mexico and became part of "American history" only after her nation's defeat in the Mexican-American War of 1848.

Part 5, "Slavery, War, and Emancipation," focuses attention on race and racism, the relation of race to gender, and the many meanings of self-determination. While these issues are addressed in documents elsewhere in the volume also, we devote this full section to them because of the lasting national importance of slavery and the Civil War. The section investigates the racial and gender order of the slaveholding South, some women's opposition to that order, and the circumstances of women North and South during and after the Civil War. Documents explore the efforts of African American women to protect themselves and their families through the most momentous changes in polity in United States history: the destruction of a state founded on the institution of racial slavery, the halting emergence and rapid decline of an experiment in the redress of racial grievance, and the rise of a new state overtly committed to equality but permissive of extreme racial oppression. The range of Southern women's experiences represented is limited, of course, because illiteracy was enforced upon slaves and was common as well among white women outside the planter elite. In this section (and not only here) we are well aware that a documentary collection illustrates primarily the history of those who had access to the tools of reading and writing.

In part 6, "Health, Medicine, and Sexuality," women appear as medical practitioners themselves, as subjects of medical consideration and treatment, and as health reformers. This section, like part 1, spans the nineteenth century, an era of "medicalization" in which the voice of the physician often replaced that of the clergyman as a guide to proper behavior. The documents in this section reveal that various approaches to the treatment and preservation of physical and mental health persisted despite the century's trend. Nonetheless, the increasing power and prestige of the medical profession show through the words of women and men as they consider such issues as abortion, public health, or female physical vulnerability.

The documents in parts 7 and 8 come from the last third of the nineteenth century. "Women's Work in an Industrial Age" illustrates women's expanding range of occupations and new consciousness of work as an element of self-definition. Predictable questions about the possibility of women's economic independence emerge from these documents, along with other questions about the extent of volition and coercion in women's labor. We may be accustomed to think of the bond-slave and no one else as a forced laborer, yet the post-Emancipation documents in this section (most directly the one on Chinese prostitutes but also those that touch on sharecropping, domestic service, household work, sweated labor, and industrial occupations) invite reflection on the nature and extent of choice in the occupations of free laborers—female or male.

The last section, "New Women, New Worlds," brings us to the turn of the century. It includes prominent women along with the anonymous and pseudonymous. Our title alludes to the various ways that women confronted new worlds: the immigrant arriving in the United States, the housewife inspired by new forms of voluntary association, the single woman finding white-collar work, the Southern black migrating north, for example. At the time, the term "new woman" typically was pinned on the prosperous, well-educated, venturesome, and young, but we propose a broader application. Our intent is to raise rather than close the issue, however. The documents make clear that much that was "old" persisted at this turning point, including conflict and bigotry based on racial and ethnic difference, and pervasive beliefs that heterosexuality, romance, and marriage encompassed all that was desirable for women.

We hope that readers will find in this book an exciting expansion of sources and possible interpretations. The arrangement of the collection is intended for the enjoyment of the browsing reader as well as for use in college courses on the history of women in the United States. Within the roughly chronological order the separation of topics is not rigid: documents on women's occupations are not confined to parts 3 and 7, nor those on health and medicine to part 6; documents on territorial and cultural expansion appear outside of part 4, and so on. Rather than using tiny snippets, we have purposely made selections long enough to reveal the patterns of argument and habits of mind of the writer. These are not documents whose meaning can be easily summarized: we would like to encourage the reader to explore the ambiguities, the complex possibilities, of each document and the person (or persons) and moment that created it. Each document has its own integrity. We hope that each will inspire curiosity and provide ground for probing large questions. The headnote preceding each document briefly sets a context for it but declines to prejudge its meanings or elicit its critical "point." On the contrary, readers may gain various kinds of knowledge and draw divergent inferences.

To convey the originals with as much authenticity as possible, we have retained spelling and punctuation as we found them in print or manuscript sources and have not used the notation *sic*. A few of these documents are almost phonetically spelled, and when read aloud convey something of the pronunciation and cadence of the speech of their times. Some of the colonial documents come from nineteenth-century printed sources, however, in which their presentation was already modernized.

The growth in recent writing of women's history, marvelous as it is, cannot replace the appeal or immediacy of the documentary source as an introduction to and confrontation with the past. What is gained in breadth, judgment, and efficacy from a fine historical analysis based on diverse sources may require sacrifice of the telling detail and emotional impact of an individual document: this is one of the ironies of the historian's craft. Documents such as these, each holding a world of its own in small compass, provide the field for modern interpretation and reinterpretation. Having lost none of their power to reveal and astonish, these documents encourage the modern reader to hold intimate conversation with voices of the past.

PART I

COLONIAL ENCOUNTERS
AND COMMUNITIES

EXAMINATION OF ANNE HUTCHINSON

Just a few years after the founding of the Massachusetts Bay Colony by English Puritans, Anne Hutchinson disrupted the social order. In Puritan orthodoxy, the distinction between mere "works" (good deeds) and "grace" (God's gift, necessary for salvation) was central. Hutchinson suggested that all the colony's ministers except John Cotton, teacher of the Boston church, preached more of the former than the latter. Her exposition of Cotton's doctrines at her home brought her a large following, which amounted to a political split in the colony and a threat to established leaders. Governor John Winthrop took the prosecutor's part in examining her before the colony's court at Newtown (now Cambridge) in 1637. Hutchinson's downfall was her heretical claim, under examination, that she had received a revelation directly from God.

Mr. Winthrop, Governor: Mrs. Hutchinson, you are called here as one of those that have troubled the peace of the commonwealth and the churches here; you are known to be a woman that hath had a great share in the promoting and divulging of those opinions that are causes of this trouble, and to be nearly joined not only in affinity and affection with some of those the court had taken notice of and passed censure upon, but you have spoken divers things as we have been informed very prejudicial to the honour of the churches and ministers thereof, and you have maintained a meeting and an assembly in your house that hath been condemned by the general assembly as a thing not tolerable nor comely in the sight of God nor fitting for your sex, and notwithstanding that was cried down you have continued the same, therefore we have thought good to send for you to understand how things are, that if you be in an erroneous way we may reduce you that so you may become a profitable member here among us, otherwise if you be obstinate in your course that then the court may take such course that you may trouble us no further, therefore I would intreat you to express whether you do not assent and hold in practice to those opinions and factions that have been handled in court already, that is to say, whether you do not justify Mr. Wheelwright's sermon and the petition.

Mrs. Hutchinson: I am called here to answer before you but I hear no things laid to my charge.

Mr. [Thomas] Hutchinson, *The History of the Province of Massachusets-Bay, from the Charter of King William and Queen Mary in 1691 until the Year 1750* (Boston: Thomas and John Fleet, 1767), app., pp. 482–91, 495–96, 504–10, 512–15, 519–20 (footnotes omitted).

Gov. I have told you some already and more I can tell you.

Mrs. H. Name one Sir.

Gov. Have I not named some already?

Mrs. H. What have I said or done?

Gov. Why for your doings, this you did harbour and countenance those that are parties in this faction that you have heard of.

Mrs. H. That's matter of conscience, Sir.

Gov. Your conscience you must keep or it must be kept for you.

Mrs. H. Must not I then entertain the saints because I must keep my conscience.

Gov. Say that one brother should commit felony or treason and come to his brother's house, if he knows him guilty and conceals him he is guilty of the same. It is his conscience to entertain him, but if his conscience comes into act in giving countenance and entertainment to him that hath broken the law he is guilty too. So if you do countenance those that are transgressors of the law you are in the same fact.

Mrs. H. What law do they transgress?

Gov. The law of God and of the state.

Mrs. H. In what particular?

Gov. Why in this among the rest, whereas the Lord doth say honour thy father and thy mother. . . .

Mrs. H. In entertaining those did I entertain them against any act (for there is the thing) or what God hath appointed? . . .

Gov. Why the fifth commandment. . . .

Mrs. H. But put the case Sir that I do fear the Lord and my parents, may not I entertain them that fear the Lord because my parents will not give me leave?

Gov. If they be the fathers of the commonwealth, and they of another religion, if you entertain them then you dishonour your parents and are justly punishable.

Mrs. H. If I entertain them, as they have dishonoured their parents I do.

Gov. No but you by countenancing them above others put honor upon them.

Mrs. H. I may put honor upon them as the children of God and as they do honor the Lord.

Gov. We do not mean to discourse with those of your sex but only this; you do adhere unto them and do endeavor to set forward this faction and so you do dishonour us.

Mrs. H. I do acknowledge no such thing neither do I think that I ever put any dishonour upon you.

Gov. Why do you keep such a meeting at your house as you do every week upon a set day?

Mrs. H. It is lawful for me so to do, as it is all your practices and can you find a warrant for yourself and condemn me for the same thing? The ground of my taking it up was, when I first came to this land because I did not go to such meetings as those were, it was presently reported that I did not allow of such meetings but held them unlawful and therefore in that regard they said I was proud and did despise all ordinances, upon that a friend came unto me and told me of it and I to prevent such aspersions took it up, but it was in practice before I came therefore I was not the first.

Gov. For this, that you appeal to our practice you need no confutation. If your meeting had answered to the former it had not been offensive, but I will say that there was no meeting of women alone, but your meeting is of another sort for there are sometimes men among you.

Mrs. H. There was never any man with us.

Gov. Well, admit there was no man at your meeting and that you was sorry for it, there is no warrant for your doings, and by what warrant do you continue such a course?

Mrs. H. I conceive there lyes a clear rule in Titus, that the elder women should instruct the younger and then I must have a time wherein I must do it.

Gov. All this I grant you, I grant you a time for it, but what is this to the purpose that you Mrs. Hutchinson must call a company together from their callings to come to be taught of you? . . .

Mrs. H. . . . if you look upon the rule in Titus it is a rule to me. If you convince me that it is no rule I shall yield.

Gov. You know that there is no rule that crosses another, but this rule crosses that in the Corinthians. But you must take it in this sense that elder women must instruct the younger about their business and to love their husbands and not to make them to clash.

Mrs. H. I do not conceive but that it is meant for some publick times.

Gov. Well, have you no more to say but this?

Mrs. H. I have said sufficient for my practice.

Gov. Your course is not to be suffered for, besides that we find such a course as this to be greatly prejudicial to the state, besides the occasion that it is to seduce many honest persons that are called to those meetings and your opinions being known to be different from the word of God may seduce many simple souls that resort unto you, besides that the occasion which hath come of late hath come from none but such as have frequented your meetings, so that now they are flown off from magistrates and ministers and this since they have come to you, and besides that it will not well stand with the commonwealth that families should be neglected for so many neighbours and dames and so much time spent, we see no rule of God for this, we see not that any should have authority to set up any other exercises besides what authority hath already set up and so what hurt comes of this you will be guilty of and we for suffering you.

Mrs. H. Sir I do not believe that to be so.

Gov. Well, we see how it is we must therefore put it away from you or restrain you from maintaining this course.

Mrs. H. If you have a rule for it from God's word you may.

Gov. We are your judges, and not you ours and we must compel you to it.

Mrs. H. If it please you by authority to put it down I will freely let you for I am subject to your authority. . . .

Dep. Gov. I would go a little higher with Mrs. Hutchinson. About three years ago we were all in peace. Mrs. Hutchinson from that time she came hath made a disturbance, and some that came over with her in the ship did inform me what she was as soon as she was landed. I being then in place dealt with the pastor and teacher of Boston and desired them to enquire of her, and then I was satisfied that she held nothing different from us, but within half a year after, she had vented divers of her strange opinions and had made parties in the country, and at length it comes that Mr. Cotton and Mr. Vane were of her judgment, but Mr. Cotton hath cleared himself that he was not of that mind, but now it appears by this woman's meeting that Mrs. Hutchinson hath so forestalled the minds of many by their resort to her meeting that now she hath a potent party in the country. Now if all these things have endangered us . . . and if she in particular hath disparaged all our ministers in the land that they have preached a covenant of works, and only Mr. Cotton a covenant of grace, why this is not to be suffered. . . .

Mr. H. I pray Sir prove it that I said they preached nothing but a covenant of works. . . .

Dep. Gov. If they do not preach a covenant of grace clearly, then they preach a covenant of works.

Mrs. H. No Sir, one may preach a covenant of grace more clearly than another, so I said. . . .

Dep. Gov. When they do preach a covenant of works do they preach truth?

Mrs. H. Yes Sir, but when they preach a covenant of works for salvation, that is not truth.

Dep. Gov. I do but ask you this, when the ministers do preach a covenant of works do they preach a way of salvation?

Mrs. H. I did not come hither to answer to questions of that sort. . . .

Dep. Gov. I will make it plain that you did say that the ministers did preach a covenant of works.

Mrs. H. I deny that.

Dep. Gov. And that you said they were not able ministers of the new testament, but Mr. Cotton only.

Mrs. H. If ever I spake that I proved it by God's word. . . .

Mr. Peters. We shall give you a fair account of what was said and desire that we may not be thought to come as informers against the gentlewoman, but as it may be serviceable for the country and our posterity to give you a brief account. This gentlewoman went under suspicion not only from her landing, that she was a woman not only difficult in her opinions, but also of an intemperate spirit. What was done at her landing I do not well remember, but as soon as Mr. Vane and ourselves came this controversy began . . . [and] we thought it good to send for this gentlewoman, and she willingly came, and at the very first we gave her notice that such reports there were that she did conceive our ministry to be different from the ministry of the gospel, and that we taught a covenant of works, &c. and this was her table talk and therefore we desired her to clear herself and deal plainly. She was very tender at the first. Some of our brethren did desire to put this upon proof, and then her words upon that were, The fear of man is a snare why should I be afraid. These were her words. . . . Briefly, she told me there was a wide and a broad difference between our brother Mr. Cotton and our selves. I desired to know the difference. She answered that he preaches the covenant of grace and you the covenant of works and that you are not able ministers of the new testament and know no more than the apostles did before the resurrection of Christ. I did then put it to her, What do you conceive of such a brother? She answered he had not the seal of the spirit. And other things we asked her but generally the frame of her course was this, that she did conceive that we were not able ministers of the gospel. . . .

[Six more ministers testify, agreeing with Peters.]

Gov. Here are six undeniable ministers who say it is true and yet you deny that you did say that they did preach a covenant of works and that they were not able ministers of the gospel, and it appears plainly that you have spoken it, and whereas you say that is was drawn from you in a way of friendship, you did profess then that it was out of conscience that you spake and said The fear of man is a snare, wherefore shall I be afraid, I will speak plainly and freely.

Mrs. H. That I absolutely deny, for the first question, was thus answered by me to them. They thought that I did conceive there was a difference between them and Mr. Cotton. At the first I was somewhat reserved, then . . . I said I would deal as plainly as I could, and whereas they say I said they were under a covenant of works and in the state of the apostles why these two speeches cross one another. I might say they might preach a covenant of works as did the apostles, but to preach a covenant of works and to be under a covenant of works is another business.

Dep. Gov. There have been six witnesses to prove this and yet you deny it.

Mrs. H. I deny that these were the first words that were spoken.

Gov. You make the case worse, for you clearly shew that the ground of your opening your mind was not to satisfy them but to satisfy your own conscience. . . .

THE NEXT MORNING

Mr. Peters. I humbly desire to remember our reverend teacher [of the Boston church, John Cotton]. May it please you to remember how this came in. Whether do you not remember that she said we were not sealed with the spirit of grace, therefore could not preach a covenant of grace, and she said further you may do it in your judgment but not in experience, but she spake plump that we were not sealed.

Mr. Cotton. You do put me in remembrance that it was asked her why cannot we preach a covenant of grace? Why, saith she, because you can preach no more than you know, or to that purpose, she spake. Now that she said you could not preach a covenant of grace I do not remember such a thing. I remember well that she said you were not sealed with the seal of the spirit. . . .

Mrs. H. If you please to give me leave I shall give you the ground of what I know to be true. . . . The Lord knows that I could not open scripture; he must by his prophetical office open it unto me. So after that being unsatisfied in the thing, the Lord was pleased to bring this scripture out of the Hebrews. He that denies the testament denies the testator, and in this did open unto me and give me to see that those which did not teach the new covenant had the spirit of antichrist, and upon this he did discover the ministry unto me and ever since, I bless the Lord, he hath let me see which was the clear ministry and which the wrong. Since that time I confess I have been more choice and he hath left me to distinguish between the voice of my beloved and the voice of Moses, the voice of John

Baptist and the voice of antichrist, for all those voices are spoken of in scripture. Now if you do condemn me for speaking what in my conscience I know to be truth I must commit myself unto the Lord.

Mr. Nowel. How do you know that that was the spirit?

Mrs. H. How did Abraham know that it was God that bid him offer his son, being a breach of the sixth commandment?

Dep. Gov. By an immediate voice.

Mrs. H. So to me by an immediate revelation.

Dep. Gov. How! an immediate revelation.

Mrs. H. By the voice of his own spirit to my soul. . . .

Gov. Daniel was delivered by miracle do you think to be deliver'd so too?

Mrs. H. I do here speak it before the court. I look that the Lord should deliver me by his providence. . . .

Mr. Bartholomew. I speak as a member of the court. I fear that her revelations will deceive.

Gov. Have you heard of any of her revelations?

Mr. Barthol. For my own part I am sorry to see her now here and I have nothing against her but what I said was to discover what manner of spirit Mrs. Hutchinson is of; only I remember as we were once going through Paul's church yard she then was very inquisitive after revelations and said that she had never had any great thing done about her but it was revealed to her beforehand.

Mrs. H. I say the same thing again.

Mr. Barthol. And also that she said that she was come to New-England but for Mr. Cotton's sake. . . .

Dep. Gov. I desire Mr. Cotton to tell us whether you do approve of Mrs. Hutchinson's revelations as she hath laid them down. . . .

Mr. Cotton. That she may have some special providence of God to help her is a thing that I cannot bear witness against.

Dep. Gov. Good Sir I do ask whether this revelation be of God or no?

Mr. Cotton. I should desire to know whether the sentence of the court will bring her to any calamity, and then I would know of her whether she expects to be delivered from that calamity by a miracle or a providence of God.

Mrs. H. By a providence of God I say I expect to be delivered from some calamity that shall come to me.

Gov. The case is altered and will not stand with us now, but I see a marvellous providence of God to bring things to this pass that they are. We have been hearkening about the trial of this thing and now the mercy of God by a providence hath answered our desires and made her to lay open her self and the ground of all these disturbances to be by revelations, . . . [so] the ground work of her revelations is the immediate revelation of the spirit and not by the ministry of the word, and that is the means by which she hath very much abused the country that they shall look for revelations and are not bound to the ministry of the word, but God will teach them by immediate revelations and this hath been the ground of all these tumults and troubles, and I would that those were all cut off from us that trouble us, for this is the thing that hath been the root of all the mischief.

Court. We all consent with you. . . .

Dep. Gov. . . . I am fully persuaded that Mrs. Hutchinson is deluded by the devil, because the spirit of God speaks truth in all his servants.

Gov. I am persuaded that the revelation she brings forth is delusion.

All the court but some two or three ministers cry out we all believe it—we all believe it. . . .

Gov. The court hath already declared themselves satisfied concerning the things you hear, and concerning the troublesomeness of her spirit and the danger of her course amongst us, which is not to be suffered. Therefore if it be the mind of the court that Mrs. Hutchinson for these things that appear before us is unfit for our society, and if it be the mind of the court that she shall be banished out of our liberties and imprisoned till she be sent away, let them hold up their hands.

All but three. . . .

Gov. Mrs. Hutchinson, the sentence of the court you hear is that you are banished from out of our jurisdiction as being a woman not fit for our society, and are to be imprisoned till the court shall send you away.

Mrs. H. I desire to know wherefore I am banished?

Gov. Say no more, the court knows wherefore and is satisfied.

CHURCH TRIAL AND EXCOMMUNICATION
OF ANN HIBBENS

*The assembled First Church of Boston examined Ann Hibbens in 1640
for offense she had given in a dispute with several of the town's joiners
(carpenters). After hiring a joiner to do some carpentry in her house, she
had judged the work poorly done and the rate excessive, and had gone to
other joiners asking their opinion of the work's value. One joiner, John
Davis, brought the issue before the church because of what he considered
false accusations and contentious behavior by Hibbens. This account of her
trial (with spelling and punctuation modernized) comes from the personal
notebook of congregant Robert Keayne.*

*In 1656, two years after the death of her husband (a respected member
of the Boston community), Hibbens was accused and convicted of witchcraft, and executed.*

Pastor: All this that you now relate is only to excuse yourself and lessen
your own fault and lay blame upon others; and therefore you have in an
unsatisfied way sent from workman to workman, and from one to another, to view the work and to [ap]praise it; and when the elders and
others that met at your own house about this did see reason that you
should be satisfied, yet you have been so suspicious and used such
speeches to accuse our Brother Davis and other workmen, when they
would not speak as you do. Yet you have continued still to be so unsatisfied, that you have caused more expense of time than all your work is
worth. And when our Teacher and the elders and myself, upon due search
and examination of the matter, we did not find that there was any great
wrong done to you—or if it were a wrong yet we thought you ought to
have been satisfied and to stir no more in it—but such has been the
unquiet frame of your spirit, that you would take no warning, nor hearken to our counsel and exhortation, but have still been stirring, to the
offense of many of the congregation whose names and credits you have
defamed, and we are unsatisfied also. Therefore consider what whether
this has been according to the rule of Christian love; and therefore if you
cannot give a better answer, you must expect the further proceedings of
the church against you, as shall be most wholesome for your soul.

Elder Oliver: Sister, methinks: the last meeting we had about this busi-

Robert Keayne's ms. "Notes on John Cotton's Sermans," transcribed into "Hibbens Typescript"
by Anita Rutman, pp. 13–19, 23, 28–41, 43–47, 55–57, 61–64, courtesy Massachusetts Historical Society and Anita Rutman.

ness when there was ten of us together, (five for you and five for our Brother Davis), and many witnesses examined, and the joiners professing as in the presence of God that they had rated it as low as ever as they could, and so low as we can get no other joiners in this town to do the like—and they brought it to ten pounds or thereabouts—and therefore methinks you should be satisfied and speak no more.

Mrs. Hibbens: There was a joiner from Salem and some others that saw it that did not reckon it above half the price of what he took for it.

Brother Penn: All that our Sister hath spoken tends not to any measure of repentance or sorrow for her sin, but to her further justification and excusing of herself, and casting blame upon others, which savors of great pride of spirit and a heart altogether untouched by any of those means that hath been used with her.

Sgt. Savage: I think if all other offenses were passed by, that hath been mentioned, yet she hath shed forth one sin in the face of the congregation worthy of reproof: and that is transgressing the rule of the apostle in usurping authority over him whom God hath made her head and husband, and in taking the power and authority which God hath given to him out of his hands; and when he was satisfied and sits down contented she is unsatisfied, and will not be content, but will stir in it, as if she were able to manage it better than her husband, which is a plain breach of the rule of Christ.

Pastor: That indeed is observed in her by diverse [people] as a great aggravation of her sin; in so much that some do think she doth but make a wisp of her husband. Yet this she alleged for herself: that her husband did give her leave to order and carry on this business to her own satisfaction.

Brother Corser: It is thought by many that it is an untruth which she speaks and yet it will be proved on oath that her husband would have had her contented and rest satisfied—and she would not.

Brother Hibbens: At the first I did give my wife leave to agree with the joiner, and to order the business with him as she thought good. Yet I must needs say in faithfulness to the church that when difference did arise about the work, my wife told me she had agreed with him to do it for forty s[hillings]—which I cannot affirm, having no witness but my wife's own affirmation, which he denied from the first. And therefore conceiving that the work was too much for the price, I told him [that] when it was done, what it came to more, I would give him, as two men should judge it worth. And I chose my Brother Davis, of whose faithfulness I am well satisfied, and was very willing to stand to that agreement he made, and did persuade my wife, and could have wished with all my heart she had been willing to have done the same. And I have had some exercise of spirit with her, that she hath not done so. . . .

Mrs. Hibbens: The Lord knoweth that in all this I have but only desired to find out the truth of a thing and to do them good with whom I had to deal. . . .

Pastor: Brother Davis, produce your witnesses, that our Sister Hibbens did accuse you and the joiners in the town of such a sinful confederacy before she dealt with you about it.

Brother Davis: She said we had committed such wickedness that the stones in the street and the beams in the house would cry for vengeance, and that the joiners had compacted together to deceive her. Our Brother Button, Mr. Oliver, and Mr. Leveret can witness. . . .

[Oliver, Leveret, and Button give witness.]

Brother Davis: If the pains and arbitrations of Brethren and godly men shall be censured, threatened, and called into question, when they have done to their best skill and judgment as in the sight of God, and have a reproach cast on their names, it will make all men unwilling to arbitrate anything. For I think she hath had at least twenty, or forty several meetings, and she rest in none of them except in one or two that speaks according to her mind, when we were not by. And so to be accused that we commit wickedness and did sin against our consciences, and that the wickedness was so great that the timbers of the house would cry to God for vengeance upon us for this unrighteous valuation of her work. . . .

Mr. Cotton: Sister Hibbens, I pray speak to this point in the fear of God and presence of His church. For the thing you are accused of, and for which you are to give satisfaction first, is in this thing: whether you have so thought and spake against our Brethren, and yet did not deal with them in a church way; and whether you do allow yourself in any such thing or do judge yourself for it before the Lord. . . .

Mrs. Hibbens: . . . my scruple is this, that they may be helped to see their evil, which I hope in time will come out; and therefore I thought it was my part to labor to search out and find the truth of it. I thought it was not ripe for church proceeding, but in that I did not show so much love to our Brother's soul as to use the right way of bringing him to a sight of his sin, but rather did speak of it to his disgrace, I confess to be my sin, and desire to judge my self and to be more sorry for it before the Lord.

Mr. Cotton: . . . I pray, speak to another point which did aggravate your offense in the church: that though you owed subjection to your husband, and to take advice and counsel from him, but when he did advise you to be quiet and sit still . . . you were unsatisfied, and did still stir up and down with an unquiet and restless spirit, as if you had more wit and care than your husband.

Mrs. Hibbens: My husband did give me leave for the satisfying of my spirit, to search farther into it, and to find out the truth.

Pastor: . . . And so it may be your husband yielded to you, but you should have been advised by your husband at first, though it was against your mind or will. . . .

Teacher: . . . the thing is this: whether if these Brethren do testify as in the sight and presence of God, that they have done justly and according to a good conscience, then whether you are not bound to believe them, and to acknowledge that you were uncharitable in thinking and speaking so of your Brethren.

Mrs. Hibbens: Yes, I think I ought to believe them, and am to judge myself for it, and lay after such thoughts.

Sgt. Oliver: The answer she makes doth not reach the thing expected from her. Her answer expresseth no more than what any may say in the point of judgment; but that which now is expected from our Sister is penitency and brokenness of spirit for that wrong she hath done them, and those evil thoughts she hath taken up against them.

Pastor: Therefore speak punctually: are you indeed convinced in your conscience that you have wronged them, and do sit as God in the consciences of your Brethren to judge their conscience, which belongs only to God?

Mrs. Hibbens: I can say no more than what I have. I leave that to their own conscience to judge. . . .

Brother Eliot: I think this should farther be pressed upon her spirit: her want of wifelike subjection to her husband, and in following his advice and not to do things contrary to it.

Mrs. Hibbens: You may remember, sir, that you have delivered it as an ordinance of God, that a man should hearken to the counsel of his wife—from that speech of God to Abraham, hearken to thy wife in all that she shall say to thee.

Mr. Cotton: Did you hear me say so, or deliver any such point?

Mrs. Hibbens: I was told you did deliver it before I came.

Mr. Cotton: If any told you so, they told you an untruth, for I dare confidently affirm that I never delivered any such thing.

Capt. Gibbens: I desire that our Sister would express who that was, which should tell her so; for myself sometimes dealing with her about her doing things contrary to the advice of her husband, she answered me thus: whether it is better to obey God or man, that judge you. By which she intimated to me that disobedience to the counsel of her godly husband was her obedience to God, and that God would have her to do what she did. So that it argues, she takes it for a principle that the husband must hearken to his wife in the counsel she shall give, and not the wife to the husband. And so she makes a cipher of her husband and his authority, which she should have in great respect.

Brother Fairbank: I conceive she is settled in that opinion, for myself having occasion to speak with her at our Pastor's house about the obedience of wives to husbands, she answered me from that speech of God to Abraham—hearken to thy wife, in all that she shall say to thee.

Mr. Cotton: That is to be understood when a wife speaks as the oracles of God, according to the mind and will of God—as indeed then the speech of godly women were as oracles, and did declare the mind and counsel of God to their husbands, and then they were to hearken to them as to God. But that wives *now* should be always God's oracles to their husband, and that the husband should obey his wife, and not the wife the husband, that is a false principle. For God hath put another law upon women: wives, be subject to your husbands in all things. Except they should require something of you that is a plain sin, or a direct breach of rule, you ought to obey them and be subject to them in all things. Are you convinced therefore that you ought to hearken to the counsel of your husband, and that it is a sin in you at any time to transgress the will and appointment of your husband?

Mrs. Hibbens: Yes, sir, I do think that I am bound to obey my husband in all lawful things, and that it is a sin to do the contrary.

Pastor: And are you also convinced that it was a sin in you not to obey your husband in being satisfied with that appraisement of brethren, without further agitation?

Mrs. Hibbens: I have said that my husband gave me leave to wade farther, to find out the sin in this business. . . .

Pastor: I would have you, Sister, consider [what] the Lord [means], by all this accusation of the brethren, which makes them so jealous of the frame of your spirit and carriage toward your husband; and whether there is not much sin this way in your carriage to your husband, and therefore God leaves you in so great jealousy in the hearts of brethren in this thing, that though you may not be guilty at this time, yet in some such carriages formerly. . . .

Mr. Cotton: . . . [Now] for your uncharitable censurings, and judgings of your brethren: they have by oath cleared themselves of your prejudice; therefore you are bound to believe them. If you do not, you take upon you to judge their consciences, and so you thrust yourself into God's throne and seat, to know the hearts of men, which is God's peculiar prerogative which he will give to no other. Do you not think it is a sin for you to sit in God's throne? I pray speak.

Mrs. Hibbens: Yes, if I should do so, it were a great sin.

Mr. Cotton: Why, you do so, if after their clearing by oath you do not clear them in your conscience—if you do not believe them, but retain your uncharitable opinion of them still. Therefore, I pray, give God the glory. Do you believe now that they have spoken the truth, and that you have done them wrong, to entertain such thoughts of them as you have done?

Mrs. Hibbens: I dare not clear them, but I leave them on their consciences to God.

Mr. Cotton: I am sorry to hear you say so, and that your heart is so prejudiced against your brethren. . . . Another offense you are to consider and to give satisfaction for, is your usurping authority over such a head and husband which God hath given to you, who is able to guide and direct you according to God. Now, do you think it is a breach of rule in a wife to transgress the will of her husband, when he requires that which is according to God?

Mrs. Hibbens: My husband did give me leave to search further into the foulness of this business. . . .

Pastor: We see the Lord hath not yet broken her spirit, nor there is nothing comes from her that tends to satisfactions. Therefore we must propound it to the church, what is farther to be done. . . .

[Several men speak their approval of the censure of excommunication.]

Mr. Hibbens: . . . If church would show their bowels of pity in sparing or respiting her censure for a time, the Lord may so bow the heart of my wife that she may give the church full satisfaction, which would be the rising of my soul. I shall wholly leave it with you.

[The church members then proceed to assent to the excommunication of Mrs. Hibbens. The Pastor delivers the sentence of excommunication.]

ORDINARY DEALINGS AT COLONIAL COUNTY COURTS

These entries from the seventeenth-century court records of Accomack-Northampton County, Virginia, and Suffolk County, Massachusetts, indicate some of the ways in which women came before the law in the British North American colonies.

ORDINARY DEALINGS AT ACCOMACK-NORTHAMPTON COUNTY COURT

January 7, 1632 [1633]

[At this] Court Jane Winlee Commenced a sute against [James] Knott for the misse usage of her sonn Pharoah [who is an] apprentice unto the said James, the said James being found delinquent after examination had[.] It is therefore ordered by the bord that the said James Knott shall remedie what had beene formerly amisse and shall pay the charges of the Court and if the said James shall here after be justly complained of and thereof convicted that the Indentures betweene the said James and Pharoah shalbe voyd, and the said Pharoah delivered to the said mother.

May 19, 1634

A suite preferred by Susan helline, widdowe against John major for satisfaction for her paynes and tyme in lookinge to his wife the tyme she did lay in Childbed and upon due Examination and the [othe] of Agnis williams it is ordered that the said John major [shall pay] unto Susan Helline 18 hens within this month

September 8, 1634

At this Cort Edward Drew preferred a petition against Joane Butler for caling of his wife common Carted hoare and upon dew examination, and the deposition of John Holloway and William Baseley who affermeth the same on oath to be true that the syd Joane Butler used those words.

Upon dew examination it is thought fit by this board that the syd Joane Butler shall be drawen over the kings Creeke at the starne of a boate or Canew from on [one] Cowpen to the other, ore else the next saboth day in the tyme of devyne servis betwixt the first and second lesson present

Susie M. Ames, ed., *County Court Records of Accomack-Northampton, Virginia, 1632–1640* (Washington, D.C.: American Historical Association, 1954), 1, 2, 15, 20, 29, 30, 42–43, 63, 67, 79, 85: and *Records of Suffolk County Court: 1671–1680*, Publications of the Colonial Society of Massachusetts, vol. 29 (Boston, 1938), pp. 223, 302, 338, 436, 492, 558, 1063.

her selfe befor the minister and say after him as followeth. I Joane Butler doe acknowledge to have called Marie Drew hoare and thereby I confesse I have done her manefest wronge, wherfor I desire before this congregation, that ye syd Marie Drew will forgive me, and also that this congregation, will joyne, and praye with me, that God may forgive me.

February 19, 1634 [1635]

A suit commenced by Richard Hudson against mirs Savage for his servis which she promised 600 lbs. of tobacco and five barrels of corne which syd corne and tobacco it is ordered that the syd Richard shall have presently.

I Hanna Scarborough of Acchawmacke widdow have barg[ained] and sold unto Capt. Thomas Graves Esq. one Cow and a calfe for which I doe acknowledge to have received satisfaction witnesss my hand this 9th day of January.
Witness John Walton   Hanna Scarborough
        Edmund Scarborough

November 16, 1635

These are to witness that whereas Ann Harmar wife of mr. Charles Harmar sold to Phillip Chapman of Accawmack tow Heyfers now in the possession of the said Phillip, I the said Charles doe for my selfe my heyres and assignes confirme ratify and establish the sale and possession of the said Heyfers with the increase unto the said Philip Chapman his heyres executors and administrators for ever in Witness whereof I have here unto set my hand this   th day of november 1635.
In the presence of Thomas Graves John Angood.   Charles Harmar

November 28, 1636

These presents shall witness that I Elizabeth Caursley of Acchawmack being left and appoynted sole and absolute executrix of my right deere and well beloved husbound Henry Caursley late deceased [doe] heereby give bequeath and make over unto my children Agnis and Francis my plantation with all other my servants goods and monies whatsoever and I doe heereby authorise my well beloved fr[iend] and father in law Henry wilson to be my true and absolute overseer of this my deed and gift. In witness of these presents I have heere unto set my hand and seale this 26th day [of] November 1635.
Signed and delivered   The mark of
in the presents of   Elizabeth Caursley
George Travelor william Roper

January 1, 1636 [1637]

Alice the wife of Henry Bagwell hath made to appeare unto our court that ther is dew unto her two hundred acres of land for the transportation of herselfe and her sone Thomas Stratton upon her owne charges and likewise for tow servants John waltum and John Crowder which right of land she doth assigne o[ver] unto her sone Thomas Stratton one hundred acres of land and one hundred acres of land to Mary Chilcott, her daughter as of right pertayning which this board doth certifie the same for a truth unto the Governor and counsell under tytell of our court.

July 3, 1637

Upon the complaint of Elizabeth Starkey unto this Court concernige diverse unjust and rigorous abuses done and offered unto her by Alexander Mountney. Shee the said Elizabeth beinge a servant unto the said Mountney and one John Holloway haveinge a halfe share in her, and haveinge disbursed halfe the payment for her. Itt is thereupon ordered that the said John Holloway shall have the said Elizabeth in his free possession and Custody and that shee shall bee freed from the said Mountney, The said Holloway payeinge unto the said Mountney the one half of what was disbursed for her.

September 25, 1637

The depositon of Anne Wilkins the wife of John Wilkins

This deponent saith that Anne Williamson the wife of Roger Williamson and Anne Stephens the wife of Christopher Stephens came to the Cowe Pen and there did in a jeering manner abuse Grace Waltham saying that John Waltham husband of the said Grace hade his Mounthly Courses as Women have, and that the said Anne Stephens shold say that John Waltham was not able to gett a child. And further she saith not. Anne Stephens the wife of Williams Stephens, *idem.*

ORDINARY DEALINGS AT SUFFOLK COUNTY COURT

Session of 28 January, 1672–73

Jasper Indian Sentanced

Jasper m^r Warren's Indian convict by his own confession in Court of committing Fornication. The Court Sentanceth him to bee whip't with fifteen Stripes or to pay Forty shillings in mony fine to the County & Fees of Court.

Joan Negro's Sentance

Joan m[r] Warren's Negro convict by her own confession in Court of committing Fornication with Jasper Indian & that she had an illegitemate Childe. The Court Sentances her to bee whip't with fifteen Stripes or to pay Forty Shillings in Mony fine to the County & Fees of Court.

Session of 29 July, 1673

Scott's Sent[a]

Sarah Scott presented for Reviling & strikeing her Mother. Vpon due hearing of the case, The Court Sentances her to stand upon a Block or Stoole of two foote high in the Markett place in Boston upon a thursday immediately after lecture with an inscription upon her breast in a faire character For undutifull abusive & reviling speeches & carriages to her naturall mother & to give bond for her good behavio[r] till the next Court of this County 10[li] herselfe & 5[li] apeice two sureties & to pay Fees of Court.

Session of 28 October, 1673

Bedwell Fin[d] 40[s]

Mary Bedwell bound over to this Court to Answer for her railing & scurrilous Language & bad Speeches of which Shee was convict in Court. The Court Sentenc[d] her to be whip't with fifteen Stripes or to pay Forty Shillings in mony as a Fine to the County & Fees of Court standing committed untill the Sentence bee performed.

Session of 28 April, 1674

Steward Admonish'[t]

Hanna Steward being committed to prison upon suspition of Stealing severall goods from her Master Jonathan Bridgham; which upon hearing could not bee fully proved ag[t] her The Court Admonished her & Order her to pay fees of Court & prison & soe dismissed her.

Stevens discharg[d]

Sarah Stevens committed to prizon upon her saying that she had Lyen with Christopher Lawson; which was fully evidenced against her; but shee denying in Court that shee had soe done The Court judging by her carriages & testimonies concerning her that shee was a distempered crazy woman discharged her.

Licenses

Anne Puglice upon certificate from the Selectmen of Boston had her Licence renewed to distill & retail strong waters by small quantities for yᵉ yeare ensuing; provided shee did not sell to any of the inhabitants of the Town to drincke it in her house and George Puglice her husband as principall in ten pounds & Richard Collicot & William Bartholmew as Sureties in five pounds apeice acknowledged themselves respectiuely bound to the Treasuroʳ of the County of Suffolke on condicion that Anne Puglice should observe all the Laws concerning distilling and retailing of strong waters & that shee should not sell any to the inhabitants of the Town to bee dranck in her house.

Session of 28 July, 1674

Order abᵗ Hitt

Jn Answer to the request of Anne Hitt widdow & Administratrix to the Estate sometime Eliphalet Hitts of Boston deceased that Shee might haue Liberty to dispose of & put to Sale some part of that Estate for the paiment of debts & Legacies & maintenance of herselfe & Children: The Court Orders & Empowres the saide Anne Hitt (with the consent & advice of those that are Sureties for her true Administracion upon the saide Estate) to dispose of & put to Sale the house & ground at Charlestown valued in the Jnventory at £:170. Shee rendring an Account of sᵈ Sale unto the Court of this County.

Session of 26 January, 1675

Hawkins Sentenced

Mary Hawkins convict in Court of bold whorish carriages & having a bastard Childe & impudent & pernicious Lying: The Court Sentenced her to bee whip't at a Carts tayle up from the dwelling house of John Hall in Boston formerly Ezekiel Foggs Lodgeing into the Town round about the Town house & soe to the prison with twenty five Stripes severely. & within one month following to bee whip't again severely with twenty Five stripes, paying Fees of Court & prison standing committed untill this Sentence bee performed.

Mary Hawkins' petition

To yᵉ honʳᵈ Court of Assistants now siting at Boston
The humble petition of Mary Hawkins Humbly sheweth
That where as yoʳ pore petitioner hath through her very great

sin & wickednes many ways agriuated, brought herselfe vnder the iust sentence of yᵉ Countie Court, one part of wᶜʰ hath bene already inflicted vpon me & though I can not but owne yᵗ I deserue nt onely yᵉ other part to be inflicted, but by reason of my sin being so agreuated as It was, neuer to haue any countenans of fauour [showne] to me either from god or [man] yet considering gods wonderfull mercy to humble peniten [sinners] (though very hainous) calls vpon them to turne from the[ir] wickednes & liue, & yᵗ yᵉ same spirit of Compashon he works in his people, imboldens me humbly to Supplicate yoʳ honʳˢ yᵗ you wil be pleased to remitt yᵗ other part of yᵉ punishment yᵗ is not yet inflicted, desireing yᵉ lord to worke still more & more in my soule a greater sence of my sin & giue me truly to repent & turne to him & to loath my selfe & sin wᶜʰ I hope in [some] weaker measure I doe, thus leaueing my condition in yᵉ lords & yoʳ hands praying for yoʳ honʳˢ I subscribe myselfe

yoʳ Honʳˢ pore afflicted prisoner

mary hokahans

In Ansʳ to this peticon this Court Judgeth it meet wᵗʰ the Consent of the [County] Court to Grant hir request & Remitts hir second punishment ordering the keep[ʳ] of the prison to Dissmiss hir from yᵉ prison & set hir at liberty

Session of 29 July, 1679

Waters' Complaint

Upon complaint made to this Court by Elizabeth Waters that her Husband Wᵐ Waters doth refuse to allow her victuals clothing or fireing necessary for her Support or liuelihood and hath acted many unkindnesses and cruelties towards her: The Court having sent for the sᵈ Wᵐ Waters and heard both partys, do Order that the sᵈ Waters bee admonish't for his cruelty and unkindness to his wife, and that hee forthwith provide Suitable meate drinke and apparrell for his sᵈ wife for future at the Judgemᵗ of mʳ Edward Rawson and mʳ Richᵈ Collacot or allow her five Shillings per weeke.

Burnell's complaint and Order

Upon complaint of Sarah Burnell Widdow of Wᵐ Burnell sometime of Boston deceᵈ that her Son Samuel Burnell hath the Estate that was left by her sᵈ Husband in his hands & refuseth to relieue her or yeild her any Succor or maintenance therefrom: The Court Orders that the sᵈ Widdow bee forthw[th] put into possession of the Chamber. Shee formerly had in her Son's house or other at the Judgem[t] of Cap[tn] John Richards and L[t] Daniel Turill and bee paid five Shillings in money per weeke by her Son untill the next Court of this County.

CASE OF SARAH TAYLOR, INDENTURED SERVANT

In 1659 Sarah Taylor's case first came before the court of Kent County, Maryland, a group of six to ten commissioners appointed by the governor to administer local justice. Indentured servitude was typical for white women of Taylor's age (about twenty) in the Chesapeake colonies at the time, but her master and mistress were exceptionally abusive and the court's resolution of her case was highly unusual. Taylor's master, Thomas Bradnox, had served since 1647 as a commissioner of the court to which she brought her complaint, although he was illiterate and was repeatedly brought before the court himself for drunkenness, assault, profanity, and hog stealing. He did not sit on the court in cases brought against him.

In this document, most contractions have been written out, the letter u *changed to* v *where needed, and a few commas inserted.*

A Court holden on Kent the first day of October 1659

Sarah Tailer Complaineth to the Majestrate mr Joseph wickes of divers wronges & abuses given her by her Master and Mrs, Capt Thomas Bradnox & Mary his wife. And upon the same was committed into the Constables costody to convey to Capt Vaughan for further examination, or to her Maister if shee ware willing to returne, which with her free consent to Constable Henry Gott delivered her to her Maister till the next Court followinge. And then Capt Bradnox did promise to stand to tryall without further somons or writt. . . .

John Jenkins sworne in Court Examined saith That he never saw Capt Bradnox or his wife strike his Servant Sarah Tailer with either Bulls pisle or Rope but he saw the said Sarah have a blacke place crosse one of her shoulders & this Deponent heard her Mrs give her som bad words. And this is what your Deponent doth affirme to the best of his knowledge.

Tobias wells on oath saith that he saw Sarah Tailer Stript & on her backe he saw severall blacke spotts and on her Arme a great blacke spott about as broad as his hand, And Further saith not.

Mr Joseph wickes doth Informe the Court that Mrs Mary Bradnox broake the peace in strikeinge her Sarvant before him beinge a Majestrate, And on the time when the said Sarvant was there to make her Complaint which the said mr wickes could not in Justice passe by or suffer, which was one blow or stroke with a Ropes ende. . . .

J. Hall Pleasants, ed., *Archives of Maryland,* vol. 54, Proceedings of the County Courts of Kent, 1648–1676, Talbot, 1662–1674, and Somerset, 1665–1674 (Baltimore: Maryland Historical Society, 1937), pp. 167–69, 178–80, 213, 224–25, 234.

Capt. Thomas Bradnox Plaintiff
John Deere Defendant

The Court findings by suffitient testimony and also the Confestion of John Deere that he is guilty in entertaininge [Sarah Taylor] the Sarvant of Capt Bradnox privatly without his concent, the Court doth Judge that John Deere for his offence shall aske Capt Thomas Bradnox Forgivenesse in open Court And promise never to commit the Like againe, And to pay Cost to suyt to the plaintiff, else Execution.

Sarah Tailer Complainant
Capt Thomas Bradnox Defendant

The Court takeinge into their Consideration the Cause of these suyts with John Deere & John Smith to arise from the runninge away of the said Sarah Tailer out of her mr & Mistris service, which was for the space of twelve dayes & noe Just Cause appearinge to the Court for the same, mr Henry Morgan doth Judge that the said Sarah shall be whipt. The rest of the Court doth Judge that her Former stripes ware suffitient Corporall punishment, And that shee shall on her Knees aske her Mr & Mrs Forgiveness, And promise amendment for the future, which the said maid there did in open Court, & her Mr to pay all the Charges in the suyte.

Capt Tho. Bradnox Plaintiff
John Smith Defendant

The Plaintiff alledgeth that the Defendant privately detained & Concealed his Sarvant Sarah Tailer, And the Conestble Henry Gott declares that he founde the said Sarvant within night in the house of John Smith. The Defendant confesseth that the maid was in his house, And that he found her in the woods & brought her home to his owne house, but beinge weary that Eveninge he could not trancporte her that night, but did intend next morninge to convey her to her Mr or the Conestable or Else to some Majestrate.

The Court havinge Debated this Matter Longe and Findeinge noe cleere proofe in the Cause to pass Judgmt upon hath with the concent of the partyes Refferanct the hereinge & Determininge hereof untill the next Court being the first day of November. . . .

Sarah Tailer absenteth her selfe From her Mr Capt Thomas Bradnox servis, & complaineth to the Majestrate Mr Joseph wickes of abuses & stripes given her by her mistres without Cause. Whereupon the Majestrate commits her to the Constable, & to send her home if Conveniently he may, or else to bring her to the next Court & the Constable said he could not gett her to her Maisters house but hath now delivered her to this Court. Mrs. Bradnox aledgeth, that for the neglecte of her Mayd Sarah in severall things, shee had given her correction & produceth the sticke in Court wherewith shee had beate her. The Sarvant Sarah Tailer Craves of the Court that shee may have the Testimony of Mecom Meconny & Thomas watts to prove her complaint. Capt Bradnox beinge agreed thereto The Court doth order that mr Phillip Conner shal Examine the Evidence & Take their Depositions, & seeing Just Cause shall send to Capt Vaughan or other of the Majestrats to Administer Justice as the Cause shall require, and the Sarvant to returne home to her maisters house. . . .

Whereas Sarah Tailer hath mayd Complainte unto me that her Mrs Mary Bradnox doth Frequently beate & abuse this Complanent as is pretended by the said Sarah, without any Cause given her said Mrs, And that her Complaint will suffitiently appeare either by the Rest of the said Sarvants of the house, which ware present somtimes when her sd Mrs gave her some part of the Blowes & Causless abuses done unto this Complanent, Besides the remarkable signes as this Complanent saith will appear upon her Body, For which Causes & Reasons the said Sarah will not be parswaded by me to returne home to her said Mrs House but resolveth whatsoever becomes of her not to serve her said Mrs any Longer, to be soe abused by her Causlessely.

These are therefore in the Name of the Lord Proprietor to will & require you to take into yowr Custody the aforesaid Sarah Tailer & if by any Lawfull meanes you may use to Convey her unto her said Maisters house, or otherwise to secure her in your Custody For her said Mr untill the next Court to be holden on Kent the first day of December next where by vertue hereof you are required to bringe her to make her Complaint appear, & that you give timely notice hereof unto her said Maister Thomas Bradnox. hereof Faile you not as you will answar the Contrary Given this 28th of November 1659. And make returne of this writt. To Morgan Williams Constable or his Deputy. [signed] Joshua Wickes. . . .

[1661] Capt Thomas Brodnox Inditeth John White and Sarah Tayler that thay have fellonioasly Runn away and stolen out of his house Diveres good as are in an Inventory in pertikculers by thayre owne Confession spetified youe of the Jeury are to Examine the Evidence and Bringe in your verdit whether the Acction be Crimminall for a further triall at the proventiall Court or not. The Inventory of the goods that wase stolne Itum on[e] wastcote Laced with gould lace, on[e] pare of Bodises, on[e] hood, on[e] scarfe, two neck handcherchifs, 3 pockett handcherchifs, three Aprons—on[e] laune, on[e] saye, on[e] blu linnene; t[w]o pare of shus, on[e] pare of stockings, on[e] holland Coyfe scollopt, two holland Lacede Coyfs—on[e] Lawne Laced, on[e] Cambrick Coyfe Laced—on[e] stock neackloth, on[e] holland Coyfe and Dresinge, on[e] band and bandstrings, two other Coyfes, on[e] shirt, on[e] canves petticot, on[e] canves Apron, on[e] pare of stokings, on[e] serge wascote, on[e] pare of Lockerum Drawers, on[e] pare of knett gloves, on[e] beaver hatt, on[e] new whit blankett, on[e] new Coverled, on[e] portinggall Cape, on[e] new Dowlas shirt. . . . The Jeury [12 men] all sworne

The Jeurys Verditt: The verditt of the Jeury is thes that we do not find it valluable to Reach the law of fellony Conserninge the good that John Whit and Sarah Tayler Did Cary away from Capt Thomas Brodnox as Doth appear to us & this is oure varditt being Jeury men. [signed] Thomas Stagwell foreman

Whereas the Jeury hath brought in thayre varditt and Doth not finde them Guilty of Felony according to thayre Inditment thes Courts sencure is acording to the vardite and Doth order that the goods be Delivered unto Capt Thomas Brodnox as they are and the sarvants to Retorne to thayre Masters sarves. . . .

Att A Court holdern upon Kent the seventh Day of August 1661 . . .

The Complaint of Sarah Tayler Servant to Capt Thomas Brodnox taken the 5th of August 1661 Saith that on Satterday Morning being the 3d of august she beinge about hur Mrs Bussiness in hur Masters kitchin: hur Master & hur Mistres came and suddenly fell uppon hur: and she helped to hold hur untell he begune to beate hure with a great ropes end: then she went and kept the doore untell hur husband hade beate her so unreasonably that theare is twenty on[e] Impresions of blowes small and great upon her backe and Armes that hath binne taken notis of and when hur Master has soe beaten hur; hur Master said now spoyle me a batch of bread againe.

Thes Complaint being read to Capt Brodnox he did acknoledg the beating of hur and that he would answer itt.

Joseph Newman Sworne in Court Saith That on on[e] Sunday morneing when he lived at Capt Thomas Brodnox house Capt Brodnox tooke up a thre futted sto[o]le and stroke Sarah Tayler on the head with it for takeing a booke in hure hand to read: and said youe disimbling Jade what doe you doe with a booke in youre hand, & further saith not [signed] Joseph Newman

Whereas Complaint hath binne made before us by Sarah Tayler servant to Capt Thomas Brodnox that her said Mr. hath Correckted hur when he hade no Caus at all as itt hath apeared before us by the testimony of

Joseph Newman: and when he hade Caus, Corrected hur above Measiour as it dide apeare by the veiw of Capt Robert Vaughan and two other Commisioners to whom she shewed the Impresion of the blowes receved from hur said Master Capt Brodnox: And thearfore we doe think fitt to discharge the said Sarah Tayler of Hur Aprentiships: In regard of the Eminent Danger likely to Insew by the Invetterat Mallice of hur Master & Mistres toward hure.

Thearfore we doe by thes present under oure hands and seales pronounce & declare that we have fore the Causes aforesaid and other Causes to us Knowne Discharge the said Sarah Tayler the Aprentise of hur Apretisehood thes 7th of August 1661. [signed] Robt Vaughan, William Leeads, James Ringgold, Nichholus pickard. . . .

[1662] Whereas the Right Honnorable Charles Calvert Leutenant Generall of thes province dirickted a Commision to us, Edward Lloyd & Henry Coursey, for the hearing and reporting of a sartine differance betwext Mary Brodnox Complainent and Capt Robert Vaughan, Capt William Leeads, Mr. James Ringgould & Mr. Nickholas pickard, Comisioners of Kent County, touching the seting free of on[e] Sarye Tayler latte sarvant to the said Brodnox: In pursuance of which Commision we the said Edward Lloyd & Henry Coursey did Sommons before us the said Complainnent and Commisioners and upon debating the matter both partyes did valluntary refer themselves to us the said Commisiors to Compose and Arbretrate the said difference: and upon hearing and Considering the severall Allegations we doe for A finall determination & Conclusion of the Same, Award that Each of the respecttive Commisioners pay unto the Complainent Mary Brodnox two hundred & twenty pounds of good casked Tobacco by the 20th of October next and she to pay the Charges. [signed] Edward Lloyde L Loyde Henry Coursey Datted the 7th of Junne 1662.

STATUTES ON SLAVE DESCENT

English settlers forcibly imported Africans to work in the Chesapeake colonies as early as the 1620s, but it was not until the 1660s that colonial laws began to fix the status of Africans and their descendants as slaves for life (in Latin, durante vita). In the event of interracial pairing, as these first statutes show, Virginia and Maryland figured the consequences differently. In Virginia, the child's status followed the mother's; in Maryland, the father's. Maryland's 1664 law, aimed to prevent white women from marrying Negro slaves, instead gave owners an incentive to urge marriages between black men and white women in order to enslave the latter and their children. In 1681, the Maryland assembly tried to rectify this problem by severely penalizing such conniving owners. By 1692 the assembly moved toward the Virginia pattern by enslaving the children of slave parents (not only fathers).

LAWS OF VIRGINIA, DECEMBER 1662—14TH CHARLES II

Act XII—Negro womens children to serve according
to the conditions of the mother.

Whereas some doubts have arrisen whether children got by any Englishman upon a Negro woman should be slave or ffree, *Be it therefore enacted and declared by the present grand assembly,* that all children borne in the country shalbe held bond or free only according to the condition of the mother, *And* that if any christian shall committ fornication with a negro man or woman, hee or shee soe offending shall pay double the ffines imposed by the former act.

MARYLAND ASSEMBLY PROCEEDINGS, SEPTEMBER 1664

An Act Concerning Negroes & other Slaves

Bee itt Enacted by the Right Honorable the Lord Proprietary by the advice and Consent of the upper and lower house of this present Generall Assembly That all Negroes or other slaves already within the Province And all Negroes and other slaves to bee hereafter imported into the Province shall serve Durante Vita. And all Children born of any Negro or other slave shall be Slaves as their ffathers were for the terme of their lives. And

William Waller Hening, *The Statutes at Large . . .of Virginia,* vol. 2 (Richmond, Va., 1823), p. 170 [this 1662 law was reenacted repeatedly during the colonial period, in 1696, 1705, 1748, and 1753]; William Browne, ed., *Archives of Maryland* (Baltimore: Maryland Historical Society), vol. 1 (1883), pp. 533–34; vol. 7 (1889), pp. 203–4; vol. 13 (1893), pp. 546–49.

foreasmuch as divers freeborne English women forgettfull of their free Condicion and to the disgrace of our Nation doe intermarry with Negro Slaves by which alsoe divers suites may arise touching the Issue of such woemen and a great damage doth defall the Masters of such Negroes for prevention whereof for deterring such freeborne women from such shamefull Matches Bee itt further Enacted by the Authority advice and Consent aforesaid That whatsoever free borne woman shall intermarry with any slave from and after the Last day of this present Assembly shall Serve the master of such slave dureing the life of her husband. And that all the Issue of such freeborne woemen soe marryed shall be Slaves as their fathers were. And Bee itt further Enacted that all the Issues of English or other freeborne woemen that have already marryed Negroes shall serve the Masters of their Parents till they be Thirty yeares of age and noe longer.

MARYLAND ASSEMBLY PROCEEDINGS, AUGUST–SEPTEMBER 1681

An Act concerning Negroes & Slaves—

Bee itt enacted by the Right Honourable the Lord Proprietor by & with the Advice & Consent of the upper & Lower houses of the present General Assembly & the authority of the same, that all Negroes & other Slaves already Imported or heereafter to bee Imported into this Province shall serve (durante vita) & all the Children already borne or heereafter to bee borne of any Negroes or other Slaves within this Province shall bee Slaves to all intents & purposes as theire fathers were for the Terme of theire naturall Lives.

And for as much a[s] diverse ffreeborne Englishe or White-woman sometimes by the Instigacion Procurement of Conievance of theire Masters Mistresses or dames, & always to the Satisfaccion of theire Lascivious & Lustful desires & to the disgrace not only of the English butt allso of many other Christian Nations, doe Intermarry with Negroes & Slaves by which means diverse Inconveniencys Controversys & suites may arise Touching the Issue or Children of such ffreeborne women aforesaid, for the prevencion whereof for the future, Bee itt further enacted by the Authority aforesaid that if any Master Mistress or dame haveing any ffreeborne Englishe or white woman Servant as aforesaid in theire possession or property, shall by any Instigacion procurement knowledge permission or Contriveance whatsoever, suffer any such ffreeborne Englishe or Whitewoman Servant in their possession & wherein they have property as aforesaid to Intermarry or Contract in Matrimony with any Slave from and after the Last day of this present Sessions of Assembly, That then the said Master Mistress or dame . . . shall forfeite & Loose all theire Claime & Title to the service & servitude of any such ffreeborne woman & alsoe the said woman Servant soe married shall bee & is by this present Act absolutely discharged manymitted & made free Instantly upon her Intermarriage as aforesaid, from the Services Imployments use Claime or demands of any such Master Mistress or dame soe offending as afforesaid. And all Children borne of such ffreeborne woman. soe manymitted . . . shall bee ffree . . . as also the said Master Mistress & dame shall forfeite the sum of Tenn Thousand pounds of Tobacco. . . .

MARYLAND ASSEMBLY PROCEEDINGS, MAY 10–JUNE 9, 1692

An Act concerning Negro Slaves.

Be it Enacted by the King and Queens most Excellent Majesties by and with the Advice and consent of this present Generall Assembly and the Authority of the same, That all negroes and other slaves already imported or hereafter to be Imported into this Province, shall serve their naturall lives and all the Children born already or hereafter to be born or any Negroes of other Slaves within this Province shall be Slaves to all intents and purposes as their parents were for the terme of their natural lives. . . . [And] Be it Enacted by and with the advice and consent aforesaid, That any freeborn English or white woman that shall after the Publication of this Law, either intermarry with or permitt herself to be begotten with children by any Negro or other Slaves, shall . . . Imediatly upon such Marriage forfeit her freedome and become a Servant during the Terme of seven years to the use and benefitt of the Ministry or the Poor of the same Parish at the discretion of the Vestry men . . . and the issues of such women shall likewise be Servants to the uses aforesaid till they arive to the Age of one and twenty years . . . And be it Enacted by the Authority aforesaid by and with the consent and advice aforesaid that any freeborn English or white man that shall from and after the Publication of this Act either inter marry or begett with Child any negro woman or Slave when proved against him shall be lyable to the same paines and penalties as in any by this Act is provided against English or white woman. And be it likewise Enacted . . . [the same punishment as in 1681] if any Master Mistress or dame having any free born English or white woman Servant as aforesaid in their Possession or propriaty shall by any Instigation procurement, knowledge premission or Coniveance whatsoever suffer any such freeborn English or white woman Servant . . . to intermarry or contract in Matrimony with any Negro or Slave. . . .

～

SUSANNA MARTIN, ON TRIAL FOR WITCHCRAFT

Although the Salem trials of 1692 are the best-known example of witch-craft hysteria in the English colonies, accusations and convictions of witches were not confined to that episode. At least a hundred individuals were complained of or indicted for witchcraft before the Salem outbreak, and fifteen executed. About two hundred more were named in Salem, and the trials there resulted in nineteen executions. More than three-quarters of the accused were women. Unquestionably, women more than men were thought to incline toward evil and toward the alliance with the devil that was called witchcraft. The Salem trial of Susanna Martin (recorded by the eminent minister Cotton Mather) shows the kinds of complaints against a female neighbor that might lead accusers to name her a witch. Martin had long been suspected of witchcraft and was executed on July 19, 1692.

I.

Susanna Martin, pleading *Not Guilty* to the Indictment of *Witchcraft*, brought in against her, there were produced the Evidences of many Persons very sensibly and grievously Bewitched; who all complained of the Prisoner at the Bar, as the Person whom they believed the cause of their Miseries. And now, as well as in the other Trials, there was an extraordinary Endeavour by *Witchcrafts*, with Cruel and frequent Fits, to hinder the poor Sufferers from giving in their Complaints, which the Court was forced with much Patience to obtain, by much waiting and watching for it. . . .

IV. *John Atkinson* testifi'd, That he exchanged a Cow with a Son of *Susanna Martin's*, whereat she muttered, and was unwilling he should have it. Going to receive this Cow, tho he Hamstring'd her, and Halter'd her, she, of a Tame Creature, grew so mad, that they could scarce get her along. She broke all the Ropes that were fastned unto her, and though she were ty'd fast unto a Tree, yet she made her escape, and gave them such further trouble, as they could ascribe to no cause but Witchcraft.

V. *Bernard Peache* testifi'd, That being in Bed, on the Lord's-day Night, he heard a scrabbling at the Window, whereat he then saw *Susanna Martin* come in, and jump down upon the Floor. She took hold of this Deponent's Feet, and drawing his Body up into an Heap, she lay upon him near Two Hours; in all which time he could neither speak nor stir. At

Cotton Mather, *The Wonders of the Invisible World* (London: J. R. Smith, 1862 [orig. 1693]), pp. 138–48.

length, when he could begin to move, he laid hold on her Hand, and pulling it up to his Mouth, he bit three of her Fingers, as he judged, unto the Bone. Whereupon she went from the Chamber, down the Stairs, out at the Door. This Deponent thereupon called unto the People of the House, to advise them of what passed; and he himself did follow her. The People saw her not; but there being a Bucket at the Left-hand of the Door, there was a drop of Blood found upon it; and several more drops of Blood upon the Snow newly fallen abroad: There was likewise the print of her 2 Feet just without the Threshold; but no more sign of any Footing further off. . . .

VI. *Robert Downer* testified, That this Prisoner being some Years ago prosecuted at Court for a Witch, he then said unto her, *He believed she was a Witch.* Whereat she being dissatisfied, said, *That some She-Devil would shortly fetch him away!* Which words were heard by others, as well as himself. The Night following, as he lay in his Bed, there came in at the Window, the likeness of a *Cat,* which flew upon him, took fast hold of his Throat, lay on him a considerable while, and almost killed him. At length he remembred what *Susanna Martin* had threatned the Day before; and with much striving he cried out, *Avoid, thou She-Devil! In the Name of God the Father, the Son, and the Holy Ghost, Avoid!* Whereupon it left him, leap'd on the Floor, and flew out at the Window.

And there also came in several Testimonies, that before ever *Downer* spoke a word of this Accident, *Susanna Martin* and her Family had related, *How this* Downer *had been handled!* . . .

VIII. *William Brown* testifi'd, That Heaven having blessed him with a most Pious and Prudent Wife, this Wife of his, one day met with *Susanna Martin;* but when she approach'd just unto her, *Martin* vanished out of sight, and left her extreamly affrighted. After which time, the said *Martin* often appear'd unto her, giving her no little trouble; and when she did come, she was visited with Birds, that sorely peck'd and prick'd her; and sometimes, a Bunch, like a Pullet's Egg, would rise in her Throat, ready to choak her, till she cry'd out, *Witch, you shan't choak me!* While this good Woman was in this extremity, the Church appointed a Day of Prayer, on her behalf; whereupon her Trouble ceas'd; she saw not *Martin* as formerly; and the Church, instead of their Fast, gave Thanks for her Deliverance. But a considerable while after, she being Summoned to give in some Evidence at the Court, against this *Martin,* quickly thereupon, this *Martin* came behind her, while she was milking her Cow, and said unto her, *For thy defaming her at Court, I'll make thee the miserablest Creature in the World.* Soon after which, she fell into a strange kind of distemper, and became horribly frantick, and uncapable of any reasonable

Action; the Physicians declaring, that her Distemper was preternatural, and that some Devil had certainly bewitched her; and in that condition she now remained.

IX. *Sarah Atkinson* testify'd, That *Susanna Martin* came from *Amesbury* to their House at *Newbury,* in an extraordinary Season, when it was not fit for any to Travel. She came (as she said, unto *Atkinson*) all that long way on Foot. She brag'd and shew'd how dry she was; nor could it be perceived that so much as the Soles of her Shoes were wet. *Atkinson* was amazed at it; and professed, that she should her self have been wet up to the knees, if she had then came so far; but *Martin* reply'd, *She scorn'd to be Drabbled!* It was noted, that this Testimony upon her Trial, cast her in a very singular Confusion.

X. *John Pressy* testify'd, That being one Evening very unaccountably Bewildred, near a Field of *Martins,* and several times, as one under an Enchantment, returning to the place he had left, at length he saw a marvellous Light, about the bigness of an Half-bushel, near two Rod, out of the way. He went, and struck at it with a Stick, and laid it on with all his might. He gave it near forty blows; and felt it a palpable substance. But going from it, his Heels were struck up, and he was laid with his Back on the Ground, sliding, as he thought, into a Pit; from whence he recover'd by taking hold on the Bush; altho' afterwards he could find no such Pit in the place. Having, after his Recovery, gone five or six Rod, he saw *Susanna Martin* standing on his Left-hand, as the Light had done before; but they changed no words with one another. He could scarce find his House in his Return; but at length he got home extreamly affrighted. The next day, it was upon Enquiry understood, that *Martin* was in a miserable condition by pains and hurts that were upon her.

It was further testify'd by this Deponent, That after he had given in some Evidence against *Susanna Martin,* many years ago, she gave him foul words about it; and said, *He should never prosper more;* particularly, *That he should never have more than two Cows; that tho' he was never so likely to have more, yet he should never have them.* And that from that very day to this, namely for twenty years together, he could never exceed that number; but some strange thing or other still prevented his having any more.

XI. *Jervis Ring* testify'd, That about seven years ago, he was oftentimes and grievously oppressed in the Night, but saw not who troubled him; until at last he Lying perfectly Awake, plainly saw *Susanna Martin* approach him. She came to him, and forceably bit him by the Finger; so that the Print of the bite is now, so long after, to be seen upon him.

XII. But besides all of these Evidences, there was a most wonderful Account of one *Joseph Ring*, produced on this occasion.

This Man has been strangely carried about by *Dæmons*, from one *Witch-meeting* to another, for near two years together; and for one quarter of this time, they have made him, and keep him Dumb, tho' he is now again able to speak. There was one *T. H.* who having, as 'tis judged, a design of engaging this *Joseph Ring* in a snare of Devillism, contrived a while, to bring this *Ring* two Shillings in Debt unto him.

Afterwards, this poor Man would be visited with unknown shapes, and this *T. H.* sometimes among them; which would force him away with them, unto unknown Places, where he saw Meetings, Feastings, Dancings; and after his return, wherein they hurried him along through the Air, he gave Demonstrations to the Neighbours, that he had indeed been so transported. When he was brought unto these hellish Meetings, one of the first Things they still did unto him, was to give him a knock on the Back, whereupon he was ever as if bound with Chains, uncapable of stirring out of the place, till they should release him. He related, that there often came to him a Man, who presented him a *Book*, whereto he would have him set his Hand; promising to him, that he should then have even what he would; and presenting him with all the delectable Things, Persons, and Places, that he could imagin. But he refusing to subscribe, the business would end with dreadful Shapes, Noises and Screeches, which almost scared him out of his Wits. Once with the Book, there was a Pen offered him, and an Ink-horn with Liquor in it, that seemed like Blood: But he never toucht it.

This Man did now affirm, That he saw the Prisoner at several of those hellish Randezvouzes.

Note, this Woman was one of the most impudent, scurrilous, wicked Creatures in the World; and she did now throughout her whole Tryal, discover her self to be such an one. Yet when she was asked, what she had to say for her self? Her chief Plea was, *That she had lead a most virtuous and holy Life.*

CAROLINA WOMEN OBSERVED

In 1700, Englishman John Lawson was appointed by the Lords Proprietor of Carolina to make a reconnaissance survey of the back country. With a few other Englishmen and an Indian guide, he embarked on a fifty-nine-day trip of about 550 miles, beginning on the coast just above Charleston, traveling west and north into the interior, and then some distance into North Carolina, turning eastward back toward the coast. These areas were populated by Native Americans, including Santees, Chickanees, Waterees, Waxhaws, Catawbas, and Tuscaroras, and by a few white traders. Lawson settled in North Carolina and was appointed Surveyor-General. He met his death in 1711 at the hands of Tuscarora Indians in retaliation for English depredations of Indian lands and settlements. Lawson's New Voyage to Carolina, *originally published in 1708, was one of the first sources of information for Europeans about the land, wildlife, and people of Carolina.*

As for the *Indian* Women, which now happen in my Way; when young, and at Maturity, they are as fine-shap'd Creatures (take them generally) as any in the Universe. They are of a tawny Complexion: their Eyes very brisk and amorous; their Smiles afford the finest Composure a Face can possess; their Hands are of the finest Make, with small long Fingers, and as soft as their Cheeks; and their whole Bodies of a smooth Nature. They are not so uncouth or unlikely, as we suppose them; nor are they Strangers or not Proficients in the soft Passion. They are most of them mercenary, except the married Women, who sometimes bestow their Favours also to some or other, in their Husbands Absence. For which they never ask any Reward. As for the Report, that they are never found unconstant, like the *Europeans,* it is wholly false; for were the old World and the new one put into a Pair of Scales (in point of Constancy) it would be a hard Matter to discern which was the heavier. As for the Trading Girls, which are those design'd to get Money by their Natural Parts, these are discernable, by the Cut of their Hair; their Tonsure differing from all others, of that Nation, who are not of their Profession; which Method is intended to prevent Mistakes: for the Savages of *America* are desirous (if possible) to keep their Wives to themselves, as well as those in other Parts of the World. When any Addresses are made to one of these Girls, she

John Lawson, *A New Voyage to Carolina,* ed. Hugh Talmage Lefler (Chapel Hill: University of North Carolina Press, 1967), pp. 189–97, 90–91. Copyright © 1967 by the University of North Carolina Press. Reprinted by permission of the publisher.

immediately acquaints her Parents therewith, and they tell the King of it, (provided he that courts her be a Stranger) his Majesty commonly being the principal Bawd of the Nation he rules over, and there seldom being any of these *Winchester*-Weddings agreed on, without his Royal Consent. He likewise advises her what Bargain to make, and if it happens to be an *Indian* Trader that wants a Bed-fellow, and has got Rum to sell, be sure, the King must have a large Dram for a Fee, to confirm the Match. These *Indians,* that are of the elder sort, when any such Question is put to them, will debate the Matter amongst themselves with all the Sobriety and Seriousness imaginable, every one of the Girl's Relations arguing the Advantage or Detriment that may ensue such a Night's Encounter; all which is done with as much Steadiness and Reality, as if it was the greatest Concern in the World, and not so much as one Person shall be seen to smile, so long as the Debate holds, making no Difference betwixt an Agreement of this Nature, and a Bargain of any other. If they comply with the Men's Desire, then a particular Bed is provided for them, either in a Cabin by themselves, or else all the young people turn out, to another Lodging, that they may not spoil Sport; and if the old People are in the same Cabin along with them all Night, they lie as unconcern'd, as if they were so many Logs of Wood. If it be an *Indian* of their own Town or Neighbourhood, that wants a Mistress, he comes to none but the Girl, who receives what she thinks fit to ask him, and so lies all Night with him, without the Consent of her Parents.

The *Indian* Traders are those which travel and abide amongst the *Indians* for a long space of time; sometimes for a Year, two, or three. These Men have commonly their *Indian* Wives, whereby they soon learn the *Indian* Tongue, keep a Friendship with the Savages; and, besides the Satisfaction of a She-Bed-Fellow, they find these *Indian* Girls very serviceable to them, on Account of dressing their Victuals, and instructing 'em in the Affairs and Customs of the Country. Moreover, such a Man gets a great Trade with the Savages; for when a Person that lives amongst them, is reserv'd from the Conversation of their Women. 'tis impossible for him ever to accomplish his Designs amongst that People.

But one great Misfortune which oftentimes attends those that converse with these Savage Women, is, that they get Children by them, which are seldom educated any otherwise than in a State of Infidelity; for it is a certain Rule and Custom, amongst all the savages of *America,* that I was ever acquainted withal, to let the Children always fall to the Woman's Lot; for it often happens, that two *Indians* that have liv'd together, as Man and Wife, in which Time they have had several Children: if they part, and another Man possesses her, all the Children go along with the Mother, and none with the Father. And therefore, on this Score, it ever seems impossible for the Christians to get their Children (which they have by these *Indian* Women) away from them; whereby they might bring them up in the Knowledge of the Christian Principles. Nevertheless, we often find, that *English* Men, and other *Europeans* that have been accustom'd to the Conversation of these savage Women, and their Way of Living, have been so allur'd with that careless sort of Life, as to be constant to their *Indian* Wife, and her Relations, so long as they liv'd, without ever desiring to return again amongst the *English,* although they had very fair Opportunities of Advantages amongst their Countrymen; of which sort I have known several.

As for the *Indian* Marriages, I have read and heard of a great deal of Form and Ceremony used, which I never saw, nor yet could learn in the Time I have been amongst them, any otherwise than I shall here give you an Account of: which is as follows.

When any young *Indian* has a Mind for such a Girl to his Wife, he, or some one for him, goes to the Young Woman's Parents, if living; if not, to her nearest Relations; where they make Offers of the Match betwixt the Couple. The Relations reply, they will consider of it, which serves for a sufficient Answer, till there be a second Meeting about the Marriage, which is generally brought into Debate before all the Relations (that are old People) on both Sides: and sometimes the King, with all his great Men, give their Opinions therein. If it be agreed on, and the young Woman approve thereof, (for these Savages never give their Children in Marriage, without their own Consent) the Man pays so much for his Wife: and the handsomer she is, the greater Price she bears. . . .

They never marry so near as a first Cousin; and although there is nothing more coveted amongst them, than to marry a Woman of their own Nation, yet when the Nation consists of a very few People (as now adays it often happens) so that they are all of them related to one another, then they look out for Husbands and Wives amongst Strangers. For if an *Indian* lies with his Sister, or any very near Relation, his Body is burnt, and his Ashes thrown into the River, as unworthy to remain on Earth; yet an *Indian* is allow'd to marry two Sisters, or his Brothers Wife. Although these People are call'd Savages, yet Sodomy is never heard of amongst them, and they are so far from the Practice of that beastly and loathsome Sin, that they have no Name for it in all their Language.

The Marriages of these *Indians* are no farther binding, than the Man and Woman agree together. Either of them has Liberty to leave the other, upon any frivolous Excuse they can make; yet whosoever takes the Woman that was another Man's before, and bought by him, as they all are, must certainly pay to her former Husband, whatsoever he gave for her. . . .

The Woman is not punish'd for Adultery, but 'tis the Man that makes the injur'd Person Satisfaction, which is the Law of Nations practis'd amongst them all; and he that strives to evade such Satisfaction as the Husband demands, lives daily in Danger of his Life; yet when discharg'd, all Animosity is laid aside, and the Cuckold is very well pleased with his Bargain, whilst the Rival is laugh'd at by the whole Nation, for carrying on his Intrigue with no better Conduct, than to be discover'd and pay so dear for his Pleasure.

The *Indians* say, that the Woman is a weak Creature, and easily drawn away by the Man's Persuasion: for which Reason, they lay no Blame upon her, but the Man (that ought to be Master of his Passion) for persuading her to it.

They are of a very hale Constitution; their Breaths are as sweet as the Air they breathe in, and the Woman seems to be of that tender Composition, as if they were design'd rather for the Bed than Bondage. Yet their Love is never of that Force and Continuance, that any of them ever runs Mad, or makes away with themselves on that score. They never love beyond Retrieving their first Indifferency, and when slighted, are as ready to untie the Knot at one end, as you are at the other. . . .

The *Indian* Womens Work is to cook the Victuals for the whole Family, and to make Mats, Baskets, Girdles of Possum-Hair, and such-like. They never plant the Corn amongst us, as they do amongst the *Iroquois*, who are always at War and Hunting; therefore, the Plantation Work is left for the Women and Slaves to perform, and look after; whilst they are wandring all over the Continent betwixt the two Bays of *Mexico* and St. *Laurence*.

The Mats the *Indian* Women make, are of Rushes, and about five Foot high, and two Fathom long, and sew'd double, that is, two together; whereby they become very commodious to lay under our Beds, or to sleep on in the Summer Season in the Day-time, and for our Slaves in the Night.

There are other Mats made of Flags, which the *Tuskeruro Indians* make, and sell to the Inhabitants.

The Baskets our Neighbouring *Indians* make, are all made of a very fine sort of Bulrushes, and sometimes of Silk-grass, which they work with Figures of Beasts, Birds, Fishes, &c.

A great way up in the Country, both Baskets and Mats are made of the split Reeds, which are only the outward shining Part of the Cane. Of these I have seen Mats, Baskets, and Dressing-Boxes, very artificially done.

The Savage Women of *America*, have very easy Travail with their Children; sometimes they bring Twins, and are brought to bed by themselves, when took at a Disadvantage; not but that they have Midwives amongst them, as well as Doctors, who make it their Profession (for Gain) to assist and deliver Women, and some of these Midwives are very knowing in several Medicines that *Carolina* affords, which certainly expedite, and make easy Births. Besides, they are unacquainted with those severe Pains which follow the Birth in our *European* Women. Their Remedies are a great Cause of this Easiness in that State: for the *Indian* Women will run up and down the Plantation, the same day, very briskly, and without any sign of Pain or Sickness; yet they look very meager and thin. Not but that we must allow a great deal owing to the Climate, and the natural Constitution of these Women, whose Course of Nature never visits them in such Quantities, as the *European* Women have. And tho' they never want Plenty of Milk, yet I never saw an *Indian* Woman with very large Breasts; neither does the youngest Wife ever fail of proving so good a Nurse, as to bring her Child up free from the Rickets and Disasters that proceed from the Teeth, with many other Distempers which attack our Infants in *England,* and other Parts of *Europe.* They let their Children suck till they are well grown, unless they prove big with Child sooner. They always nurse their own Children themselves, unless Sickness or Death prevents. I once saw a Nurse hired to give Suck to an *Indian* Woman's Child, which you have in my Journal. After Delivery, they absent the Company of a Man for forty days. As soon as the Child is born, they wash it in cold Water at the next Stream, and then bedawb it, as I have mention'd before. After which, the Husband takes care to provide a Cradle, which is soon made, consisting of a Piece of flat Wood, which they hew with their Hatchets to the Likeness of a Board: it is about two Foot long, and a Foot broad; to this they brace and tie the Child down very close, having, near the middle, a Stick fasten'd about two Inches from the Board, which is for the child's Breech to rest on, under which they put a Wad of Moss, that receives the Child's Excrements, by which means they can shift the Moss, and keep all clean and sweet. Some Nations have very flat Heads, as you have heard in my Journal, which is made whilst tied on this Cradle, as that Relation informs you. These Cradles are apt to make the Body flat: yet they are the most portable things that can be invented; for there is a String which goes from one Corner of the Board to the other, whereby the Mother slings her Child on her back; so the Infant's Back is towards hers, and its Face looks up towards the Sky. If it rains, she throws her Leather or Woollen Match-coat, over her Head, which covers the Child all over, and secures her and it from the Injuries of rainy Weather. The Savage Women quit all Company, and dress not their own Victuals, during their Purgations.

As for those of our own Country in *Carolina,* some of the Men are very laborious, and make great Improvements in their Way; but I dare hardly give 'em that Character in general. The easy Way of living in that plentiful Country, makes a great many Planters very negligent, which, were they otherwise, that Colony might now have been in a far better Condition than it is, (as to Trade, and other Advantages) which an universal Industry would have led them into.

The Women are the most industrious Sex in that Place, and, by their good Houswifry, make a great deal of Cloath of their own Cotton, Wool and Flax; some of them keeping their Families (though large) very decently apparel'd, both with Linnens and Woollens, so that they have no occasion to run into the Merchant's Debt, or lay their Money out on Stores for Cloathing.

The *Christian* Natives of *Carolina* are a straight, clean-limb'd People; the Children being seldom or never troubled with Rickets, or those other Distempers, that the *Europeans* are visted withal. 'Tis next to a Miracle, to see one of them deform'd in Body. The Vicinity of the Sun makes Impression on the Men, who labour out of doors, or use the Water. As for those Women, that do not expose themselves to the Weather, they are often very fair, and generally as well featur'd, as you shall see any where, and have very brisk charming Eyes, which sets them off to Advantage. They marry very young; some at Thirteen or Fourteen; and She that stays till Twenty, is reckon'd a stale Maid; which is a very indifferent Character in that warm Country. The Women are very fruitful; most Houses being full of Little Ones. It has been observ'd, that Women long marry'd, and without Children, in other Places, have remov'd to *Carolina,* and become joyful Mothers. They have very easy Travail in their Child-bearing, in which they are so happy, as seldom to miscarry.

. . . Many of the Women are very handy in Canoes, and will manage them with great Dexterity and Skill, which they become accustomed to in this watry Country. They are ready to help their Husbands in any servile Work, as Planting, when the Season of the Weather requires Expedition; Pride seldom banishing good Houswifry. The Girls are not bred up to the Wheel, and Sewing only; but the Dairy and Affairs of the House they are very well acquainted withal; so that you shall see them, whilst very young, manage their Business with a great deal of Conduct and Alacrity.

~

A RAPE ON THE BODY OF ANNE EASTWORTHY

Rape was a capital crime in the English colonies in the seventeenth and eighteenth centuries. Because of this and because colonial juries were reluctant to judge a sexual act to be against a woman's will if she had in any way made herself available for assault, rapists were rarely prosecuted successfully. Documentation of rape is hard to find, but that does not mean that rape did not occur. As this newspaper report suggests, women who worked outside their own households were especially vulnerable.

Burlington [New Jersey], November 10 [1729]. On Friday last, at our Supream Court, came on the Tryal of *James Burnside,* an *Irishman,* for a Rape on the Body of *Anne Eastworthy,* Widow of——*Eastworthy.*

The said *Anne Eastworthy* being brought into Court in a Chair, depos'd, That going from Philadelphia in a Boat to A. Goforth's Plantation, she enquir'd for some Spinning; that the said James Burnside being in the Boat with her and several others, told her, He could help her to half a Year's Work: That afterwards landing on the Jersey Shore, near Ancocus, about Dusk, she went with him in Hopes to get Work; but he led her thro' several Woods and Fields, and at last into a Cow-Pen; that upon her telling him, She would make him Amends if he could assist her, he told her, He desir'd Nothing but a Night's Lodging, which, as she said, very much surprize'd her; and thereupon he took her in his Arms, and —— (N.B. We omit those Expressions which, tho' used in open Court, we apprehend may be offensive to the Ear of a modest Reader.) That she struggled, resisted, and cry'd out bitterly, begging him for Christ's sake not to abuse her, but rather to kill her, saying, For Christ's sake, Man, don't abuse me thus, but rather kill me; that after he had ravish'd her, they walk'd on for some Time, she being, as she said, in a miserable Condition, and in Fear of her Life, he asked her, Whether she would tell of it or no, and she saying No, he —— ravished her again; That they then walk'd on further till they came to a House, where the Good Man took her in.

The said Person depos'd, that she came in his House about the same Time before depos'd, in a seeming weak Condition; that she remained in his House Two Weeks and upwards, weak and languishing. It was also sworn, that the said James Burnside offer'd to pay for her Keeping, and to make it up with her.

Pennsylvania Gazette 49 (November 10–13, 1729) and 60 (December 30, 1729–January 6, 1730).

The Prisoner made little Defence himself; but having Counsel allow'd by the Lenity of the Court, several Witnesses were call'd, particularly Mr. E. R. Price, who depos'd, that some Years since, when he was Deputy to the Attorney-General, the said Anne Eastworthy had swore a Rape against one Hill at Salem; that she and her Husband being bound to prosecute, or appear as Evidence, absconded and forfeited their Recognizances, upon which the Grand Jury brought in the Bill Ignoramus.

Titan Leeds, Esq; Sheriff, depos'd, that having a Writ for the said Anne Eastworthy, he found her in Bed; That several Persons being in the Room, Discourse began about the aforesaid Rape, and the said Anne declar'd, That if the aforesaid Burnside would come and marry her in the Condition she was in, he should not be hang'd; or Words to that Purpose.

This was confirm'd by another Evidence; and the Fellow had several appear'd to his Reputation, particularly his Master, who gave him the Character of an honest, faithful, civil Fellow; and another Evidence, who told the Court bluntly, If they wanted to be inform'd further, they might ask the Prisoner's greatest Enemy in Court, who had several Daughters with whom he us'd to keep Company.

The Counsel offer'd to prove that the said Anne Eastworthy had been an infamous Woman; but that not being allow'd by the Court, after a Tryal of about four Hours, the Jury brought him in Guilty. *Death.*

The next Day the Prisoner being brought into Court to receive Sentence, his Counsel offer'd several Arguments in Arrest of Judgement, and particularly that the Indictment was insufficient, by Reason, that after the Word Ravish, the Words, against her Will were left out; whereupon it was order'd, that the Pleadings on both Sides should be put off till next Court, and the Prisoner was remanded back again, and order'd to be put in Irons.

[December 30, 1729.] The Man who was found guilty of a Rape at the last Court at Burlington, has broken Prison and made his Escape.

A LAW FOR REGULATING MIDWIVES

Most health care and healing in the colonial period were provided by women: from the mothers, sisters, wives, and neighbors who "watched" by the bedside of the sick and employed family remedies for illness, to the skilled midwives and "doctoresses" who learned their craft through years of observation and apprenticeship under other women. Midwives were best known for delivering babies, but the range of their medical services might include virtually everything offered by male physicians except invasive techniques such as bleeding and surgery. Midwives were pivotal members of their communities and, as those communities grew larger, were regulated by laws such as this one enacted in New York City in 1716.

City of
New York ⎱ SS

ATT a Common Council held Att the City Hall of the Said City on fryday the 27ᵗʰ day of July Anno Dom̄ 1716.

. . .

THE following Law was this day Read Agreed to & after the Ringing of Three Bells published At the City Hall in the usual Manner (Viz.ᵗ)

A Law for Regulating Mid Wives within the City of New York

BE IT ORDAINED by the Mayor Recorder Aldermen and Assistants of the City of New York Convened in Common Council and it is hereby Ordained by the Authority of the same that No Woman whatsoever within this Corporation of the City of New York Shall be Capable of, or in any manner whatsoever Use or Exercise the Office or Imploy of A Mid Wife within the said Corporation untill She Shall before the Mayor Recorder and Aldermen of the said Corporation for the time being or any One of them take the Oath of a Midwife hereafter Mentioned which Oath they or any one of them have hereby power to Administer in the Words following (Viz.ᵗ)

You Shall swear, first that you Shall be Dilligent and faithfull And Ready to help Every Woman Labouring of Child As well the poor as the Rich; And that in time of Necessity you shall not for sake or Leave the poor Woman to go to the Rich   ITEM you Shall Neither Cause nor suffer any Woman to Name or put any other father to the Child, but only him which is the Very true father thereof Indeed According to the Uttmost of your power. ITEM you shall not Suffer any Woman to Pretend feign or surmise her self to be Delivered of a Child who is not Indeed, Neither to Claim any other Womans Child for her own. ITEM You Shall not suffer any Womans Child to be Murthered Maimed or Otherwise hurt as much as you may And so often as you shall perceive any perill or Jeopardy Either in the Woman or in the Child in any such wise as you Shall be in Doubt what shall Chance thereof you shall thenceforth in Due time send for other Midwifes and Expert Women in that faculty and use their Advice Councel and Assistance in that behalf. ITEM You Shall not Give any Counsel or Administer any Herb Medicine or Potion or any other thing to any Woman being with Child whereby She Should Destroy or Miscarry of that she goeth withall before her time. ITEM You Shall not Enforce any Woman being with Child by any pain or by any UnGodly Ways or Means to give you any more for your pains or labour in bringing her A Bed than they would Otherwise Do. ITEM You Shall not Consent Agree Give or Keep Counsel that any Woman be Delivered secretly of that which she goeth with but in the presence of Two or three Witnesses ready ITEM You shall be secret and not Open any matter Appertaining to your Office in the presence of any Man unless Nessessity or Great Urgent Cause do Constrain you so to do. ITEM. If you shall know any MidWife using or doing any thing Contrary to any of the premisses or in any otherwise then shall be seemly or Convenient You shall forthwith Detect and Openly shew the same to the Mayor Recorder and Aldermen of the City of New York for the time being or one of them. ITEM you shall use yourself in honest behaviour unto the Woman being Lawfully Admitted to the Room and Office of A Mid Wife in all things Accordingly. ITEM You Shall not make or Assign any Deputy or Deputies to Exercise or Occupy under you in your Absence the Office or Room of a Mid Wife but such as you shall perfectly know to be of Right honest and Discreet behaviour as also Apt Able and having sufficient knowledge and Experience to Exercise the said Room and Office. ITEM if any Woman in Labour under your Care Shall Desire the Advise or Assistance of any other Mid Wife or Mid Wifes you Shall Readily Consent to the Same and use their Advice Counsell and Assistance in that behalf if in your Conscience you think it for the Benifitt of such Woman in Labour. ITEM You Shall not Conceal the Birth of any Bastard Child within the Corporation of the City of New York but Shall forthwith upon Understanding thereof Give Knowledge of the same to the Mayor Recorder and Aldermen of the City of New York for the time being or any one of them or to the Alderman or Chief Magistrate of the Ward where such Bastard Child Shall be born All which Articles and Charge you Shall faithfully Observe &

keep So help you God.   AND be it Ordained by the Authority Aforesaid that the Mayor Recorder & Aldermen of the City of New York for the time being or any one of them before whom such Oath Shall be taken Shall Certifie the taking of such Oath to the Mayors Next Court there to be Recorded AND be it Ordained by the Authority Aforesaid that if any Woman within the said Corporation of the City of New York Shall after the third Day of August Next Ensueing the Date hereof Use Occupy or Exersize the Office of A Mid Wife within the said Corporation of the City of New York before the Oath before Mentioned hath been Duely Administred unto her by the Mayor Recorder and Aldermen of the said City of New York for the time being or one of them that then And in such Case such Woman so useing Occupying or Exersizeing the Office of A Mid-Wife within the said Corporation of the City of New York for Every Default shall forfeit and pay the sum of forty shillings of Lawfull Money of the province of New York to be Recovered before the Mayor Recorder and Aldermen of the said City of New York for the time being or any one of them by A summary proceeding which forfeiture shall be Levyed by Distress and sale of the Goods and Chattells of such Offender against the Tenor of this Law by Warrant under the hand & seal of the said Mayor Recorder and Aldermen of the City of New York for the time being or any one of them and shall be Disposed of in manner following that is to say one half of the said forfeiture to the Treasurer of the City of New York for the time being for the use of the Corporation of the said City of New York And the Other half to the person or persons who Shall sue for or prosecute the same And in Case such Offender against the Tenor of this Law shall not have sufficient goods and Chattells to be found within the said Corporation to satisfie the said forfeiture then and in such Case It shall And may be Lawfull for the Mayor Recorder and Aldermen of the City of New York for the time being or any one of them by Warrant under hand and seal to Committ such Offender to the Common Goal of the Said City there to Remain without Bail or Mainprize for the Space of Thirty Days After the Date of such Warrant Unless the said forfeiture be in the Mean time paid and satisfyed Dated att the City Hall of the said City the Twenty Seventh day of July in the second year of his Ma^tyes Reigne Anno Dom̄ 1716.

PART II

TRANSITIONS TO
A NEW REPUBLIC

SARAH OSBORN'S RELIGIOUS CONVERSION

Sarah Osborn, noted for her piety during her long life in Newport, Rhode Island, was born in London in 1714. Her family emigrated to the colonies in 1722 and settled in Newport in 1729. The following part of her memoirs, in which she recounts her experiences during the religious revivals that came to be called the "Great Awakening" in New England, was completed in 1743. She lived until 1796, acting as religious mentor to younger people, giving religious instruction in her home (to African American slaves, among others), and teaching school to support herself.

I thought I trusted in God; and used frequently, in times of trial, to go and pour out my complaints to him, thinking he was my only support. But I dare not now be positive, or really conclude, that I know what it was to put my trust in God; for my conduct after this seems so inconsistent with grace, that I dare not say I had one spark of it then; but rather think I was only under a common work of the Spirit: Though some times I think I had true grace, though very weak. . . . After this (O that with deep humility of soul, with sorrow and shame, I could speak of it) I relapsed again, and was full of vanity. I kept company with a young man, something against my parents' will. But that was owing to false reports raised of him; for at first they liked him. I made resolutions, that, after I was married, I would lead a new life, flattering myself that then I should not have the hinderances which I now had. I used bitterly to reflect upon myself, when I had given myself liberty to be merry; for though I appeared outwardly so, I had no real pleasure: But still put off repentance, or an entire breaking off from vanity, till a more convenient season; and so resisted the Spirit of God.

. . . In process of time, I was married to Mr. Samuel Wheaten, being in my eighteenth year, October 21, 1731, and went with my husband, the next winter, to see his friends in the country; where I stayed almost five months; and was almost all the time under strong convictions. Oh, how I did sweat and tremble for fear my convictions should wear off again, and plead with God to set home strong convictions, and never, never suffer them to cease, till they ended in a sound and saving conversion. . . .

. . . From this time I had a hope again, at times, that Christ was mine. But it was some years after before it pleased God to answer it fully, by giving me an assurance of it. . . .

Samuel Hopkins, ed., *Memoirs of the Life of Mrs. Sarah Osborn* (Worcester, Mass.: Leonard Worcester, 1799), pp. 15–21, 39, 42–43, 45–46, 49–55.

After I came home, I met with much affliction in many respects. It seemed to me that the whole world were in arms against me. I thought I was the most despised creature living upon earth. I used to pray to God in secret to relieve me; but did not, as I ought, see his hand in permitting it so to be, as a just punishment for my vile sins: And therefore was not humbled under it as I ought; but let nature rise, and acted very imprudently, in many respects. I was then with child, and often lamented that I was to bring a child into such a world of sorrow: But some times found a disposition to dedicate my babe to God, while in the womb; and did so, at all seasons of secret prayer. And after it was born, my husband being at sea, I could not rest till I had solemnly given it up to God in baptism. And I thought that I did indeed give up both myself and it to God.

I met with many trials in my lying in, it being an extreme cold season. My child was born on Oct. 27, 1732. The next spring, my husband returned home; but went to sea again, and died abroad in November, 1733. I was then in my twentieth year. The news of my husband's death came to me on the first of the next April. . . . But God appeared wonderfully for my support. I saw his hand, and was enabled to submit with patience to his will. I daily looked round me, to see how much heavier the hand of God was laid on some others, than it was on me, where they were left with a large number of children, and much involved in debt. And I had but one to maintain; and, though poor, yet not involved. Others, I saw, as well as myself, had their friends snatched from them by sudden accidents. The consideration of these things, together with the thoughts of what I deserved, stilled me so, that though the loss of my companion, whom I dearly loved, was great; yet the veins of mercy, which I saw running through all my afflictions, were so great likewise, that, with Job, I could say, "The Lord gave, and the Lord hath taken away, and blessed be the name of the Lord."

. . . As before this affliction every one seemed to be enemies to me, so from that time, all became friends. My parents treated me very tenderly; and God inclined every one who saw me to be kind to me. My brother was come into New-England: And being a single man, we went to housekeeping together. But in three months after he married, and I soon found it would not do to live as before; and began to be thoughtful how I should do. I could see no way in which I could get a living. All doors seemed to be shut. But I verily believed that God would point out a way for me. And accordingly, the very day I came to a resolution to move as soon as I could, a stranger to my case, who kept a school a little way off, came to me, and told me that she only waited for a fair wind to go to Carolina; and, if it would suit me, I should have her chamber and schollars; which

I joyfully accepted. Thus the widow's God remarkably provided for me. This was on Nov. 19, 1734. I was then placed in a family, who discovered a great deal of affection for me; and in all respects used me as tenderly as if I had been a near relation.

. . . The instances of the remarkable hand of God in his providence, in ordering my temporal affairs, are innumerable. But, oh vile wretch! after all this I grew slack again, and got into a cold, lifeless frame. As I grew better in bodily health, my soul grew sick. I daily laid up a stock for repentance. But, through rich grace, I was again convinced of my stupidity, and began to be more diligent in attending on the means of grace. But I found I could not profit by the word preached: Nothing reached my heart; all seemed but skin deep: And the more I went to meeting, the more I found it so. Then I began to think I must take some other course. . . .

. . . [And] O, when I had finished writing my covenant, which was on the 26th of March, 1737, and came to spread it before God, and with prayers and tears to deliver it to him as my own act and deed, it verily seemed to me that all the heavens rang with acclamations of joy, that such a prodigal as I was returned to my God and Father. . . .

These were happy days—But now how shall I speak! Oh, that I may do it with a heart truly broken for my sins! After all this, I began to grow more conformed to the world. Things which, when I was thus lively, appeared insipid, and indeed odious to me, began to grow more tolerable, and by degrees in a measure pleasant. And depraved nature and Satan together pleaded for them thus, "That there was a time for all things; and singing and dancing now and then, with a particular friend, was an innocent diversion. Who did I see, besides myself, so precise and strict? Other christians allowed themselves in such things, who, I had reason to think, were far superior to me in grace; especially one with whom I was very intimate. Sure, if it was sin, she would not allow herself in it. It was for extraordinary christians, such as ministers, and others who were eminent for piety, to avoid the practice of such things, and not for *me*. Who did I think I was, that I should pretend to outdo other christians? They could talk of worldly things. What ailed me?" Thus the devil and carnal reasoning argued me out of a great part of my resolutions for strict godliness; and, in short, made me, in a sort, believe that it was only pride and hypocrisy, and to be seen of men, that had ever made me pretend to it.

Thus I sunk by degrees lower and lower, till I had at last almost lost all sense of my former experiences. I had only the bare remembrance of them, and they seemed like dreams or delusion; at some times. At others again, I had some revivals. . . . But I knew I was a dreadful backslider, and had dealt treacherously with God. . . .

In Sept. 1740, God in mercy sent his dear servant Whitefield[1] here, which in some measure stirred me up. But when Mr. Tennent[2] came soon after, it pleased God to bless his preaching so to me, that it roused me. But I was all the winter after exercised with dreadful doubts and fears about my state. I questioned the truth of all I had experienced, and feared I had never yet passed through the pangs of the new birth, or ever had one spark of grace.

. . . I continued thus till March, 1741. And then it pleased God to return Mr. Tennent to us again, and he preached twenty one sermons here. But while he was here, I was more than ever distressed. I had lost the sensible manifestations of Christ's love. . . . And [Mr. Tennent] struck directly at those things, for which I had so foolishly and wickedly pleaded christian example, such as singing songs, dancing and foolish jesting, which is not convenient. He said, he would not say there was no such thing as a dancing christian, but he had a very mean opinion of such as could bear to spend their time so, when it is so short, and the work for eternity so great. Then, and not till then, was I fully convinced what prodigal wasters of precious time such things were. And, through grace, I have abhorred them all ever since.

. . . After I was thus revived, my longings to be made useful in the world returned, and I earnestly pleaded with God that he would not suffer me to live any longer an unprofitable servant; but would point out some way, in which I might be useful: And that I might now be as exemplary for piety, as I had been for folly. And it pleased God so to order it, that I had room to hope my petitions were both heard, and in a measure answered. For soon after this a number of young women, who were awakened to a concern for their souls, came to me, and desired my advice and assistance, and proposed to join in a society, provided I would take the care of them. To which, I trust with a sense of my own unworthiness, I joyfully consented. And much sweetness we enjoyed in these meetings. . . .

About this time I had the offer of a second marriage, with one who appeared to be a real christian (and I could not think of being unequally

---

1. George Whitefield, English evangelical preacher who undertook a speaking tour in the American colonies in 1739–41. He kindled the "great and general revival of religion" in the 1740s.—Ed.
2. Gilbert Tennent, a "New Light" Presbyterian minister from New Jersey who benefited in prestige and following from his association with Whitefield during the latter's visits to America.—Ed.

yoked with one who was not such). I took the matter into serious consideration. I foresaw there were difficulties which I must unavoidably encounter; and many duties would be incumbent on me, to which I had been a stranger: Particularly, in my being a mother in law to three sons, which my proposed husband had by a first wife. But after weighing all circumstances, as well as I could, in my mind, and earnest prayer, which God enabled me to continue in for some time, I concluded it was the will of God, that I should accept of the offer, and accordingly was married to Mr. Henry Osborn, on the fifth day of May, 1742. . . .

Soon after this, we fell into disagreeable and difficult worldly circumstances, with respect to living and paying the debts we owed. My greatest concern was with respect to the latter, lest we should not be able to do justice, and so wrong our creditors, and bring dishonor on God, and our profession. Under this pressure and distress, I was relieved and supported by the following words of Scripture, "Let your conversation be without covetousness, and be content with such things as ye have; for he hath said, I will never leave thee, nor forsake thee." I lived cheerfully, upon this promise, for a considerable time. And God ordered things so that our creditors were paid to their satisfaction.

I have often thought God has so ordered it throughout my days hitherto, that I should be in an afflicted, low condition, as to worldly circumstances, and inclined the hearts of others to relieve me in all my distresses, on purpose to suppress that pride of my nature, which doubtless would have been acted out greatly to his dishonor, had I enjoyed health, and had prosperity, so as to live independent of others. I will therefore think it best for me; . . . [and], on account of my poverty, I never was despised.

QUERY TO THE PHILADELPHIA
BAPTIST ASSOCIATION

Although women predominated in church membership in many colonies (especially in New England) as early as the middle of the seventeenth century, there is little evidence that as church members they voted or held office in church governments. The following discussion occurred among representatives of Calvinist Baptist churches in the middle colonies, convened to provide guidance to local congregations on matters of belief and polity—in this case, the question whether women should vote in the church. Its tenor is likely a product of temporary egalitarian impulses emanating from the evangelical enthusiasms of the 1740s.

The elders and messengers of the congregations baptized upon profession of faith, in Pennsylvania and the Jerseys, met at Philadelphia, the 24th day of September 1746. . . .

Query: Whether women may or ought to have their votes in the church, in such matters as the church shall agree to be decided by votes?

Solution. As that in 1 Cor. xiv. 34, 35, and other parallel texts, are urged against their votes, as a rule, and ought, therefore, to be maturely considered.

If, then, the silence enjoined on women be taken so absolute, as that they must keep entire silence in all respects whatever; yet, notwithstanding, it is to be hoped they may have, as members of the body of the church, liberty to give a mute voice, by standing or lifting up of the hands, or the contrary, to signify their assent or dissent to the thing proposed, and so augment the number of the one or both sides of the question. But, with the consent of authors and casuists, such absolute silence in all respects cannot be intended; for if so, how shall a woman make a confession of her faith to the satisfaction of the whole church? or how shall the church judge whether a woman be in the faith or no? How shall a woman offended, after regular private proceeding with an offending member, tell the church, as she is bound to do, if the offender be obstinate, according to the rule, Matt. xviii. 17? How shall a woman do, if she be an evidence to a matter of fact? Shall the church grope in the dark for want of her evidence to clear the doubt? Surely not. Again, how shall a woman defend herself if wrongfully accused, if she must not speak? This is a privilege of

Minutes of the Philadelphia Baptist Association, from A.D. *1797 to* A.D. *1807* (Philadelphia: Baptist Publication Society, 1851), pp. 49, 53. The editors wish to thank Jon Butler for advice on this document.

all human creatures by the laws of nature, not abrogated by the law of God.

Therefore there must be times and ways in and by which women, as members of the body, may discharge their conscience and duty towards God and men, as in the cases above said and the like. And a woman may, at least, make a brother a mouth to ask leave to speak, if not ask it herself; and a time of hearing is to be allowed, for that is not inconsistent with the silence and subjection enjoined on them by the law of God and nature, yet ought not they to open the floodgate of speech in an imperious, tumultuous, masterly manner. Hence the silence, with subjection, enjoined on all women in the church of God, is such a silence as excludes all women whomsoever from all degrees of teaching, ruling, governing, dictating, and leading in the church of God; yet may their voice be taken as above said. But if a woman's vote be singular, her reasons ought to be called for, heard, and maturely considered, without contempt.

SARAH HARLAN'S WILL

Sarah Harlan lived in Kennett Township in Chester County, Pennsylvania, in the mid-eighteenth century. Her will, dated 1747/8, and the inventory of her belongings following her death suggest what a farm woman of that time and place needed to do her work and how one widow distributed the goods she had helped to accumulate during her life.

I Sarah Harlan of the Township of Kennett in the County of Chester & province of Pensilvania, Being weak of Body but of perfect mind & memory, & calling to mind the mortality of the Body, & the Immortality of the Soul do make & ordain this my Last will and Testament as followeth, first I commit my Soul to the hand of God that gave it & my Body to the Earth to be Decently Buried according to the Discretion of my Executrix hereafter named. And as to my Worldly Estates which it hath pleased God to Bless me with, I Give & Dispose of the Same in the following manner & form, that is to say first & foremost after my just Debts & funeral Charges are fully payed and Discharged I Give & Bequeath unto my three Sons to wit, George Samuel & Aaron Each of them the Sum of five Shillings Lawfull Money to be payed to Each of them within one year after my Decease, & I Likewise Give & Bequeath unto my three Daughters, to witt, Charity Baldwin, Mary Evans, & Elizabeth Hollingsworth, Each of them the Sum of Twenty Pounds Lawfull Money to be payed to Each of them within one year after my Decease. I also Give unto my Cuzon Martha Way the Sum of four Pounds Lawfull Money to be payed to her when shee arive to the age of Eighteen years, and as for the Remainder of my Estate my will is that the same be Equally Divided between all my Grand Children that is now Born, that is the Children of my Sons & Daughters above named. And Lastly I nominate Constitute & Appoint my welbeloved Daughter Mary Evins my Executrix wholy & solely to see this my Last will & Testament, Justly & truly exicuted & I do hereby [illegible] & make void all other former Will or wills by me made, Ratifying & Confirming this to be my Last Will & Testament, Sealed with my Seal and Dated this fifth day of february in the year of our Lord one Thousand Seven Hundred & fourty Seven—Eight

Signed Sealed pronounced   Sarah Harlan
and declared to be the Last   her
will & Testament of Sarah   mark

Sarah Harlan, will, dated 1747/8, no. 1089, Chester County Archives, West Chester, Pa.

Harlan in the presence of
(signed) John Clark
(signed) Francis Clark . . .

An Inventory of the Goods Effects & Credits belonging to the Estate of
Sarah Harlan of Kennitt Deceased & appraised by us whose Names are
Hereunto Subscribed this fourth Day of March 1747/8

	£	S	D
To the purse & apparel	5	0	0
To her Hackney Mair & Saddle & bridle	8	0	0
To Bonds & Bills With their Interest	33	10	0
To the Book Debts	8	15	3
To the Best Bed & furniture	10	0	0
To the other Bed & furniture	7	0	0
To a Black walnut Chest	0	15	0
To 1 Black walnut Table	1	0	0
To the other Table	0	10	0
To 1 pair of old Case of Draws	1	0	0
To the Chairs	0	12	0
To 31 yards of Dursy Not Milld nor Coulored @ 3s per yd	4	13	0
To 40 yds of Linnon Cloath @ 2s per yd	4	0	0
To 18 yds of Linsey @ 2s per yd	1	16	0
To 1 Looking Glass	0	6	0
To 1 Table & Mail Chest	0	10	0
To 2 Brass Kettles	2	0	0
To 3 Brass pans & a Warming pan	2	15	0
To 15 plates & 5 pewter Dishes with old puter	2	0	0
To 2 Small Iron pots & pot Racks	0	14	0
To 2 Tubs & 2 pails	0	4	0
To 1 Large Bible	1	10	0
To 1 Box Iron & 3 Candle Sticks	0	5	0
To 3 Wheels & Reel	0	15	0
To 1 three year old Colt	5	10	0
To 9 Sheep	3	0	0
To a Hackel Long Wheel	0	7	0
To a pide Heipher	2	0	0
To 1 Brown Dto	1	5	0
To 3 Cows	4	10	0

	£		
To 1 Spring Calf	0	8	0
. . .			
To a Sow & pigg	0	10	0
To 4 Stocks & half of Bees	1	0	0
To 14 yards of Dursy @ 4 s per yd	2	16	0
To 3 yards of flanell @ 3s per yd	0	9	0
To 5 pounds of flax @ 1s per pound	0	5	0
£	119	10	3

Joseph Harlan
Joseph Mendenhall

LETTER FROM AN INDENTURED SERVANT

Between the 1690s and the 1750s the labor system of the Chesapeake colonies was transformed, as the supply of white indentured servants dwindled and white planters bought African slaves to replace them. Nonetheless, some white men and women continued to emigrate from England as indentured servants all through the eighteenth century. This 1756 letter, one of the few available firsthand accounts from a woman servant (since most were illiterate), suggests that things had changed little since Sarah Taylor's time a hundred years earlier.

To Mr. John Sprigs White Smith in White Cross Street near Cripple Gate London

Honred Father   Maryland Sept'r 22'd 1756.
My being for ever banished from your sight, will I hope pardon the Boldness I now take of troubling you with these, my long silence has been purely owing to my undutifullness to you, and well knowing I had offended in the highest Degree, put a tie to my tongue and pen, for fear I should be extinct from your good Graces and add a further Trouble to you, but too well knowing your care and tenderness for me so long as I retain my Duty to you, induced me once again to endeavour if possible, to kindle up that flame again. O Dear Father, belive what I am going to relate the words of truth and sincerity, and Ballance my former bad Conduct [to] my sufferings here, and then I am sure you'll pitty your Destress[ed] Daughter, What we unfortunat English People suffer here is beyond the probility of you in England to Conceive, let it suffice that I one of the unhappy Number, am toiling almost Day and Night, and very often in the Horses druggery, with only this comfort that you Bitch you do not halfe enough, and then tied up and whipp'd to that Degree that you'd not serve an Annimal, scarce any thing but Indian Corn and Salt to eat and that even begrudged nay many Negroes are better used, almost naked no shoes nor stockings to wear, and the comfort after slaving dureing Masters pleasure, what rest we can get is to rap ourselves up in a Blanket and ly upon the Ground, this is the deplorable Condition your poor Betty endures, and now I beg if you have any Bowels of Compassion left show it by sending me some Relief, C[l]othing is the principal thing wanting, which if you should condiscend to, may easely send them to me

Isabel Calder, ed., *Colonial Captivities, Marches, and Journeys* (New York: Macmillan, 1935), pp. 151–52.

by any of the ships bound to Baltimore Town Patapsco River Maryland, and give me leave to conclude in Duty to you and Uncles and Aunts, and Respect to all Friends

Honred Father
Your undutifull and Disobedient Child
Elizabeth Sprigs

DIARY OF MARY COOPER

*Mary Cooper and her husband, Joseph, lived on a Long Island farm at the
brisk commercial nexus of southern New England and New York City. This
location accounts for the steady stream of people and preaching flowing
through Cooper's life and the level of market activity of her household:
selling crops, purchasing items at a store, taking in travelers, and hiring
workers (Joseph also owned four slaves—the "people" referred to in the
diary). Commercial transactions may have caused the debts that so worried Mary. Fifty-five years old, she had borne six children, only one of
whom, daughter Esther, remained alive. Esther was separated from her
husband (and first cousin), Simon Cooper, and living in her parents' house
in 1769.*

1 June the 1, 1769, Thirsday. A most vemant cold north east wind
[struck out: and rain]. We all went to the Quaker meeten where a multitude were geathered to here a woman preach that lately came from England, and a most amebel woman she is. Tex: 'Of the leaven put in three
masuess of meal.'

2 Friday. A fine clear day but not hot. I went early to town to see Isreal.
He is goin to Nine Parners. The first swarme of bees.

3 Saterday. Clear and cool with an east wind.

4 June the 4, 1769, Sabbath. A fine clear morning, like to be hot. Two
swarmes of bees hendered me from going to meeten. One Indan preacher
in town. No company here but old Abbe Wood.

5 Moonday. A fine cleare hot day. No company here.

6 Tuesday. Very winde weather. Our men gon to Hogisland to raise
Tom Smith's barne. The girls gon to Salle Wheeler. The being alone has
been no great happyness to me. I have been unwell and could dow but
littel.

7 Wednsday. Fine weather. No company here.

8 Thirsday. Fine clear weather: Salle Wheler here. . . .

[14] [Wednsday]. Very dry. The bees swarme. . . .

[16] Friday. Hot clear weather. Two swarmes of bees. Evening, I put
them in one hive. . . .

The Diary of Mary Cooper: Life on a Long Island Farm, 1768–1773, ed. Field Horne (Oyster Bay,
N.Y.: Oyster Bay Historical Society, 1981), pp. 13–18, 20–21, 23–25, reprinted courtesy of the
Oyster Bay Historical Society.

25 June the 25, Sabbath.   Clear and very hot. Ester is gon to Hammon's meeten. I stay at home. This day no body here but Salle Wheler and Ab Colwell. No dinner and a very slender repact in the afternoon, weak tea and a few crusts of breade and butter, no way eaqueal to our appititues. Ester staid out all night. Simon come home much out of humor. . . .

29 June the 29, Thursday.   Extreemely hot and dry. Every thing is all most redy to perrish for want of rain. . . .

1 July the 1, 1769, Saterday.   A fine clear day. Very hot. I have been unwell all the weeke, dirty and tired allmost to death.

2 July the 2, Sabbath.   I went a foot to town. Got to the afternoon meeten extreemely tired and enexpressabel hot.

3 Moonday.   I am much freted with Ester prepareing the house for some yong women, Doctor Laourence daughters and Salle Wright and some others.

4 Tuesday.   Extreeme hot and dry. Bet and Deb L., Ester and Deb T., Ab and Nep Y. here and stay all night. My Salle Wright here to stay some time.

5 Wednsday.   Extreeme hot and dry. The girls gon home, all but Salle Wright.

6 Thirsday.   Melting hot and dry. O, I am tired almost to death. Up late makeing wine.

7 Friday.   Hot as yesterday. I am dirty and distressed, almost weared to death. Dear Lord, deliver mee.

8 Saterday.   Extreemely hot and dry. If the Lord dose not look in mercy upon the earth and send some rain we shall soon perish. Isreal and Nick came here.

9 July the 9, Sabbath day.   Somthing cloudy. I and Ester walk to the New Light meeten parte of the way in the rain. A fine rain all the after noon. I felt very dul and unsensabal all the day and I belive all the rest was much so. . . .

11 Tuesday.   Clear and very hot. O, I am very unwell, tiered almost to death cooking for so many peopel.

12 Wednsday.   Fine clear weather. Much freting a bout dinner.

13 July the 13, 1769, Thirsday.   This day is forty years sinc I left my father's house and come here, and here have I seene littel els but harde labour and sorrow, crosses of every kind. I think in every repect the state of my affairs is more than forty times worse then when I came here first, except that I am nearer the desierered haven. A fine clear cool day. I am un well. . . .

19 Wednsday.   A fine clear and still morning. Mis Sillick and her husband here. They are gon home. Ptr, Linde, Isreal here to get cheres. Frances has a strange ide this night that something is the matter with her son Barsilla.

20 Thirsday.   A fine clear morning. We began to dry cheares. 14 young peopel from Cold Spring came here to get cheres. Evening, grows cloudy and like for rain. . . .

23 July the 23, 1769, Sabbath.   A fine clear still morning, Very tired with harde worke. I did not go to meeten.

24 Moonday.   I am drying cheres. Afternoon, exceeding high wind and a very greate shower of rain. I am much distrest with hard worke.

25 Tuesday.   A fine clear and coole day. I am drying cheres. Still very greateliy distrest giting dinner.

26 Wednsday.   A fine clear still morning. We are drying cheres. Sal and Pol Birdsaul and Nep Youngs here. I am very unwell. . . .

30 July the 30, Sabbath.   I went throw much difculty to meeten. Ptr tx: 'Thare is a path which no sowl knoweth.' Sis tx: 'I sow one like the son of man walking a midst the golden candelstiks.' I feel extreeme dul and lifeless. Salle Wright took leve of us to go home. Ester and Salle is gon to Seder Swamp with her. Clouday most of the day. Some thunder, rain this night. . . .

1 August the 1.   New moon this morning. Tuesday. A fine clear cool morning. I feele much distrest, fearing I shall here from some of my credtors. Afternoon, I have done my worke and feele something more comfortabl. I went to Salle Wheeler's to meet Ester and Salle but am sent after in greate hurre. Ben Hildrith is come here in a littel boate with two men with him. I am up late and much freted them and thier two dogs which they keep att tabel and in the bedroom with them.

2 Wednsday.   The first I herde this morning was Ben's dogs barking and yeling in the bed room. They did nothing but drink them selves drunk all the day long and sent for more rum.

3 Thursday.   The wind is not fare to go home, so they cary the girls to town in the boate. Ben behaved like a blackgarde scound[rel] and as if he had been hurred by the devel.

4 Friday.   They set sail to go home to my great joy, and I desier I may never se them here again. I greately dread the cleaning of [illegible] hous after this detested gang.

5 Saterday.   A fin clear cool day. Much hard worke cleaneing the house. An old Indian come here to day that lets fortans and ueses charmes to

cure tooth ach and drive away rats. O Lord, thou knowest that my soul abhors these abominations. Lay not this sin to my charge. On Thirsday I had an extreme pain in my back and hip so th I could not go with out cryin out. . . .

23 Wednsday.   A fine clear morning with a cold north wind. My hearte is burnt with anger and discontent, want of every nessesary thing in life and in constant feare of gapeing credtors consums my strenth and wasts my days. The horrer of these things with the continuel cross of my famaly, like to so many horse leeches, prays upon my vitals, and if the Lord does not prevent will bring me to the house appointed for all liveing. Salle Burtis here. . . .

27 August the 27, 1769, Sabbath.   Very gretely hurred geting this company a way to Greate Meten. I went to the New Light meeten to here a Black man preach. Felt nothing but distres. Very greatly tired and freted, walkin home so fast.

28 Moonday.   Clear weather but not a fair wind for New England. Up late this night. I am much distrist and know not what to dow. O Lord, lead my ways and let my life be [illegible] in thy sight. Doctor Wright come here this day.

29 August the 29, Tuesday.   We are hurred to set sail for New England, very greatly aganst my will. The tumulting waves look frightfull. But thro infinate mercy we came safe to Mr. Hildrith house in two hours wheare we weare recived with many welcoms and used with the utmost kindness by all the famaly. Cloudy and like for rain every day this wekee but none come except some small showers, not more than due. Nothing remarkabel except that we had the heavyest bread I had every seene. . . .

29 [September] Friday.   Fair weather. Simon Cooper is going to make a [? choping] frolic tomorrow afternoon. . . .

30 Saterday.   Very high north east wind. Very cloudy most of the day. Afternoon, changes to a south wind. We are very busie cooking for the work men. Evening, they eate ther supper. The more parte went away. Some stay to dance, very greately aganst my will. Some anger about the danceing. Some time in the night come up a shower of rain and thunder. Easter and Salle was frighted very greatly and come down. Easter like to have fits.

1 October the 1, 1769, Sabbath.   West wind and like for fair weather. Simon Cooper quarel very greatly about Ester dancing. He got in a unxpresabel rage and struck her. I am going to meeten but no not how to get over the Broock, the tide is so high. I come to meeten just as the [illegi-

ble] ware coming out of the house. I did not stay to the evening meeten and yet come home sometime in the night. . . .

9 Moonday. I went to town in the rain but did no buisness. I and Esther come home late. Both wet and distrest. She waded over the Brook. . . .

7 [November] Tuesday. A cleare fine morning. Whipo came to mend the house. Very harde west wind all day long. The girls gon to spin at Salle Wheeler's.

8 Wednsday. A fine clear still day. Whippo took of the roof of the old house.

9 November the 9. This day is ten years since my father departed this life. . . .

15 [struck out: Thirsday]. Wednsday. I am heshling flacks.

16 Thirsday. I am very busey trying tallow. Cold west wind. Frose hard last night. . . .

21 Tuesday. Rain but clears some time in the afternoon. The girls come home. The two Indan preachers had a meeten here this night.

22 November the ??, 1769. Wednesday. The two preachers went from here this morning to Metenicok where they had a call to preach at the Widdow Weekses, at Ben Latten's and some other places. They were kindly recived and greate numbers flocked to here them.

23 Thirsday. Very cold. We are very buesy killing hogs. Master Vande Waters and some other man come here.

25 Saterday. We are busey and very dirty. The preachers come to town this evening. We went to town to meeten. Extreeme cold. We come home late in the night.

26 November the 25, Sabbath. Very cold. We hurred away early to meeten where we found a very greate milttitude of peopel. Had a very happy meeten. Some ware much afected and all behaved very soberly. Yong Doctor Lawrence envited them to come and preach at his house the next day. We staid to the evening meeten with greate delight and come home late in the night. . . .

1 December the 1, 1769, Friday. A fine warme day but very mire walking.

2 Saterday. A fine warme day. Oh, I am distressed with harde worke makeing sassages and boile souse, bakeing and cooking.

3 December the 3, Sabbath. Hurred all most to death cooking. I walked to meeten and when I come there the meeten was out. Phebe Weekes gave herself a member this day.

We had a meeten this evening about some reprochfull talk among the members. I and Frances com home late in the night. . . .

11 Moonday.   Cloudy but warme. I am dirty and buesy as ever. Cloudy and like for rain. Some small rain all night.

12 Tuesday.   Mist and small rain all day long. I am very buse boiling sope.

13 Wednsday.   Clear with a most frightfull harde west wind. Groes extreeme cold and freses hard all of a suding. This day is thirty seven years since my dear and amibel sister Elisabeth departed this life.

14 Thirsday.   Cold but not so windy or cold as yesterday. Full of freting, discontent, dirty and meresabel both yesterday and to day.

15 Friday. Cloudy and cold. Still I have got some clean cloths on thro mercy. Very littel done to clean the house.

MOLL PLACKET-HOLE

Printed privately in Philadelphia in 1765, Hilliad Magna. Being the Life and Adventures of Moll Placket-Hole was typical of eighteenth-century bawdy sexual satire. The pamphlet displayed a candor on sexual matters that went hand in hand with a form of misogyny common in urban life in the new republic. Despite the pamphlet's fictional tone, brothels did exist in colonial cities from their earliest days. As in this account, they were sometimes the target of mob violence.

MOLL PLACKET-HOLE was born in a *Bawdy House* in a *Lane* in the City of *Brotherly Love* about the latter End of the Year, the great Frost destroyed the *Potatoes* in *Ireland.* Who her Father was is as uncertain, as the Father of *Catharine* the late Empress of all the *Russias.* Her Mother kept a Port of Trade; and as the Duties were all paid down, she had no Clerks in her Custom-House; and therefore could not remember all who *entered,* and *unloaded their freights* there. She was a hospital sort of a Woman. She entertained Men of all Ranks and Stations. She lived in an *Alley,* and (as was said before) kept the *Port.*

It happened, while she was pregnant, that she dreamed of her delivery and that the Child was presented by a Customer, with a rich silken Robe adorned with the finest Ermine: From whence she prognosticated that her Daughter would one Day be related to Advocates and Judges.

Nothing remarkable appeared in *Moll* the three first Years of her Life. She spent that Time, like *Gargantua* and most other Children, in the frequent Repetitions of Eating, Drinking, P——g Shi——g and Sleeping.

The next three Years of her Life, were spent in romping about with Children of her Age; and it was remarked, that she was never without Pennies to buy Cakes Pears *&c.* which she received from them that frequented the House.

From six to ten she discovered a great Curiosity in prying into the *Mystical* imployment of her Mother's Customers of different Sexes; and found out every Crevice that she might peep through. The Scenes were too indecent to be described here. Let it suffice that they were such as have a natural Tendency to fire the Blood, and Root out every Virtuous Principle.

From ten to twelve she shewed all the Eagerness for forbidden Joy, which a warm Constitution, prompted by Example, and unchecked by

Hilliad Magna. Being the Life and Adventures of Moll Placket-Hole ([Philadelphia]: 1765). The editors are indebted to Clare Lyons for locating and providing a copy of this document.

Conscience could excite. And yet for a Reason, easier to be imagined, than decent to express, *She Feared to try the grand Experiment.*

The Custom of her Mother's *Port* failing, at the Age of twelve (Shocking to consider!) this same Mother *sold* her Virginity—*sold* it for the Trifling Consideration of *Ten Pounds.*

Her purchaser was soon cloyed and abandoned her. Virtue lost and good Reputation (if ever she had it) gone, she commenced open Prostitute and dealt out her Favours to the highest Bidder. This Course of Life, she followed about seven Years, in which nothing very remarkable happened. The common Occurences to Women of her Profession, such as *Poxes, Claps, Salivations, [Kickings?], Houses of Correction, &c.* fell frequently to her share.

Her Body being broken of Disease, she could not get a Livelihood any longer in this Way. However as she had been conversant from her Infancy in Houses, where Gain was got by procuring lewd Women for the Use of Men, in perpetrating Acts of Uncleanness, she thought, she understood the Trade and set up a *Bawdy-House.* Having furnished herself with handsome Husseys, she had much Custom, and the *Rich*, who were furnished by her in that Way, paid her so largerly, that she herself became *Rich*, and bought a House and sundry Lots of Ground. It was necessary however, that a Man should live with her, that they might appear to the Publick, as *honest* Housekeepers. Such an one was found. Whether they were married or not, is uncertain: but they shared the Gains.

The Trade became at last so publick, that it gave Offence to her sober Neighbours. *Matrons* mourned for their Children, unguarded Youths, who had been drawn in there; *Ministers of the Gospel* declaimed against the Vice, both in publick Assemblies and private Companies; and the *Magistrates* resolved to punish *all* such Offenders as could be found out. *Moll* had Friends, who advised her of the impending Danger, and disappeared, 'till the Storm blew over, and then returned in Triumph.

It would be endless to relate the Arts she used to inveigle unwary Girls. Let two instances suffice.

One of her *Rich* Customers saw a pretty Country Girl in Market. Her modest Deportment (strange!) and ruddy Complexion fired him so, that he resolved to glut a brutal Appetite with her, cost what it might. He inquired, who she was, found her to be a wealthy Farmer's Daughter, who lived some Miles out of Town, he described her to *Moll*, and swore he must have her, and she should have her Price. *Moll* put on her best Duds, and in the Character of a sickly Gentlewoman, came to the Farmer's House, under pretence of taking the Benefit of Country Air. After staying some Days, and paying handsomely for her Entertainment, she obtained Leave of the Farmer and his Wife to permit their Daughter to spend a Week with her in Town. But the good Girl (being blessed with some Penetration), before she fell a Sacrifice, discovered the Design.— Here (thanks to divine Providence!) *Moll* was disappointed.

The other instance is of the same Sort, with other Circumstances.

Moll saw a handsome Girl in Market, she thought she would suit her purpose, she bought all she had to sell, and pretending she had not Money sufficient to pay her, without changing a *Five Pound Bill*, she persuaded the Girl to go home with her; invited her pressingly to stay Dinner; and after Dinner, prevailed on her to be dressed in her own flaunting Cloaths; and invented every Amusement to delay her, 'till it should be too late for her to return Home. She then told her, she should be welcome to lodge with her, and sent Orders for taking Care of her Horse. The Girl consented with Reluctance. In the Evening, a Person (who is esteemed a Gentleman) for whom she was designed, came. He fell in Conversation with her, and thinking he had spent Time enough in *Civility*, began to treat her *rudely*: Which she resented. He was surprized at her Coyness; and let her understand such Nicety was not to be observed, *in the Place where she was*. Upon which, bursting into Tears, she implored his Mercy; told her Story, and who her Parents were. But oh! think of the Confusion of the Man, when he found her the Daughter of his Friend thus inveigled, and on the Brink of Destruction! Lust no more inflamed him. The *Man* returned. (*Tho' you force Nature back, as it were, with a Pitchforck it will return*). He cursed himself, he cursed *Moll*; and conducted the unwary Girl safe to her Lodging at the Inn.

The bad Effects of her House-Keeping appeared in a Thousand Instances; but in none more than the misfortune of a miserable young Woman, now languishing in a Hospital, the particulars of whose Case are well known to the Town; and 'tis a Matter of Credit to the Place, that the Inhabitants have in Imitation of the Almighty (so far as he can be imitated) who causes his *Sun to Shine and his Rain to fall upon the just and the unjust*, have rejected no Object of Compassion, whether the Distress arose from Misfortune, Indiscretion or Vice.

On *Moll's* appearance after her short Eclipse, she endeavoured to shine away. She exulted; and insulted every one who she believed, had complained against her, and their Relatives and Friends also. Till the Town tired out with her Insolence, and her Escape from Justice in a regular Manner, set a Mob (many of whom had been her Beneficiaries) upon her. They pulled down her House, and destroyed her Furniture &c.

She stormed and raged and swore if her Customers would not build her a better House, she would expose them. A Sense of Shame remains after the greatest Debaucheries. They opened a Subscription, and a hundred Pounds were subscribed in one Day.

What the latter Part of her Life may be God knows.

REFLECTIONS.

Brothel-Houses are Seats of Idleness and Debauchery. Independent of the divine Law which declares that *Whoremongers and Adulterers God will judge*, such Practices destroy the Bodies and Estates of the People; and discourage Matrimony, the best Seminary for raising good Members of a Common Weal. A good Woman who has suffered a Mother's Throes, carefully dandled her Infant on her Knees, and looked on the pleasing Care, the pledge of her Love, as a Comfort in her Strength, and Support of her declining Years, must feel Anguish not to be expressed, on finding her deluded by such Mercenary Harpies.

The Miseries of Poverty, Contempt and Disease are the sad Consequences that must follow the poor Wretches themselves. &c. &c. &c.

ABIGAIL ADAMS'S LETTERS FROM
THE HOME FRONT

*When military and political obligations of the American Revolution kept
men away from their homes, women bore the burdens of keeping the economy going and families together. In 1776 Abigail Adams was thirty-two
and the mother of four children. She was pregnant again in 1777 (as she
notes by reference to her "confinement," the period of time during and just
after childbirth) but the baby did not survive. Her letters to her husband,
John, who was serving in Philadelphia as Massachusetts delegate to the
Continental Congress, describe life on their farm in Braintree, Massachusetts, just before and during the first year of the Revolutionary War.*

Braintree March 31 1776

I wish you would ever write me a Letter half as long as I write you; and
tell me if you may where your Fleet are gone? What sort of Defence
Virginia can make against our common Enemy? Whether it is so situated
as to make an able Defence? Are not the Gentery Lords and the common
people vassals, are they not like the uncivilized Natives Brittain represents
us to be? I hope their Riffel Men who have shewen themselves very savage
and even Blood thirsty; are not a specimen of the Generality of the people.

I am willing to allow the Colony great merit for having produced a
Washington but they have been shamefully duped by a Dunmore.

I have sometimes been ready to think that the passion for Liberty cannot be Eaquelly Strong in the Breasts of those who have been accustomed
to deprive their fellow Creatures of theirs. Of this I am certain that it is
not founded upon that generous and christian principal of doing to others as we would that others should do unto us.

Do not you want to see Boston; I am fearfull of the small pox, or I
should have been in before this time. I got Mr. Crane to go to our House
and see what state it was in. I find it has been occupied by one of the
Doctors of a Regiment, very dirty, but no other damage has been done to
it. The few things which were left in it are all gone. Cranch has the key
which he never deliverd up. I have wrote to him for it and am determined
to get it cleand as soon as possible and shut it up. I look upon it a new
acquisition of property, a property which one month ago I did not value
at a single Shilling, and could with pleasure have seen it in flames.

The Book of Abigail and John: Selected Letters of the Adams Family, 1762–1784, ed. L. H. Butter-
field (Cambridge, Mass.: Harvard University Press, 1975), pp. 120–21, 177–78, 182–83, 189–
91. Reprinted by permission of the publishers. Copyright © 1975 by the Massachusetts
Historical Society.

The Town in General is left in a better state than we expected, more oweing to a percipitate flight than any Regard to the inhabitants, tho some individuals discoverd a sense of honour and justice and have left the rent of the Houses in which they were, for the owners and the furniture unhurt, or if damaged sufficient to make it good.

Others have committed abominable Ravages. The Mansion House of your President is safe and the furniture unhurt whilst both the House and Furniture of the Solisiter General have fallen a prey to their own merciless party. Surely the very Fiends feel a Reverential awe for Virtue and patriotism, whilst they Detest the paricide and traitor.

I feel very differently at the approach of spring to what I did a month ago. We knew not then whether we could plant or sow with safety, whether when we had toild we could reap the fruits of our own industry, whether we could rest in our own Cottages, or whether we should not be driven from the sea coasts to seek shelter in the wilderness, but now we feel as if we might sit under our own vine and eat the good of the land.

I feel a gaieti de Coar to which before I was a stranger. I think the Sun looks brighter, the Birds sing more melodiously, and Nature puts on a more chearfull countanance. We feel a temporary peace, and the poor fugitives are returning to their deserted habitations.

Tho we felicitate ourselves, we sympathize with those who are trembling least the Lot of Boston should be theirs. But they cannot be in similar circumstances unless pusilanimity and cowardise should take possession of them. They have time and warning given them to see the Evil and shun it.—I long to hear that you have declared an independancy—and by the way in the new Code of Laws which I suppose it will be necessary for you to make I desire you would Remember the Ladies, and be more generous and favourable to them than your ancestors. Do not put such unlimited power into the hands of the Husbands. Remember all Men would be tyrants if they could. If perticuliar care and attention is not paid to the Laidies we are determined to foment a Rebelion, and will not hold ourselves bound by any Laws in which we have no voice, or Representation.

That your Sex are Naturally Tyrannical is a Truth so thoroughly established as to admit of no dispute, but such of you as wish to be happy willingly give up the harsh title of Master for the more tender and endearing one of Friend. Why then, not put it out of the power of the vicious and the Lawless to use us with cruelty and indignity with impunity. Men of Sense in all Ages abhor those customs which treat us only as the vassals of your Sex. Regard us then as Beings placed by providence under your protection and in immitation of the Supreem Being make use of that power only for our happiness.

June 23 1777

I have just retird to my Chamber, but an impulce seazes me to write you a few lines before I close my Eye's. Here I often come and sit myself down alone to think of my absent Friend, to ruminate over past scenes, to read over Letters, journals &c.

Tis a melancholy kind of pleasure I find in this amusement, whilst the weighty cares of state scarcly leave room for a tender recollection or sentiment to steal into the Bosome of my Friend.

In my last I expressd some fears least the Enemy should soon invade us here. My apprehensions are in a great measure abated by late accounts received from the General.

We have a very fine Season here, rather cold for a fortnight, but nothing like a drought. You would smile to see what a Farmer our Brother C[ranc]h makes, his whole attention is as much engaged in it, as it ever was in Spermacity Works, Watch Work, or Prophesies. You must know he has purchased, (in spight of the C[olone]lls Threats) that Farm he talkd of. He gave a large price for it tis True, but tis a neat, profitable place, 300 sterling, but money is lookd upon of very little value, and you can scarcly purchase any article now but by Barter. You shall have wool for flax or flax for wool, you shall have veal, Beaf or pork for salt, for sugar, for Rum, &c. but mony we will not take, is the daily language. I will work for you for Corn, for flax or wool, but if I work for money you must give a cart load of it be sure.

What can be done, and which way shall we help ourselves? Every article and necessary of life is rising daily. Gold dear Gold would soon lessen the Evils. I was offerd an article the other day for two dollors in silver for which they askd me six in paper.

I have no more to purchase with than if every dollor was a silver one. Every paper dollor cost a silver one, why then cannot it be eaquelly valuable? You will refer me to Lord Kames I know, who solves the matter. I hope in favour you will not Emit any more paper, till what we have at least becomes more valuable.

Nothing remarkable has occurd since I wrote you last. You do not in your last Letters mention how you do—I will hope better. I want a companion a Nights, many of them are wakefull and Lonesome, and "tierd Natures sweet restorer, Balmy Sleep," flies me. How hard it is to reconcile myself to six months longer absence! Do you feel it urksome? Do you sigh for Home? And would you willingly share with me what I have to pass through? Perhaps before this reaches you and meets with a Return, —— I wish the day passt, yet dread its arrival.—Adieu most sincerely most affectionately Yours.

My dearest Friend   July 23 1777

Notwithstanding my confinement I think I have not omitted writing you by every post. I have recoverd Health and strength beyond expectation; and never was so well in so short a time before. Could I see my Friend in reality as I often do in immagination I think I should feel a happiness beyond expression; I had pleasd myself with the Idea of presenting him a fine son or daughter upon his return, and had figurd to myself the smiles of joy and pleasure with which he would receive it, but [those?] dreams are buried in the Grave, transitory as the morning Cloud, short lived as the Dew Drops.

Heaven continue to us those we already have and make them blessings. I think I feel more solicitious for their welfare than ever, and more anxious if posible for the life and Health of their parent. I fear the extreem Heat of the season, and the different temperament of the climate and the continual application to Buisness will finish a constitution naturally feeble.

I know not in what manner you will be affected at the loss, Evacuation, sale, giving up—which of the terms befits the late conduct at Tycondoroga. You may know more of the reasons for this conduct (as I hear the commanding officer went immediately to Congress) than we can devine this way; but this I can truly say no Event since the commencement of the War has appeard so allarming to me, or given me eaquel uneasiness. Had the Enemy fought and conquerd the fort, I could have borne it, but to leave it with all the stores before it was even attackd, has exited a thousand Suspicions, and gives room for more wrath than despondency.

We every day look for an attack upon us this way. The reports of this week are that a number of Transports with Troops have a[rriv]ed at Newport. Some expresses went through this Town yesterday.

Yours of June 30 reach'd me last week. I am not a little surprizd that you have not received Letters from me later than the 9 of June. I have never faild for this two months writing you once a week. Tho they contain matters of no great importance I should be glad to know when you receive them.

We have had a remarkable fine Season here, no drought this summer. The Corn looks well, and english Grain promiseing. We cannot be sufficently thankfull to a Bountifull providence that the Horrours of famine are not added to those of war, and that so much more Health prevails in our Camps than in the year past.

Many of your Friends desire to be rememberd to you. Some complain that you do not write them. Adieu. Master Tom stands by and sends duty—he often recollects How *par* used to put him to Jail as he calls it. They are all very Healthy this summer, and are in expectation of a Letter every packet that arrives. Yours, ever yours,

PS Price Current!! This day I gave 4 dollors a peice for Sythes and a Guiney a Gallon for New england Rum. We come on here finely. What do you think will become of us. If you will come Home and turn Farmer, I will be dairy woman. You will make more than is allowd you, and we shall grow wealthy. Our Boys shall go into the Feild and work with you, and my Girl shall stay in the House and assist me.

My dearest Friend   Boston August 22 1777

I came yesterday to this Town for a ride after my confinement, and to see my Friends. I have not been into it since I had the happiness of spending a week here with you. I am feeble and faint with the Heat of the weather, but otherways very well. I feel very anxious for your Health and almost fear to hear from you least I should hear you were sick; but hope your temperance and caution will preserve your Health. I hope, if you can get any way through these Hot months you will recruit. Tis very Healthy throughout Town and Country for the Season, the chin cough prevails in Town among children but has not yet reachd the Country.

Your Letters of August 1, 3 and 4th came by last nights post, and I have to acknowledge the recept of yours of july 27, 28 and 30th by last wedensdays post. I acknowledge my self greatly indebted to you for so frequently writing amidst all your other cares and attentions. I would fain believe that tis a releafe to you after the cares of the day, to converse with your Friend. I most sincerely wish your situation was such that the amusements your family could afford you, might have been intermixed with the weighty cares that oppress you.—

> "My Bosome is thy dearest home;
> I'd lull you there to rest."

As to *How* I wish we could know what he means that we might be able to gaurd against him. I hope however that he will not come this way, and I believe the Season is so far advanced, that he will not venture.

At the Northward our affairs look more favorable. We have been successfull in several of our late engagements. Heaven preserve our dear

Countrymen who behave worthy of us and reward them both here and hereafter. Our Militia are chiefly raisd, and will I hope be marchd of immediately. There has been a most shamefull neglect some where. This continent has paid thousands to officers and Men who have been loitering about playing foot-Ball and nine pins, and doing their own private buisness whilst they ought to have been defending our forts and we are now suffering for the neglect.

The late call of Men from us will distress us in our Husbandry. I am a great sufferer as the High Bounty one hundred dollars, has tempted of my Negro Head, and left me just in the midst of our Hay. The english and fresh indeed we have finishd, but the salt is just comeing on, and How to turn my self, or what to do I know not. His going away would not worry me so much if it was not for the rapid depretiation of our money. We can scarcly get a days work done for money and if money is paid tis at such a rate that tis almost imposible to live. I live as I never did before, but I am not agoing to complain. Heaven has blessd us with fine crops. I hope to have 200 hundred Bushels of corn and a hundred & 50 weight of flax. English Hay we have more than we had last year, notwithstanding your ground wants manure. We are like to have a plenty of sause. I shall fat Beaf and pork enough, make butter and cheesse enough. If I have neither Sugar, molasses, coffe nor Tea I have no right to complain. I can live without any of them and if what I enjoy I can share with my partner and with Liberty, I can sing o be joyfull and sit down content—

> "Man wants but little here below
> Nor wants that little long."

As to cloathing I have heithertoo procured materials sufficent to cloath my children and servants which I have done wholy in Home Spun. I have contracted no debts that I have not discharg'd, and one of our Labourers Prince I have paid seven months wages to since you left me. Besides that I have paid Bracket near all we owed him which was to the amount of 15 pounds lawfull money, set up a cider press &c., besides procuring and repairing many other articles in the Husbandery way, which you know are constantly wanted. I should do exceeding well if we could but keep the money good, but at the rate we go on I know not what will become of us.

But I must bid you adieu or the post will go of without my Letter.— Dearest Friend, adieu. Words cannot convey to you the tenderness of my affection.

∿

AN ADOLESCENT'S WARTIME DIARY

Women's usual employments changed during the Revolutionary War, not only because many men were away but also because women had a necessary role in supplying the army with food, clothing, and, in some cases, shelter. The practice of quartering officers in private households meant additional work for many women, but for fifteen-year-old Sally Wister, daughter of a prosperous Philadelphia Quaker family, it meant mainly excitement, flirting, and romantic fantasy. The Wister family, fearing a British occupation of Philadelphia (the new nation's capital), had relocated to a relative's house in Gwynedd, outside the city. It was there that Sally kept this journal in the form of letters to her friend Deborah Morris.

September, 1777

Yesterday, which was the 24th of September, two Virginia officers called at our house, and informed us that the British army had crossed the Schuylkill. Presently after, another person stopped, and confirmed what they had said, and that General Washington and army were near Pottsgrove. Well, thee may be sure we were sufficiently scared; however, the road was very still till evening. About seven o'clock we heard a great noise. To the door we all went. A large number of waggons, with about three hundred of the Philadelphia militia. They begged for drink, and several pushed into the house. One of those that entered was a little tipsy, and had a mind to be saucy. I then thought it time for me to retreat; so figure me (mightily scared, as not having presence of mind enough to face so many of the military) running in at one door, and out at another, all in a shake with fear; but after a little, seeing the officers appear gentlemanly and the soldiers civil, I called reason to my aid. My fears were in some measure dispelled, tho' my teeth rattled, and my hand shook like an aspen leaf. They did not offer to take their quarters with us; so, with many blessings, and as many adieus, they marched off. . . .

Fifth Day, September 26th.

We were unusually silent all the morning; no passengers came by the house, except to the mill, and we don't place much dependence on mill news. About 12 o'clock, cousin Jesse heard that General Howe's army had moved down towards Philadelphia. Then, my dear, our hopes and fears were engaged for you. However, my advice is, summon up all your resolu-

"Journal of Miss Sally Wister," as published in *Pennsylvania Magazine of History and Biography* 9 (1885), pp. 319–24, 326–27, 332–33; 10 (1886), pp. 51–52, 55–57.

tion, call Fortitude to your aid, don't suffer your spirits to sink, my dear; there's nothing like courage; 'tis what I stand in need of myself, but unfortunately have but little of it in my composition. I was standing in the kitchen about 12, when somebody came to me in a hurry, screaming, "Sally, Sally, here are the light horse!" This was by far the greatest fright I had endured; fear tack'd wings to my feet; I was at the house in a moment; at the porch I stopt, and it really was the light horse. I ran immediately to the western door, where the family were assembled, anxiously waiting for the event. They rode up to the door and halted, and enquired if we had horses to sell; he answered negatively. "Have not you, sir," to my father, "two black horses?"—"Yes, but have no mind to dispose of them." My terror had by this time nearly subsided. The officer and men behaved perfectly civil; the first drank two glasses of wine, rode away, bidding his men to follow, which, after adieus in number, they did. The officer was Lieutenant Lindsay, of Bland's regiment, Lee's troop. The men, to our great joy, were Americans, and but 4 in all. What made us imagine them British, they wore blue and red, which with us is not common. It has rained all this afternoon, and, to present appearances, will all night. In all probability the English will take possession of the city tomorrow or next day. What a change it will be! . . .

Nothing worth relating has occurred this afternoon. Now for trifles. I have set a stocking on the needles, and intend to be mighty industrious. This evening our folks heard a very heavy cannon. We suppose it to be fired by the English. The report seem'd to come from Philadelphia. We hear the American army will be within five miles of us tonight. The uncertainty of our position engrosses me quite. Perhaps to be in the midst of war, and ruin, and the clang of arms. But we must hope the best. . . .

Second Day, October 19th.

Now for new and uncommon scenes. As I was lying in bed, and ruminating on past and present events, and thinking how happy I should be if I could see you, Liddy came running into the room, and said there was the greatest drumming, fifing, and rattling of waggons that ever she had heard. What to make of this we were at a loss. We dress'd and down stairs in a hurry. Our wonder ceased. The British had left Germantown, and our army were marching to take possession. It was the general opinion they would evacuate the capital. Sister B. and myself, and G. E. went about half a mile from home, where we cou'd see the army pass. Thee will stare at my going, but no impropriety, in my opine, or I should not have gone. We made no great stay, but return'd with excellent appetites for our breakfast. Several officers call'd to get some refreshments, but none of consequence till the afternoon. Cousin P. and myself were sitting at the door; I in a green skirt, dark short gown, etc. Two genteel men of the military order rode up to the door: "Your servant, ladies," etc.; ask'd if they could have quarters for General Smallwood. Aunt F. thought she could accommodate them as well as most of her neighbors,—said they could. One of the officers dismounted, and wrote "Smallwood's Quarters" over the door, which secured us from straggling soldiers. After this he mounted his steed and rode away. When we were alone, our dress and lips were put in order for conquest, and the hopes of adventures gave brightness to each before passive countenance. . . . Dr. Gould usher'd the gentlemen into our parlour, and introduc'd them,—"General Smallwood, Captain Furnival, Major Stodard, Mr. Prig, Captain Finley, and Mr. Clagan, Colonel Wood, and Colonel Line." These last two did not come with the General. They are Virginians, and both indispos'd. The General and suite, are Marylanders. Be assur'd, I did not stay long with so many men, but secur'd a good retreat, heart-safe, so far. Some sup'd with us, others at Jesse's. They retir'd about ten, in good order. How new is our situation! I feel in good spirits, though surrounded by an army, the house full of officers, the yard alive with soldiers,—very peaceable sort of people, tho'. They eat like other folks, talk like them, and behave themselves with elegance; so I will not be afraid of them, that I won't. Adieu. I am going to my chamber to dream, I suppose, of bayonets and swords, sashes, guns, and epaulets. . . .

Second Day, 26th October.

The General and officers drank tea with us, and stay'd part of the evening. After supper I went with aunt, where sat the General, Colonel Line, and Major Stodard. So Liddy and I seated ourselves at the table in order to read a verse-book. The Major was holding a candle for the General, who was reading a newspaper. He look'd at us, turn'd away his eyes, look'd again, put the candlestick down, up he jumps, out of the door he went. "Well," said I to Liddy, "he will join us when he comes in." Presently he return'd, and seated himself on the table. "Pray, ladies, is there any songs in that book?" "Yes, many." "Can't you favor me with a sight of it?" "No, Major; 'tis a borrow'd book." "Miss Sally, can't you sing?" "No." Thee may be sure I told the truth there. Liddy, saucy girl, told him I could. He beg'd, and I deny'd; for my voice is not much better than the voice of a raven. We talk'd and laugh'd for an hour. He is clever, amiable, and polite. He has the softest voice, never pronounces the r at all.

I must tell thee, to-day arriv'd Colonel Guest and Major Leatherberry; the former a smart widower, the latter a lawyer, a sensible young fellow, and will never swing for want of tongue. Dr. Diggs came Second day; a mighty disagreeable man. We were oblig'd to ask him to tea. He must needs pop himself between the Major and me, for which I did not thank him. After I had drank tea, I jump'd from the table, and seated myself at the fire. The Major follow'd my example, drew his chair close to mine, and entertain'd me very agreeably. Oh, Debby; I have a thousand things to tell thee. I shall give thee so droll an account of my adventures that thee will smile. "No occasion of that, Sally," methinks I hear thee say, "for thee tells me every trifle." But, child, thee is mistaken, for I have not told thee half the civil things that are said of us *sweet* creatures at "General Smallwood's Quarters.". . .

December 5th, Sixth Day.

Oh, gracious Debby, I am all alive with fear. The English have come out to attack (as we imagine) our army, three miles this side. What will become of us, only six miles distant? We are in hourly expectation of an engagement. I fear we shall be in the midst of it. Heaven defend us from so dreadful a sight. The battle of Germantown, and the horrors of that day, are recent in my mind. It will be sufficiently dreadful, if we are only in hearing of the firing, to think how many of our fellow creatures are plung'd into the boundless ocean of eternity, few of them prepar'd to meet their fate. But they are summon'd before an all-merciful judge, from whom they have a great deal to hope.

Seventh Day, December 6th.

No firing this morn. I hope for one more quiet day.

Seventh Day, Noon, 4 o'clock.

I was much alarm'd just now, sitting in the parlour, indulging melancholy reflections, when somebody burst open the door. "Sally, here's Major Stodard." I jumped. Our conjectures were various concerning his coming. The poor fellow, from great fatigue and want of rest, together with being expos'd to the night air, had caught cold, which brought on a fever. He cou'd scarcely walk, and I went into aunt's to see him. I was surpris'd. Instead of the lively, alert, blooming Stodard, who was on his feet the instant we enter'd, he look'd pale, thin, and dejected, too weak to rise, and "How are you, Miss Sally?" "How does thee do, Major?" I seated myself near him, inquir'd the cause of his indisposition, ask'd for the General, receiv'd his compliments. Not willing to fatigue him with too much chat, I bid him adieu. . . .

First Day, Morn, December 7th.

I trip'd into aunt's. There sat the Major, rather more like himself. How natural it was to see him. "Good morning, Miss Sally." "Good morrow, Major, how does thee do to-day?" "I feel quite recover'd, Sally." "Well, I fancy this indisposition has sav'd thy head this time." Major: "No ma'am; for if I hear a firing, I shall soon be with them." That was heroic. About eleven I dress'd myself, silk and cotton gown. It is made without an apron. I feel quite awkwardish, and prefer the girlish dress. . . .

Fourth Day, June 3, 1778

. . . About nine I took my work and seated myself in the parlour. Not long had I sat, when in came Dandridge,—the handsomest man in existence, at least that I had ever seen. But stop here, while I just say, the night before, chatting upon dress, he said he had no patience with those officers who, every morn, before they went on detachments, would wait to be dress'd and powder'd. "I am," said I, "excessively fond of powder, and think it very becoming." "Are you?" he reply'd. "I am very careless, as often wearing my cap thus" (turning the back part before) "as any way." I left off where he came in. He was powder'd very white, a (pretty colored) brown coat, lapell'd with green, and white waistcoat, etc. . . . He made a truly elegant figure. "Good morning, Miss Sally. You are very well, I hope." "Very well. Pray sit down," which he did, close by me. "Oh, dear," said I, "I see thee is powder'd." "Yes, ma'am. I have dress'd myself off for you." Will I be excused, Debby, if I look upon his being powder'd in the light of a compliment to me? . . .

'Tis impossible to write a regular account of our conversation. Be it sufficient to say that we had a multiplicity of chat.

About an hour since, sister H. came to me and said Captain Dandridge was in the parlour, and had ask'd for me. I went in. He met me, caught my hands. "Oh, Miss Sally, I have a beautiful sweetheart for you." "Poh! ridiculous! Loose my hands." "Well, but don't be so cross." "Who is he?" "Major Clough. I have seen him. Ain't he pretty, to be sure? I am going to headquarters. Have you any commands there?" "None at all; but" (recollecting), "yes, I have. Pray, who is your commanding officer?" "Colonel Bland, ma'am." "Please give my compliments to him, and I shou'd be glad if he would send thee back with a little more manners." He reply'd wickedly, and told me I had a little spiteful heart. But he was intolerably saucy; said he never met with such ladies. "You're very ill-natur'd, Sally." And, putting on the sauciest face, "Sally, if Tacy V*nd*r*n won't have me, will you?" "No, really; none of her discarded lovers." "But, provided I prefer you to her, will you consent?" "No, I won't." "Very well, madam." And after saying he would return to-morrow, among a hundred other things, he elegantly walk'd out of the room. . . .

Sixth Day, June 5th, Morn, 11 o'clock.

Last night we were a little alarm'd. I was awaken'd about 12, with somebody's opening the chamber door. I observ'd cousin Prissa talking to mamma. I asked what was the matter. "Only a party of light horse." "Are they Americans?" I quickly said. She answer'd in the affirmative, (which dispell'd my fears), and told me Major Jameson commanded, and that Captains Call and Nixon were with him. With that intelligence she left us. I revolved in my mind whether or not Jameson would renew his acquaintance; but Morpheus buried all my ideas, and this morning I rose by, or near seven, dress'd in my light chintz, which is made gown-fashion, kenton handkerchief, and linen apron. . . .

Dress'd as above, down I came, and went down to our kitchen, which is a small distance from the house. As I came back, I saw Jameson at the window. He met me in the entry, bow'd:—"How do you do, Miss Sally?" After the compliments usual on such occasions had pass'd, I invited him into our parlour. He followed me in. We chatted very sociably. . . .

I ask'd him whether Dandridge was on this side the Delaware. He said, "Yes." I wanted sadly to hear his opinion, but he said not a word. The conversation turn'd upon the British leaving Philadelphia. He firmly believ'd they were going. I sincerely wish'd it might be true, but was afraid to flatter myself. I had heard it so often that I was quite faithless, and express'd my approbation of Pope's 12th beatitude, "Blessed are they that expect nothing, for they shall not be disappointed." He smil'd, and assur'd me they *were* going away.

He was summon'd to breakfast. I ask'd him to stay with us. He declin'd the invitation with politeness, adding that he was in a hurry,—oblig'd to go to camp as soon as he could. He bow'd, "Your servant, ladies," and withdrew immediately. After breakfast they set off for Valley Forge, where Gen'l Washington's army still are.

LEARNING BY DOING WOMEN'S WORK

The diary of fifteen-year-old Elizabeth Fuller, daughter of an impecunious minister in the small Massachusetts town of Princeton, reveals patterns of work and sociability common in the homes of the early American republic. For women, an important part of that work was the production of clothing, from the initial breaking and carding of natural fibers to the cutting, sewing, and quilting of garments. Spinning had so much been the labor of the young and unmarried, like Fuller, in early modern England that the name "spinsters" was deeded to those who never married. At the time Fuller wrote, some parts of clothing production had already begun to be commercialized.

1791
Jan.   1—A very severe snow storm to-day.

2—Sabbath Fair & cold.

3—Cloudy & warm. Elisha Brooks here this afternoon.

6—warm & foggy the snow wastes very fast. Sam Mirick & Asaph Perry here a getting up wood

8—Cold to-day. Timmy went to Mr. Perrys. Hannah Brooks here.

9—Sabbath. I went to Meeting, rode on the colt.—I have not been before since October 17.

(eve seven o'clock) Revd. Mr. Tucker, Mr. Johnes of Gerry, Lieut. Mirick & Lieutenant Russell came here to spend the eve.

10—Mr. Thomson here this P.M. Wareham Hastings and Sam Brooks here this eve.

11—Ephraim Mirick & Asaph Perry at work here.

12—I went to Mrs. Miricks to make a visit. Charles Mirick there. Nathan Perry here, *this to divide newspapers.*

13—Hannah Brooks here borrowed half a pound of wool. David Perry here to get Timmy to go to singing school.

14—I am a Passing Grammar. David Perry here.

15—Enoch Brooks here, brought home the wool. I am a studying today

16—Sabbath very warm and pleasant no meeting in town. I wish

Francis Everett Blake, *History of the Town of Princeton in the County of Worcester and Commonwealth of Massachusetts, 1759–1915,* vol. 1 (Princeton, Mass., published by the town, 1915), pp. 305–11.

Mr. Crafts Brains would make haste and grow stronger for I really hate to stay at home such fine Sleighing riding & walking as 'tis now.

17—The Severest snow storm there has been this winter. I washed.

18—Fair but cold. I studied in the afternoon. Mr. Uriah Moore to get Pa to go to Lieut. Miricks to assist Mr. Ben. Clark in a law Suit between him & Amos Clark, said Amos is black Tonys son. it is called a Rule of law.

19—Pa went to Lieut. Miricks to assist Mr. Benja^m Clark.

20—I am writing Grammar. Nathan Perry had Pa's Horse to carry Caty and Lucretia Mirick to Col. Whetcombs.

21—I am a writing Grammar to-day. Pleasant weather. Nathan Perry put our Horse into their sleigh and carried Me to the singing school & back again. I had a fine ride and a fine evening; they sung a great many Tunes, I sang with them.

22—Nathan Perry here this eve. till eight o'clock.

23—Sabbath. I went to church. Mr. Davis Preached.

24—I washed. Timmy went to Mr. Perrys in the eve.

27—Pa went to Mr. Cuttings this evening.

28—Pa went to Leominster.

29—Mrs. Hastings here and drank tea with us.

30—Sabbath snowy dull weather. Timmy went to church. Mr. Davis Preached. Pa & all the rest of our Family staid at home.

31—Mr. Benjamin Clark here to-day.

1791
Feb.
1—Mr. Cutting here last eve.—Mr. Tom Ralph here this morn.—Mr. Hadley here to Dine.

2—James Mirick here to get our Colt.—Asaph Perry here, Pa paid him.

3—Tom Ralph here this morn. Nathan Perry came here about nine o'clock & staid until one.

4—Pa & Timmy Gone to Hubbardston after Rye. (eve.) Pa & Tim came home have bought fifteen Bushels Rye. John Brooks here.

5—Nathan Perry here this eve till seven o'clock.

6—Sabbath. I went to church in the P.M. Mr. Payson of Ringe Preached.

8—cold a severe storm. James Mirick here.

9—storm weather. I am a picking blue wool. Nathan Perry here to-day.

11—Pleasant but cold. Mr. Parmenter here this eve.

12—Nathan Perry here.

13—Sabbath. I went to church Mr. Estabrook Preached

14—Mr. Perry here this eve.

17—Excessive cold, I do not know as there ever was a colder day. I picked wool.

18—Cold. I finished picking wool.

19—stormy. Nathan Perry here, brought some letters from Sally, they came by way of Worcester.

20—Sabbath. no Meeting but of antipedo baptists.

21—David Perry here. Mr. Perry here this eve a few moments. Pa is gone to Westminster.

22—I began to break the blue wool for Pa's coat, broke a pound & three quarters in the P.M. Pa went to Sterling.

23—I broke four Pounds of blue Wool to-day.

24—I finished breaking wool. Mr. Stephen Brigham here.

26—Elisha Brooks here.

27—Sabbath no Preaching.

28—very warm South wind & rain. I washed to-day.

1791

Mar.   1—Pa went to Mr. Stephen Brighams to write his will. Ma began to spin the wool for Pa's coat. I card for her & do the household work.

2—Ma is a spinning.

3—Ma spun three skeins.—Nathan Perry here.—Pa is gone to Mr. Hastings this eve.

4—Mrs. Perry here to spend the afternoon.

5—Ma spun.

6—Sabbath. no Meeting in Town.

7—very warm. Anna Perry here visiting.—I made 18 dozen of candles & washed.

8—Ma spun.

9—Miss Eunice Mirick here a visiting this afternoon.

10—Warm and rainy.—Francis Eveleth here to borrow our singing Book. Ma spun.

11—Rainy weather. Mr. Thomson here to-day after rates. Mr. Parmenter here, bought two calf skins of Pa, gave him ten shillings apiece.—David Perry here.—Timmy went to Mr. Brooks.

12—David Perry here to-day.

13—Sabbath no Meeting.

14—March Meeting Mr. Crafts asked a dismission, had his request granted without the least difficulty, so now we are once more a free people ha ha, he is going to Weymouth to keep shop a going out of Town this week 'tis thought he has not much to carry with him I do not know nor care what he has.

15—Revd. Mr. Rice & Mr. Isaac Thomson here. Mr. Rice Dined here.

16—Pa went to Mr. Bangs to-day.

18—Capt. Clark here this evening.

19—John Brooks here to-day.—Nathan Perry here for the newspaper.—Ma spun two skeins & an half of filling yarn.

20—Sabbath. Pa went to church Mr. Saunders Preached, he is one of Stephen Baxters classmates. the going was so bad that none of the rest of our Family went to hear him.

21—Cold. Mr. Brooks here.

22—Pa went to Mr. Bangs.

23—Pa went to Mr. Rolphs to-day. On the 13th inst. Miss Caty Mirick was Married to Mr. Joshua Eveleth.

24—Mr. Brooks here to-day to get Pa to write a Deed of Mr. Hastingses Farm for him.

25—Ma finished spinning her blue Wool to-day.

26—Ma went to Mrs. Miricks to get a slay Harness. Mrs. Caty Eveleth came home with her.

27—Sabbath very pleasant I went to church. Mr. Rolph Preached.—Esqr. Woolson here to tarry all night.

28—Esqr. Woolson went from here this morning. A man here to-day that was both deaf and dumb, he is Son to a Merchant in London, he went to sea & the ship was struck with Lightning & which occasioned his being deaf & dumb, he could write wrote a good deal here. He was a good looking young Man, about 25 he wrote his name Joel Smith. I really pitied him. I went to Mrs. Miricks & warped the piece.

29—Mrs. Garfield came here to show me how to draw in Piece did not stay but about half an hour.

30—I tyed in the Piece & wove two yards.

31—Fast. I went to Meeting all day. Mr. Rolph preached half of the day & Mr. Saunders the other half. Mr. Saunders is a very good Preacher & a handsome Man.—David Perry here this evening to sing with us.

1791

April 1—I wove two yards and three quarters & three inches to-day & I think I did pretty well considering it was April Fool day. Mr. Brooks & Mr. Hastings here to get Pa to do some writing for them.

2—I wove three yards and a quarter.

3—Sabbath. I went to church.—an anular eclipse of the sun, it was fair weather.

4—I wove five yards & a quarter. Mr. Cutting here this eve.

5—I wove four yards. Mrs. Garfield & Mrs. Eveleth who was once Caty Mirick here a visiting.—The real estate of Mr. Josiah Mirick deceased is vendued to-day.

(eve) Timmy has got home from the vendue Mr. Cutting has bought the Farm gave 255£ Sam Matthews has bought the part of the Pew gave eight dollars.

6—I got out the White piece Mrs. Garfield warped the blue, came here & began to draw in the Piece.

7—I finished drawing in the Piece & wove a yard & a half. Sam Matthews here to-day.

8—I wove two yards & a quarter.

9—I wove two yards & a quarter.

10—Sabbath. I went to church in the A.M. Mamma went in the P.M. she has not been before since she came from Sandwich.

11—I wove a yard & a half. Parmela Mirick here to see me.

12—I wove to-day.

13—Mrs. Brooks here a visiting. I wove.

14—I got out the Piece in the A.M. Pa carried it to Mr. Deadmans. Miss Eliza Harris here.

15—I began to spin Linnen spun 21 knots. I went to Mr. Perrys on an errand. Pa went to Mr. Matthews to write his will & some deeds. He has sold Dr. Wilson 20 acres of Land & given Sam a deed of some I believe about 25 acres.

16—Pa went to Mr. Matthews again.—I spun 21 knots.

17—Sabbath I went to church all day Mr. Davis Preached Mr. Saunders is sick.

18—I spun two double skeins of Linnen.

19—I spun two double skeins.

20—I spun two double skeins.—Ma went to Mrs. Miricks for a visit was sent for home.—Revd. Daniel Fuller of Cape Ann here to see us.

21—Revd. Mr. Fuller went from here this morn. Ma went to Mrs. Miricks again.—I spun two skeins.—Sukey Eveleth & Nabby here to see Nancy.

22—I spun two double skeins O dear
Quadville has murdered wit, & work will do as bad, for wit is always merry, but work does make me sad.

23—I spun two skeins. Nathan Perry here.—Wareham Hastings at work here.

24—I went to church. Mr. Thurston Preached.—Mr. Saunders is sick.

25—Leonard Woods here all this forenoon, brought Holyokes singing Book. Left it here.

26—Pa went to see Mr. Saunders. I Pricked some tunes out of Holyokes Singing Book.

27—I spun five skeins of linnen yarn.

28—I spun five skeins of linnen yarn. Pa went to Sterling.

29—I pricked some Tunes out of Holyokes singing Book. I spun some.

30—I spun four skeins to-day.

1791

May   1—Sabbath I went to Meeting to-day.

2—I spun five skeins to-day.

3—I spun five skeins to-day.

4—I spun two skeins to-day finished the Warp for this Piece.— Nathan Perry worked here this P.M.

5—I spun four skeins of tow for the filling to the Piece I have been spinning. Pa went to Worcester to get the newspaper. Nathan Perry here this eve.

6—I spun four Skeins to-day.

7—I spun four Skeins to-day.

8—Sabbath. I went to church A.M. Mr. Thurston preached. Mr. John Rolph & his Lady & Mr. Osburn her Brother & a Miss Anna Strong (a Lady courted by said Osbourn) came here after Meeting and drank Tea.

9—I spun four skeins. Mr. Thurston here this P.M. a visiting he is an agreeable Man appears much better out of the Pulpit than in.

10—I spun four Skeins to-day.

11—I spun four skeins.

12—I spun four skeins. Lucy Matthews here.

13—I spun four skeins.—Ma is making Soap. Rainy.

14—I spun four skeins. Ma finished making soap and it is very good.

15—I went to church A.M. Mr. Thurston Preached he is a ——. —Mr. Rolph drank Tea here.

17—I spun four skeins to-day.

18—I spun four skeins of linnen yarn to Make a Harness of.—Ma is a breaking.

19—I spun two skeins and twisted the harness yarn.

20—Mrs. Garfield came here this Morning to show me how to make a Harness, did not stay but about half an Hour.— Mrs. Perry & Miss Eliza Harris here a visiting.

21—I went to Mrs. Miricks and warped the Piece.

22—I went to church in the A.M. Mr. Saunders preached gave us a good sermon his text Romans 6th Chap. 23 verse. For the wages of Sin is Death.

23—I got in my Piece to-day wove a yard.

24—Wove two yards & an half.

25—Election. I wove three Yards to-day.—Mrs. Perry here a few moments.

26—I wove three Yards to-day. The two Mrs. Matthews here to Day. I liked Sam's Wife much better than I expected to.— Miss. Eliza Harris here about two Hours.

27—I wove five Yards to-day.

29—Pleasant weather. Pa went to Sterling. My Cousin Jacob Kembal of Amherst came here to-day.

30—General Election at Bolton.—Mr. Josiah Eveleth & Wife & Mrs. Garfield here on a visit.

1791
June

1—Moses Harrington carried off Mr. Hastings old shop.

2—Elisha Brooks here to-day.

5—I made myself a Shift.—Mrs. Perry here a visiting. Nathan Perry here this evening.

6—Sabbath. No Meeting in Town. Elisha Brooks here to see if there was a meeting.

7—I made myself a blue worsted Coat.

8—Aaron & Nathan Perry here.—Pamela Mirick here a visiting this afternoon.

9—Mrs. Brooks here a visiting.—I helped Sally make me a blue worsted Gown.

10—I helped Sally make me a brown Woolen Gown.

12—Sally cut out a striped lutestring Gown for me.

13—Sabbath I went to church. Mr. Green Preached.

14—Aaron Perry here.

15—I cut out a striped linnen Gown.—Sally finished my lute-string.

16—Rainy weather. Ma cut out a Coattee for me.—Salmon Houghton breakfasted with us.—Elisha Brooks spent the afternoon here.

17—Ma, Sally & I spent the afternoon at Mrs. Miricks.

18—Cool. Sally finished my Coattee.

19—I finished my striped linnen Gown. Mr. Soloman Davis here.

20—Sabbath. I went to Church. wore my lutestring, Sally wore hers we went to Mr. Richardsons & Dined.—rained at night.

21—Pleasant weather. Mr. Bush here.

22—Capt. Moore here to-day. Put in my dwiant Coat & Sally & I quilted it out before night.

23—Sally put in a Worsted Coat for herself and we quilted it out by the middle of the afternoon. Very pleasant weather.

24—I made myself a Shift.

25—Very hot weather.—Abishai Eveleth here.

27—Rainy, unpleasant weather. I stayed at home all day.

A FATHER'S ADVICE TO HIS DAUGHTER

While traveling on business in Philadelphia, North Carolinian A. Jocelin learned of his daughter's recent marriage. Beset by financial difficulties—and thus unable to provide for his children in the expected ways—he wrote to express his confidence in her judgment in this important decision and took the opportunity to advise her on how women's virtues could guarantee a prosperous and happy home.

Philadelphia. Sept. [illegible] 1788

Dear Child.

I understand since I left home, that you have left your Fathers house. [illegible] have literally forsaken father and Mother, and joined your self to an Husband. I confess the Event doth not displease me, because I doubt not your judgement concerned with your inclination in determining that it would be productive of your greatest temporal felicity. That you may not be Disappointed I sincerely wish and pray; for, if I know my own heart, the greatest happiness of my Children is by no means the least or last of my wishes. It hurts me Exceedingly however that by a remarkable series of misfortunes, it is out of my power to do that for them, and for you in particular on this Occasion, which my inclination would lead me to do. I hope nevertheless that, at a future period of time, I may have it in my power to Demonstrate to them by some substantial testimonials, that I love them most tenderly.

Give my Affectionate Compliments to your Husband, tell him I sincerely wish him every happiness on the Occasion, which he could expect in a Marriage relation; and inform him, that from what I know of his family, and what I have heard of him in particular, I feel myself happy in the Connection. . . .

You have now Dear Child entered on a new mode of living—have entered into a new relationship, and consequently have involved yourself in new cares, and laid yourself under new duties and obligations. Thus Circumstanced, I feel myself under some kind of obligation to observe a few things to you which possibly may be found of service to attend to [torn] journey through this life.

The visionary bliss, which young people anticipate in general before their Marriage, they are most commonly Disappointed in. The happiest

A. Jocelin to his daughter, September 1788, Giles Family Papers, no. 3391, Southern Historical Collection, University of North Carolina at Chapel Hill. The editors are indebted to Charlotte Haller for locating and providing a copy of this letter.

and pleasantest path if Married is planted with thornes, and the real comforts and pleasures of matrimony are not to be found, where they were at first supposed to be deposited. To be disappointed in Visionary, or immaginary felicity is on the whole the best, because it naturally lends the mind to seek for Happiness in those things which are capable of giving the most rational and most substantial Satisfaction, the pleasures arising from being Agreeably Circumstanced in life—and from agreeable reflections on a faithful Discharge of duties are much more exquisite and permanent than those which are produced by the gratification of the senses. A woman therefore ought to consider her greatest happiness in the Marriage state to consist of her being united to a Man of Virtue and Honour, who is her protector—her supporter—Affectionate friend—Bosom companion—participator in enjoyments—sharer in sorrow, and whose friendly and affectionate care will be continued, not for a month, or a year only, for so long as life shall render such friendly Offices necessary. . . . The intimate and inseperable union which subsist between a Man and his Wife is such that it is impossible to divide their interest and happiness—they are mutual, and in the nature of things cannot be otherwise, what is therefore done to promote the others happiness is done to promote their own—and so on the other hand what one does to interrupt, or destroy the happiness of the other, is but injuring in an equal degree, in most cases the happiness of the other—much more depends on the disposition and conduct of a woman to promote her own happiness, than many wives are aware of—the mans reputation, his interest and peace are often injured and sometimes totally ruined, by the errors, follys and vices of his Wife, in such a Case what becomes of the reputation, interest and peace of the woman? Is she not sunk much deeper (if possible) in misery than her Husband? . . .

Virtue in a woman has often been considered as that alone in which a good and perfect female Character consist. To this I add but then so far am I from confining my idea of female virtue to [that] which is commonly understood by it, that I consider it an Assembl[age?] of Virtues, or rather, I consider a virtuous woman to be one who is disposed to discharge, to the utmost of her power, all the relative and social duties which as a woman, a wife, a mother &c may be incumbent on her, and those who have such a disposition in the highest degree, may be Esteemed in the highest degree a Virtuous woman.

Were I to enlarge on the subject, I might write a considerable volume but, as I have nothing further in view than to direct your attention to some things, which I conceive may contribute to your welfare and happiness I shall confine myself to a few particulars.

A woman should consider it one of the most essential objects of her Views and conduct to secure and keep alive the love and affection of her Husband—for it is a Virtue in its nature, and the very act of doing those things which are necessary for this, produces mutual pleasure and satisfaction, this is a point which many, many overlook and neglect, and that very unadvisedly, for when that affection, which first brought a man and woman together, becomes alienated, [illegible] they might as well separate themselves—their living together with alienated Affections produces nothing but misery and torment—many women who are sensible of the importance of securing the affections of their husbands, oftentimes mistake the means of affecting it—they often immagine that the beauty and decorations of their persons was that which at the first attracted the notice of the Husbands and therefore, it is necessary to keep up the same appearance . . . , but such kinds of deceptions are too gross and flimsy to have the desired effect on discerning minds. The glowing warmth of love and friendship is not to be kept alive by any such artifices, nor was it ever lighted up by such a spark. . . . Remember therefore, that an amiable and Virtuous disposition, with a Correspondant conversation and deportment, constitute that which a woman is principally to depend upon, for a continuation of that love and Affection, which made her the wife of the man of her choice—such a disposition and behavior will allways have its proper effect on the mind of any man whose esteem and Affectionate friendship are worth having. But a woman who is out of humour with every little untoward incident—who is continually [brawling?] like Xantippes Wife—who is constantly blowing up the sparks of ill humour, discord and dispute, and who is displeased and discontented in all Circumstances, will soon weary the patience of a Job, and drive a man Abroad to seek that tranquility which he allways ought to find at home—let your face therefore allways be clothed with good humour—and your tongue speak nought but the words of Affection Condescension and kindness— . . . —the first words of an Affectionate friend, well timed, will soon disarm a man of his passion—will melt even a heart of stone, if the least spark of sensibility [illegible] and often it will reclaim a profligate. . . .

Above all things never let there [be] any witness to any ill natured dispute which may happen, nor disclose any family discord to your nearest friends, neither let your father or mother know your complaints, unless an offense be too gross to be put up with, and there should be a probability of redress be obtained in such a way. . . .

Another thing I would recommend to you as a female Virtue, and essential to the interest and Convenience of a family, is Industry. I flatter myself however that I have no great occasion to urge this upon you, for I think you are industriously disposed, but I will tell you the advantages of it that you may not want motives to prevent you from falling into a habit of slothfullness if events and circumstances should render your industry not absolutely necessary. Female industry greatly promotes the interest and convenience of a Family; for tho' it may not be directly so productive of profit as the labour of a Man, yet in its consequences it is advantageous, because it saves that which would be otherways lost, and doubles the value of family necessaries by prolonging the usefulness of many things, besides these by the industry of a woman a family is actually supplied with many necessaries and Conveniences—that you may have some just idea of the importance of female industry in a family, look at the children of an industrious woman; they are neat, clean, and whole tho perhaps made so with many a patch on their clothes, but no matter, it answers every necessary purpose and besides such clothes rendered usefull and comfortable Even until they are outgrown—then View the children of a careless idle woman—they were all clothed the other day with new clothes, but they are now become dirty, with a hole here, a rent there, and a strip flying at another place—and so they will remain til the dirt [rot] one part, and the winds drive the remainer away, which will be before the winter is half over—in this particular half the expense of supporting a family of children with Clothes may be saved by the industry of the mother, and such are the advantages of female industry in every particular, when female industry can be applied. . . .

I would also recommend Oeconomy to you as an essential Virtue, the interest of a man is much under the influence of his wife's conduct. She may contribute much to its increase, or she may materially [damage] it and that particularily in two respects, viz by a prudent or imprudent expenditures in the family; and by limiting, or not limiting her wants to her Husbands circumstances. A discreet woman, who wishes to promote her husbands interest, will allways pay such particular attention to the affairs of her house; as to spend with prudence and judgement that which is particularly commited to her care, and management, which may be done in such a manner as not to betray a niggardly disposition, which would dishonour a mans house, nor on the other hand to be guilty of profusion and waste—make it therefore your study to know how to turn everything to the best account, so as to save the most, and at the same time not to discover a spirit of meaness, this art is to be acquired by a studious attention—and by progressive experience. And as it is of consequence to a family, I could beg you to Attend to it. It may further be considered a Virtue of the Oeconomical kind in a woman, not to extend her ambition, and wants beyond the convenience of her Husbands Circumstances—his circumstances may at times be such that the full gratifications of the requisitions of his wife, might fatally injure his interest, in such a case it would be highly criminal in a wife, and but a miserable proof of her regard to him, and his interest, were she to extend her demands beyond the bounds of his abilities. . . . A man who regards his wife with affection will allways gratify her (with pleasure) as far as reason and his abilities will permit him to do, and with this every woman of sense who regards the interest and happiness of her husband as she ought to do will be content.

If providence should prosper your Husband in his business, and he should flourish, let your demands be circumscribed within the bounds of reason and moderation. . . .

If Misfortunes should befal your Husband, and he should be reduced in his Circumstances, I can say nothing more to the purpose than to refer you to your Dear Mother for an example in such a case. She has allways considered repeated and distressing Misfortunes as providential. She has submitted to them with a Christian Spirit, not been discont[ent]ed under them, Has reduced her requisitions to such circumstances, and by her own industry, and good oeconomy, has alleviated the distress of such severe Misfortunes as many women would have sunk under.

Moderation in the article of visiting, I would reckon one of the number of female Virtues—an overfondness for visiting, is the same in a woman as that of gambling in a man, and is equally inconvenient to the interest of a family and may be equally ruinous. . . .

I would consider neatness and cleanliness another female Virtue and highly Ornamental. A cleanly house, and a neat cleanly woman, are the best ornament, a man can be possessed of. A man of true taste never esteemed a woman for being adorned with gaudy fripperies, but he cannot but be pleased with a woman who is careful to cloth herself in a neat and cleanly manner, and to keep everything about her neat and cleanly also, . . . this neatness and cleanliness ought not to be of the Deceptive kind—it ought not to be a holy Day but an every day appearance and it ought to extend to manners. If I was going to satisfy myself of the disposition and real Character of any woman in this particular, I should not go into her Parlour, nor examine her Sunday dress, but I should go into her kitchen, and examine the furniture of that room; for tho she might not have occasion to do the work of the Kitchen herself, yet the kitchen will most commonly bear the image of the Mistress disposition, let the work be done by whom it will. I should also be inclined to look into pantry, perhaps into her bedchamber and closet, and instead of Visiting her in the afternoon, I would pay her an occas[ional] Visit early in the morning, if in such an enquiry, . . . I found nothing to be dissatisfied with, I should pronounce the woman neat in person, and delicate in mind. . . .

I will add once more what I esteem a female Virtue, a moderation in dress and fashion. Extravagance in fashion was originally intended to hide some [natural?] deformity, or blemish, or to attract the notice of other people and however excuseable it may be in a young woman in order to deceive a man into a likeing of her person it can never be excused in a married woman, who can no longer have Occasion for artifice, and who ought not to be anxious about the notice and attention of the multitudes. A woman of comeliness and Beauty can add nothing by extravagant fashions, to render herself beautiful, but often by this eclipses the beauty which nature has bestowed on her. . . .

. . . Your duties and cares may be augmented by an increased family, you may be involved in the cares, and laid under the duties and Obligations of a parent—this increases ones domestic happiness but at the same time, it produces an anxious care and solicitude about the welfare and conduct of your Children. Children early discover a wicked perverse spirit—a spirit of wilful Obstinacy, and often times, a lying, fraudulent, thieving, frightful, malicious, vengeful, deceitful, proud and profane spirit, which if suffered to remain and grow up with them, produces melancholy effects. Such Children often times become the grief of their parents, a nuisance to society, a burden on the earth, and finally they will suffer the future Miserable consequences of such evil and unres[t]rained dispositions—it is a duty therefore which parents owe to themselves—to their Children and to the world, to suppress such [illegible] dispositions. . . .

. . . I now should close. But as you are now gone from me, and put it out of my power to give you frequent direction and advice, and that I may in some measure discharge the duty which I owe to you, I would add something respecting your immortal interest and concerns, which of all others is the most important, and worthy the first attention of the Mind. . . .

Consider therefore the love and favour of God, and the security of your future and endless felicity, as the first and greatest object of your Life. . . . In all your thoughts, wishes and purposes—If a state of future happiness be the great object of your desires, you will esteem the Visisitudes of this life, and the pleasures of time, and sense, as matter of but little consequences, compared with matters of futurity—and indeed you will render every thing in this life subservient to your future interest.

. . . after all that hath or can be said about it, genuine religion consists in a conformity of the temper and disposition of the mind to the nature, character and will of God, the great origin and fountain of Spiritual excellence. . . .

. . . Labour earnestly to acquire such a divine, habitual temper and disposition. . . . Real religion is manifested by an earnest desire to perform all the duties, and services, we owe to God, and to our fellow creatures, which comprehends every thing we understand by external religion—the discharge of these duties are of importance but then, there is not real religion in them—nothing meritorious, and nothing acceptable, unless they proceed from true and unfeigned Love for God and man—what these duties are, and how to be performed, our reason, but especially the Scriptures teach and direct us—apply therefore, constantly to these oracles for knowledge and instruction, and that with an earnest desire to be instructed. Consider one thing further, you are accountable to God yourself. [No] other [can] answer for you, your religious faith and practice ought to be the result of your own reflect[ions] and not those of another . . . form your own Judgement to that which shall appear to you to be truth, after all the light and information you can Obtain, without paying an implicit regard to the peculiar Opinion of any person on earth; for the Opinion of others will stand you in no stead in the day of Account. . . .

I have met with nothing [but] a continued series of misfortune since I left home, and now find myself [more] distressed and embarrassed than I ever was in my life—[How] long the Afflictive hand of providence will lie upon [me] I know not, I still retain my sentiment, however, that although the ways of providence are to us, dark and intricate, yet perfect wisdom and goodness, govern all the events which befal us in this life, and notwithstanding we cannot see the designs, and harmony of the divine administration, yet I believe our greatest good is the intention of such afflictive dispensations. I know not as yet how I shall proceed from here, or when I shall come home—It grieves me to the heart that I have a family, whom I love most tenderly, involved in the Calamities which have befallen me. I hope however we shall all still rely on the goodness of God for the removal of our [burden] in his own time—for to whom else shall we go for relief.

With sincere wishes for your welfare, and of your Husband, to whom remember me.

I am, Dear Child, your Affectionate Father, A. Jocelin

∾

ELIZA SOUTHGATE REFLECTS ON THE SEXES

Born in 1783 in Scarborough, Maine, Eliza Southgate had the advantages of wealth and family connections. Her father, a doctor with some knowledge of the law, was eventually appointed a judge; her mother was from a large landholding family. Eliza was educated at Susanna Rowson's prestigious Young Ladies Academy in Boston. She wrote these letters to a male cousin, Moses Porter, of about her own age and comparable background.

September 1800

. . . As I look around me I am surprised at the happiness which is so generally enjoyed in families, and that marriages which have not love for a foundation on more than one side at most, should produce so much apparent harmony. I may be censured for declaring it as my opinion that not one woman in a hundred marries for love. A woman of taste and sentiment will surely see but a very few whom she could love, and it is altogether uncertain whether either of them will particularly distinguish her. If they should, surely she is very fortunate, but it would be one of fortune's random favors and such as we have no right to expect. The female mind I believe is of a very pliable texture; if it were not we should be wretched indeed. Admitting as a known truth that few women marry those whom they would prefer to all the world if they could be viewed by them with equal affection, or rather that there are often others whom they could have preferred if they had felt that affection for them which would have induced them to offer themselves,—admitting this as a truth not to be disputed,—is it not a subject of astonishment that happiness is not almost banished from this connexion? Gratitude is undoubtedly the foundation of the esteem we commonly feel for a husband. One that has preferred us to all the world, one that has thought us possessed of every quality to render him happy, surely merits our gratitude. If his character is good—if he is not displeasing in his person or manners—what objection can we make that will not be thought frivolous by the greater part of the world?—yet I think there are many other things necessary for happiness, and the world should never compel me to marry a man because I could not give satisfactory reasons for not liking him. I do not esteem marriage absolutely essential to happiness, and that it does not always bring happiness we must every day witness in our acquaintance. A single life is considered too generally as a reproach; but let me ask you, which

Clarence Cook, ed., *A Girl's Life Eighty Years Ago: Letters of Eliza Southgate Bowne* (New York: C. Scribner's Sons, 1887), pp. 37–41, 55–57, 58–62, 101–2, 104–5.

is the most despicable—she who marries a man she scarcely thinks *well* of—to avoid the reputation of an old maid—or she, who with more delicacy, than marry one she could not highly esteem, preferred to live single all her life, and had wisdom enough to despise so mean a sacrifice, to the opinion of the rabble, as the woman who marries a man she has not much love for—must make. I wish not to alter the laws of nature—neither will I quarrel with the rules which custom has established and rendered indispensably necessary to the harmony of society. But every being who has contemplated human nature on a large scale will certainly justify me when I declare that the inequality of privilege between the sexes is very sensibly felt by us females, and in no instance is it greater than in the liberty of choosing a partner in marriage; true, we have the liberty of refusing those we don't like, but not of selecting those we do. This is undoubtedly as it should be. But let me ask you, what must be that love which is altogether voluntary, which we can withhold or give which sleeps in dullness and apathy till it is requested to brighten into life? Is it not a cold, lifeless dictate of the head,—do we not weigh all the conveniences and inconveniences which will attend it? And after a long calculation, in which the heart never was consulted, we determine whether it is most prudent to love or not. . . . I am confident in my own mind that no person whom I could love would ever think me sufficiently worthy to love me. But I congratulate myself that I am at liberty to refuse those I don't like, and that I have firmness enough to brave the sneers of the world and live an old maid, if I never find one I can love. . . .

May 1801

. . . I believe I possess decent talents and should have been quite another being had they been properly cultivated. But as it is, I can never get over some little prejudices which I have imbibed long since, and which warp all the faculties of my mind. I was pushed on to the stage of action without one principle to guide my actions,—the impulse of the moment was the only incitement. I have never committed any grossly imprudent action, yet I have been folly's darling child. I trust they were rather errors of the head than the heart, for we have all a kind of inherent power to distinguish between right and wrong, and if before the heart becomes contaminated by the maxims of society it is left to act from impulse though it have no fixt principle, yet it will not materially err. Possessing a gay lively disposition, I pursued pleasure with ardor. I wished for admiration, and took the means which would be most likely to obtain it. I found the mind of a female, if such a thing existed, was thought not worth cultivating. I disliked the trouble of thinking for myself and therefore adopted the sentiments of others—fully convinced to adorn my person and acquire a few little accomplishments was sufficient to secure me the admiration of the society I frequented. I cared but little about the mind. I learned to flutter about with a thoughtless gaiety—a mere feather which every breath had power to move. I left school with a head full of something, tumbled in without order or connection. I returned home with a determination to put it in more order; I set about the great work of culling the best part to make a few sentiments out of—to serve as a little ready change in my commerce with the world. But I soon lost all patience (a virtue I do not possess in an eminent degree), for the greater part of my ideas I was obliged to throw away without knowing where I got them or what I should do with them; what remained I pieced as ingeniously as I could into a few patchwork opinions,—they are now almost worn threadbare, and as I am about quilting a few more, I beg you will send me any spare ideas you may chance to have that will answer my turn. . . .

June 1801

As to the qualities of mind peculiar to each sex, I agree with you that sprightliness is in favor of females and profundity of males. Their education, their pursuits would create such a quality even tho' nature had not implanted it. The business and pursuits of men require deep thinking, judgment, and moderation, while, on the other hand, females are under no necessity of dipping deep, but merely "skim the surface," and we too commonly spare ourselves the exertion which deep researches require, unless they are absolutely necessary to our pursuits in life. We rarely find one giving themselves up to profound investigation for amusement merely. Necessity is the nurse of all the great qualities of the mind; it explores all the hidden treasures and by its stimulating power they are "polished into brightness." Women who have no such incentives to action suffer all the strong energetic qualities of the mind to sleep in obscurity; sometimes a ray of genius gleams through the thick clouds with which it is enveloped, and irradiates for a moment the darkness of mental night; yet, like a comet that shoots wildly from its sphere, it excites our wonder, and we place it among the phenomenons of nature, without searching for a natural cause. Thus it is the qualities with which nature has endowed us, as a support amid the misfortunes of life and a shield from the allurements of vice, are left to moulder in ruin. In this dormant state they become enervated and impaired, and at last die for *want of exercise*. The little airy qualities which produce sprightliness are left to flutter about like feathers in the wind, the sport of every breeze.

Women have more fancy, more lively imaginations than men. That is easily accounted for: a person of correct judgment and accurate discernment will never have that flow of ideas which one of a different character might,—every object has not the power to introduce into his mind such a variety of ideas, he rejects all but those closely connected with it. On the other hand, a person of small discernment will receive every idea that arises in the mind, making no distinction between those nearly related and those more distant, they are all equally welcome, and consequently such a mind abounds with fanciful, out-of-the-way ideas. Women have more imaginations, more sprightliness, because they have less discernment. I never was of opinion that the pursuits of the sexes ought to be the same; on the contrary, I believe it would be destructive to happiness, there would a degree of rivalry exist, incompatible with the harmony we wish to establish. I have ever thought it necessary that each should have a separate sphere of action,—in such a case there could be no clashing unless one or the other should leap their respective bounds. Yet to cultivate the qualities with which we are endowed can never be called infringing the prerogatives of man. Why, my dear Cousin, were we furnished with such powers, unless the improvement of them would conduce to the happiness of society? Do you suppose the mind of woman the only work of God that was "made in vain." The cultivation of the powers we possess, I have ever thought a privilege (or I may say duty) that belonged to the human species, and not man's exclusive prerogative. Far from destroying the harmony that ought to subsist, it would fix it on a foundation that would not totter at every jar. Women would be under the same degree of subordination that they now are; enlighten and expand their minds, and they would perceive the necessity of such a regulation to preserve the order and happiness of society. Yet you require that their conduct should be always guided by that reason which you refuse them the power of exercising. I know it is generally thought that in such a case women would assume the right of commanding. But I see no foundation for such a supposition. . . .

I am aware of the censure that will ever await the female that attempts the vindication of her sex, yet I dare to brave that censure that I know to be undeserved. It does not follow (O what a pen!) that every female who vindicates the capacity of the sex is a disciple of Mary Wolstoncraft. Though I allow her to have said many things which I cannot but approve, yet the very foundation on which she builds her work will be apt to prejudice us so against her that we will not allow her the merit she really deserves,—yet, prejudice set aside, I confess I admire many of her sentiments, notwithstanding I believe should any one adopt her principles, they would conduct in the same manner, and upon the whole her life is the best comment on her writings. Her style is nervous and commanding, her sentiments appear to carry conviction along with them, but they will not bear analyzing.

[1802]

I hardly know what to say to you, Cousin, you have attacked my system with a kind of fury that has entirely obscured your judgment, and instead of being convinced of its impracticability, you appear to fear its justness. You tell me of some excellent effects of my system, but pardon me for thinking they are dictated by prejudice rather than reason. I feel fully convinced in my own mind that no such effects could be produced. You ask if this plan of education will render one a more dutiful child, a more affectionate wife, &c, &c., surely it will,—those virtues which now are merely practised from the momentary impulse of the heart, will then be adhered to from principle, a sense of duty, and a mind sufficiently strengthened not to yield implicitly to every impulse, will give a degree of uniformity, of stability to the female character, which it evidently at present does not possess. From having no fixed guide for our conduct we have acquired a reputation for caprice, which we justly deserve. I can hardly believe you serious when you say that "the enlargement of the mind will inevitably produce superciliousness and a desire of ascendancy,"—I should much sooner expect it from an ignorant, uncultivated mind. We cannot enlarge and improve our minds without perceiving our weakness, and wisdom is always modest and unassuming,—on the contrary a mind that has never been exerted knows not its deficiencies and presumes much more on its powers than it otherwise would. . . .

You undoubtedly think I am acting out of my sphere in attempting to discuss this subject, and my presumption probably gave rise to that idea, which you expressed in your last, that however unqualified a woman might be she was always equipt for the discussion of any subject and overwhelmed her hearers with her "clack." On what subjects shall I write you? I shall either fatigue and disgust you with female trifles, or shock you by stepping beyond the limits you have prescribed.

⁓

PETITION ON BEHALF OF FANNY, A SLAVE WOMAN

This unusual petition, signed in 1815 by seventeen citizens of Loudoun County, Virginia, asked that a slave woman named Fanny and her two children be permitted to remain in Virginia after their manumission. Virginia law of 1806 required that freed slaves leave the state within six months. Both the law and this petition reflect the wave of individual emancipations, especially of women, that took place in the upper South during the generation following the Revolution. As a result of those emancipations—and in spite of laws that demanded former slaves' removal from the states where they were freed—these years saw the emergence of free African American communities in Virginia and elsewhere.

To the General Assembly of Virginia the Memorial & Petition, of the Undersigned, in behalf of Fanny a woman of Colour, in the Custody of Thomas Chapel of Loudon County, and her infant children Ellen and Harriott respectfully represent:

That the said Fanny was brought into Fauquier County in this state from Harford County, Maryland, by a certain Robert Whiteford about the year of our Lord 1797, and was about ten years afterwards sold by the Heirs of the said Whiteford to the aforenamed Thomas Chapel, but the said Chapel on searching the records of Fauquier County aforesaid and finding that she was not registered according to Law, gave her up to those persons of whom he purchased her. that the said Chapel having found the said Fanny to be a remarkably steady & industrious woman, has for several years since that period hired her of the Heirs of the said Whiteford; and that during the whole time she has been in the said Chapel's services and for about two years before, a negro man belonging to the said Chapel has regularly cohabitated with her as his wife. The extraordinary character of the said Fanny and her husband induced the said Chapel about two years ago when she was likely to be separated from her husband, in consequence of the removal of her Master, who was nevertheless willing to sell her and her then youngest child, Ellen, to encourage her in endeavoring to raise money by subscription to purchase herself & her said child. The said Thomas Chapel, who is one of your petitioners, subscribed a considerable sum for the purpose and many of your other

Petition, Inhabitants of Loudoun County, December 6, 1815, Legislative Petitions, General Assembly, Legislative Department, Archives and Records Division, Library of Virginia, Richmond, Va. The editors are indebted to Brenda Stevenson for locating and providing a copy of this document.

Petitioners also subscribed. By this means, and by her own indefatigable industry, the said Fanny has raised money sufficient to procure a transfer of herself and her said infant child Ellen to the said Thomas Chapel, which transfer has been legally effected. This transfer has been made solely for her benefit the said Chapel being desirous to manumit her and also her infant children Ellen and Harriott, the latter born since said transfer was made; and the only obstacle to such manumission being effected is that which the Law interposes.

Your Petitioners do not wish to call in question the expediency of any Law, which derives its sanction from the wisdom of your honorable body. They know that many of the descendants from Africa are far too debased to be fit for freedom, but they see in this case no such obstacle. They see an individual under a solemn contract to liberate a woman, of unexceptionable character and her children, who by Law are liable to be detained in his service, and to "entail" the miserable condition of *Slavery* "on the endless generations proceeding from them." They see this individual willing to fulfull his contract, willing, even now to indulge his Slave with every comfortable privilege that he can, but Alas! they know that *Virtue* cannot be entailed like Slavery. They therefore ask that your honorable body will be pleased to pass an Act authorizing the said Thomas Chapel to manumit the said Fanny and her infant children Ellen and Harriott. They conceive that *Justice* and *Humanity* require this at your hands, and that no Plea of expediency can with propriety be urged against it. They trust it will *never* be said that the Legislature of *Virginia*—of the State which boasts as her Son, the Man who assisted by a band of *Patriots* united with him in the cause of freedom, achieved the *Independence* of our Beloved Country—that the Legislature of this State have suffered a legal obstruction, to be interposed to the performance of an act so obviously required by the best of motives, but that the "wisdom which cometh from *above*" and is profitable to direct in all things will be vouchsafed to guide your deliberations: And that this may be the case your petitioners as in duty bound will ever Pray.

WOMEN'S WORK IN THE MARKET ECONOMY

These excerpts from several issues of the New York Evening Post *of 1824 illustrate the new possibilities and risks for urban women associated with the expanding market economy of the early nineteenth century.*

March 5, 1824

WANTED, a Lady capable of teaching Drawing, Painting, and Embroidery, in an Academy in a healthy part of the state of North Carolina. Terms, &c., will be made known on application to this office.

March 5, 1824

VALUABLE REAL ESTATE FOR SALE. For sale, at auction, on the 30th day of March inst. at 12 o'clock on the premises, a valuable Mill and about 20 acres of first rate upland and salt meadows, situated on New Town Creek, in the Township of Bushwick, King's County, Long Island, two miles from Williamsburgh Ferry—There is now three run of stone in said mill, which, with little expence, may be increased to five, as there is an inexhaustible stream of water. On the premises is a good House, Barn, Hovel and other out-buildings. Also, the privilege of the water right 150 feet below the Williamsburgh Turnpike and where another mill may be erected, if desirable. The situation is pleasant, and the mill pond abounds with shell and scale fish, of all kinds, and from its proximity to the city, is considered as a very desirable residence. Also, the privilege of erecting a stone house at Millers' landing, near Williamsburgh Ferry. The title of the above property is indisputable. For further particulars, apply on the premises, or to

SARAH SCHENCK, 41 Cliff St.

New York

March 10, 1824

WANTED, a woman of good character, to do plain Cooking, and other work connected with a kitchen. Apply at 96 Broadway.

March 11, 1824

A NURSE WANTED—wanted, a middle aged woman, capable of taking care of children. Apply at No. 77 Fulton street.

New York Evening Post, 1824.

March 12, 1824

WANTED, a middle aged woman of respectable connection, to superintend and make herself useful in a small family. She must be a good seamstress and be able to produce unqualified recommendations as to character and abilities. A line addressed to R. L. stating name, references, and residence, will meet with immediate attention, if left at this office.

March 12, 1824

WANTED, a smart active Woman to take charge of a dairy, about 9 miles from the city, and to assist in the work of a small family. Enquire at No. 45 Franklin street.

March 26, 1824

TO THE LADIES. MRS. ALLAIN & CO. 120 Broadway, have the honour to inform the ladies, that on Monday 29th inst. they will open a handsome choice of Spring Fashions. Wanted, 2 or 3 apprentices in the millinary line.

April 14, 1824

Grass Bonnets—A number of females and children are now employed at Baltimore in fabricating grass bonnets and hats, in imitation of the various qualities of Leghorn, and the manufacture appears to have been attended with much success. The introduction last year, into that city, of a grass bonnet manufactured by a lady of Tioga county, in this state, is said to have had the happy effect of directing the attention and ingenuity of the people of Baltimore, to the same branch of domestic industry. Judge Drake, of Tioga, had arrived there a few days ago by way of the Susquehanna bridge, having with him another grass bonnet, made by the same lady that produced the other, and which is described to be greatly superior in colour, texture, and workmanship, and surpassing any Leghorn hat ever seen in this country.

May 6, 1824

REMOVAL—Miss E. Beers, Ladies Dress Maker, has removed to No. 36 Dey street, where she will be pleased to receive and execute the commands of her friends. Wanted, 2 or 3 young Ladies apprentices to the Dress making business.

May 14, 1824

MRS. BARBER, Corset, Dress & Habit Maker, begs leave to inform the Ladies of New York, and those from the Southward, that she has removed from 19 Courtland St. to No. 13 Maiden lane, a few doors from Broadway—where she intends continuing the above business, in all its branches. N.B. A few respectable young persons wanted to learn the above business. None need apply, but those who can produce the most unexceptionable recommendations.

May 19, 1824

WANTED, a young woman capable of taking charge of a store, & a good seamstress, none need apply but such as can give good references as to character & abilities. Apply at the Corset Warehouse 27 Chatham st.

June 9, 1824

WET NURSE. A Healthy young woman, with a good fresh breast of milk, wants a situation in the above capacity, in a respectable family. The most respectable references can be produced, as to character, ability, &c. Apply at No. 1 State street.

June 30, 1824

A SITUATION is wanted by a young woman to wait upon one or more ladies, and to do needlework, she likewise is well acquainted with dress making, and would have no objection to traveling to any part. Good recommendations can be referred to from her last place. Inquire at No. 54 William street.

July 22, 1824

GLOVE SEWERS WANTED

WANTED immediately, 18 or 20 Glove and Mitten Sewers. Also, a Girl to help do house work. Apply at 258 Broadway.

August 5, 1824

NOTICE.—All persons having claims against the estate of Capt. DAVID MANN, deceased, are requested to present the same to George W. Niven, Esq, 281 Greenwich street, or to the subscriber, 54 Elizabeth street, for settlement, and those indebted to said estate are requested to make immediate payment. MARGARET MANN, Administratrix.

August 26, 1824

WANTED, a woman, well acquainted with the millinery business, to superintend a respectable establishment in the city. A liberal salary will be given to one who can produce satisfactory recommendations. Apply at 218 1–2 Bowery.

September 10, 1824

MISS LOCKE, No. 62 Broadway, respectfully informs her friends and the public that she has just received a handsome assortment of MILLINERY from Paris, consisting of Bonnets, Turbans, and Ribbons, which will be opened on Monday, 13th September, at 10 o'clock, and to which she solicits their attention. N.B. Apprentices for the Dress-making business wanted. Apply as above.

October 19, 1824

WANTED, 300 Tailoresses, at No. 6 Wall-street, immediately.

October 28, 1824

WANTED, a respectable woman about 30 years of age, who is able and willing to make herself useful in a small family. She must be a good seamstress, and somewhat acquainted with tailoring. Also, a capable, active white woman, who can cook, wash and iron. Good recommendations will be required. Apply at No. 70 Chatham street.

November 9, 1824

TO JOURNEYMEN TAILORS.—Wanted immediately, 100 first rate Coat makers, also 100 Tailoresses, who are first rate vest and pantaloons makers—to such liberal prices and constant employment will be given. Apply to

J. T. JACOBS & CO.
corner Maiden lane & Nassau st.

November 26, 1824

It is the duty of the Board of Managers on this the 27th anniversary, to present to the Society for the relief of Poor Widows with Small Children, their

REPORT

And at seasons like this, the important question must always recur—what is the best method of assisting the poor? After the experience of many years we can only answer, much must be left to the intelligence and prudence of the managers.—As your Board has generally, if not exclusively, been formed of professing Christians, influenced by the principles of the Bible, we have reason to believe the precept of the Apostle has been adopted by them—"If a man will not work let him not eat." It has been their endeavor to exclude all idle and immoral persons from partaking of the bounty of the Society.

Our resources appear large, but in truth they are so limited as to form the most discouraging trait to those who wish to take an active part in the distribution of your bounty.

This city, extending so rapidly in population and in riches, has its increase also of poor widows with small children; an interesting class of poor certainly, and it has been a question often agitated in the Board of Managers whether it would not be expedient to limit the number assisted, rather than to excite hopes to relief which cannot be realized to any comfortable degree, by reason of the number of those who have a claim to the very small pittance we have to bestow.

There are 230 widows and 568 children now on the books of the managers, and who, last winter were assisted by them. . . .

PART III

WOMAN'S SPHERE
AND WOMEN'S EMPLOYMENTS

MARIA STEWART SEES CHAINS ON THE SOUL

Maria W. Miller Stewart, born in 1803 in Hartford, Connecticut, was one of the first American women to address a public audience of both men and women for a political purpose. Her four speeches, all published in the antislavery Liberator, *combined deep religious conviction with zealous commitment to improving the situation of her fellow free African Americans. Employing biblical images and messages, Stewart exhorted free African Americans to lift themselves from circumstances she viewed as little better than slavery, urged them to prove wrong those whites who claimed that blacks could be neither educated nor respectable, and insisted on reinterpreting biblical injunctions restricting women's right to speak out on behalf of the oppressed.*

LECTURE,
DELIVERED AT THE FRANKLIN HALL,
Boston, Sept. 21, 1832.

Why sit ye here and die? If we say we will go to a foreign land, the famine and the pestilence are there, and there we shall die. If we sit here, we shall die. Come let us plead our cause before the whites: if they save us alive, we shall live—and if they kill us, we shall but die.

Methinks I heard a spiritual interrogation—'Who shall go forward, and take off the reproach that is cast upon the people of color? Shall it be a woman?' And my heart made this reply—'If it is thy will, be it even so, Lord Jesus!'

I have heard much respecting the horrors of slavery; but may Heaven forbid that the generality of my color throughout these United States should experience any more of its horrors than to be a servant of servants, or hewers of wood and drawers of water! Tell us no more of southern slavery; for with few exceptions, although I may be very erroneous in my opinion, yet I consider our condition but little better than that. Yet, after all, methinks there are no chains so galling as the chains of ignorance—no fetters so binding as those that bind the soul, and exclude it from the vast field of useful and scientific knowledge. O, had I received the advantages of early education, my ideas would, ere now, have expanded far and wide; but, alas! I possess nothing but moral capability—no teachings but the teachings of the Holy Spirit.

Productions of Mrs. Maria W. Stewart, Presented to the First African Baptist Church & Society, of the City of Boston (Boston: Friends of Freedom and Virtue, 1835), pp. 51–56.

I have asked several individuals of my sex, who transact business for themselves, if providing our girls were to give them the most satisfactory references, they would not be willing to grant them an equal opportunity with others? Their reply has been—for their own part, they had no objection; but as it was not the custom, were they to take them into their employ, they would be in danger of losing the public patronage.

And such is the powerful force of prejudice. Let our girls possess what amiable qualities of soul they may; let their characters be fair and spotless as innocence itself; let their natural taste and ingenuity be what they may; it is impossible for scarce an individual of them to rise above the condition of servants. Ah! why is this cruel and unfeeling distinction? Is it merely because God has made our complexion to vary? If it be, O shame to soft, relenting humanity! "Tell it not in Gath! publish it not in the streets of Askelon!" Yet, after all, methinks were the American free people of color to turn their attention more assiduously to moral worth and intellectual improvement, this would be the result: prejudice would gradually diminish, and the whites would be compelled to say, unloose those fetters!

> Though black their skins as shades of night,
> Their hearts are pure, their souls are white.

Few white persons of either sex, who are calculated for any thing else, are willing to spend their lives and bury their talents in performing mean, servile labor. And such is the horrible idea that I entertain respecting a life of servitude, that if I conceived of there being no possibility of my rising above the condition of a servant, I would gladly hail death as a welcome messenger. O, horrible idea, indeed! to possess noble souls aspiring after high and honorable acquirements, yet confined by the chains of ignorance and poverty to lives of continual drudgery and toil. Neither do I know of any who have enriched themselves by spending their lives as house-domestics, washing windows, shaking carpets, brushing boots, or tending upon gentlemen's tables. I can but die for expressing my sentiments; and I am as willing to die by the sword as the pestilence; for I am a true born American; your blood flows in my veins, and your spirit fires my breast.

I observed a piece in the Liberator a few months since, stating that the colonizationists had published a work respecting us, asserting that we were lazy and idle. I confute them on that point. Take us generally as a people, we are neither lazy nor idle; and considering how little we have to excite or stimulate us, I am almost astonished that there are so many industrious and ambitious ones to be found; although I acknowledge, with extreme sorrow, that there are some who never were and never will be serviceable to society. And have you not a similar class among yourselves?

Again. It was asserted that we were "a ragged set, crying for liberty." I reply to it, the whites have so long and so loudly proclaimed the theme of equal rights and privileges, that our souls have caught the flame also, ragged as we are. As far as our merit deserves, we feel a common desire to rise above the condition of servants and drudges. I have learnt, by bitter experience, that continual hard labor deadens the energies of the soul, and benumbs the faculties of the mind; the ideas become confined, the mind barren, and, like the scorching sands of Arabia, produces nothing; or, like the uncultivated soil, brings forth thorns and thistles.

Again, continual hard labor irritates our tempers and sours our dispositions; the whole system becomes worn out with toil and fatigue; nature herself becomes almost exhausted, and we care but little whether we live or die. It is true, that the free people of color throughout these United States are neither bought nor sold, nor under the lash of the cruel driver; many obtain a comfortable support; but few, if any, have an opportunity of becoming rich and independent; and the employments we most pursue are as unprofitable to us as the spider's web or the floating bubbles that vanish into air. As servants, we are respected; but let us presume to aspire any higher, our employer regards us no longer. And were it not that the King eternal has declared that Ethiopia shall stretch forth her hands unto God, I should indeed despair.

I do not consider it derogatory, my friends, for persons to live out to service. There are many whose inclination leads them to aspire no higher; and I would highly commend the performance of almost any thing for an honest livelihood; but where constitutional strength is wanting, labor of this kind, in its mildest form, is painful. And doubtless many are the prayers that have ascended to Heaven from Afric's daughters for strength to perform their work. Oh, many are the tears that have been shed for the want of that strength! Most of our color have dragged out a miserable existence of servitude from the cradle to the grave. And what literary acquirements can be made, or useful knowledge derived, from either maps, books or charts, by those who continually drudge from Monday morning until Sunday noon? O, ye fairer sisters, whose hands are never soiled, whose nerves and muscles are never strained, go learn by experience! Had we had the opportunity that you have had, to improve our moral and mental faculties, what would have hindered our intellects from being as bright, and our manners from being as dignified as yours? Had it been our lot to have been nursed in the lap of affluence and ease, and to have basked beneath the smiles and sunshine of fortune, should we not have naturally supposed that we were never made to toil? And why are not our forms as delicate, and our constitutions as slender, as yours? Is not the workmanship as curious and complete? Have pity upon us, have pity upon us, O ye who have hearts to feel for other's woes; for the hand of God has touched us. Owing to the disadvantages under which we labor, there are many flowers among us that are

> "————born to bloom unseen,
> And waste their fragrance on the desert air."

My beloved brethren, as Christ has died in vain for those who will not accept of offered mercy, so will it be vain for the advocates of freedom to spend their breath in our behalf, unless with united hearts and souls you make some mighty efforts to raise your sons and daughters from the horrible state of servitude and degradation in which they are placed. It is upon you that woman depends; she can do but little besides using her influence; and it is for her sake and yours that I have come forward and made myself a hissing and a reproach among the people; for I am also one of the wretched and miserable daughters of the descendants of fallen Africa. Do you ask, why are you wretched and miserable? I reply, look at many of the most worthy and interesting of us doomed to spend our lives in gentlemen's kitchens. Look at our young men, smart, active and energetic, with souls filled with ambitious fire; if they look forward, alas! what are their prospects? They can be nothing but the humblest laborers, on account of their dark complexions; hence many of them lose their ambition, and become worthless. Look at our middle-aged men, clad in their rusty plaids and coats; in winter, every cent they earn goes to buy their wood and pay their rents; their poor wives also toil beyond their strength, to help support their families. Look at our aged sires, whose heads are whitened with the frosts of seventy winters, with their old wood-saws on their backs. Alas, what keeps us so? Prejudice, ignorance and poverty. But ah! methinks our oppression is soon to come to an end; yea, before the Majesty of heaven, our groans and cries have reached the ears of the Lord of Sabaoth. As the prayers and tears of Christians will avail the finally impenitent nothing; neither will the prayers and tears of the friends of humanity avail us any thing, unless we possess a spirit of virtuous emulation within our breasts. Did the pilgrims, when they first landed on these shores, quietly compose themselves, and say, "the Britons have all the money and all the power, and we must continue their servants forever?" Did they sluggishly sigh and say, "our lot is hard, the Indians own the soil, and we cannot cultivate it?" No; they first made powerful efforts to raise themselves, and then God raised up those illustrious patriots, WASHINGTON and LAFAYETTE, to assist and defend them. And, my brethren, have you made a powerful effort? Have you prayed the Legislature for mercy's sake to grant you all the rights and privileges of free citizens, that your daughters may rise to that degree of respectability which true merit deserves, and your sons above the servile situations which most of them fill?

STRIKING TAILORESSES SPEAK

Aside from domestic service, needlework was the most common form of urban women's employment both before and during industrialization. Sewingwomen and tailoresses (those who specialized in pantaloons and men's vests) were chronically oppressed by low wages, debilitating competition, and periodic unemployment. New York City tailoresses, joining a wave of female labor activism on the east coast, cooperated with one another in a "turn-out" (strike) in the spring of 1831 to try to establish a standard list of prices for their work. The following speeches by strike leaders were printed in a newspaper sympathetic to the Workingmen's Party in New York.

ADDRESS OF SARAH MONROE

[delivered at the Friends' Academy]

We have been told, my friends, that it is impossible for us to do any thing at present to improve our miserable condition. That it will be impracticable without a union—without a cooperation, I am well aware. But if we fail, my friends, it will not be without a good cause, but because its advocates are poor and inexperienced. That we are oppressed, and *very much* oppressed, *all*, who have eyes and ears, will acknowledge. That our burthens are becoming heavier and heavier every succeeding year, is a truth that cannot be denied—That we are not used to asking charity, is well known—and that we are not in the practice of pleading our own cause, our employers are well aware.

But, my friends, let us not be discouraged. Our cause is one that the tailors themselves dare not openly slander; and I think they would be ashamed openly to oppose.

We shall have all the honest and humane part of the community in our favor. The voice of the righteous will be heard in our defence, not in this city only, but throughout the United States. Let us turn a deaf ear to the slander of our enemies; for enemies we have, no doubt: but if we are true to ourselves and each other, they cannot harm us. After all, my friends, who is to stand between us and oppression? If we do not come forth in our own defence, what will become of us? Need I ask what is to become of us—let us bring back to our recollection the scenes of distress that have been exhibited in this city during the past winter—let us remember the widow that is making round jackets for one shilling and sixpence

New York Daily Sentinel, March 3 and June 25, 1831.

each. What is to find *her* food and clothing, to say nothing of *her children?* Long have the poor tailoresses of this city borne this oppression in silence; until *patience* is no longer a virtue—and in *my* opinion to be longer silent would be a *crime.* High time is it, my friends, that we awake—high time is it that we were up and doing; and that we take our cause into consideration. Let us trust no longer to the generosity of our employers; seeing that they are men in whose heads or hearts the thought of doing justice to a fellow being never seems to enter. Yes, my fellow sufferers, let us unite—let us organize ourselves—let us do all in our power to increase our members; for on that the success of our cause depends. Are there any here who think us presumptuous in coming forward in our own defence,—let them place themselves in our situation—let them be obliged to endure all the confinement, fatigue, privations and sufferings that we must necessarily endure in consequence of our getting only partly paid for our labor, and I think they will be disposed to applaud rather than censure us.

We have been told, my friends, that we should coolly and calmly consider our present undertaking. Some of us have done so: and though our minds are awakened, and our bodily strength demolished with incessant toil, we have come to the determination to leave no fair, honest and honorable means untried to secure to ourselves an adequate and permanent reward for our labors. It needs no small share of courage for us, who have been used to impositions and oppression from our youth up to the present day, to come before the public in the defence of our own rights: but, my friends, if it is unfashionable for the men to bear oppression in silence, why should it not also become unfashionable with the women? or do they deem us more able to endure hardships than they themselves?

My friends, I am under the necessity of informing you that we have unfortunately, though innocently, incurred the displeasure of the Friends, who have been so kind as to let us have this house to meet in. I said we had incurred their displeasure, or disapprobation; and I appeal to all who were present at our last meeting, how innocently it was done! Perhaps you will be surprised, when I tell you, that the resolutions, handed by some stranger to our Chairman, which were read and laid on the table at the close of our last meeting, are, or will be the cause of our having to seek another place to meet in. The friends say that the resolutions read from that paper were agrarian! I now assert, and without the fear of contradiction, there were not ten women in the room who so much as understood the meaning of the word *agrarianism!* But, my friends, if we had been aware of all the wiles and snares set for the unwary and inexperienced, we should have read those articles by a committee, previous to their coming before the public. Had the Friends been as much interested as I think we had reason to believe and hope they were, they would have first known whether we were traduced or not. That they have always been the friends of the poor and the oppressed, even of the poor African, we know. I say, had they been as interested as we had reason to believe, they would have given us a hearing before they condemned us— they would have shown us more brotherly love, kindness and charity, than by dismissing us in this way. This is not all. For if we cannot look up to the Friends, or such men as these, to countenance and uphold us, to whom, I ask, shall we look? to whom shall we go? What does reason, religion and virtue require, but *to unloose heavy burdens—to break every yoke of bondage—to let the oppressed go free—to do justice to the poor, the widow and the afflicted?* This, my friends, is all we ask; and shall we ask it in vain?

AN ADDRESS

Delivered before the United Tailoresses Society,
by the Secretary [Louise Mitchell]

I consider it a duty encumbent on all who feel an interest in this our infant society, to promote as far as possible its rise and progress; for this purpose we are here assembled, and for this purpose I now attempt a few remarks, which I hope will meet the approbation of those in whose service I am for a term engaged, and whose approval with regard to my official duties, I am proud to merit. But to the purpose. In the first place, I would recommend (as the only firm basis on which we can establish ourselves) patience and perseverance, with a determination to be united, not only as a society, but in the interest of every circumstance connected with our present important undertaking. If union is strength, why should we be weak? let this be our motto, "United we stand divided we fall." Secondly, suffer me to urge the necessity of a free and candid avowal of opinion on the part of the members, respecting every subject in discussion; let each individual consider this her duty, as well as her right. I am aware that many are averse to this measure, feeling themselves incapacitated for public business, and acknowledge their inability to act without the aid of man—but they will do well to remember who are our oppressors;—that it would be worse than useless to seek redress through their instrumentality. Let us, then, have more confidence in our own abilities, and less in the sincerity of man. 'Tis true, custom and education have assisted to intimidate us, but our energies once roused, we shall find ourselves less deficient than we were wont to believe, and have we not

sufficient excitement to arouse those energies? Oppression! and its consequent attendant, misery, call loud for our utmost exertions. Can we
resist so urgent an appeal to our feelings? no—if we have one solitary
spark of female spirit in our composition, now is the time to exert it.
Suffer it to emerge from obscurity and unite our unwearied efforts to
accomplish our purpose. Undoubtedly a great number (from their hitherto secluded lives) feel a reluctance to come forward, fearful of having
their names made public. Excuse me, if I say I consider this a timidity
unworthy of us; for in my estimation, the publicity of a respectable name
can be no injury to the lady, or the cause she advocates; and is not this a
cause worthy to be advocated by all who bear the name of woman? Are
we not a species of the human race, and is not this a free country? Then
why may not we enjoy that freedom? Because we have been taught to
believe ourselves far less noble and far less wise than the other sex. They
have taken advantage of this weakness, and, tyrant like, have stept from
one ascendancy to another, till finally, and without resistance, they have
us in their power; and severely have they abused that power; nay, they
have even trampled us under their feet, (comparatively speaking,) and we
have made no resistance; our supposed helplessness has heretofore
caused us to remain silent and submissive, but I hope and believe our
eyes are now open to a scene of injury too glaring to be overlooked, and
too painful to be submitted to. When we complain to our employers and
others, of the inequality of our wages with that of the men's, the excuse
is, they have families to support, from which females are exempt. Now
this is either a sad mistake, or a wilful oversight; for how many females
are there who have families to support, and how many single men who
have none, and who, having no other use for the fruits of their employers'
generosity, they child like, waste it; while the industrious mother, having
the care of a helpless offspring, finds (with all the economy she is necessi-
tated to practice) the scanty reward of her labors scarcely sufficient to
support nature! To this argument, when forced to acknowledge its truth,
the reply is, the fault is our own; we will admit it, inasmuch as we have
suffered their imposition. This, then, ought to stimulate us to unheard of
exertions.—Then again let me urge the necessity of a joint interest in this
our common cause, to enable us to go through with a mighty work began,
namely, that of gaining our liberty; for we are, literally, *slaves,* and I know
of nothing at present so essential as punctual attendance to our meetings;
each night of appointment let not one be missing. In this way we will
express the interest we feel, and thereby encourage others to join so
prosperous a cause—for prosperous it will be, if we persevere. Fear not
public opinion; trust me, it will be in our favor; our proceedings will be

garnished with a title no less formidable than that of female heroism—
excited by oppression, and exerted in behalf of their just claim to a share
of the boasted Independence.

SARAH GRIMKÉ ON THE CONDITION OF WOMEN IN THE UNITED STATES

Sarah Moore Grimké (1792–1873) was born into a wealthy slaveholding family in South Carolina. In revulsion against slavery she left the South, adopted the Quaker faith, and found friends among Quaker antislavery sympathizers in Philadelphia. She was, with her younger sister Angelina, deeply involved in the antislavery movement when she wrote Letters on the Equality of the Sexes and the Condition of Women *(1838). Her book was the first by an American woman to examine women's status and circumstances around the globe. Written in the form of letters to a close friend, Grimké's book anticipated many of the arguments for women's equality that would be taken up by woman's rights proponents during the next several decades.*

Brookline, 1837

My Dear Sister,—I have now taken a brief survey of the condition of woman in various parts of the world. I regret that my time has been so much occupied by other things, that I have been unable to bestow that attention upon the subject which it merits, and that my constant change of place has prevented me from having access to books, which might probably have assisted me in this part of my work. I hope that the principles I have asserted will claim the attention of some of my sex, who may be able to bring into view, more thoroughly than I have done, the situation and degradation of woman. I shall now proceed to make a few remarks on the condition of women in my own country.

During the early part of my life, my lot was cast among the butterflies of the *fashionable* world; and of this class of women, I am constrained to say, both from experience and observation, that their education is miserably deficient; that they are taught to regard marriage as the one thing needful, the only avenue to distinction; hence to attract the notice and win the attentions of men, by their external charms, is the chief business of fashionable girls. They seldom think that men will be allured by intellectual acquirements, because they find, that where any mental superiority exists, a woman is generally shunned and regarded as stepping out of her "appropriate sphere," which, in their view, is to dress, to dance, and to set out to the best possible advantage her person, to read the novels which inundate the press, and which do more to destroy her character

Sarah M. Grimké, *Letters on the Equality of the Sexes and the Condition of Women* (Boston: Isaac Knapp, 1838), pp. 46–55.

as a rational creature, than any thing else. Fashionable women regard themselves, and are regarded by men, as pretty toys or as mere instruments of pleasure; and the vacuity of mind, the heartlessness, the frivolity which is the necessary result of this false and debasing estimate of women, can only be fully understood by those who have mingled in the folly and wickedness of fashionable life; and who have been called from such pursuits by the voice of the Lord Jesus, inviting their weary and heavy laden souls to come unto Him and learn of Him, that they may find something worthy of their immortal spirit, and their intellectual powers; that they may learn the high and holy purposes of their creation, and consecrate themselves unto the service of God; and not, as is now the case, to the pleasure of man.

There is another and much more numerous class in this country, who are withdrawn by education or circumstances from the circle of fashionable amusements, but who are brought up with the dangerous and absurd idea, that *marriage* is a kind of preferment; and that to be able to keep their husband's house, and render his situation comfortable, is the end of her being. Much that she does and says and thinks is done in reference to this situation; and to be married is too often held up to the view of girls as the sine qua non of human happiness and human existence. For this purpose more than for any other, I verily believe the majority of girls are trained. This is demonstrated by the imperfect education which is bestowed upon them, and the little time allowed them for reading, and by the idea being constantly inculcated, that although all household concerns should be attended to with scrupulous punctuality at particular seasons, the improvement of their intellectual capacities is only a secondary consideration, and may serve as an occupation to fill up the odds and ends of time. In most families, it is considered a matter of far more consequence to call a girl off from making a pie, or a pudding, than to interrupt her whilst engaged in her studies. This mode of training necessarily exalts, in their view, the animal above the intellectual and spiritual nature, and teaches women to regard themselves as a kind of machinery, necessary to keep the domestic engine in order, but of little value as the *intelligent* companions of men.

Let no one think, from these remarks, that I regard a knowledge of housewifery as beneath the acquisition of women. Far from it: I believe that a complete knowledge of household affairs is an indispensable requisite in a woman's education—that by the mistress of a family, whether married or single, doing her duty thoroughly and *understandingly*, the happiness of the family is increased to an incalculable degree, as well as a vast amount of time and money saved. All I complain of is, that our education consists so almost exclusively in culinary and other manual operations. I do long to see the time, when it will no longer be necessary for women to expend so many precious hours in furnishing "a well spread table," but that their husbands will forgo some of their accustomed indulgences in this way, and encourage their wives to devote some portion of their time to mental cultivation, even at the expense of having to dine sometimes on baked potatoes, or bread and butter. . . .

There is another way in which the general opinion, that women are inferior to men, is manifested, that bears with tremendous effect on the laboring class, and indeed on almost all who are obliged to earn a subsistence, whether it be by mental or physical exertion—I allude to the disproportionate value set on the time and labor of men and of women. A man who is engaged in teaching, can always, I believe, command a higher price for tuition than a woman—even when he teaches the same branches, and is not in any respect superior to the woman. This I know is the case in boarding and other schools with which I have been acquainted, and it is so in every occupation in which the sexes engage indiscriminately. As for example, in tailoring, a man has twice, or three times as much for making a waistcoat or pantaloons as a woman, although the work done by each may be equally good. In those employments which are peculiar to women, their time is estimated at only half the value of that of men. A woman who goes out to wash, works as hard in proportion as a wood sawyer, or a coal heaver, but she is not generally able to make more than half as much by a day's work. The low remuneration which women receive for their work, has claimed the attention of a few philanthropists, and I hope it will continue to do so until some remedy is applied for this enormous evil. I have known a widow, left with four or five children, to provide for, unable to leave home because her helpless babes demand her attention, compelled to earn a scanty subsistence, by making coarse shirts at 12½ cents a piece, or by taking in washing, for which she was paid by some wealthy persons 12½ cents per dozen. All these things evince the low estimation in which woman is held. There is yet another and more disastrous consequence arising from this unscriptural notion—women being educated, from earliest childhood, to regard themselves as inferior creatures, have not that self-respect which conscious equality would engender, and hence when their virtue is assailed, they yield to temptation with facility, under the idea that it rather exalts than debases them, to be connected with a superior being.

There is another class of women in this country, to whom I cannot refer, without feelings of the deepest shame and sorrow. I allude to our female slaves. Our southern cities are whelmed beneath a tide of pollution; the virtue of female slaves is wholly at the mercy of irresponsible tyrants, and women are bought and sold in our slave markets, to gratify the brutal lust of those who bear the name of Christians. In our slave States, if amid all her degradation, and ignorance, a woman desires to preserve her virtue unsullied, she is either bribed or whipped into compliance, or if she dares resist her seducer, her life by the laws of some of the slave States may be, and has actually been sacrificed to the fury of disappointed passion. Where such laws do not exist, the power which is necessarily vested in the master over his property, leaves the defenceless slave entirely at his mercy, and the sufferings of some females on this account, both physical and mental, are intense. Mr. Gholson, in the House of Delegates of Virginia, in 1832, said, "He really had been under the impression that he owned his slaves. He had lately purchased four women and ten children, in whom he thought he had obtained a great bargain; for he supposed they were his own property, *as were his brood mares.*" But even if any laws existed in the United States, as in Athens formerly, for the protection of female slaves, they would be null and void, because the evidence of a colored person is not admitted against a white, in any of our Courts of Justice in the slave States. . . . In Christian America, the slave has no refuge from unbridled cruelty and lust. . . .

Nor does the colored woman suffer alone: the moral purity of the white woman is deeply contaminated. In the daily habit of seeing the virtue of her enslaved sister sacrificed without hesitancy or remorse, she looks upon the crimes of seduction and illicit intercourse without horror, and although not personally involved in the guilt, she loses that value for innocence in her own, as well as the other sex, which is one of the strongest safeguards to virtue. She lives in habitual intercourse with men, whom she knows to be polluted by licentiousness, and often is she compelled to witness in her own domestic circle, those disgusting and heart-sickening jealousies and strifes which disgraced and distracted the family of Abraham. In addition to all this, the female slaves suffer every species of degradation and cruelty, which the most wanton barbarity can inflict; they are indecently divested of their clothing, sometimes tied up and severely whipped, sometimes prostrated on the earth, while their naked bodies are torn by the scorpion lash. . . . Can any American woman look at these scenes of shocking licentiousness and cruelty, and fold her hands in apathy, and say, "I have nothing to do with slavery"? *She cannot and be guiltless.*

I cannot close this letter, without saying a few words on the benefits to be derived by men, as well as women, from the opinions I advocate relative to the equality of the sexes. Many women are now supported, in idleness and extravagance, by the industry of their husbands, fathers, or brothers, who are compelled to toil out their existence, at the counting house, or in the printing office, or some other laborious occupation, while the wife and daughters and sisters take no part in the support of the family, and appear to think that their sole business is to spend the hard bought earnings of their male friends. I deeply regret such a state of things, because I believe that if women felt their responsibilty, for the support of themselves, or their families, it would add strength and dignity to their characters, and teach them more true sympathy for their husbands, than is now generally manifested—a sympathy which would be exhibited by actions as well as words. Our brethren may reject my doctrine, because it runs counter to some common opinions, and because it wounds their pride; but I believe they would be 'partakers of the benefit' resulting from the Equality of the Sexes, and would find that woman, as their equal, was unspeakably more valuable than woman as their inferior, both as a moral and an intellectual being.

Thine in the bonds of womanhood,   Sarah M. Grimké

THE LEGAL RIGHTS AND WRONGS OF WOMEN

Simon Greenleaf became the Royall Professor of Law at Harvard Law School in 1833, after many years as a lawyer in Maine. In 1839, apparently in response to Sarah and Angelina Grimké's Massachusetts lectures, which had linked the legal status of women to that of slaves, he gave a lyceum lecture on the legal rights of women. His justification of existing common-law provisions for women irked the writer of the following letter, who probably was not named Keziah Kendall although she signed that way (spelling her first name differently at the beginning and end of the letter). That Keziah and her sisters bear the names of the three daughters of Job in the Old Testament raises some suspicion; and scholars have not been able to find records of the Kendall family or their property holdings in the Cambridge area. Nonetheless, someone who believed Greenleaf's attitude needed changing wrote him a four-page letter in a neat feminine hand.

I take the liberty to write to you on the subject of the Lyceum lecture you delivered last Feb. but as you are not acquainted with me I think I will introduce myself. My name is Kezia Kendall. I live not many miles from Cambridge, on a farm with two sisters, one older, one younger than myself. I am thirty two. Our parents and only brother are dead—we have a good estate—comfortable house—nice barn, garden, orchard &c and money in the bank besides. Jemima is a very good manager in the house, keeps everything comfortable—sees that the milk is nicely prepared for market—looks after everything herself, and rises before day, winter and summer—but she never had any head for figures, and always expects me to keep all accounts, and attend to all business concerns. Keranhappuck, (who is called Kerry) is quite young, only nineteen, and as she was a little girl when mother died, we've always petted her, and let her do as she pleased, and now she's courted. Under these circumstances the whole responsibility of our property, not less than twenty five thousand dollars rests upon me. I am not over fond of money, but I have worked hard ever since I was a little girl, and tried to do all in my power to help earn, and help save, and it would be strange if I did not think more of it than those who never earned anything, and never saved anything they could get to

Keziah Kendall to Simon Greenleaf, Greenleaf Papers, box 3, folder 10, Harvard Law School Library; reprinted with permission of the library. See also Dianne Avery and Alfred S. Konefsky, "The Daughters of Job: Property Rights and Women's Lives in Mid-Nineteenth-Century Massachusetts," *Law and History Review* 10, no. 2 (Fall 1992), pp. 350–56.

spend, and you know Sir, there are many such girls nowadays. Well—our milkman brought word when he came from market that you were a going to lecture on the legal rights of women, and so I thought I would go and learn. Now I hope you wont think me bold when I say, I did not like that lecture much. I dont speak of the manner, it was pretty spoken enough, but there was nothing in it but what every body knows. We all know about a widow's thirds, and we all know that a man must maintain his wife, and we all know that he must pay her debts, if she has any—but I never heard of a yankee woman marrying in debt. What I wanted to know, was good reasons for some of those laws that I cant account for. I do hope if you are ever to lecture at the Lyceum again, that you will give us some. I must tell my story to make you understand what I mean. One Lyceum lecture that I heard in C. stated that the Americans went to war with the British, because they were taxed without being represented in Parliament. Now we are taxed every year to the full amount of every dollar we possess—town, county, state taxes—taxes for land, for movables, for money and all. Now I dont want to go representative or any thing else, any more than I do to be a "constable or a sheriff," but I have no voice about public improvements, and I dont see the justice of being taxed any more than the "revolutionary heroes" did. You mention that women here, are not treated like heathen and Indian women—we know that—nor do I think we are treated as Christian women ought to be, according to the Bible rule of doing to others as you would others should do unto you. I am told (not by you) that if a woman dies a week after she's married that her husband takes all her personal property and the use of the real estate as long as he lives—if a man dies his wife can have her thirds—*this* does not come up to the Gospel rule. Now the young fellow that is engaged to our Kerry, is a pleasant clever fellow, but he is not quite one and twenty, and I dont s'pose he ever earned a coat in his life. Uncle told me there was a way for a woman to have her property trustee'd, and I told it to Kerry—but she, poor girl has romantic notions owing to reading too many novels, and when I told her of it, she would not hear of such a thing—"What take the law to keep my property away from James before I marry him—if it was a million of dollars he should have it all." So you see I think the law is in fault here—to tell you the truth I do not think young men are near so careful about getting in debt as girls, and I have known more than one that used their wife's money to pay off old scores. I had a young friend who was without parents, married when she was twenty years old. She had sixteen thousand dollars all in Bank stock. She has lived in a good house, and dressed well since, but I have never known her to have a five dollar bill to give away, and I know she had an own Aunt sent to the poor-house last year. She is a generous woman and this would not have been if she had her own money. I had rather go to my mantua maker to borrow twenty dollars if I needed it, than to the richest married woman I know. Another thing I have to tell you—when I was young I had a lover, Jos. Thompson, he went into business in a neighboring town, and after a year or two while I was getting the wedding things—Joe failed, he met with misfortunes that he did not expect,—he could have concealed it from me and married, but he did not—he was honorable, and so we delayed. He lived along here two or three years, and tried all he could to settle with his creditors, but some were stiff and held out, and thought by the by we would marry, and they should get my property. Uncle said he knew if we were married, there were those who would take my cattle and the improvement of my land. Joseph used to visit me often those years, but he lost his spirits and he could not get into business again, and he thought he must go to sea. I begged him not to, and told him we should be able to manage things in time, but he said no—he must try his luck, and at least get enough to settle off old scores, and then he would come here and live and we would make the best of what I had. We parted—but it pleased God he should be lost at sea. What I have suffered, I cannot tell you. Now Joe was no sailor when I engaged with him, and if it had been a thing known that I should always have a right to keep possession of my own, he need never have gone to sea, and we might have lived happily together, and in time with industry and economy, he might have paid off all. I am one that cant be convinced without better reasons that I have heard of, that women are dealt with by the "gospel rule." There is more might than right in such laws as far as I can see—if you see differently, do tell us next time you lecture. Another thing—you made some reflections upon women following the Anti's. When the fuss was about Antimasonry, the women did nothing about it, because there were no female masons, and it was none of their business. Women have joined the Antislavery societies, and why? women are kept for slaves as well as men—it is a common cause, deny the justice of it, who can! To be sure I do not wish to go about lecturing like the Misses Grimkie, but I have not the knowledge they have, and I verily believe that if I had been brought up among slaves as they were, and knew all that they know, and felt a call from humanity to speak, I should run the venture of your displeasure, and that of a good many others like you. I told Uncle that I thought your lecture was a onesided thing—and he said, "why Keziah, Squire Greenleaf is an advocate, not a judge, you must get him to take t'other side next time." Now I have taken this opportunity to ask you to give us a remedy for the "legal wrongs" of women, whenever you have a chance. The fathers of the land should look to these things—who knows but your daughter may be placed in the sad situation I am in, or the dangerous one Kerry is in. I hear you are a good man, to make it certain—do all the good you can, and justify no wrong thing.

Yours with regard
Keziah Kendall.

THE PECULIAR RESPONSIBILITIES, AND DIFFICULTIES, OF AMERICAN WOMEN

Daughter of preacher Lyman Beecher and sister of Harriet Beecher Stowe, Catharine Beecher (1800–1878) made a name for herself by advancing both women's education and the vocation of domesticity. Her Treatise on Domestic Economy, *from which this selection is taken, discussed every conceivable aspect of domestic responsibilities and arts. Reprinted almost every year between 1841 and 1856, the book sold so well that it brought Beecher (who never married) financial independence.*

THE PECULIAR RESPONSIBILITIES OF AMERICAN WOMEN

There are some reasons, why American women should feel an interest in the support of the democratic institutions of their Country, which it is important that they should consider. The great maxim, which is the basis of all our civil and political institutions, is, that "all men are created equal," and that they are equally entitled to "life, liberty, and the pursuit of happiness."

But it can readily be seen, that this is only another mode of expressing the fundamental principle which the Great Ruler of the Universe has established, as the laws of His eternal government. "Thou shalt love thy neighbor as thyself"; and "Whatsoever ye would that men should do to you, do ye even so to them," are the Scripture forms, by which the Supreme Lawgiver requires that each individual of our race shall regard the happiness of others, as of the same value as his own; and which forbid any institution, in private or civil life, which secures advantages to one class, by sacrificing the interests of another.

The principles of democracy, then, are identical with the principles of Christianity.

But, in order that each individual may pursue and secure the highest degree of happiness within his reach, unimpeded by the selfish interests of others, a system of laws must be established, which sustain certain relations and dependencies in social and civil life. What these relations and their attending obligations shall be, are to be determined, not with reference to the wishes and interests of a few, but solely with reference to the general good of all; so that each individual shall have his own interest, as well as the public benefit, secured by them.

Catharine E. Beecher, *Treatise on Domestic Economy*, rev. 3d ed. (New York: Harper & Brothers, 1847), pp. 25–27, 33–34, 36–43.

For this purpose, it is needful that certain relations be sustained, which involve the duties of subordination. There must be the magistrate and the subject, one of whom is the superior, and the other the inferior. There must be the relations of husband and wife, parent and child, teacher and pupil, employer and employed, each involving the relative duties of subordination. The superior, in certain particulars, is to direct, and the inferior is to yield obedience. Society could never go forward, harmoniously, nor could any craft or profession be successfully pursued, unless these superior and subordinate relations be instituted and sustained.

But who shall take the higher, and who the subordinate, stations in social and civil life? This matter, in the case of parents and children, is decided by the Creator. He has given children to the control of parents, as their superiors, and to them they remain subordinate, to a certain age, or so long as they are members of their household. And parents can delegate such a portion of their authority to teachers and employers, as the interests of their children require.

In most other cases, in a truly democratic state, each individual is allowed to choose for himself, who shall take the position of his superior. No woman is forced to obey any husband but the one she chooses for herself; nor is she obliged to take a husband, if she prefers to remain single. So every domestic, and every artisan or laborer, after passing from parental control, can choose the employer to whom he is to accord obedience, or, if he prefers to relinquish certain advantages, he can remain without taking a subordinate place to any employer.

Each subject, also, has equal power with every other, to decide who shall be his superior as a ruler. The weakest, the poorest, the most illiterate, has the same opportunity to determine this question, as the richest, the most learned, and the most exalted.

And the various privileges that wealth secures, are equally open to all classes. Every man may aim at riches, unimpeded by any law or institution which secures peculiar privileges to a favored class, at the expense of another. Every law, and every institution, is tested by examining whether it secures equal advantages to all; and, if the people become convinced that any regulation sacrifices the good of the majority to the interests of the smaller number, they have power to abolish it. . . .

The tendencies of democratic institutions, in reference to the rights and interests of the female sex, have been fully developed in the United States; and it is in this aspect, that the subject is one of peculiar interest to American women. In this Country, it is established, both by opinion and by practice, that woman has an equal interest in all social and civil concerns; and that no domestic, civil, or political, institution, is right, which sacrifices her interest to promote that of the other sex. But in order to secure her the more firmly in all these privileges, it is decided, that, in the domestic relation, she take a subordinate station, and that, in civil and political concerns, her interests be intrusted to the other sex, without her taking any part in voting, or in making and administering laws. . . .

It appears, then, that it is in America, alone, that women are raised to an equality with the other sex; and that, both in theory and practice, their interests are regarded as of equal value. They are made subordinate in station, only where a regard to their best interest demands it, while, as if in compensatiion for this, by custom and courtesy, they are always treated as superiors. Universally, in this Country, through every class of society, precedence is given to woman, in all the comforts, conveniences, and courtesies, of life.

In civil and political affairs, American women take no interest or concern, except so far as they sympathize with their family and personal friends; but in all cases, in which they do feel a concern, their opinions and feelings have a consideration, equal, or even superior, to that of the other sex.

In matters pertaining to the education of their children, in the selection and support of a clergyman, in all benevolent enterprises, and in all questions relating to morals or manners, they have a superior influence. In such concerns, it would be impossible to carry a point, contrary to their judgement and feelings; while an enterprise, sustained by them, will seldom fail of success.

If those who are bewailing themselves over the fancied wrongs and injuries of women in this Nation, could only see things as they are, they would know, that, whatever remnants of a barbarous or aristocratic age may remain in our civil institutions, in reference to the interests of women, it is only because they are ignorant of them, or do not use their influence to have them rectified; for it is very certain that there is nothing reasonable, which American women would unite in asking, that would not readily be bestowed.

The preceding remarks, then, illustrate the position, that the democratic institutions of this Country are in reality no other than the principles of Christianity carried into operation, and that they tend to place woman in her true position in society, as having equal rights with the other sex; and that, in fact, they have secured to American women a lofty and fortunate position, which, as yet, has been attained by the women of no other nation. . . .

The success of democratic institutions, as is conceded by all, depends upon the intellectual and moral character of the mass of the people. If they are intelligent and virtuous, democracy is a blessing; but if they are ignorant and wicked, it is only a curse, and as much more dreadful than any other form of civil government, as a thousand tyrants are more to be dreaded than one. It is equally conceded, that the formation of the moral and intellectual character of the young is committed mainly to the female hand. The mother forms the character of the future man; the sister bends the fibres that are hereafter to be the forest tree; the wife sways the heart, whose energies may turn for good or for evil the destinies of a nation. Let the women of a country be made virtuous and intelligent, and the men will certainly be the same. The proper education of a man decides the welfare of an individual; but educate a woman, and the interests of a whole family are secured.

If this be so, as none will deny, then to American women, more than to any others on earth, is committed the exalted privilege of extending over the world those blessed influences, which are to renovate degraded man, and "clothe all climes with beauty."

No American woman, then, has any occasion for feeling that hers is an humble or insignificant lot. The value of what an individual accomplishes, is to be estimated by the importance of the enterprise achieved, and not by the particular position of the laborer. The drops of heaven which freshen the earth, are each of equal value, whether they fall in the lowland meadow, or the princely parterre. The builders of a temple are of equal importance, whether they labor on the foundations, or toil upon the dome.

Thus, also, with those labors which are to be made effectual in the regeneration of the Earth. And it is by forming a habit of regarding the apparently insignificant efforts of each isolated laborer, in a comprehensive manner, as indispensable portions of a grand result, that the minds of all, however humble their sphere of service, can be invigorated and cheered. The woman, who is rearing a family of children; the woman, who labors in the schoolroom; the woman, who, in her retired chamber, earns, with her needle, the mite, which contributes to the intellectual and moral elevation of her Country; even the humble domestic, whose example and influence may be moulding and forming young minds, while her faithful services sustain a prosperous domestic state;—each and all may be animated by the consciousness, that they are agents in accomplishing the greatest work that ever was committed to human responsibility. It is the building of a glorious temple, whose base shall be coextensive with the bounds of the earth, whose summit shall pierce the skies, whose splendor shall beam on all lands; and those who hew the lowliest stone, as much as those who carve the highest capital, will be equally honored, when its top-stone shall be laid, with new rejoicings of the morning stars, and shouting of the sons of God.

DIFFICULTIES PECULIAR TO AMERICAN WOMEN

And as it has been shown, that American women have a loftier position, and a more elevated object of enterprise, than the females of any other nation, so it will appear, that they have greater trials and difficulties to overcome, than any other women are called to encounter. . . .

Now, the larger portion of American women are the descendants of English progenitors, who, as a nation, are distinguished by systematic housekeeping, and for a great love of order, cleanliness, and comfort. And American women, to a greater or less extent, have inherited similar tastes and habits. But the prosperity and democratic tendencies of this Country produce results, materially affecting the comfort of housekeepers, which the females of monarchical and aristocratic lands are not called to meet. In such countries, all ranks and classes are fixed in a given position, and each person is educated for a particular sphere and style of living. And the dwellings, conveniences, and customs of life, remain very nearly the same, from generation to generation. This secures the preparation of all classes for their particular station, and makes the lower orders more dependent, and more subservient to employers.

But how different is the state of things in this Country. Every thing is moving and changing. Persons in poverty, are rising to opulence, and persons of wealth, are sinking to poverty. The children of common laborers, by their talents and enterprise, are becoming nobles in intellect, or wealth, or office, while the children of the wealthy, enervated by indulgence, are sinking to humbler stations. The sons of the wealthy are leaving the rich mansions of their fathers, to dwell in the log cabins of the forest, where very soon they bear away the daughters of ease and refinement, to share the privations of a new settlement. Meantime, even in the more stationary portions of the community, there is a mingling of all grades of wealth, intellect, and education. There are no distinct classes, as in aristocratic lands, whose bounds are protected by distinct and impassable lines, but all are thrown into promiscuous masses. Thus, persons of humble means are brought into contact with those of vast wealth, while all intervening grades are placed side by side. Thus, too, there is a constant comparison of conditions, among equals, and a constant temptation presented to imitate the customs, and to strive for the enjoyments, of those who possess larger means.

In addition to this, the flow of wealth, among all classes, is constantly increasing the number of those who live in a style demanding much hired service, while the number of those, who are compelled to go to service, is constantly diminishing. Our manufactories, also, are making increased demands for female labor, and offering larger compensation. In consequence of these things, there is such a disproportion between those who wish to hire, and those who are willing to go to domestic service, that, in the non-slaveholding States were it not for the supply of poverty-stricken foreigners, there would not be a domestic for each family who demands one. And this resort to foreigners, poor as it is, scarcely meets the demand; while the disproportion must every year increase, especially if our prosperity increases. For, just in proportion as wealth rolls in upon us, the number of those, who will give up their own independent homes to serve strangers, will be diminished.

The difficulties and sufferings, which have accrued to American women, from this cause, are almost incalculable. There is nothing, which so much demands system and regularity, as the affairs of a housekeeper, made up, as they are, of ten thousand desultory and minute items; and yet, this perpetually fluctuating state of society seems forever to bar any such system and regularity. The anxieties, vexations, perplexities, and even hard labor, which come upon American women, from this state of domestic service, are endless; and many a woman has, in consequence, been disheartened, discouraged, and ruined in health.

"SWEETHEARTS AND WIVES": A STORY FROM *GODEY'S LADY'S BOOK*

Under the editorship of Sarah Josepha Hale, the magazine called Godey's Lady's Book *became an acknowledged arbiter of female responsibility and genteel conduct in the mid-nineteenth century. It contained fiction, editorial comments, information on the latest fashions, and advice on domestic management. T. S. Arthur's didactic stories "Written for the Lady's Book" appeared frequently through the 1840s.*

"When you come to deal with the sober realities of a married life, Agnes, you will, I fear, find less of sunshine than you fondly hope for."

"Aunt Mildred, how can you talk so! Surely, you ought to have more regard for William Fairfield's true character, than to insinuate, as you evidently intend to do, that he will not be the same to me after we are married, than he now is."

"Sweethearts and wives, are, somehow or other, looked at with different eyes, Agnes."

"Aunt Mildred, you will offend me if you talk so!"

"You are willing to be offended, because I speak the truth. I had hoped more from the good sense of my niece"—Aunt Mildred said, in a tone of rather more seriousness than that in which she had, at first, spoken.

"But, Aunt Mildred," said her niece, looking into her face, while the moisture gathered in her eyes, "How can I bear to hear you talk so! Do I not know that William Fairfield loves me, as he loves his own life, and that he would sooner die than give me a moment's pain?"

"You must not be offended at me when I speak what I feel to be the truth, my dear child. I have lived longer, and have seen more of the world than you have. It is not, then, let me tell you, according to the nature of men to love any one as they love their own lives, nor to prefer death to giving pain to those they do love. This is all romance, Agnes, and the sooner you get it out of your head, the better. It will take itself out, if you don't mark my word for it!" . . .

"O Aunt, you will kill me if you talk so! If I thought that William did not love me as deeply as he says that he does, I would never see him again. I never can and never will be satisfied with any thing but a love that will sacrifice all for me. *I* will give such a pure, fervent love—nothing less than a like return can make me happy."

T. S. Arthur, "Sweethearts and Wives," *Godey's Lady's Book* 23 (December 1841), pp. 264–69.

"You do not know yourself my child. You offer more than you will be able to give, and ask more than you ever can receive. None of us are perfect; all of us are selfish. You are, in a certain degree, selfish, so is William. And in just so far as this selfish principle comes into activity, will both of you expect to receive more from the other, than you are willing to give. . . . I have not lived thus long in the world . . . without having learned many of its painful secrets; and one of these is that young love's promise is never realized. I have known many as full of the romance of love as you, and yet, all have been disappointed."

"And I know a good many, too, aunt, whose marriage promise has utterly failed. But, then, how could it have been otherwise; where there was no character or principle in the husband? I have built my happiness on a safer foundation. No one, I am sure, can breathe ought against William Fairfield."

"He is, if I judge him rightly, Agnes, a young man of a good heart, and sound principles. Indeed, I know of no one to whom I had rather commit the happiness of my niece."

"Thank you, my dear aunt, for that admission! And do not trouble yourself; I shall be as happy as I expect," . . . said the now laughing girl, kissing fondly the cheek of her who had been from early years to her, a mother and friend; and then danced lightly from the room, humming a pleasant ditty.

That evening her lover came as usual. It need not be denied that Aunt Mildred's warning had made some impression upon her mind, notwithstanding her effort to throw it off. . . .

"You do not seem as lively as usual," William said, half an hour, perhaps, after he had come in.

"Don't I? Well, the fact is, Aunt Mildred has been saying something to me, that, if I could believe there was any truth in it, would make me feel gloomy enough."

"Indeed! And what is that, Agnes?"

"Why, she says," replied the simple-hearted maiden looking him in the face, "that you will not love me after we are married, as you do now."

"She is right there, dear Agnes! for I will love you a thousand times more"; the lover responded fervently, kissing at the same time the glowing cheek of his affianced bride.

Agnes did not reply; but her heart seemed too large for her bosom.

"And you did not believe it?"

"O no, no, not for a moment!" said the warm-hearted girl. . . .

Our fond lovers are now united; and, as the honey moon is over, it becomes necessary for them to come down from their romance, and enter upon the sober duties of a married life. Aunt Mildred, though a very sensible woman, had not acted with her usual good sense towards her niece. She had thoroughly accomplished her in every thing but what she most needed, to make her competent to fill the place of wife and mother. She had not failed to warn her of the coming sober realities of a married lift, but had, alas! neglected to prepare her to encounter them aright.

It was not long, therefore, before her husband began to experience little annoyances, in consequence of her want of domestic knowledge; and what was worse, from her distaste for the practical duties required of every wife. She seemed to have looked forward to the married state, as one that was to elevate her to a higher degree of happiness, and yet bring with it no cares nor duties. When, therefore, repeated irregularities in the household economy occurred, and were felt by the husband as annoyances, he could not help thinking, sometimes, that the wife he so dearly loved, was not as thoughtful of his comfort, as he was of her's. Such thoughts will always produce corresponding feelings, and these latter cannot exist without in some way showing themselves. In the case of William Fairfield, they were exhibited in the form of a reserve, sometimes, that, while it existed, was exceedingly painful to his young wife. Besides this cause, fruitful in domestic disquietude, there was another that too frequently intrudes itself upon the first few years of marriage, a desire to lead, rather than to be led by the husband, in little things,—a habit of expecting him to consult, in all things, the will and tastes of the wife even at the sacrifice, sometimes, of duty and judgment. In fact, the wife, unconscious that in the marriage relation the husband should be looked to as of some consequence and consideration, as possessing claims upon her will to be guided by his understanding,—still imagines that all the power and peculiar influence which she possessed over him in the sweetheart-state, must of right continue. . . .

Fairfield installed his wife mistress of a neatly furnished house, and both settled themselves down in it, brimfull of present pleasure, and delightful anticipations. The two servants managed things pretty well for the first few weeks, but after that, many irregularities became apparent. The meals were often half an hour beyond the usual and set time, and were frequently very badly cooked. The sweeping and dusting were carelessly done, and the furniture, from want of attention, began to look a little dingy, much to the annoyance of Mrs. Fairfield. Still, it did not occur to her, that she was wrong in leaving every thing to her servants. It never came into her thoughts that her mind should be the governing one of her household, in *all things,* great and small, as much as was her husband's the governing mind in his business. The idea, that she was to take pleasure in exemption from domestic duties, and not in the performance of them, was fully entertained by her, and this her husband soon perceived, and it pained him much, for he saw that in this false idea was an active germ of future disquietude.

Punctual, almost, some would say, to a fault, he felt much the want of regularity, which was daily growing worse instead of better. Too frequently he was kept from his store in the morning, half an hour later than business required him to be there, in consequence of breakfast not being ready. Whenever this happened, he usually hurried away without the parting kiss which young wives most usually expect, for he did not feel like giving it. Sometimes Agnes would claim the token of love, but she felt that it was coldly given, and its price was a gush of tears, as soon as he had passed from her sight.

But the evening usually compensated for the disquietude of the day. Then, no duties unperformed vexed the feelings of either. Agnes sung, and played sweetly, and had, besides these accomplishments a mind well stored, and a taste highly cultivated. Home was to each a little paradise and they felt how happy they were in each other. Gradually, however, the shadows, too frequently cast over their feelings, passed not off entirely, even when all duties and cares were laid aside.

"Why does not Agnes think!" Fairfield would sometimes exclaim internally. "Surely, she cannot but perceive that these things annoy me very much. I spare no toil or pains to make her happy, and, surely, she ought to be willing to assume some cares and duties for my sake!"

"I fear he does not love me!" the young wife would often say, bursting into tears, as she closed her chamber door after her, and sat down to weep in abandonment of feelings after her husband had gone out to his business. "What would I not do to retain the love once given me so freely! But he is, I fear, disappointed in me. O I would rather die than lose the pure love he once lavished upon me!" . . .

One day, perhaps six months after their marriage, Fairfield, much pressed and perplexed with business, left his store at the usual hour for dinner. On his way home, his mind was still intent upon business affairs, and he walked faster than usual, anxious to get back as soon as possible, as his presence was needed. Much to his disappointment, he found the cloth not even laid for dinner.

"It isn't dinner time, surely?" Agnes said, as he came into the parlor, where she was practising a new piece upon the piano.

"Indeed then, it is," he replied in a tone of disappointment.

"Why, I'm sure it can't be two o'clock," responded Agnes, getting up and examining a time-piece on the mantel, that struck the hour regularly.

"It is, as I live! Why how swiftly the time has passed, I had no idea that it was so late." Then ringing the bell, she directed the cook to get dinner immediately.

"It won't be done for half an hour," the cook replied carelessly.

"Half an hour! that is too bad!" Fairfield said, impatiently.

"Indeed, Sally, you must be more punctual," said Mrs. Fairfield, her cheek colouring, for she always felt distressed when her husband was moved to displeasure.

"I've got it as quick as I could," Sally replied, tartly, gliding off to the kitchen.

An oppressive silence followed the withdrawal of the cook.

"Why don't she go down and hurry the dinner?" the husband could not help saying, after some fifteen minutes had elapsed, and there was no reappearance of Sally, for the purpose of arranging the table. "If I were to leave every thing in my store to clerks and porters, my business would soon run into disorder." . . .

It was near three o'clock when the meal was ready, but neither had any appetite for it. After swallowing a few mouthfuls, Fairfield hurried away to his store, and got there just too late to meet an important customer, who he knew was in town, and had been expecting all the morning. Mrs. Fairfield, who had been left sitting at the table, got up instantly and retired to her chamber, to spend the afternoon in weeping. She knew that her husband blamed her, but this she could not help feeling to be unreasonable.

"How could I help it?" she asked herself, as a fresh gush of tears streamed down her cheeks, "am I not dependent upon worthless servants? Surely, he don't expect me to go into the kitchen! If he does, he is much mistaken!" This last sentence was uttered in a calm, and somewhat indignant tone.

That evening, the supper passed off in moody silence. Fairfield, though disposed, when he came in, to lay aside, if possible, his vexed and unpleasant feelings, found a cloud upon his wife's face, and this created a positive indisposition on his part, to say even the first kind word that was to bring about a reaction. She felt that he blamed her, and she thought unjustly, and this prevented her from speaking in her usual kind and affectionate tone.

Evening passed away, and they retired for the night, still oppressed and gloomy, and each still disposed to blame the other. The morning found them in a much calmer frame of mind, and the husband's affectionate tones restored the light to Agnes' countenance. After conversing freely at the breakfast table, Fairfield said, just before rising, "I wish, Agnes, you would try to have dinner on the table punctually at two; my business requires all my attention just now, and a little delay is often a serious disadvantage to me."

The face of Agnes coloured deeply, and for a few moments she was too much disturbed to speak. At last she said, "I know you blame me, William. But how can I help it? Sally will have her own way. I can't go into the kitchen myself and do the cooking."

"But, then, Agnes, you know you could keep an eye over Sally, and when you see she is likely to be behindhand, hurry her on a little."

"Yes, and I might be at it everlastingly," Agnes responded, rather warmly. "If I have got to be at the heels of servants all the while, I might as well give up at once."

"But, Agnes, how do other ladies get along with their domestics?"

"I don't know any that get along better than I do. They have to put up with them, and we will have to do the same."

William Fairfield felt that it would be useless to urge the matter further on his young wife, and so did not reply. But he felt a good deal discouraged as he left the house, and hurried along to his store. . . .

Causes of unpleasant feeling, other than those relating to the domestic arrangements of the family, were in existence. For the first few months, the tastes and preferences of Agnes were consulted by her husband, in every thing. But now he began to feel that she expected too much, and considered him too little. She evidently preferred, in all things, her own will, to his; and expected him, as a matter of course, always to yield to her inclinations. This began to annoy him, and its impropriety to force itself upon his thoughts. He also began to yield to her with less apparent willingness. This was, of course, perceived, and thought to be an evidence of declining affection, and its discovery was a new source of pain to the heart of Agnes. . . . Still, she never seemed to imagine the true cause. No more attention was given to domestic affairs, and when the kind manner of her husband would return, after a temporary reserve, she would be as wilful, and as exacting as ever. . . .

Then, as she seemed so much determined on having her own will, he would not resist. But he condemned in his mind her conduct, distinctly. With all this she would be full of expressions and tokens of love, would tell him how dear he was to her, and how she could not live without him. Sometimes, while thus lavishing upon him acts of affection, and words of love, he would ask almost involuntarily, "If she so really loved me, would it not lead her to do more for my comfort, to consult my wishes more. Love, it is said, speaks plainer in actions than words. I fear she is too selfish, too much disposed to seek for happiness away from, instead of in, her duties." . . .

And they did, really love one another, but had not yet learned to accommodate themselves to each other's peculiarities. Fairfield was to blame, as well as Agnes. He should have been open and candid towards her, and have explained to her rationally, calmly, and affectionately, her duty; but he shrunk from this for fear of wounding her, thus wounding her a thousand times more acutely, in permitting her to go on in actions and omissions the natural results of which, were exceedingly painful to the heart of a young and loving wife.

One evening they started out to take a walk, neither of them feeling as happy as once they did, when, as lover and maiden, they had strolled along under the soft light of a quiet moon. Fairfield was silent, and Agnes but little inclined to talk, and each was too much occupied in mind with the other's peculiarities and faults. It so happened that, as the husband made a movement to turn down a certain street, as they were going home, that the wife objected and held back. The husband persevered, and the wife continued to resist; when, finding that he was not at all disposed to yield, she let go, saying, "Well, I am going this way, you can go that, if you would rather."

Surprised, yet irritated, and too much under the influence of the latter feeling to pause a moment for reflection, Fairfield, without replying, kept on, and Agnes, repenting her wilfulness, but too proud to pause, went another direction. Both arrived at home nearly at the same moment; and both had experienced in the five minutes since they parted, an age of misery. Neither of them spoke as they entered the house together. Agnes went up to her chamber, and her husband seated himself in the parlour below. In about half an hour, the excitement of the young wife's feelings began to subside, and with this calmer mood, came a distinct perception that she had done wrong; and with this consciousness, arose the determination to tell the husband so, as soon as he came up stairs. But the time continued to wear away, and yet he came not. Wearied and anxious, she laid herself across the bed and fell asleep.

In the mean time, Fairfield sat in the parlour, an agitated and miserable man. An open rupture had at last occurred, and he was reasoning himself into the determination not to suffer it to be healed until there was a full explanation and understanding between them. . . .

Startled by a painful dream, Agnes awoke about midnight, and rousing herself up, looked around in alarm for her husband. When she recovered her bewildered senses, the scene of the evening previous came up vividly before her mind.

"Where is he?" she asked herself, in a husky whisper.

Then catching up the light she hurried down stairs. The sound of her hastening feet startled her husband, who instantly thought, truly, that she had fallen asleep, and had just awakened; and now, in surprise and fear at his absence, had come to seek him. This thought at once modified and tendered his feelings towards her.

"O William! William!" she exclaimed, springing foward towards him, "can you, will you forgive me!"

Then sinking into his arms, she buried her head in his bosom, and lay trembling and sobbing like a frightened child.

After this excitement had, in a degree, subsided, Fairfield bent down, and kissing her cheek, whispered—"All is forgiven, dear Agnes! But let us now try so to understand each other, that no further cause for unhappiness may exist. We have not been happy during the past year, the first of our marriage—and yet, we love each other, and desire to make each other happy. Something must, then, be wrong in both of us. Now, let us lay aside all reserves, and be open, honest, and candid with each other. . . .

He then, as she would not bring a word against him, reluctantly entered upon his complaints against her, in regard to her want of due attention to the concerns of her household. This roused her up a little.

"Surely," she said "William, you do not wish to see your wife a drudge?"

"Not by any means, Agnes. But, then, I wish to see her engaged in the steady performance of every duty required by her station; because I know that only by doing so, can she render herself and family truly happy. No station, my dear wife, is exempt from its cares and its duties; if these are faithfully and willingly assumed, peace of mind will follow; if neglected, pain. As the mistress of a family, the comfort of others is placed in your hands, and, particularly, that of your husband. If you put aside your care and responsibility, and refer them to hired servants, you are in the neglect of plain and important duties; and one of the consequences which follows is, that your domestic arrangements are disturbed, and your family subjected to many annoyances. Suppose, for instance, during the past year, instead of trusting every thing to your cook, you had yourself had a careful eye, every day, over her department—had superintended the cooking so far as to know that dinner went on in time, and was properly served up at the exact hour, do you not perceive that the care which this would have subjected you to, would have been happiness compared with the feelings you have experienced in seeing me, almost daily, annoyed by irregularities which I saw you could correct, and blamed you for not correcting?"

Agnes heaved a long, deep sigh, but made no answer.

"I speak thus plain," continued the husband, "because I think it best for our happiness that I should do so. Your error lies in a false idea which you have entertained, that your happiness was to come somewhere from out of your domestic duties, instead of in the performance of them—that they were not part of a wife's obligations, but something that she could put aside if she were able to hire enough servants. I cannot, thus, delegate my business duties to any one; without my governing mind and constant attention, every thing would soon be in disorder, and an utter failure, instead of prosperity, be the result of my efforts. By my carefulness and constant devotion to business, I am enabled to provide you with every comfort; surely, then, you should be willing also to give careful attention to your department, that I may feel home to be a pleasant place. Under this view, my dear Agnes, do you conceive that I am ungenerous or unkind in wishing to see you take upon yourself more cares, and to perform more domestic duties?"

"Oh, no—no—no, dear husband!" said his wife, twining her arms around his neck, and kissing his cheek fondly. "I see very plainly how wrong I have been, and how false the views were that I have entertained. Hereafter I will strive to find my delight in what I now perceive, plainly, to be my duties. And if, at any time, I grow weary or think them irksome, I will say to myself—'I am but trying to make my husband happy, and his home a home indeed.' Only keep an unclouded brow, William—only love me, and I ask nothing more."

"I have always loved you tenderly, Agnes, although you sometimes tried me sorely."

"I know I have, my dear husband. And now, if there is any thing else, speak out plainly; I would know my faults, that I may correct them. It will be true charity for you to do so now."

"I believe it will, Agnes," he said, touching his lips to hers; "and if I pain you, remember it is only that you may be freed from a greater and lasting pain. Do not think me selfish in what I am about to say, or that I desire to rule over you tyrannically. In the wise order of Providence, there is a distinct and important difference in the relation of the sexes; and, particularly, in that which a man and his wife bear to each other. He is stronger, and his mind is a form receptive of more wisdom; she is weaker, and her mind is a form receptive of more affection. Thus they are radically different. As husband and wife, his wisdom becomes, as it were, joined to her affection, and her affection to his wisdom; thus they mutually act and react upon each other, and in just so far as each acts in a true position, do they become one, and happy in the marriage union. But if the wife attempt to guide or to force his understanding, then discord will occur, in the very nature of things; for only in just so far as her will is united with his understanding, can they, or will they act in harmony. Now one fault which you have, Agnes, is a disposition to have little things your own way, even in opposition to my expressed or implied preference. Whenever you do this, I feel as if you were unwilling to be influenced at all by me—as if you wished to be understanding and will both; thus making me a mere cypher. No man can or ought to bear this, without feeling that it is wrong. Do you understand me, Agnes?"

"I think I understand you perfectly, William. And what is better, you will say I see my fault distinctly, and will try my best to correct it. I did not think, before, that I was so selfish and wilful as I now perceive myself to be. You will forgive me the past, dear husband, will you not?"

"All—all is forgiven," he said, earnestly, again kissing her tear-moistened cheek. "And now let us begin life anew, each trying to make the other happy."

A PARLOR BALLAD

Singing in church and at home was a standard pastime and an admired feminine accomplishment by the late eighteenth century. As a form of women's cultural production and imaginative projection, music was arguably as prominent as writing during the nineteenth century, but is much more difficult to document because performance was evanescent. By mid-century women composers became visible. They have left a record in their parlor ballads, written to be sung in the middle-class family circle. This quasi-operatic example, intended for a female voice, was published both as sheet music and in Godey's Lady's Book in 1830, and was included in a series called Gems of our Time *in 1868. Whether the lyrics allude to an unrequited heterosexual love or to an intense relationship between two women is left intriguingly ambiguous; but certainly the practice of learning and playing music together fostered female friendships, and ballads on this theme—dedicated by one woman to another—were not uncommon.*

"Our Friendship," Yale Music Library. Used by permission. The editors are grateful to Judith Tick for alerting us to and providing a copy of this document.

"OUR FRIENDSHIP," a favourite Song Composed for the Piano Forte, And affectionately Dedicated to her Pupil Virginia J. S. Johnston BY Mrs. TOWNSHEND STITH.

Philada. Pub. & sold by Geo. Willig 171 Chesnut St.

Andante.

Ad lib: A tem:

Entered According to Act of Congress the twenty sixth day of August 1830 by G. Willig state of Penn.

2

It died in beauty, like a rose blown from its pa – rent

stem; It died in beauty like a pearl drop'd – – from some

di – – – – a – dem, It died in beauty like a lay, A –

–long a moon lit – lake; It died in beau –ty like the

"Our Friendship."

"Our Friendship".

MARGARET McCARTHY WRITES HOME

The first wave of Irish immigration to the United States started in the 1830s and was greatly augmented as a result of the Irish potato famine beginning in 1848. One of the things that distinguished Irish immigrants was the high proportion of single women among them. The writer of the following letter came from Kingwilliamstown, County Cork. Her letter does not indicate what kind of occupation she found (the great majority of single Irish women were domestic servants), but whatever work she did enabled her to send money to her parents, to encourage them to join her.

Michael Boyan Esqre.
Kingwilliamstown Kanturk Post Office
County of Cork, Ireland
to be forwarded to Mr Alexander MCarthy, of same place.

New York September 22nd, 1850.

My Dr. Father and Mother Brothers and Sisters,

I write these few lines to you hopeing That these few lines may find you all in as good State of health as I am at present thank God I received your welcome letter To me Dated 22nd. of May which was A Credit to me for the Stile and Elligence of its Fluent Language but I must Say Rather Flattering My Dr. Father I must only say that this is a good place and A good Country for if one place does not Suit A man he can go to Another and can very easy please himself But there is one thing thats Ruining this place Especially the Frontirs towns and Cities where the Flow of Emmigration is most the Emmigrants has not money enough to Take them to the Interior of the Country which oblidges them to Remain here in New York and the like places for which Reason Causes the less demand for Labour and also the great Reduction in wages for this Reason I would advise no one to Come to America that would not have Some Money after landing here that (would) Enable them to go west in case they would get no work to do here but any man or woman without a family are fools that would not venture and Come to this plentyful Coun-try where no man or woman ever Hungerd or ever will and where you will not be Seen Naked, but I can asure you there are Dangers upon Dangers Attending Comeing here but my Friends nothing Venture noth-

Diamaid O. Muirthe, *A Seat behind the Coachman: Travellers in Ireland, 1800–1900* (Dublin: Gill & Macmillan, 1977), pp. 138–42. Reprinted by permission of the publisher. The editors are grateful to Christine Stansell for locating and providing a copy of this document.

ing have Fortune will favour the brave have Courage and prepare yourself for the next time that, that worthy man Mr. Boyen is Sending out the next lot, and Come you all Together Couragiously and bid adieu to that lovely place the land of our Birth, that place where the young and old joined Together in one Common Union, both night and day Engaged in Innocent Amusement, But alas. I am now Told its the Gulf of Misersry oppression Degradetion and Ruin of evry Discription which I am Sorry to hear of so Doleful a History to Be told of our Dr. Country This my Dr. Father induces me to Remit to you in this Letter 20 Dollars that is four Pounds thinking it might be Some Acquisition to you untill you might Be Clearing away from that place all together and the Sooner the Better for Believe me I could not Express how great would be my joy at seeing you all here Together where you would never want or be at a loss for a good Breakfast and Dinner. So prepare as soon as possible for this will be my last Remittince untill I see you all here. Bring with you as much Tools as you can as it will cost you nothing to Bring them And as for your Clothing you need not care much But that I would like that yourself would Bring one good Shoot of Cloth that you would spare until you come here And as for Mary She need not mind much as I will have for her A Silk Dress A Bonnet and Viel according and Ellen I need not mention what I will have for her I can fit her well you are to Bring Enough Flannels and do not form it at home as the way the weay Flannel at home and here is quite different for which reason I would Rather that you would not form any of it untill you Come, with the Exception of whatever Quantity of Drawers you have you can make them at ahome But make them Roomly Enough But Make No Jackets.

My Dr. Father I am Still in the Same place but do not Intend to Stop here for the winter. I mean to come into New York and there Spend the winter Thade Houlehan wrote to me Saying that if I wished to go up the Country that he would send me money but I declined so doing untill you Come and then after you Coming if you think it may be Better for us to Remain here or go west it will be for you to judge but untill then I will Remain here. Dan Keliher Tells me that you Knew more of the House Carpentery than he did himself and he can earn from twelve to fourteen Shilling a day that is seven Shilling British and he also Tells me that Florence will do very well and that Michl can get a place Right off as you will not be In the Second day when you can Bind him to any Trade you wish And as for John he will Be Very Shortly Able to Be Bound two So that I have Every Reason to Believe that we will all do will Together So as that I am sure its not for Slavery I want you to Come here no its for affording My Brothers and Sisters And I an oppertunity of Showing our

Kindness and Gratitude and Comeing on your Seniour days that we would be placed in that possision that you my Dr. Father and Mother could walk about Lesuirly and Indepenly without Requireing your Labour an object which I am Sure will not fail even by Myself if I was oblidged to do it without the assistance of Brother or Sister for my Dr. Father and Mother.

I am proud and happy to Be away from where the County Charges man or the poor Rates man or any other Rates man would have the Satisfaction of once Inpounding my cow or any other article of mine Oh how happy I feel and am sure to have look as The Lord had not it destined for me to get married to Some Loammun or another at home that after a few months he and I may be an Incumberance upon you or perhaps in the poor house by this, So my Dr. Father according as I had Stated to you I hope that whilst you are at home I hope that you will give my Sister Mary that privelage of Injoying herself Innocently on any occasion that She pleases so far as I have said Innocently and as for my Dr. Ellen I am in Raptures of joy when I think of one day Seeing her and you all at the dock in New York and if I do not have a good Bottle of Brandy for you Awaiting your arrival its a Causion.

Well I have only to tell my Dr. Mother to Bring all her bed Close and also to bring the Kittle and an oven and have handles to them and do not forget the Smoothing Irons and Beware when you are on board to Bring some good floor and Ingage with the Captain Cook and he will do it Better for you for very little and also Bring some whiskey and give them the Cook and some Sailors that you may think would do you any good to give them a Glass once in a time and it may be no harm.

And Dr. Father when you are Comeing here if you Possiblely can Bring My Uncle Con I would Be glad that you would and I am sure he would be of the greatest acquisision to you on board and also Tell Mary Keeffe that if her Child died that I will pay her passage very Shortly and when you are Comeing do not be frightened Take Courage and be Determined and bold in your Undertaking as the first two or three days will be the worst to you and mind whatever happens on board Keep your own temper and do not speak angry to any or hasty the Mildest Man has the best chance on board So you make your way with evey one and further you are to speak to Mr Boyan and he I am sure will get one Request for you Mr Boyan will do it for me, when you are to Come ask Mr Boyan to give you a few lines to the Agent or Berth Master of the Ship that will Secure to you the Second Cabin which I am sure Mr Boyan will do and as soon as you Receive this letter write to me and let me know about every thing when you are to come and what time and state Particulars of evry thing to me and Direct as before. And if you are to come Shortly when you come to Liberpool wright to me also and let me know when you are to sail and the name of the Ship you sail in as I will be uneasy untill I get an answer.

No more at present But that you will give Mr and Mrs Boyan my best love and respect And let me know how they and family are as they would or will not Be ever Better than I would wish them to be also Mrs. Milton and Charles Mr and Mrs Roche and family Mr and Mrs day and family Mr Walsh and as for his family I am sure are all well Mr and Mrs Sullivan and family Mrs O Brien Con Sheehan wife and family all the Hearlihys and familys Tim Leahy and family own Sullivan of Cariganes and family Darby Guinee and family John Calleghan and family Timoth Calleghan and family Timothy Sheehan and Mother So no more at present form your Ever Dear and Loveing Child.

Margaret MCarthy.

PETITION FOR A TEN-HOUR WORKDAY

When the first textile factories in the United States were established in the 1820s in Lowell, Massachusetts, young women, recruited from New England farms, formed the majority of the operatives. The move of some women's labor from household to factory was essential to early industrialization. By the 1840s, employee resistance to speed-ups and pay cuts became visible in the organization of Female Labor Reform Associations in Lowell and other mill towns. Sarah Bagley, one of the editors of the Voice of Industry, *a millworkers' newspaper, was also a leader in the 1845 campaign to petition the Massachusetts legislature for a law restricting the workday to ten hours. It was not until 1874 that Massachusetts passed such a law, however—and then, not for all workers, but only for women and minors.*

House of Representatives, March 12, 1845

The Special Committee to which was referred sundry petitions relating to the hours of labor, have considered the same and submit the following

REPORT

The first petition which was referred to your committee, came from the city of Lowell, and was signed by Mr. John Quincy Adams Thayer, and eight hundred and fifty others, "peaceable, industrious, hard working men and women of Lowell." The petitioners declare that they are confined "from thirteen to fourteen hours per day in unhealthy apartments," and are thereby "hastening through pain, disease and privation, down to a premature grave." They therefore ask the Legislature "to pass a law providing that ten hours shall constitute a day's work," and that no corporation or private citizen "shall be allowed, except in cases of emergency, to employ one set of hands more than ten hours per day."

The second petition came from the town of Fall River, and is signed by John Gregory and four hundred and eighty-eight others. These petitions ask for the passage of a law to constitute "ten hours a day's work in *all corporations* created by the Legislature."

The third petition signed by Samuel W. Clark and five hundred others, citizens of Andover, is in precisely the same words as the one from Fall River.

The fourth petition is from Lowell, and is signed by James Carle and

Documents Printed by Order of the House of Representatives of the Commonwealth of Massachusetts during the Session of the General Court, A.D. *1845,* no. 50 (Boston: Dutton and Wentworth, 1845).

three hundred others. The petitioners ask for the enactment of a law making "ten hours a day's work, where no specific agreement is entered into between the parties."

The whole number of names on the several petitions is 2,139, of which 1,151 are from Lowell. A very large proportion of the Lowell petitioners are females. Nearly one half of the Andover petitioners are females. The petition from Fall River is signed exclusively by males. . . .

On the 13th of February, the Committee held a session to hear the petitioners from the city of Lowell. . . .

The first petitioner who testified was Eliza R. Hemmingway. She had worked 2 years and 9 months in the Lowell Factories; 2 years in the Middlesex, and 9 months in the Hamilton Corporations. Her employment is weaving,—works by the piece. The Hamilton Mill manufactures cotton fabrics. The Middlesex, woollen fabrics. She is now at work in the Middlesex Mills, and attends one loom. Her wages average from $16 to $23 a month exclusive of board. She complained of the hours for labor being too many, and the time for meals too limited. In the summer season, the work is commenced at 5 o'clock, A.M., and continued till 7 o'clock, P.M., with half an hour for breakfast and three quarters of an hour for dinner. During eight months of the year, but half an hour is allowed for dinner. The air in the room she considered not to be wholesome. There were 293 small lamps and 61 large lamps lighted in the room in which she worked, when evening work is required. These lamps are also lighted sometimes in the morning.—About 130 females, 11 men, and 12 children (between the ages of 11 and 14,) work in the room with her. She thought the children enjoyed about as good health as children generally do. The children work but 9 months out of 12. The other 3 months they must attend school. Thinks that there is no day when there are less than six of the females out of the mill from sickness. Has known as many as thirty. She, herself, is out quite often, on account of sickness. There was more sickness in the Summer than in Winter months; though in the Summer, lamps are not lighted. She thought there was a general desire among the females to work but ten hours, regardless of pay. Most of the girls are from the country, who work in the Lowell Mills. The average time which they remain there is about three years. She knew one girl who had worked there 14 years. Her health was poor when she left. Miss Hemmingway said her health was better where she now worked, than it was when she worked on the Hamilton Corporation.

She knew of one girl who last winter went into the mill at half past 4 o'clock, A.M. and worked till half past 7 o'clock P.M. She did so to make more money. She earned from $25 to $30 per month. There is always a large number of girls at the gate wishing to get in before the bell rings. On the Middlesex Corporation one fourth part of the females go into the mill before they are obliged to. They do this to make more wages. A large number come to Lowell to make money to aid their parents who are poor. She knew of many cases where married women came to Lowell and worked in the mills to assist their husbands to pay for their farms. The moral character of the operatives is good. There was only one American female in the room with her who could not write her name.

Miss Sarah G. Bagley said she had worked in the Lowell Mills eight years and a half,—six years and a half on the Hamilton Corporation, and two years on the Middlesex. She is a weaver, and works by the piece. She worked in the mills three years before her health began to fail. She is a native of New Hampshire, and went home six weeks during the summer. Last year she was out of the mill a third of the time. She thinks the health of the operatives is not so good as the health of females who do house-work or millinery business. The chief evil, so far as health is concerned, is the shortness of time allowed for meals. The next evil is the length of time employed—not giving them time to cultivate their minds. She spoke of the high moral and intellectual character of the girls. That many were engaged as teachers in the Sunday schools. That many attended the lectures of the Lowell Institute; and she thought, if more time was allowed, that more lectures would be given and more girls attend. She thought that the girls generally were favorable to the ten hour system. She had presented a petition, same as the one before the Committee, to 132 girls, most of whom said that they would prefer to work but ten hours. In a pecuniary point of view, it would be better, as their health would be improved. They would have more time for sewing. Their intellectual, moral, and religious habits would also be benefited by the change.

Miss Bagley said, in addition to her labor in the mills, she had kept evening school during the winter months, for four years, and thought that this extra labor must have injured her health.

Miss Judith Payne testified that she came to Lowell 16 years ago, and worked a year and a half in the Merrimack Cotton Mills, left there on account of ill health, and remained out over seven years. She was sick most of the time she was out. Seven years ago she went to work in the Boott Mills, and has remained there ever since; works by the piece. She has lost, during the last seven years, about one year from ill health. She is a weaver, and attends three looms. Last pay-day she drew $14.66 for

five weeks work; this was exclusive of board. She was absent during the
five weeks but half a day. She says there is a general feeling in favor of
the ten hour system among the operatives. She attributes her ill health to
the long hours of labor, the shortness of time for meals, and the bad air
of the mills. She had never spoken to Mr. French, the agent, or to the
overseer of her room, in relation to these matters. She could not say that
more operatives died in Lowell than other people. . . .

The only witnesses whom the Committee examined, whose names
were not on the petition, were Mr. Adams and Mr. Isaac Cooper, a member of the House from Lowell, and also has worked as an overseer in the
Lawrence Cotton Mills for nine years. His evidence was very full. He gave
it as his opinion that the girls in the mills enjoy the best health, for the
reason that they rise early, go to bed early, and have three meals regular.
In his room there are 60 girls, and since 1837, has known of only one
girl who went home from Lowell and died. He does not find that those
who stay the longest in the mill grow sickly and weak. The rooms are
heated by steampipes, and the temperature of the rooms is regulated by
a thermometer. It is so he believes in all the mills. The heat of the room
varies from 62 to 68 degrees. . . .

From Mr. Clark, the agent of the Merrimack Corporation, we obtained
the following table of the time which the mills run during the year.

Begin work.—From 1st May to 31st August, at 5 o'clock.
From 1st September to 30th April, as soon as they can see.
Breakfast.—From 1st November to 28th February, before going to work.
From 1st March to 31st of March, at 7½ o'clock.
From 1st April to 19th September, at 7 o'clock.
From 20th Sept. to 31st October, at 7½ o'clock.
Return in half an hour.
Dinner.—Through the year at 12½ o'clock.
From 1st May to 31st Aug., return in 45 minutes.
From 1st Sept. to 30th April, return in 30 minutes.
Quit work.—From 1st May to 31st August, at 7 o'clock.
From 1st September to 19th Sept., at dark.
From 20th Sept. to 19th March, at 7½ o'clock.
From 20th March to 30th April, at dark.

Lamps are never lighted on Saturday evenings. The above is the time
which is kept in all the mills in Lowell, with a slight difference in the
machine shop; and it makes the average daily time throughout the year,
of running the mills, to be 12 hours and ten minutes.

There are four days in the year which are observed as holidays, and on which the mills are never put in motion. These are Fast Day, Fourth of July, Thanksgiving Day, and Christmas Day. These make one day more than is usually devoted to pastime in any other place in New England. The following table shows the average hours of work per day, throughout the year, in the Lowell Mills:

	Hours	Min.		Hours	Min.
January	11	24	July	12	45
February	12		August	12	45
March*	11	52	September	12	23
April	13	31	October	12	10
May	12	45	November	11	56
June	12	45	December	11	24

*The hours of labor on the 1st of March are less than in February, even though the days are a little longer, because 30 minutes are allowed for breakfast from the 1st of March to the 1st of September.

DOMESTIC MANAGEMENT IN THE LETTERS OF
MARTHA COFFIN WRIGHT

Reared in a Philadelphia Quaker family, Martha Coffin Wright was almost thirty-five when she wrote the following letters. She was the wife of an upstate New York lawyer (David Wright) and the mother of four children: Marianna (born 1825), Eliza (born 1830), Tallman (born 1832), and Ellen (born 1840). Maria, much mentioned, was a domestic servant. In 1848 Wright joined her sister Lucretia Mott, to whom these letters are written, and Elizabeth Cady Stanton in planning the first women's rights convention, held at Seneca Falls. From then on she was active in the women's rights movement.

Auburn, Nov. 7th, 1841 . . . Yesterday passed like all the rest in brushing up, straightening the green cloth, holding fast the table Cover that Ellen should not put it off, resting, reading & sewing—I made 3 pumpkin pies & one apple. Maria has really done well & I hope she will continue to, for I had much rather keep her, for many reasons. . . .

Maria got through with her washing by dinner time on Monday & got the meals in order too—she was up at 5. I made the starch & made bread. She does much better than she did, & Ellen is not afraid of her now. Yesterday being the first dry day since Friday I shook the green cloth & pieces & swept the parlor & dining room thoroughly—other days I made the hand brush and dust pan answer. Mrs. Crossnell called in the afternoon—was sorry she was out when Miss Temple called but she had engagements every day which had prevented her calling as she & Mr. C. intended &c &c I forgot today that I drove nails over the tops of some of the doors in the dining room & made a nice line out of Tallman's ex-kite string—not the one Uncle Thomas gave him. The day being rainy, all the clothes were dried in the dining room by night. . . .

Thursday 11th   At the dawn of each day, how much sewing I plan to accomplish before night & how little I do. Today I was going to make any quantity of aprons and frocks for Ellen & all I have made out has been to make 6 seed bags for D. after putting things in order, making Tallman's bed, trimming lamps, &c. While Ellen slept I ran down and in a jiffy had two pans full of first rate gingerbreads made for D. & the children. . . .

Martha Coffin Wright to Lucretia Mott, November 7, 18, 1841; [Dec.?] 18, [1841?]; Garrison Collection, Sophia Smith Collection, Smith College. Reprinted by permission of the Sophia Smith Collection.

Evening—I don't feel half as amiable as I did, because my baboon came to me at 3 o'clock, . . . & in a mellifluous voice, informed me that she was going out a little while but wd. be back in time to get tea, and after watching out of the window till David came (the view is not at all handsome from these windows when you are watching for refractory apes) I reluctantly went down & soon had a fire & got tea. To be sure, it is a trifle to get tea, when you have first rate bread & butter, only one feels so mad to be outwitted. . . .

12th   As I was looking over my letter, whack! went the stove equal to a cannon & now both windows are open to let out the smoke . . . Bang! goes the *blamed* stove again I had got all the smoke out & closed the windows, and then raised the door to get the stove hot again—before it was too hot. I shut it nearly down & it chosed to puff. We really don't know whether to keep it or not—it has answered as well for a few days back, but I have managed it today precisely as I did yesterday. . . . Ellen sits in the chair at the window amusing herself with making bubbles. Most of the time I keep the dining room door open, & if I sing plenty, she stays there a long time, playing in the wood box and pulling the cloth off of the table. When I am still she comes to see whether I have left the room, which I often do for a few minutes when I have to see to something. She frequently comes & insists on having my hand to lay her cheek against & if I am ever so busy, I must stop for I would not refuse the little affectionate pet if I could. She has two new under teeth just thro'. . . .

[P.S.] The carpet and oil cloth & tin round the stove were such podge work & the carpet so hard to sweep that my chief business out to-day was to get a piece of oil cloth as long as the rug so as to dispense with that. I got a piece 8 feet long & a yd & qr wide for wh[ich] I gave $5. It seems a good deal, but it will last a great while & do me a great deal of good—it is very pretty, white ground with bright vines red blue & green. . . .

Auburn, Nov. 19th.   12 o'clock & I have not had time since breakfast to rest, having the dining room to sweep, my bed room &c &c—before which I left Ellen in Eliza's care, & made some gingerbread which was very good with the slight omission of *ginger*—so I went to work & made another batch remembering that important ingredient. . . . 17 years yesterday since I was first married & 12 since the last. Ellen is 15 m[onth]s old to-day, & the snip is just waking when she has only slept while I wrote the above.

26th   . . . I am not at all disposed to dispute the truth of Mother's remark that hateful as Maria was, it was better to have her & be mad than to have to work hard,—*and be mad*—but I bore with her as long as I could, and when she sneaked out, vehemently dressed in a very light dress in a driving snow storm, just when she ought to have been making her fire to get tea, I felt so mad that I could not resist the temptation to tell her that if she did not come back at tea time, she should not at all—for I had told her in the morning that as David was away, we would have early tea, and she could then have a long evening if she wished to go out—to which she made no reply. You are too good, all of you, have your feelings too well disciplined ever to feel so angry as I did when I opened the window as she was sneaking off, and spoke to her. I know I never found it so difficult to speak the few words that I did & when I closed the window—my heart beat so that I could hardly breathe, from the effort I had made to *appear pacific*. I wanted to look in the glass to see if I did not *look like Byron*, but the children being present I *read the newspaper*. Byron said that when he felt himself paling with anger, he was dangerous or something like it. Mother knows just how mad we used to feel with Maria. David said I ought to have dismissed her long ago & he did not know how I had done to keep her so long as I did. When she came to pack up her things late the next morning I told her I would give her one more trial if she wd promise to do better but she wd make no such promise—she had always gone out when she pleased to spend the afternoon & night, and always would. I went down in the afternoon to see Aunt Clara. She was not surprised and expressed much regret that I had had so much trouble, wd try & get another girl for me, if her Irish girl knew of any. I shall keep Eliza at home this quarter. She assists in the care of Ellen & washes most of the dishes—gets tea & toasts bread—sets the table &c. David had to leave in the cars at 10 o'clock Sunday night for Waterloo—he only returned the day before from Seneca Falls. I never felt more lonely than when I locked the door after him—only myself & the children in the house & I did not rest much that night, as every noise woke me, & the wind being high there were plenty of all sorts of noises. It was delightful to see him with his valise on his way home at 2 o'clock yesterday—3 days & a half and as I had been teaching Eliza how to roast chickens while Ellen slept, there were three that I had just set away on the hanging shelf—fearing they would not keep I had them all roasted & set away to warm over—the other three I cut up and stewed. Day before yesterday I was engaged some time in the *laundry*, having selected from the basket of clothes that await a washer 2 dozen that would be needed before one came. I dried them in the kitchen, and ironed them the next day & thought I was a bug, as I never washed so much before. . . . Sarah having taken the chief care of all such things for 12 years, I have not fairly got my hand in yet. My bread has been excellent—we got a new barrel of flour to-day. . . .

To-day I was sweeping the porch when a spare young woman presented herself, to know if I wanted a girl. After seating her & settling a few preliminaries I ventured to suggest a hope that she was steady, as I had just dismissed a girl very capable & satisfactory in other respects. She sd she should think she was old enough to be steady—she was 27. So much the better thought I perhaps she has sowed her wild oats. Mrs. Dennis recommended her, she had formerly lived with her. . . . So it was settled that she wd come tomorrow afternoon, so as to be here ready to go to washing. My first business after she left was to run in & inquire of Eunice [Dennis] why she didn't take her herself. She told me she was a most excellent girl to work & neat BUT her chracter was not good when she lived with her. She begged her to take her & assured her she was not as she used to be, & Eunice said she told Caroline perhaps she had reformed & she was almost sorry she had not taken her, but as she had a young girl in the kitchen she thought it would not answer, tho' if she had been able to be about herself she should not have hesitated. Thinks I, are there none good in Auburn? no, not one? However perhaps she told the truth & had reformed, & if so it wd be cruel not to give her a trial—and my hands were so shock'n rough, so to short & long I feel pretty well satisfied. Eunice sd she was one that wd take good care of things & be good with the children—that she had a good disposition. From there I went over to see Miss Townsend & let her know why Eliza had not been. As soon as she [Eliza] heard of the girl she sd "now I can to to school this yr." I told Miss T that I had thought before [when] I was without a girl of keeping Eliza out. . . .

29th   Yesterday I rose a little earlier than usual so as to have every thing in the order I wished my Magdalen to find it, & kept the kitchen warm all day but she ne-er came—this morning David put on the boiler for me & I hoped to see her after breakfast, but when D. came up to dinner he found me busy, & wanted to know if he was not a prophet when he sd she wd not come—but toward night she appeared & I have been showing her how we manage about washing &c—a doleful task. Tallman is a pretty good auxiliary as he knows the places of things pretty well. . . . She tells the children she can't read, her sight not being good, for which I am sorry as I was going to lend her "Live & Let Live" and *"some novels."* The first evening Henrietta came to live with me two yrs ago, she sent one of the children to me to know if I wd *please to lend her some novels.* Esther wished to know if I wd please to lend her a sharp pen knife to cut her corns—Sylvia wanted a comb—Lucinda a shawl—Mercy a pair of gloves—Maria, a thimble—Nancy Anna wanted a trunk to journey to the Eastward &c &c. My present Magdalen, like her prototype, rejoices in the name of Polly—Polly Magdalen! . . . Ellen does not seem so much afraid of Polly Mag as she did of Maria. I have entirely done feeding her thickened milk. She eats a great deal of bread & three or four times a day, drinks a little cup of milk, unboiled—since the cold weather I found it necessary to make that change in her diet. N.B. Polly smokes a pipe. . . .

Polly seems disposed to do her best—and is a very good cook, & saving but her health is not good & she is pretty slow—she says "jest" let her keep steady on & she can do a great deal of work but she "aint as swift as some" & that is a fact—but I don't care, as long as she does as well as she has, & is contented. She spent one evening out "to a party" promising to be back by 10 & was as good as her word. I was going out this morning and she wished to know if I was going 'up street,' "cause if ye are I will be very much obliged to ye if ye'll just stop at the milliners if ye go by there, and *see if my hat's done.*" Imagine sister Lucretia stopping at the milliners to inquire for a "hat" for one of the Paphaan damsels next door to Ann Frosh's. I rather think I didn't stop. . . . I have finished all Ellen's little green aprons, four in all. I made Eliza a quilted hat to race about with, out of one breadth—myself a nice apron out of one & a half, & made Ellen two cunning little Machester frocks out of the one Marianne wore on her journey to Kimberton, afterward her blackberrying dress. Last winter, it was Eliza's everyday dress & now it looks as neat on Ellen as Lydia Davis' three-breadths-of-muslin-de-laine ones. Moreover I have knit a pr of gloves for Thomas to wear at the factory & finished a pr of long stockings for Ellen as her little legs were quite rough. My mending, in addition to the above, has kept me as busy as I could be, for most of the afternoon I have to give up everything & amuse Ellen as she gets lonesome. . . .

[Dec. 1841?] . . . The conversation at tea was on women having the property that their parents had accumulated for them, secured to them before marriage—a measure wh Mrs. Satterlee & Mrs. G. advocated & David & Mrs. Worden opposed. I agreed with the former, that instead of showing a want of confidence in a husband it was providing a sure means for his comfort in case of those contingencies always liable to recur where a man is engaged in business of any kind. David thought a wife shared in her husband's good fortune, & should be willing to share his reverses—& *in nine cases out of ten where a man failed in business it was traceable to a wife's extravagances.* Now I think it a great shame for David to make so ungallant a speech as that even if it was the truth which it is not. Women are very apt to look on with apprehension & endeavor to avert by such arguments as they can use, the mania of speculation, the reckless endorsing for others & the thousand unprofitable schemes that are busying them to ruin—but those arguments are not spoken thro' a trumpet, nor on the housetop, and the unnumerable acts of self-denial that they practice with the hope of keeping back the crisis, are untold & when it comes at length, involving the wife & helpless children in the general ruin, when "all their household gods are shivered around" why then forsooth it is the "wife's extravagance". I have been so busy since, that I have forgotten to scold David for maligning wives, but I mean to tell him that men who make such speeches *deserve* such feather vestments as the New Orleans gentleman proposes to don.

A NEW YORK WOMAN ON A
NORTH CAROLINA PLANTATION

*In 1853 at the age of twenty-six, Sarah Hicks of New Hartford, New York,
married Benjamin Franklin Williams, a North Carolina planter-physician.
The couple had met in Albany, where Sarah was attending the Albany
Female Academy and Ben, seven years older, was studying medicine. It
took him eight years to convince her to marry him, because of her reluctance to move south. These letters recount her first impressions after the
couple moved to Greene County, one of the richest agricultural regions of
North Carolina. They settled temporarily at Ben's widowed mother's
home, Clifton Grove, a working plantation with thirty-seven slaves. As
wife and mother, Sarah Hicks Williams lived the rest of her life in the
South.*

Clifton Grove, Oct. 10, 1853
Monday

My dear Parents:

I arrived safely at my new home on Friday last, but have had no time
to write until now. . . . You may imagine I have seen many strange things.
As for my opinions, in so short a time, it would not be fair to give them.
I have seen no unkind treatment of servants. Indeed, I think they are
treated with more familiarity than many Northern servants. They are in
the parlor, in your room and all over. The first of the nights we spent in
the Slave Holding States, we slept in a room without a lock. Twice before
we were up a waiting girl came into the room, and while I was dressing,
in she came to look at me. She seemed perfectly at home, took up the
locket with your miniatures in it and wanted to know if it was a watch. I
showed it to her. "Well," she said, "I should think your mother and father
are mighty old folks." Just before we arrived home, one old Negro caught
a glimpse of us and came tearing out of the pine woods to touch his hat
to us. All along the road we met them and their salutation of "Howdy
(meaning How do you) Massa Ben," and they seemed so glad to see him,
that I felt assured that they were well treated. As we came to the house, I
found Mother Williams ready to extend a mother's welcome. Mary and
Harriett were both here and delighted to see me. I felt at home. At dinner
we had everything very nice. It is customary when the waiting girl is not

James C. Bonner, ed., "Plantation Experiences of a New York Woman," *North Carolina Historical
Review* 33, no. 3 (July 1956), pp. 389–98. Reprinted by permission of the North Carolina Division of Archives and History.

passing things at table, to keep a large broom of peacock feathers in motion over our heads to keep off flies, etc. I feel confused. Everything is so different that I do not know which way to stir for fear of making a blunder. I have determined to keep still and look on for a while, at any rate. Yesterday I went to Church in a very handsome carriage, servants before and behind. I began to realize yesterday how much I had lost in the way of religious privileges. We went six miles to church, as they have preaching at Snow Hill only every one or two Sabbaths.. On arriving I found a rough framed building in the midst of woods, with a large congregation, consisting of about equal numbers of white and black. These meetings are held about one a month and then addressed by two or three exhorters, who are uneducated, and each speaks long enough for any common sermon. The singing is horrible. Prize your religious privileges. They are great and you would realize it by attending Church here once. I shall miss these much. Things that Northerners consider essential are of no importance here. The house and furniture is of little consequence. To all these differences I expect to become accustomed in time. My husband is all kindness and loves me more than I am worthy. With him I could be happy anywhere. I have seen enough to convince me that the ill-treatment of the Slaves is exaggerated at the North but I have not seen enough to make me like the institution. I am quite the talk of the day, not only in the whole County, but on the plantation. Yesterday I was out in the yard and an old Negro woman came up to me, "Howdy, Miss Sara, are you the Lady that won my young Master. Well, I raised him." Her name was Chaney and she was the family nurse. Between you and me, my husband is better off than I ever dreamed of. I am glad I didn't know it before we were married. He owns 2000 acres of land in this vicinity, but you must bear in mind that land here is not as valuable as with you. But I'll leave these things to talk of when I see you, which I hope may be before many months. I will write you more fully when I have the time. Some of our friends leave this morning and I must go and see them. Write soon, very soon. Ben sends love. Love to all. Ever your

Sara

I wish you could see the cotton fields. The bolls are just opening. I cannot compare their appearance to anything but fields of white roses. As to the cotton picking, I should think it very light and pleasant work. Our house is very unassuming. Not larger than Mary's. I shall feel unsettled until my furniture comes and after our return from Charleston next month. Then I hope to settle down and be quiet for a while. The house has been full of relatives ever since we came and more friends are expected tomorrow. Direct to Clifton Grove, near Snow Hill, Green Co., N.C.

Clifton Grove, Oct. 22, 1853
Saturday Morning

My dear Parents:

Your letter enclosing others has been received and ere this you have received one from me informing you of our safe arrival here. It would be wrong, perhaps, for me to form or express an opinion in regard to the manners and customs of the people, after only two weeks tarry among them. I shall not speak for or against, but will state things as I have seen them and you may form your own opinions. . . .

Ambition is satisfied here by numbering its thousands of dollars, acres of land and hundreds of negroes. Houses, furniture, dress are nothing. For instance, the Dr.'s brother, a very wealthy man, lives in a brown wood house without lathing or plastering. To be sure, he has a handsome sofa, sideboard and chairs in his parlor, which contrast strangely with the unfinished state of the house. However, he purposes building soon. This, I might say, is the common style of house, and ours, which is finished, the exception. As to household arrangements, I have discovered no system. Wash, bake or iron, just as the fit takes. . . . Baking is all done in bake kettles and cooking at a fire place. Chimneys are all built on the outside of the houses. The Negroes are certainly not overtasked on this plantation. One house girl at the North will accomplish more than two here. But I think the great fault lies in the want of system. Mother Williams works harder than any Northern farmer's wife, I know. She sees to everything. The Dr. has another place, seven miles from here, mostly pine land. That with his other business demands a good share of his time. He has gone with his brother to Greenville to engage his turpentine, which is selling for $4.00 per barrel. I don't expect him back until Monday. As to the treatment of servants, the overseer that Ben employed while he was away, struck one of the Negroes, and his mother would not speak to him afterwards, and had him discharged. They are not diffident, either. One of the field hands asked me to fix a dress for her the other day. Another servant wanted to know if Massa Ben and I couldn't ride over to Snow Hill and get her a new dress. They have plots of ground they cultivate and have what they make from them. They can go to Church (Preaching, as they say) on the Sabbath. Indeed, a majority of the congregation is colored. On Sundays they dress up and many of them look very nice. They leave off work at sundown during the week. You will not wonder, finding everything here so entirely different, if I should feel like a stranger in a strange land. It must take time for me to become accustomed to such an utter change, but with a husband who has proved so devoted, I could not be unhappy anywhere. I think I can appreciate Miss Ophelia's feelings for I have not approached any of the little negroes very closely yet, like her I should wish a good application of soap and water, comb & clean clothes.

. . . My paper is full and I have just room to say to both Write often to your

Sara

Clifton Grove, Nov. 7, 1853
Monday Morning

My dear Parents:

. . . Before this you have received another letter from me, but as I have forgotten now what I wrote, I shall answer your questions in order. . . . Our travelling South was entirely by railroad. We passed through Richmond and Petersburg, stopping only long enough to get dinner and tea. We came by cars to Wilson, twenty miles from here, where the Dr. expected his carriage to meet us, but was disappointed and so hired a carriage and came to within seven miles by plank road. The rest of the way is good common road. In the whole of that twenty miles I don't think we passed over a half dozen houses. The road on both sides was bounded by woods, mostly pine, and the trees are much taller and larger than ours. Well, Mother, you like quiet. If you come and see me I'll promise you a plenty of it. Ben was gone eight days with Richard to Beaufort on business and there were just three persons in the house, besides Mrs. Williams, myself and the servants. These were John, a nephew and a niece of the Dr.'s. For a week after we came we had company a plenty in the house. . . . But since the first week, we have been very quiet. I ride horseback very often and enjoy it much. Have been twice to the Dr.'s brother's and stayed all night once. Have also called twice at Mr. Dowell's in Snow Hill, the teacher in the Academy. I find my wardrobe quite too extravagant, I assure you, but Experience is a good teacher and I don't intend to cry over what can't be helped. You have no idea how entirely different everything here is. If you call Long Island behind the times, I don't know what you would call North Carolina. It has been rightly termed Rip Van Winkle. I am a regular curiosity. You can imagine how thickly the country is settled when I tell you that in the whole of Greene County there are only about as many inhabitants as there are in the town of New Hartford, and more than half of these colored. There are only two hundred voters in the county. If you want to know about the country and people you must come and see for I cannot give you a description. The servants are treated better in most respects than I expected. We have one that can read. I asked who taught her "My young mistress, before I came here." She told me that she had had four and they were all kind to her. As for religious privileges, they enjoy all that their masters do. I should say more, for all the preaching I have heard has been more suited to the illiterate than to the educated.

Clifton Grove, Nov. 18, 1853

My dear Parents:

You have before this received mine mailed at Wilmington. We had a very pleasant time there. . . . Our furniture arrived during our absence, all but one bureau & I feel most tired out putting things to order. There is but one closet in our house, so you can imagine that I find some difficulty in knowing where to put things. And Mother William's ways are so entirely different from anything I have ever been used to that I sometimes feel disheartened and discouraged. She is very kind to me & I intend making my will bend to hers in every respect, but I assure you I miss the order and neatness which pervades a Northern home. I can but feel that it would have been much better for us to have gone to housekeeping at once, even if we had deferred our marriage a year. I do not pretend to know much of housekeeping, but I know I could improve on some things here in the way of order. The weather today is summerlike. I have windows up all through the house and doors open. The Dr. and I sat on the piazza for a long time this morning and our roses are still blossoming in the yard. The Synod was in session in Wilmington & we attended several of its meetings. You may imagine I appreciated the opportunity once more of attending an orderly religious service. In the gallery were the colored (I should say slave population, for some are quite too light-colored to be Negroes) people & quite a large proportion of them found their places in the hymn books & joined the singing. So, it seems, that some at least can read. I think I told you in my last, of one (a house servant) in our family who reads and asked me for a Testament. I gave her one, and a tract. But the print of the former is too fine and I intend getting her a larger one. I told my husband and he approved my course. . . . I have been helping to make pumpkin pies, a new dish here, and they promise to be good. We made some a short time since and they were very good. Write soon to your affectionate daughter

Sara

I had forgotten to tell you that servants here have some means for self support. Dr. has one man who will probably lay by fifty or sixty dollars this year. He attended the pine trees and Ben gave him a certain share & he told me the other day he would make that sum.

Clifton Grove, Dec. 10th, 1853

My dear Parents:

   Your last was received Tuesday evening. . . . You ask if I am allowed to do anything. I attend to the part of the house I am in. Keep it in order. However, in it Mrs. Williams has furniture and a right, though she seldom enters it. At present there is sewing a plenty on hands for the servants. At this season the women have each a thick dress, chemise, shoes, & a blanket given them. The men pantaloons & jacket, shirt, blanket & shoes, besides caps & bonnets. The children, too, are clothed in the same materials. Now, many keep a seamstress to do this, but Mother Williams has always done it herself with the assistance of her daughters when they were home. Of course, I choose to do my part. One week we made seven dresses & a few jackets and pantaloons we sent to a poor white woman. I have made two pairs of pantaloons and we are now to work on the underclothes. The servants have three suits of clothes a year and as much more in clothes and money as they choose to earn. But as a whole, they are naturally filthy & it is discouraging to make for them, for it is soon in dirt & rags. There are exceptions, of course. You wish a description of my house—the part I stay in. On the lower floor is the parlor and my room. . . . I have not yet quite regulated upstairs & can't until my things come. I feel the need of good closets, I assure you, but the houses here are built with only a small one under the stairs. On my bed I have the dark quilt you gave me. I assure you I shall be very glad of the petticoat you spoke of giving me. I am sorry I did not bring the cotton one. We need quite as thick clothing as you do. The houses are not as tightly built as with us, and they use fireplaces altogether, and there is a chill in the air. I have been very sorry I did not bring my woolen sack. Then, too, the people most always sit with open doors, even though they sit over the fire shivering. . . . I almost forgot to tell you of my baking. I have made pumpkin pies, or helped, twice & the last, which are best, I made all alone, crust & all. They never had had them before & Ben particularly liked them. So, of course, my success pleased me. Soda biscuits, I have made twice with good success and measure cake. Not until you come here can you imagine how entirely different is their mode of living from the North. They live more heartily. There must always be two or three different kinds of meats on Mrs. Williams' table for breakfast & dinner. Red pepper is much used to flavor meat with the famous "barbecue" of the South & which I believe they esteem above all dishes is roasted pig dressed with red pepper & vinegar. Their bread is corn bread, just meal wet with water & without yeast or saleratus, & biscuit with shortening and without anything to make them light and beaten like crackers. The bread and biscuit are always brought to the table hot. . . .

Every day we speak and think of you and at nights I often dream of you and the pleasant home we have left. I really flatter myself that not many years hence, if our lives are spared, we may remove North. Ben likes the idea & I do, of course. . . . Your affectionate daughter

Sara

PART IV

WOMEN AND
THE NATIONAL MISSION

CHEROKEE WOMEN ADDRESS THEIR NATION

Although official removal did not occur until the 1830s, the United States began pressuring the Cherokees to sell their lands in the east as early as 1808. This 1817 address, presented to the council of head chiefs and warriors and endorsed by Nancy Ward, Beloved Woman of the Cherokee Nation, expresses the opposition of Cherokee women in what is now Georgia to any additional sales. The petition's reference to the land as "ours" may reflect an earlier gender division of labor (changing at the time of this petition) in which women were the agriculturalists.

Amovey [Tenn.] in Council 2nd May 1817

A True Copy}   The Cherokee ladys now being present at the meeting of the Chiefs and warriors in council have thought it their duties as mothers to address their beloved Chiefs and warriors now assembled.

Our beloved children and head men of the Cherokee nation we address you warriors in council we have raised all of you on the land which we now have, which God gave us to inhabit and raise provisions we know that our country has once been extensive but by repeated sales has become circumscribed to a small tract and never thought it our duty to interfere in the disposition of it till now, if a father or mother was to sell all their lands which they had to depend on which their children had to raise their living on which would be indeed bad and to be removed to another country we do not wish to go to an unknown country which we have understood some of our children wish to go over the Mississippi but this act of our children would be like destroying your mothers. You mothers your sisters ask and beg of you not to part with any more of our lands, we say ours you are descendants and take pity on our request, but keep it for our growing children for it was the good will of our creator to place here and you know our father the great president will not allow his white children to take our country away only keep your hands off of paper talks for it is our own country for if it was not they would not ask you to put your hands to paper for it would be impossible to remove us all for as soon as one child is raised we have others in our arms for such is our situation and will consider our circumstance.

Therefore children don't part with any more of our lands but continue

Cherokee Women to Cherokee Council, May 2, 1817, series 1, Andrew Jackson Presidential Papers. Microfilm reel 22. Library of Congress, Manuscripts Division, Washington, D.C.

on it and enlarge your farms and cultivate and raise corn and cotton and we your mothers and sisters will make clothing for you which our father the president has recommended to us all we don't charge anybody for selling our lands, but we have heard such intentions of our children but your talks become true at last and it was our desire to forewarn you all not to part with our lands.

Nancy Ward to her children Warriors to take pity and listen to the talks of your sisters, although I am very old yet cannot but pity the situation in which you will hear of their minds. I have great many grand children which I wish they to do well on our land

Nancy Ward

Attested
A McCoy Clk.   }
Thos. Wilson Secty }

Jenny McIntosh	Widow Tarpin
Caty Harlan	Ally Critington
Elizabeth walker	Cun, o, ah
Susanna Fox	Miss Asty walker
Widow Gunrod	Mrs. M. Morgan
Widow Woman Holder	Mrs. Nancy Fields

Jerusha Swain, a native of Vermont, was a missionary schoolteacher to the Cherokee Indians at Dwight Mission in Indian Territory (now Oklahoma). The Cherokees had been "removed" from the southeastern United States in the relocation of the 1830s known as "The Trail of Tears," in which as many as one-quarter of the Cherokees died. Swain's presence in the Cherokee Nation reflected both the reach of the American home missionary movement and new opportunities in the 1850s for women in the field of education.

Dwight Mission, March 26th, 1852
My dear Mother,

Your kind letter of the 28th of Feb. was very joyfully welcomed last evening. I suppose that we may not expect to get letters much short of about 24 days, they have been known to come in 18 days but not often, they have not in this part of the world the facilities for transporting the mail that they have in New England. . . .

Sabbath Eve 28th. I am thinking that perhaps you would like to know how we spend our Sabbaths here, so I will give you a history of today. At ten o'clock in the morning we have a Sabbath school, which lasts about an hour, had today about twenty scholars, most of them my day scholars, the preaching service commences at twelve. We have but one sermon, I like Mr. Willey very much but have not yet got so that I can enjoy preaching with an interpreter very much. The interuption seems to break up the connection, just now he is very much troubled to get a good interpreter, the one that he has employed has left him to enter the seminary. I should like to have you see our congregation just once, I know that you would be interested in them, for they are an interesting people. But they do not look much like a New England congregation either in dress or appearance. The men almost all wear a sort of hunting frock instead of a coat, they are made generally of calico and ruffled all round, but sometimes of some kind of checked flannel which they manufacture themselves. They are made about like your old calico sack that you wear to wash in, the women some of them wear sunbonnets, but the full blooded Cherokees all wear handkerchiefs on their heads, they will come in & sit till they get tired & then perhaps jump up & run out, sometimes the same ones going out & coming in two or three times during service.

Jerusha Swain, letters, 1851–1860, State Historical Society of Wisconsin, Archives Division, Madison, Wisc. The editors are grateful to Kathy Borkowski for her help in locating this document.

Sat. April 3d. . . . I have 30 very interesting scholars, nearly all of them very anxious to improve, & ready to make a good deal of exertion for it, they are of all ages from 4 to 20. I supposed that I had got my number completed two weeks ago, but yesterday a tall fellow made his appearance, some 18 or 20 years old, dressed in an orange coat faced with mazarine blue, whom I suppose I shall have to number with my pupils. O what a solemn thought, that they have all of their immortal souls to be saved or lost. How much may be depending on me on the influence that I exert on their souls, what shall be their future state, fearful responsibility! Who is sufficient for these things? Three of my dear pupils have lately hoped that they had given their hearts to the Savior. Pray for them my dear Mother that they may hold out to the end, and will you not pray for me to that I may be fitted for my work, I fear I have not in my heart any real love for souls, or desire for their salvation. I have such a reluctance to saying any thing to them on the subject.

Your affectionate daughter Jerusha . . .

Dwight, Friday Eve, May 14, 1852

Sat. 22 . . . I got to housekeeping thursday night, I have a good large room and chamber over it, my room has three windows & two doors directly oposite to each other, one of them opening into a piazza, in it is a bed with a good cotton mattress on it, six chairs and a large rocking chair and table and lounge, a fire place with a closet on one side and cupboard on the other, a wash stand, wash bowl & pitcher, two candle sticks snuffer bellows, shovel & tongs, a broom, dust brush & floor brush, together with some smaller articles not worthy of mention. I have the furniture left by Miss Stetson, a teacher who was here nearly thirty years & died a few years ago, there is a good yarn carpet that she made, that I can have whenever I am a mind to put it down, & a beauro that I could have had, if I had not taken one. It is a log house of course but quite a comfortable one, the post office is on the other end of it, so you can see that I can get the mail without much trouble, Now for *my family,* it consists of two girls, the older Rosella Tally is 16 years old, I have been acquainted with her but a few days, but I think I shall like her very well, her mother was educated here, and of course has been able to teach her more than most Cherokee mothers can, she is quite anxious to be in school, and has been begging for a long time to get in here, this was one reason of my changing sooner than I should otherwise have done, you would not think to see her that she had any Cherokee blood about her, indeed I have but few scholars that do look it. I have no more than three or four full blooded Cherokees. My other girl is Nancy Watts, she is about

10 years old, she has been to school most of the time since I commenced, and I have felt a good deal of interest in her especially because she had no one to care for her, her parents both died when she was quite young, and since that she has lived with her grandmother, till last summer she died, and the only person in the world who takes any interest in her is an uncle, who is a wild young man a gambler & drunkerd, you can judge how well fitted he is to bring her up, he says himself that he cannot bring her up as she ought to be and is very anxious that I should take her, she is staying with me now but I have not yet told him whether I will keep her or not. I think that I shall tell him that I will if he will let me have her per capita[1] to clothe her with. I presume he will be willing to although I have not yet seen him, if I keep her I have got every thing to do for her, she has but one decent dress & not a change of under garments, & then it will take as much as two or three weeks to get her clean, head and all, you know I have not a very good faculty for getting along with sewing when I am in school, She can read very well but cannot talk much english, and I do not suppose can understand much that she reads, I have a good deal of difficulty in making her understand what I say to her, I have to do it by signs more than any other way, but she has industrious habits, & is very quick to learn and anxious to do everything she can to please me. . . .

Dwight Mission June 17th [1852]
    . . . Nancy is I think improving fast, I find that I am getting to love her very much, she begins to talk a very little & understands more [of] what I say to her, she sews remarkably well for a girl of her age, & has a good deal of tact in planning and fixing her work she is very anxious [to] please me, I have but one difficulty with her & that is a disposition a little sullen when she is not suited, how shall I get along with such a trait of character. I should like a little of mothers advice, it is a trait of character which the cherokee girls are very apt to have. . . .
    Wed. 30th.   We have had a female prayer meeting this P.M. at my room it is the first one, & we had but a few present but I cannot but hope that it will be fully attended & be attended with good results, there are quite a number of Cherokee women who are members of the church & that I think will attend. . . .
    In haste, Yours Truly, Jerusha

Dwight Mission, Dec. 12th /52
    . . . What would you say if I should tell you that I had taken another [Cherokee girl into the household]. I almost felt as though I might be

1. Federal payments negotiated as part of land cession or removal treaties.

doing wrong to make any addition to my cares; for they are now more than any teacher ought to have out of school, & do justice to her school, but I could not resist the temptation, for I wanted some one to love that would return a small [torn]—of it & I am not sorry that I have taken her, as yet, & hope I shall not be, her name is Ellen Coval. She is six years old, and the most affectionate disposition that I have met with in the Nation, her father was a public school teacher, a New England man & well educated, his wife died soon after he came to this country & he married, a Cherokee girl (Ellen's mother) that had been educated at the Mission. He died about two years ago, & since that her mother has most sadly fallen from the paths of virtue, & rectitude. Mrs. Hitchcock had taken Mary her sister two years older, and she had left Ellen with an indian woman who could not speak a word of english. She came here week before last to see Mary & staid a few days, it did seem hard to have the two sisters parted, & to have her left too, to go to ruin, as she most certainly would, that the appeal was more than I could resist, she seemed to think that I liked her, and she would look up in to my face with such an inquiring expression, as though . . . she thought I would let her stay with me. She sleeps with me, & I do not have her away from my side night or day. I mean to keep her from associating with the other girls, except in my presence, as little as possible, she has not a bit of indian disposition about her now, & I do not mean she shall imbibe any of it, if I can help it. It is pleasant to have some one that I can caress, & treat a little as a mother would a child. Nancy I never can, for she has too much indian pride to allow it.

I begin to understand a little dear Mother of the trials that you must have had with me when I was young, though perhaps in a different way, for my disposition was not like these girls, but I know that I cannot know all of a mothers anxiety, however slight a taste I may now have of it. I know this, that I never can repay a one hundredth part of all that you have done and suffered & borne with me. I wish sometimes that I could sit down & have a good talk with you about the girls, a Cherokee girls disposition is the worst to get along with that I know any thing about, they are either all of the time angry with one another or else on such intimate terms that they are silly, & then you never know whether what you say will offend or be taken in good humor. Then any kind of reproof is of course scolding & your considdered cross. I used to be rather sensitive about being called cross but I believe that I am getting bravely over it, I am even getting to consider it quite an honor. . . .

In haste your affectionate Daughter Jerusha . . .

Dwight, Oct. 1st, 1856
My own dear Mother,

. . . I have let Nancy go up to help Mrs. David Palmer a while, & I find that I miss her a great deal. I did not reallize before how much she helped me, since I was sick the 1st of Sept. she has done all of my washing besides a great deal of other work. . . .

What would you or Kate say to my bringing you a little girl in case I should go home next summer. I think that perhaps Mrs. Petit would be willing to have me take her little Nancy. She is a very good disposition, & is quite a pretty child is about 8 years old, has light hair, blue eyes & a good skin. She has always been my favorite among Mrs. Petits children, especially the girls. I think her mother would like to have her where she could get a good education & would be well cared for. I thought perhaps Kate would like to have a little girl, she would find one a great help to her. I am not certain that her mother would let her go, but I thought I would speak of it so that in case she would, I would know what either of you thought of it. . . .

Love to all, Your aff daughter, J E Swain

Dwight Mission, Apr. 6th 1858
My dear Mother & Sister,

. . . I wish you could be here for a little while and see the change in many of the people about us. . . . The meetings are much more fully attended than they were when I went away. One great characteristic of the converts seems to be a desire to be useful, they are becoming interested in the operations of the Board, & are beginning to think that they can do something themselves. One of the members of the church gave five dollars the other day, & there has been about twenty dollars contributed in the monthly concert the past year. The childrens sewing society has earned six, and the women in the neighborhood have made a quilt & sold it for twelve, so you see that all together it makes quite a little sum, and if you could see out of what poverty it has all come you would wonder at it still more. . . .

Tuesday eve. 13th. Two or three nights ago I heard a knock at the door, and who should come in but Ellen Coval, it seems her mother had heard that I had come and sent her back without waiting to hear from me, just like her. I am sorry, for I cannot keep her. I had decided that I would not keep any girls except Nancy and Mary Whirlwind. I do not think I am strong enough to endure the care of a large family out of school. . . .

With a great deal of love for all, J. E. Swain

Dwight, March 6th/61

My own dear mother,

. . . I have today decided that I will go home this spring. . . . I have a good many plans in my head that I want to carry out before I go, among others I want to help Nancy all I can towards getting ready to settle in life, which she probably will do about the time I get ready to start.

. . . I feel sad at the thought of leaving for I have been here so long that I have some very dear friends that it will be hard to part from, & I have become so much assimilated to the people that I feel more like a Cherokee than anything else. I hardly know how I can act in civilized society. . . .

Yours Truly, J. E. Swain

EULALIA PÉREZ IN MEXICAN CALIFORNIA

This rare early nineteenth-century memoir of a Spanish-Mexican woman in Alta California, then a northern province of Mexico, offers some insights into the social relationships and racial and gender hierarchies of Spanish colonial North America. In addition to sending soldier-settlers to exploit the land, Spain set up Catholic friars' missions, like the one where Eulalia Pérez lived, to convert the indigenous population to Christianity and harness their labor. Both the workers and the "neophytes" (newly converted) referred to by Pérez were Indians. The United States acquired Alta California through the Treaty of Guadalupe Hidalgo, which ended the Mexican-American War of 1846–48.

I, Eulalia Pérez, was born in the Presidio of Loreto in Baja California.

My father's name was Diego Pérez, and he was employed in the Navy Department of said presidio; my mother's name was Antonia Rosalia Cota. Both were pure white.

I do not remember the date of my birth, but I do know that I was fifteen years old when I married Miguel Antonio Guillén, a soldier of the garrison at Loreto Presidio. During the time of my stay at Loreto I had three children—two boys, who died there in infancy, one girl, Petra, who was eleven years old when we moved to San Diego, and another boy, Isidoro, who came with us to this [Alta] California.

I lived eight years in San Diego with my husband, who continued his service in the garrison of the presidio, and I attended women in childbirth.

I had relatives in the vicinity of Los Angeles, and even farther north, and asked my husband repeatedly to take me to see them. My husband did not want to come along, and the commandant of the presidio did not allow me to go, either, because there was no other woman who knew midwifery.

In San Diego everyone seemed to like me very much, and in the most important homes they treated me affectionately. Although I had my own house, they arranged for me to be with those families almost all the time, even including my children.

In 1812 I was in San Juan Capistrano attending Mass in church when

Eulalia Pérez, "An Old Woman and Her Recollections," in *Three Memoirs of Mexican California*, trans. Vivian C. Fisher and others ([Berkeley, Calif.]: Friends of the Bancroft Library, University of California, 1988; [San Francisco]: Arion Press), pp. 74–82. From the original manuscript, in Spanish, "Una Vieja y Sus Recuerdos," in the Bancroft Library.

a big earthquake occurred, and the tower fell down. I dashed through the sacristy, and in the doorway the people knocked me down and stepped over me. I was pregnant and could not move. Soon afterwards I returned to San Diego and almost immediately gave birth to my daughter María Antonia who still lives here in San Gabriel.

After being in San Diego eight years, we came to the Mission of San Gabriel, where my husband had been serving in the guard. In 1814, on the first of October, my daughter María del Rosario was born, the one who is the wife if Michael White and in whose home I am now living. . . .

When I first came to San Diego the only house in the presidio was that of the commandant and the barracks where the soldiers lived.

There was no church, and Mass was said in a shelter made out of some old walls covered with branches, by the missionary who came from the Mission of San Diego.

The first sturdy house built in San Diego belonged to a certain Sánchez, the father of Don Vicente Sánchez, alcalde of Los Angeles and deputy of the Territorial Council. The house was very small, and everyone went to look at it as though it were a palace. That house was built about a year after I arrived in San Diego.

My last trip to San Diego would have been in the year 1818, when my daughter María del Rosario was four years old. I seem to remember that I was there when the revolutionaries came to California. I recall that they put a stranger in irons and that afterwards they took them off.

Some three years later I came back to San Gabriel. The reason for my return was that the missionary at San Gabriel, Father José Sánchez, wrote to Father Fernando at San Diego—who was his cousin or uncle—asking him to speak to the commandant of the presidio at San Diego requesting him to give my son Isidoro Guillén a guard to escort me here with all my family. The commandant agreed.

When we arrived here Father José Sánchez lodged me and my family temporarily in a small house until work could be found for me. There I was with my five daughters—my son Isidoro Guillén was taken into service as a soldier in the mission guard.

At that time Father Sánchez was between sixty and seventy years of age—a white Spaniard, heavy set, of medium stature—a very good, kind, charitable man. He, as well as his companion Father José María Zalvidea, treated the Indians very well, and the two were much loved by the Spanish-speaking people and by the neophytes and other Indians.

Father Zalvidea was very tall, a little heavy, white; he was a man of advanced age. I heard it said that they summoned Zalvidea to San Juan Capistrano because there was no missionary priest there. Many years

later, when Father Antonio Peyri fled from San Luis Obispo—it was rumored that they were going to kill the priests—I learned that Zalvidea
was very sick, and that actually he had been out of his mind ever since
they took him away from San Gabriel, for he did not want to abandon
the mission. I repeat that the father was afraid, and two Indians came
from San Luis Rey to San Juan Capistrano; in a rawhide cart, making him
as comfortable as they could, they took him to San Luis, where he died
soon after from the grueling hardships he had suffered on the way.

Father Zalvidea was very much attached to his children at the mission,
as he called the Indians that he himself had converted to Christianity. He
traveled personally, sometimes on horseback and at other times on foot,
and crossed mountains until he came to remote Indian settlements, in
order to bring them to our religion.

Father Zalvidea introduced many improvements in the Mission of San
Gabriel and made it progress a very great deal in every way. Not content
with providing abundantly for the neophytes, he planted [fruit] trees in
the mountains, far away from the mission, in order that the untamed
Indians might have food when they passed by those spots.

When I came to San Gabriel the last time, there were only two women
in this part of California who knew how to cook [well]. One was María
Luisa Cota, wife of Claudio López, superintendent of the mission; the
other was María Ignacia Amador, wife of Francisco Javier Alvarado. She
knew how to cook, sew, read and write and take care of the sick. She was
a good healer. She did needlework and took care of the church vestments.
She taught a few children to read and write in her home, but did not
conduct a formal school.

On special holidays, such as the day of our patron saint, Easter, etc.,
the two women were called upon to prepare the feast and to make the
meat dishes, sweets, etc.

The priests wanted to help me out because I was a widow burdened
with a family. They looked for some way to give me work without offending the other women. Fathers Sánchez and Zalvidea conferred and decided that they would have first one woman, then the other and finally
me, do the cooking, in order to determine who did it best, with the aim
of putting the one who surpassed the others in charge of the Indian cooks
so as to teach them how to cook. With that idea in mind, the gentlemen
who were to decide on the merits of the three dinners were warned ahead
of time. One of these gentlemen was Don Ignacio Tenorio, whom they
called the Royal Judge, and who came to live and die in the company of
Father Sánchez. He was a very old man, and when he went out, wrapped

up in a muffler, he walked very slowly with the aid of a cane. His walk consisted only of going from the missionary's house to the church.

The other judges who also were to give their opinions were Don Ignacio Mancisidor, merchant; Don Pedro Narváez, naval official; Sergeant José Antonio Pico—who later became lieutenant, brother of Governor Pío Pico; Don Domingo Romero, who was my assistant when I was housekeeper at the mission; Claudio López, superintendent at the mission; besides the missionaries. These gentlemen, whenever they were at the mission, were accustomed to eat with the missionaries.

On the days agreed upon for the three dinners, they attended. No one told me anything regarding what it was all about, until one day Father Sánchez called me and said, "Look, Eulalia, tomorrow it is your turn to prepare dinner—because María Ignacia and Luisa have already done so. We shall see what kind of a dinner you will give us tomorrow."

The next day I went to prepare the food. I made several kinds of soup, a variety of meat dishes and whatever else happened to pop into my head and I knew how to prepare. The Indian cook, named Tomás, watched me attentively, as the missionary had told him to do.

At dinner time those mentioned came. When the meal was concluded, Father Sánchez asked for their opinions about it, beginning with the eldest, Don Ignacio Tenorio. This gentleman pondered awhile, saying that for many years he had not eaten the way he had eaten that day—that he doubted that they ate any better at the King's table. The others also praised the dinner highly.

Then the missionary called Tomás and asked him which of the three women he liked best—which one of them knew the most about cooking. He answered that I did.

Because of all this, employment was provided for me at the mission. At first they assigned me two Indians so that I could show them how to cook, the one named Tomás and the other called "The Gentile." I taught them so well that I had the satisfaction of seeing them turn out to be very good cooks, perhaps the best in all this part of the country.

The missionaries were very satisfied; this made them think more highly of me. I spent about a year teaching those two Indians. I did not have to do the work, only direct them, because they already had learned a few of the fundamentals.

After this, the missionaries conferred among themselves and agreed to hand over the mission keys to me. This was in 1821, if I remember correctly. I recall that my daughter María del Rosario was seven years old when she became seriously ill and was attended by Father José Sánchez, who took such excellent care of her that finally we could rejoice at not having lost her. At that time I was already the housekeeper.

The duties of the housekeeper were many. In the first place, every day she handed out the rations for the mess hut. To do this she had to count the unmarried women, bachelors, day-laborers, vaqueros—both those with saddles and those who rode bareback. Besides that, she had to hand out daily rations to the heads of households. In short, she was responsible for the distribution of supplies to the Indian population and to the missionaries' kitchen. She was in charge of the key to the clothing storehouse where materials were given out for dresses for the unmarried and married women and children. Then she also had to take care of cutting and making clothes for the men.

Furthermore, she was in charge of cutting and making the vaqueros' outfits, from head to foot—that is, for the vaqueros who rode in saddles. Those who rode bareback received nothing more than their cotton blanket and loin-cloth, while those who rode in saddles were dressed the same way as the Spanish-speaking inhabitants; that is, they were given shirt, vest, jacket, trousers, hat, cowboy boots, shoes and spurs; and a saddle, bridle and lariat for the horse. Besides, each vaquero was given a big silk or cotton handkerchief, and a sash of Chinese silk or Canton crepe, or whatever there happened to be in the storehouse.

They put under my charge everything having to do with clothing. I cut and fitted, and my five daughters sewed up the pieces. When they could not handle everything, the father was told, and then women from the town of Los Angeles were employed, and the father paid them.

Besides this, I had to attend to the soap-house, which was very large, to the wine-presses, and to the olive-crushers that produced oil, which I worked in myself. Under my direction and responsibility, Domingo Romero took care of changing the liquid.

Luis the soap-maker had charge of the soap-house, but I directed everything.

I handled the distribution of leather, calf-skin, chamois, sheepskin, Morocco leather, fine scarlet cloth, nails, thread, silk, etc.—everything having to do with the making of saddles, shoes and what was needed for the belt- and shoe-making shops.

Every week I delivered supplies for the troops and Spanish-speaking servants. These consisted of beans, corn, garbanzos, lentils, candles, soap and lard. To carry out this distribution, they placed at my disposal an Indian servant named Lucio, who was trusted completely by the missionaries.

When it was necessary, some of my daughters did what I could not find the time to do. Generally, the one who was always at my side was my daughter María del Rosario.

After all my daughters were married—the last one was Rita, about 1832 or 1833—Father Sánchez undertook to persuade me to marry First Lieutenant Juan Mariné, a Spaniard from Catalonia, a widower with family who had served in the artillery. I did not want to get married, but the father told me that Mariné was a very good man—as, in fact, he turned out to be—besides, he had some money, although he never turned his cash-box over to me. I gave in to the father's wishes because I did not have the heart to deny him anything when he had been father and mother to me and to all my family.

I served as housekeeper of the mission for twelve or fourteen years, until about two years after the death of Father José Sánchez, which occurred in this same mission. . . .

In the Mission of San Gabriel there was a large number of neophytes. The married ones lived on their rancherías with their small children. There were two divisions for the unmarried ones: one for the women, called the nunnery, and another for the men. They brought girls from the ages of seven, eight or nine years to the nunnery, and they were brought up there. They left to get married. They were under the care of a mother in the nunnery, an Indian. During the time I was at the mission this matron was named Polonia—they called her "Mother Superior." The alcalde was in charge of the unmarried men's division. Every night both divisions were locked up, the keys were delivered to me, and I handed them over to the missionaries.

A blind Indian named Andresillo stood at the door of the nunnery and called out each girl's name, telling her to come in. If any girl was missing at admission time, they looked for her the following day and brought her to the nunnery. Her mother, if she had one, was brought in and punished for having detained her, and the girl was locked up for having been careless in not coming in punctually.

In the morning the girls were let out. First they went to Father Zalvidea's Mass, for he spoke the Indian language; afterwards they went to the mess hut to have breakfast, which sometimes consisted of corn gruel with chocolate, and on holidays with sweets and bread. On other days, ordinarily they had boiled barley and beans and meat. After eating breakfast each girl began the task that had been assigned to her beforehand—sometimes it was at the looms, or unloading, or sewing, or whatever there was to be done.

When they worked at unloading, at eleven o'clock they had to come up to one or two of the carts that carried refreshments out to the Indians working in the fields. This refreshment was made of water with vinegar and sugar, or sometimes with lemon and sugar. I was the one who made up that refreshment and sent it out, so the Indians would not get sick. That is what the missionaries ordered.

All work stopped at eleven, and at twelve o'clock the Indians came to the mess hut to eat barley and beans with meat and vegetables. At one o'clock they returned to their work, which ended for the day at sunset. Then all came to the mess hut to eat supper, which consisted of gruel with meat, sometimes just pure gruel. Each Indian carried his own bowl and the mess attendant filled it up with the allotted portion. . . .

The Indians were taught the various jobs for which they showed an aptitude. Others worked in the fields, or took care of the horses, cattle, etc. Still others were carters, oxherds, etc.

At the mission, coarse cloth, serapes, and blankets were woven, and saddles, bridles, boots, shoes and similar things were made. There was a soap-house, and a big carpenter shop as well as a small one, where those who were just beginning to learn carpentry worked; when they had mastered enough they were transferred to the big shop.

Wine and oil, bricks and adobe bricks were also made. Chocolate was manufactured from cocoa, brought in from the outside; and sweets were made. Many of these sweets, made by my own hands, were sent to Spain by Father Sánchez.

There was a rancher in every department, an instructed Indian who was Christianized. A white man headed the looms, but when the Indians were finally skilled, he withdrew.

My daughters and I made the chocolate, oil, sweets, lemonade and other things ourselves. I made plenty of lemonade—it was even bottled and sent to Spain.

The Indians also were taught to pray. A few of the more intelligent ones were taught to read and write. Father Zalvidea taught the Indians to pray in their Indian tongue; some Indians learned music and played instruments and sang at Mass. The sextons and pages who helped with Mass were Indians of the mission.

The punishments that were meted out were the stocks and confinement. When the misdemeanor was serious, the delinquent was taken to the guard, where they tied him to a pipe or a post and gave him twenty-five or more lashes, depending on his crime. Sometimes they put them in the head-stocks; other times they passed a musket from one leg to the other and fastened it there, and also they tied their hands. That punishment, called "The Law of Bayona," was very painful.

But Fathers Sánchez and Zalvidea were always very considerate with the Indians. I would not want to say what others did because they did not live in the mission. . . .

REACHING OREGON

More than a quarter of a million migrants traveled the overland route from the midwest to Oregon and California between 1840 and 1860, leaving behind their homes and communities in hopes of gaining land and wealth in unknown territories. Married women, for whom such a move might easily mean increased drudgery without correspondingly improved opportunity, were often very reluctant to leave their friends and neighbors. And many of these ventures—like the one described below—did not turn out as planned. Elizabeth Geer (then Elizabeth Smith) promised to keep a diary of her experiences to send back to her friends in La Porte, Indiana. She wrote at the close of the day, after her children were asleep.

Dear Friends—By your request I have endeavored to keep a record of our journey from "the States" to Oregon, though it is poorly done, owing to my having a young babe and besides a large family to do for; and, worst of all, my education is very limited.

April 21, 1847—Commenced our journey from La Porte, Indiana, to Oregon; made fourteen miles

[After six months of overland travel the party has reached the Columbia River.]

November 9—Finds us still in trouble. Waves dashing over our raft and we already stinting ourselves in provisions. My husband started this morning to hunt provisions. Left no man with us except our oldest boy. It is very cold. The icicles are hanging from our wagon beds to the water. Tonight about dusk Adam Polk expired. No one with him but his wife and myself. We sat up all night with him while the waves was dashing below.

November 10—Finds us still waiting for calm weather. My husband returned at 2 o'clock. Brought 50 pounds of beef on his back 12 miles, which he had bought from another company. By this time the water became calm and we started once more, but the wind soon began to blow and we were forced to land. My husband and boy were an hour and a half after dark getting the raft landed and made fast while the water ran knee deep over our raft, the wind blew, and was freezing cold. We women and children did not attempt to get out of our wagons tonight.

November 11—Laid by most all day. Started this evening. Ran about three miles and landed after dark. Here we found Welch and our boys

Transactions of the 35th Annual Reunion of the Oregon Pioneer Association (Portland, Ore.: Chausse-Prudhomme, 1908), pp. 153, 171–78.

with our cattle, for they could be driven no farther on this side for mountains. Here was a ferry for the purpose of ferrying immigrants' cattle.

November 12—Ferried our cattle over the river and buried Mr. Polk. Rain all day. We are living entirely on beef.

November 18—My husband is sick. It rains and snows. We start this morning around the falls with our wagons. We have 5 miles to go. I carry my babe and lead, or rather carry, another through snow, mud and water, almost to my knees. It is the worst road that a team could possibly travel. I went ahead with my children and I was afraid to look behind me for fear of seeing the wagons turn over into the mud and water with everything in them. My children gave out with cold and fatigue and could not travel, and the boys had to unhitch the oxen and bring them and carry the children on to camp. I was so cold and numb that I could not tell by the feeling that I had any feet at all. We started this morning at sunrise and did not get to camp until after dark, and there was not one dry thread on one of us—not even my babe. I had carried my babe and I was so fatigued that I could scarcely speak or step. When I got here I found my husband lying in Welch's wagon, very sick. He had brought Mrs. Polk down the day before and was taken sick here. We had to stay up all night tonight for our wagons are left half-way back. I have not told half we suffered. I am not adequate to the task. Here was some hundreds camped, waiting for boats to come and take them down the Columbia to Vancouver or Portland or Oregon City.

November 19—My husband is sick and can have but little care. Rain all day.

November 20—Rain all day. It is almost an impossibility to cook, and quite so to keep warm or dry. I froze or chilled my feet so that I cannot wear a shoe, so I have to go around in the cold water barefooted.

November 21—Rain all day. The whole care of everything falls upon my shoulders. I cannot write any more at present.

November 27—Embarked once more on the Columbia on a flatboat. Ran all day, though the waves threatened hard to sink us. Passed Fort Vancouver in the night. Landed a mile below. My husband never has left his bed since he was taken sick.

November 28—Still moving on the water.

November 29—Landed at Portland on the Willamette, 12 miles above the mouth, at 11 o'clock at night.

November 30—Raining. This morning I ran about trying to get a house to get into with my sick husband. At last I found a small, leaky concern, with two families already in it. Mrs. Polk had got down before us. She and another widow was in this house. My family and Welch's went in with them, and you could have stirred us with a stick. Welch and my oldest boy was driving the cattle around. My children and I carried up a bed. The distance was nearly a quarter of a mile. Made it down on the floor in the mud. I got some men to carry my husband up through the rain and lay him on it, and he never was out of that shed until he was carried out in his coffin. Here lay five us us bedfast at one time . . . and we had no money, and what few things we had left that would bring money, I had to sell. I had to give 10 cents a pound for fresh pork, 75 cents per bushel for potatoes, 4 cents a pound for fish. There are so many of us sick that I cannot write any more at present. I have not time to write much, but I thought it would be interesting to know what kind of weather we have in the winter.

1848—January 14—Rain this morning. Warm weather. We suppose it has rained half of the time that I have neglected writing.

January 15—My husband is still alive, but very sick. There is no medicine here except at Fort Vancouver, and the people there will not sell one bit—not even a bottle of wine.

January 16—Warm and dry. We are still living in the old, leaky shed in Portland. It is six miles below Vancouver, down the Columbia and 12 miles up the Willamette. Portland has two white houses and one brick and three wood-colored frame houses and a few cabins. . . .

January 20—Cool and dry. Soldiers are collecting here from every part of Oregon to go and fight the Indians in middle Oregon in consequence of the massacre at Whitman's mission. I think there were 17 men killed at the massacre, but no women or children, except Whitman's wife. They killed every white man there except one, and he was an Englishman. They took all the young women for wives. Robbed them of their clothing and everything. The Oregon government bought the prisoners at a dear rate, and then gave the Indians fight; but one white man, I believe, was killed in the war, and not many Indians. The murderers escaped. . . .

January 31—Rain all day. If I could tell you how we suffer you would not believe it. Our house, or rather a shed joined to a house, leaks all over. The roof descends in such a manner as to make the rain run right down into the fire. I have dipped as much as six pails of water off of our dirt hearth in one night. Here I sit up, night after night, with my poor sick husband, all alone, and expecting him every day to die. I neglected to tell you that Welch's and all the rest moved off and left us. Mr. Smith has not been moved off his bed for six weeks only by lifting him by each corner of the sheet, and I had hard work to get help enough for that, let alone getting watchers. I have not undressed to lie down for six weeks.

Besides all our sickness, I had a cross little babe to take care of. Indeed, I cannot tell you half.

February 1—Rain all day. This day my dear husband, my last remaining friend, died.

February 2—Today we buried my earthly companion. Now I know what none but widows know; that is, how comfortless is that of a widow's life, especially when left in a strange land, without money or friends, and the care of seven children. Cloudy. . . .

Butteville, Oregon Territory, Yamhill County, September 2, 1850
Dear and Estimable Friends, Mrs. Paulina Foster and Mrs. Cynthia Ames:

I promised when I saw you last to write to you when I got to Oregon, and I done it faithfully, but as I never have received an answer, I do not know whether you got my letter and diary or not, consequently I do not know what to write now. I wrote four sheets full and sent it to you, but now I have not time to write. I write now to know whether you got my letter; and I will try to state a few things again. My husband was taken sick before we got to any settlement, and never was able to walk afterwards. He died at Portland, on the Willamette River, after an illness of two months. I will not attempt to describe my troubles since I saw you. Suffice it to say that I was left a widow with the care of seven children in a foreign land, without one solitary friend, as one might say, in the land of the living; but this time I will only endeavor to hold up the bright side of the picture. I lived a widow one year and four months. My three boys started for the gold mines, and it was doubtful to me whether I ever saw them again. Perhaps you will think it strange that I let such young boys go; but I was willing and helped them off in as good style as I could. They packed through by land. Russell Welch went by water. The boys never saw Russell in the mines. Well, after the boys were gone, it is true I had plenty of cows and hogs and plenty of wheat to feed them on and to make my bread. Indeed, I was well off if I had only known it; but I lived in a remote place where my strength was of little use to me. I could get nothing to do, and you know I could not live without work. I employed myself in teaching my children: yet that did not fully occupy my mind. I became as poor as a snake, yet I was in good health, and never was so nimble since I was a child. I could run a half a mile without stopping to breathe. Well, I thought perhaps I had better try my fortune again; so on the 24th of June, 1849, I was married to a Mr. Joseph Geer, a man 14 years older than myself, though young enough for me. He is the father of ten children. They are all married, but two boys and two girls. He is a Yankee from Connecticut and he is a Yankee in every sense of the word, as I told you he would be if it ever proved my lot to marry again. I did not marry rich, but my husband is very industrious, and is as kind to me as I can ask. Indeed, he sometimes provokes me for trying to humor me so much. He is a stout, healthy man for one of his age.

. . . At this time we are all well but Perley. I cannot answer for him; he has gone to the Umpqua for some money due him. The other two are working for four dollars a day. The two oldest boys have got three town lots in quite a stirring place called Lafayette in Yamhill County. Perley has four horses. A good Indian horse is worth one hundred dollars. A good American cow is worth sixty dollars. My boys live about 25 miles from me, so that I cannot act in the capacity of a mother to them; so you will guess it is not all sunshine with me, for you know my boys are not old enough to do without a mother. Russell Welch done very well in the mines. He made about twenty hundred dollars. He lives 30 miles below me in a little town called Portland on the Willamette River. Sarah has got her third son. It has been one year since I saw her. Adam Polk's two youngest boys live about wherever they see fit. The oldest, if he is alive, is in California. There is some ague in this country this season, but neither I nor my children, except those that went to California, have had a day's sickness since we came to Oregon.

I believe I will say no more until I hear from you. Write as soon as possible and tell me everything. My husband will close this epistle.

Elizabeth Geer

A MORAL REFORMER MAKES HER ROUNDS

Margaret Prior (1773–1842) served as city missionary for the New York Female Moral Reform Society, a voluntary association dedicated to converting prostitutes and to abolishing the double standard of morality for men and women. These accounts of her visits appeared in the 1830s in the society's widely circulated newspaper, the Advocate of Moral Reform, *which also published the names of men who patronized prostitutes or seduced unmarried women.*

Case of a dying wife. — .... An unhappy mother called to-day and related the afflicting circumstances in which she was placed, and requested some aid in her attempts to find a poor lost daughter. She said she had four children, lived in a miserable basement in Church street, and obtained bread for her family by selling small articles in the market. Her eldest daughter was away, and she had been in the habit of leaving the second girl (who was in her fifteenth year) to look after two young children, while she went out to attend to her business. Some weeks since, she came home at night as usual, and to her surprise and grief, found this daughter missing. She soon learned from the neighbors sufficient to satisfy her, that she had been decoyed away through the artifices of a vile woman who lived near. She had sought her in different parts of the city, but as yet utterly in vain. She seemed to think that in some places to which she had been directed, the child had been secreted and a story framed to deceive her. Her heart seemed agonized in view of the condition of her wretched lost one, and how could it be otherwise. Truly this "mother's feelings could not be conceived, but by a mother." From her conversation one would suppose that she had found some consolation in God, in this hour of darkness. . . .

Interview with a family of Jews. — . . . Calling at one stately edifice near, I found it occupied by intelligent and benevolent Jews. I was conducted to an upper room where I found a mother, grandmother, and great-grandmother. The room was hung round with ancient pictures, according well with the appearance of its occupants. The Lord prepared the way for me to converse freely with them respecting Jesus Christ and his salvation. The old ladies entirely rejected me, and expressed themselves strong in the faith of a Messiah yet to come; still they treated me with great polite-

Margaret Prior, *Walks of Usefulness; or, Reminiscences of Mrs. Margaret Prior,* comp. S. R. Ingraham (New York: Am. F.M.R. Society, 1853), pp. 87–89, 90–91, 95–97, 123–25, 139–40, 202–4, 206–7.

ness. When I left, the younger lady accompanied me down stairs and then stated that she did not believe as her friends did; that the word of Jesus affected her much; that she often prayed to him in her heart, and longed for the day to come when she might teach him to her children, but was not yet sufficiently strong. I left, with an invitation to call again, and much encouraged with the hope that the redemption of this ancient people of God is drawing nigh. . . .

Conversion of a Catholic. — 17th. . . . In——street, near Broadway, I found some time since, in a large house where every room was occupied by a different family, a very interesting young female, whose little children (twins) were both sick. She seemed willing to converse, and told me with tears that she would pray, but was unable to find time to read her prayer-book, for she was a Catholic. Her youthful and lovely appearance interested me deeply, and I inquired into her former history. She is a well-educated and highly respectable woman from Ireland, and having formed no acquaintances among her inferior neighbors, she is desolate indeed. She said she was reaping the bitter fruits of disobedience to parents, as she had married a young man who lived in her father's family, and fled with him to this country. He could now get very little employment, and they were suffering for the necessaries of life. I spent several hours with her, and begged of her to repent, and humble herself before God, and her parents, as that sin seemed to lie so heavy on her heart; assuring her that God would teach her to pray without a prayer-book, if she would look to him for direction and assistance. Since that time I have visited her repeatedly, and have been enabled to be of some service to her in her poverty and affliction. To-day she met me with a cheerful, happy countenance, and told me what the Lord had done for her soul. 'He has taught me to pray without my book, and I can now have comfort all the time, even when my hands are occupied with my sick children. I now feel that justice of all I have suffered, and am willing to humble myself before my offended parents, and submit entirely to their will.' I requested her to write immediately to her parents, and state her situation without reserve, and promised to unite with her in pleading at the throne of grace for a favorable answer to her petition to be received again by them as a child. When I left her, my heart was raised to God in devout thanksgiving, that the bread thus cast on the waters, had been found before "many days." Let no Christian despise the day of small things. To the eye of sense, the daily visits of a few weak females, seems a feeble instrumentality to move on such a mass of sin and corruption as this city presents; but if angels rejoice over one sinner that repents, there is much to excite our gratitude and joy in the results of this system of visitation. The Lord alone hath done it; to his holy name be all the glory! . . .

20th. A pious lady called and requested me to go with her to E——st., to assist in removing her sick niece from a house of death, to a place where she might with propriety be favored with Christian counsel, and efforts be made for the salvation of her soul. It was a sad errand, but we went together and performed the task. The house was large, and as we passed from room to room the looks of shame and sorrow that met us, were sufficient to draw pity from any heart that had been wont to beat with a mother's or a sister's love. All the inmates were young—some less than 15 years of age. When the misery of their condition was alluded to, several wept, and expressed a wish that they had never been in existence, but said their case was now hopeless. They were told of a way to escape and urged to embrace it; but it was apparently as much in vain as preaching to the spirits in prison. It was a touching fact, that a majority of their number were orphans or fatherless. The poor sufferer whose case had brought us there was wasting away with consumption. To my inquiries respecting how she came here, her aunt replied briefly, that she was the only daughter of a beloved sister, long since laid in the grave; that she had now no near relations but herself, and that in this season of extremity she had desired her aid. When quite young she was extravagantly fond of balls, parties, and other vain amusements, and allowed to go and come as she pleased. Several years since she received the addresses of a young gentleman, and, under promise of marriage, was seduced and ruined. Her downward progress for a time was gradual, but recently it had been more rapid. She supported an infant son for a year or two, by means of her needle, but afterward abandoned herself to vice. This child is now seven years old, has been boarded in a respectable family by his mother, and knows not that she has ever swerved from the path of rectitude. The aunt seemed to be actuated only by Christian principle in her conduct toward this unfortunate relative. . . .

Alliance of vice and misery. — Another affecting scene witnessed this afternoon, was a family of five children, with a sick mother, in a damp, dark basement, left to suffer for the necessaries of life, because of the beastly intemperance of their natural guardian and protector. While endeavoring to sympathize in their distresses, the father was brought in so inebriated that he was as helpless as an infant; and yet his little ones were so agitated at his approach, that they crept under a bed in one corner of the room, trembling with fear.

If the Christians in our land could see at one view, the mass of unutterable misery that is endured in a single day by those who suffer from the intemperance of relatives to whom they are nearly allied, they would surely awake to the cause of temperance. . . .

15th. In W—— street I found a sick woman with several small children, who was anxious about her soul. She requested me, with much earnestness, to pray for her. To avoid interruption I had the door locked, and then engaged in prayer. Before rising, the father came, and finding the door closed, rapped violently, at the same time demanding admittance. One of the children obeyed him, and he entered much enraged, came near me and asked what I was about; and because unheeded, talked very rudely. I did not mind him till my prayer was finished. He then said if I "was *a man* he would put me out of doors." I told him I was there about my Master's business, in a good cause, and not at all ashamed or afraid; his wife had asked me to pray for her, and I had done so, and should pray again both for her and her wicked husband and the dear children. I told him I was old enough to be his mother, and I thought his conduct had been very unbecoming. At length he confessed, with some "confusion of face," that he had acted improperly, and asked me to come again. He also consented to let me bring his daughter a Bible that she might read it to her mother. . . .

Guilt betrayed — *Oct. 24th.* A lady called to solicit counsel and assistance. She had an unfaithful husband, and for the sake of her children and herself, she wished to take a judicious course, whatever might be the sacrifice. She had grieved over his guilt, but had sometimes told him his sin might find him out ere he was aware of it. He affected to despise the Advocate, and its disclosures, and often used reproachful language concerning it. She had watched him from time to time, and was well convinced that he made frequent calls at No. —, and had seen him enter at this No., on her way to my house. She wished me, if I had sufficient courage, to go with her, that she might meet him there before evidence. We went together, and gained admittance. The person who met us at the door, on inquiry, gave her name, and proved to be the individual whom we wished to see. The paper and tracts were offered and received. The wife then remarked that she came to see her husband, and supposed he was within. His being there was denied, but we followed to her room. Here we found everything in proper order, and the woman put on the appearance of so much innocence, that, to a person not versed in the knowledge of corrupt human nature, she would have seemed above suspicion. However the wife was not easily satisfied, and frankly alleged her charges. Both were much agitated, but the woman maintained the stand first taken, viz., that she was *unjustly accused.* Finding the point at issue not likely to be settled, I proposed prayer. After we knelt, it was ascertained by the wife that her husband was concealed under the bed. A conversation ensued between them, during which he promised reformation, if his name might not be exposed; but refused to leave his hiding-place, till "that moral reform woman had left the room." O! that he may forsake sin and repent, "lest iniquity prove his ruin."

Nov. 4th. In a disreputable house, where I had visited before, and removed some of the inmates, I found a child thirteen years old, so ill that she could not walk; and on this account the mistress had beaten her, to induce her to leave the place, but she knew not where to go. I found, by inquiry, that there were *six* miserable children of want in this den of vice, between the ages of twelve and sixteen. The woman who kept them, said she had so little patronage of late, that she could scarce give them food; and as for the sick one, she was only a bill of expence, and she cared not where she went. I asked if she would go to the Refuge. The child wept, and replied, she "had a mother in New Jersey, and perhaps she would forgive and receive her." I took her in the stage to the ferry, and thence obtained a conveyance to take her to her home. The mother had not known where she was for the last six months. Her excuse was, that she considered her old enough to take care of herself. . . . The account given by the child is this: She was allowed to go out alone evenings, and one night was met by a milliner's girl, who had been led astray, and persuaded to go with her to the place where I found her. The mother seemed almost destitute of maternal feelings, and was unwilling to receive her, lest her stepfather should be displeased. Through much entreaty, she was permitted to remain until he should come home, and decide what must be done. . . .

20th. Entered this afternoon forty-four dwellings, and left tracts and papers. This district has been considered so degraded, that the tract agent could find no visitor willing to take it. Have had the privilege of praying with several, of giving bibles to some, and securing three young girls from a course of sin and shame. . . .

25th. Went by request to see an unfortunate young woman, from a country village not far distant. But a few months since, she left clandestinely the paternal roof, and came to this city with a man who had gained her affections, and promised marriage. Instead of fulfilling his engagements, after her ruin was effected, he provided her a home among the fallen, and here I found her. I was made the bearer of a letter to her from a near relative. She was too much affected to read it, and while it was read to her, wept excessively. She acknowledged the extent of her sin and shame, the kindness of her injured friends, her ingratitude in leaving them—and gave, as her only apology, the regard she felt for her destroyer.

She was young, and previous to her fall, had been considered beautiful. At this house and the one adjoining, I conversed with ten young creatures who had been recently induced to come from the country and enter these chambers of death. It was painful and heart-sickening to behold the wreck of so much youth and loveliness.

AN AFTERNOON CALL

Mary Ann Sadlier (1820–1903) was one of the millions of single Irish women who emigrated to North America during the nineteenth century. Like many American women of her generation, she earned a living by writing fiction, publishing twenty novels as well as other works. Several of her novels, including the one from which this excerpt is taken, reflect the concerns of Irish men and women who came to live in the United States.

The door opened, and Jan appeared to announce two ladies who respectively announced themselves as Mrs. Susanna L. Bumford and Mrs. Jedediah Hopington. There was an air of respectability about these ladies, that is to say they were richly and gravely clad, and their demeanor was that of well-bred persons, so that Madam Von Wiegel and her daughter stood up to receive them, and having exchanged distant but polite salutations with the visitors, requested them to be seated—then quietly waited to ascertain the object of their visit.

Mrs. Bumford spoke first, very slowly and very distinctly. "We took the liberty of calling Madam Von Wiegel on behalf of the ——— Ward Mission, and the schools connected with it." She took out a book and pencil. "May we hope to have the honor of your name and—"

"And the benefit of my subscription," said Madam Von Wiegel with a smile. "Well! ladies, I have no objection to subscribe, but I should like to know exactly what I am subscribing *for*. Pray what is the nature of this Mission?"

"It is rather strange, madam! that you should not have heard before now of an institution so every way important," observed Mrs. Hopington in a strong nasal twang indicative of Down-East origin.

"It is rather unfortunate, at least," said the old lady still smiling, "but having admitted my ignorance, will *you* be so good as to enlighten me? What is the nature of the Mission—what are its objects?"

"The nature of the Mission," began Mrs. S. L. Bumford, pitching her voice on a somewhat higher key—

"Thank you," said Bertha speaking for the first time, "but my mother is *not* deaf, her hearing is remarkably good." And she smiled blandly.

More than a little disconcerted by this quiet sarcasm, good Mrs. Bumford found it necessary to cough once or twice before she recovered the thread of her discourse.

Mary Ann Sadlier, *Old and New: or Taste Versus Fashion* (New York: P. J. Kennedy & Sons, 1862), pp. 116–23. The editors are grateful to Colleen McDannell for locating this document.

"The nature of the Mission—is—benevolent," said she, "and its objects—strictly charitable."

"Strictly charitable, are they?"

"Yes, except in so far as they are industrial."

"Very good, indeed, and very laudable. And who are principally the recipients of the Mission's bounty?"

"The degraded—and utterly abandoned creatures—who are huddled together—in the wretched—and some of them ruinous—abodes—so common in that Ward."

"Of course, my dear Mrs. Bumford, you mean the *children* of those unhappy people," suggested her colleague; "you know it would not be possible for the Mission to do anything with the parents."

"And why, my dear madam?" questioned her attentive listener very, very calmly.

"Oh dear, Madam Von Wiegel! *they* are hopeless;—so addicted are they to idleness, drunkenness, blasphemy, and, in short, everything bad, that there a'nt any chance whatsoever of benefiting *their* condition. The degrading superstitions of Popery have besotted them to such a degree that their blindness is incurable—it really is; they are of those of whom it is written that they are abandoned to their own wickedness—yes, to the perversity of their evil ways."

"Who *are* these unfortunate people?" demanded the old lady.

"Chiefly low Irish and Italians."

"And you have no hope of benefiting *them,* but count on saving their children?"

"Precisely, madam!" said Mrs. Bumford; "the wretched parents are beyond the reach of spiritual succor. What do you think a horrid low Irishwoman told one of our fellow-laborers the other day, when she endeavored to move her hardened heart to repentance?"

"I really cannot guess, but I should like to hear."

"Well! she told her, my dear madam!—Excuse me—I actually tremble, so that I can—hardly—venture to—repeat the wicked words. They are too shocking for Christian ears to hear or Christian tongue to utter."

"Pray compose yourself, and favor us so far! My daughter and I have tolerably strong nerves."

"Well!" said Mrs. Bumford, making a desperate effort to expel the soul-defiling words from her Christian mouth: "She told our dear Christian sister that *the devil was the first Protestant*—she did, indeed, Madam Von Wiegel! and that people could get to heaven without ever reading the Bible—"

"What a degree of hardihood she must have had, that 'low Irish-woman!' "

"But that wasn't the worst of it, my dear madam!" said Mrs. Hopington, coming to the rescue of her dear exhausted sister.

"Indeed! Why I should think, after throwing the Bible overboard, and tracing the pedigree of Protestantism up to the arch-rebel Lucifer, your 'low Irishwoman' could go no farther."

"She did, though. She told us we were all a set of humbugs, going about preaching religion to them that had the true religion, if they only had the grace to practice it, and that it would be fitter for us be at home darning our stockings than trying to inveigle poor children from their lawful parents, and get them in by hook or by crook to our Mission-house."

"How insulting!"

"How shockingly rude!" ejaculated the mother and daughter.

"Was it not?—but what do you think the vile creature called our Mission?"

"I'm sure I don't know."

"Well! she called it a man-trap."

"*Soul-trap,* dear! I think was the word," suggested the other Missionary very gently.

"Yes, so it was,—well! she called it a soul-trap, and said it would be better for the poor children caught in it that they died of hunger on the streets than eat bread and meat of our providing. Wasn't that fearful, Madam Von Wiegel?"

"Very fearful, indeed!—but may I ask—in order to ascertain how far the woman was wrong and how far right—how do you provide for these children so tenderly cared for, as you say, by the ladies and gentlemen of the Mission? You cannot keep them always as pensioners on your bounty?"

"Of course not, madam! we have another society called The Children's Aid Society which takes charge of them after we have given them a certain amount of education, and sends them out West where, being disentangled from the evil surroundings of their miserable home and those degraded connections who could only prove a curse to them in after life and retard their progress in every way, they can enter on a new career with a fair chance for success."

"Very prudent on the part of the Mission!—And the friends so cut off—do they never give any trouble in the way of claiming their own flesh and blood?"

"Once in a while they do, but they are generally so poor—owing to their vicious way of living—that they cannot do much. Of course, the authorities are all with us; having a truly paternal interest in the unfortunate victims they are well disposed to protect them even against their own wretched parents, so that we have nothing to fear from *them*."

"And so—?"

"And so we—that is the Society—changes the children's names and sends them off to the branch-societies in various parts of the Union—"

"Where their relatives and friends lose all trace of them, and they grow up—anything and everything except Romanists?"

"Just so, madam!" And forthwith the pocketbook was opened, and the pencil held in readiness. "And now that we have explained the nature and the objects of our excellent institution in as satisfactory a manner as our poor abilities would permit, shall we not have the honor of receiving your subscription? How much shall I say, madam?"

"*Nothing!*"

"Nothing!" repeated both the Missionaries aghast. "Nothing? did you say 'nothing?' "

"I did," said Madam Von Wiegel, "and I mean what I say."

"Are we, then, to understand that you refuse to subscribe?"

"I do refuse."

"And on what grounds, pray?"

"On very simple grounds," said Madam Von Wiegel rising with dignity, "because I am a Catholic."

"You a Catholic! you, a German lady of high standing and connected with a family so long and so honorably known here."

"I am fain to hope that German ladies of higher standing than mine are good Catholics," said the old lady with a half smile, "but as it happens, I am *not* German, though my husband *was*."

"And pray what *are* you, then?" said Mrs. Bumford pertly.

"The question is rather impertinent," said Madam Von Wiegel calmly, "but I will not refuse to answer it. I am a countrywoman of that controversial friend of yours who made so uncivilly free with your sectional origin, and I know not but you will set *me* down, too, as 'a low Irishwoman,' for I must own that I have no greater respect than she for religious *humbugs,* and pious kidnappers. Bertha, my dear! be so good as to touch the bell."

Jan appeared on the instant.

"Show those ladies to the door, Jan!" said his mistress.

～

A DAUGHTER OF TEMPERANCE EXHORTS HER SEX

Mary Vaughan, a temperance advocate, occasional short-story writer, and, later, coauthor with Linus Brockett of Woman's Work in the Civil War *(1867), wrote these letters to Amelia Bloomer, editor of the* Lily, *a temperance paper published in Seneca Falls, New York. After taking part in the celebrated Woman's Rights Convention of 1848, Bloomer made the* Lily *a vehicle for discussion of many women's causes in addition to temperance; her advocacy of dress reform put her name on the flowing, pants-like "divided skirt" for women.*

Oswego, November 18, 1850

My Dear Mrs. Bloomer— . . . [A]llow me to add that I feel proud of one of my sex who dares in this day and age to assert her intellectual equality with the sterner sex; and to congratulate you upon the fearless and able manner with which you support the claims of woman. Yet I must be permitted to say that I think you and others mistake the true dignity of female character in calling peremptorily for the right of suffrage, and admittance to the learned professions. Like yourself I contend that females should receive nearly the same education, physically and intellectually, as males. Then let them become teachers—let them wield the pen—and that they can do it, and ably, does not now remain to be proved—and let them practice as physicians among their own sex. That, I consider a proper and desirable sphere for female effort. But let them beware how they so far denude them of the delicacy which covers the female character as a garment, and adds the truest ornament to all its virtues and graces, by mingling in the turmoil of political strife, or in the varied scenes of the court-room, or even by arrogating to themselves the station of spiritual teachers. . . .

Such is my opinion, and I give it frankly, though it may be of little worth. I am and ever shall be, however, a firm and unflinching advocate for 'Woman's Rights'—in property, educational privileges, and in the acknowledgement of her intellectual equality as far as her physical inferiority will allow. . . .

Yet even now, in the present state of affairs, she can exert an immense influence for good, publicly. She can, without outstepping the limits of delicacy, identify herself with most, if not all, of the great efforts of the day for the emancipation of the race, and its enlightenment. She can labor

Letters to the editor, *Lily* 2, no. 12 (December 1850), 3, no. 1 (January 1851), 3, no. 6 (June 1851), 3, no. 10 (October 1851), 3, no. 12 (December 1851).

actively in the Temperance reform, and in all the educational movements of the day. Oh! she can do much good, even if she cannot vote or hold office; and who shall say she is not far more useful and far more happy thus and more, that she is not fulfilling her true mission? In the Temperance reform, especially, should she labor actively; for who is a greater sufferer than she from the deadly curse it wars against. . . .

Praying God to prosper you, my dear Mrs. Bloomer, in the good work you have undertaken, I am sincerely

Your friend and well-wisher,
Mary C. Vaughan.

Oswego, Dec. 7, 1850

My Dear Mrs. Bloomer, To-day is our first really wintry one in Oswego. The snow is whirling down in eddying masses, and the keen northwest wind comes howling and roaring over the broad angry surface of the lake. . . . And we who sit by our warm fire-sides listen complacently as it howls forth the story of its wanderings, and snuggle down more deeply into the bosom of our comforts, or wrapped in furs, defy abroad its fierce, rude onslaughts, while thoughts of home burn cheerily upon the altars of our hearts.

But, alas! for the poor, this bitter, bitter day! To them the ceaseless struggle for the bare necessities of life, the constant thought whence will come food, raiment, fuel, leaves no room for the workings of the imagination. To them the howling north wind speaks not, save to admonish that winter with its snows and biting frosts has come, to bring them months of suffering. Many a care-worn mother gather to-day her little ones scantily clothed about her, and as they cower shivering around their miserable fire, lifts to heaven a silent prayer for aid. Perhaps the mother who does this is the wife of an inebriate, (alas! there are many such in our city, and our land,) and has seen her husband go forth this very morning, to spend in some haunt of dissipation, the earnings of many days labor, long hoarded for her children's wants; which, instead, go to swell the gains of that libel on humanity, a rumseller. And yet, forsooth, she must endure this patiently—she must suffer cold and hunger—she must pass wearily along life's highway with a body bowed by ceaseless labor, and an intellect debased by grovelling associations,—she must see her ragged, half-starved children the jeer and scoff of the child of luxury, whose soul is no more precious, and who mind has received no nobler stamp from the hand of Deity. And why? Because the *thing* whose name she and her children bear, to whom while he was yet a man she gave her heart's best affections, is a miserable sot, with nearly every semblance of humanity poisoned out of him by Alcohol, and battered out of him in bar-room fights; with no love for anything but his own degraded self, no higher aim than to procure in any way the price of his daily drams. And yet the law pronounces that *animal* her husband. Public opinion assures her she is fulfilling 'Woman's mission' in bearing patiently the pangs of a thousand deaths, and in submitting to all the degradations and nameless woes that render her life one long torment, both in her own person and that of her little ones.—And is this her duty? Is she thus fulfilling her true mission? Women of America! do the chains of old prejudices yet bind you so strongly that you can see your Sister thus suffer and endure, and say with calm smiles upon your lips: she only performs a wife's duty—only fulfills her marriage vows! Sisters, cheerful and prosperous, dwelling in your happy homes—Sisters! was it not to a MAN—man made in the image of his Creator, a 'little lower than the angels,' yet having the stamp of Divinity upon his proud front—that she pledged her vows, and entrusted her happiness! And now, is this degraded brute wallowing in gutters, sleeping in pig-stys, mouthing forth unintelligible nonsense, or in his drunken fury blaspheming the name of his Creator, entirely unmindful of his obligations, demanding all sacrifices of her, and making none in return—is this he? Does not a mutual contract cease to be binding when one party fails in its fulfillment? . . . Let your voices be raised—let your potent influence so sway the current of public opinion, that woman shall not be forced by it to endure a thraldom more horrible than would be hers, were her living, sentient body chained to a loathsome corpse.

. . . It is true we hear at the altar, the solumn injunction, 'What God has joined together, let not man put asunder,' but I do not believe God ever joined a meek, pure-minded, gentle, loving woman to a drunkard, and the sooner such ties are sundered the better for all parties concerned. And legal enactments should be made, whereby in many, if not most cases, the separation might be entire. . . .

Meanwhile I am yours truly,
Mary C. Vaughan

Oswego, May 8th, 1851

My Dear Mrs. Bloomer,

. . . I notice the holding of a Women's Rights Convention at Akron, Ohio, and I am glad our sisters are on the alert. These frequent conventions cannot fail to be of some service; they call forth the reliable talent and energy of the sex, if they can do no more.

The more I see, and think, and feel, of Woman's necessities and wrong, the more I desire to see them righted. The more I see how beautifully, how benevolently, her talents develop themselves when once directed toward the alleviation of those wrongs, the more completely I recognize her capabilities, and the more ardently long for their full expansion.

Yours, truly, Mary C. Vaughan.

Oswego, Sept. 16, 1851

My Dear Mrs. Bloomer:—My thoughts have of late been much turned to the subject of woman's influence upon the cause of temperance, and I am convinced that she can do little except through the medium of the ballot box. True, there is the powerful though quiet influence she exerts at home, as an educator, but beyond the precincts of her own family circle, what is she accomplishing toward the arrest of this formidable evil? Alas, very, *very* little. The effect of moral suasion upon men's habits and prejudices is daily lessening. Man has discovered it, and is commencing to act on the discovery. Every where, from our large cities and villages, swells up the cry, '*Intemperance is increasing.*' Our young men are grown more bold in seeking the saloon and bar-room. They disturb the quiet of our streets with their nightly brawls, as they emerge from these haunts of iniquity. They pollute our drawing rooms, and come into the presence of our sisters and daughters, with faces flushed, and breath reeking with the fumes of intoxicating drinks. They are fast hastening down, down to ruin. . . .

Less than a year since, as yourself and readers well know, the idea that women should go to the polls, was utterly repugnant to me. But when once convinced that she could act in no other way to any extent in the Temperance reform, there came a complete change over my feelings upon that subject. I am not ashamed to change opinions when convinced that those heretofore held are erroneous—as in this case I am, most sincerely. But then comes the thought if she should enjoy the right of voting for Temperance measures, why not for every reform? why not for all things that affect the public weal, if she choose to use that right? I for one have no ambition at present to approach the ballot-box, except for cast into it a vote which might have its bearing upon Temperance. Yet while I feel that I have a right, which, though withheld, is not the less mine, to do that, I cannot deny that I have the same right to vote on other questions. . . .

May God prosper you in every good purpose and mete out to you your reward. Truly yours,

Mary C. Vaughan.

Oswego, Oct. 20, 1851

Dear Mrs. Bloomer:—

. . . We must warn, exhort, and beseech our sex, to discountenance practices which may by any means lead men to an unrestrained indulgence in intoxicating drinks. No sense of our powerlessness to accomplish fully a great work should deter us from doing our little all toward that accomplishment. Every act, every word, has its influence. . . . And till we are allowed to advance this and other reforms through the ballot-box, let us not cease doing what we can. I grant the inefficiency of female temperance organizations toward staying the desolating tide of the ocean of drunkenness. But they help on the work of self-improvement, which must be the stepping stone to reach our elevation to the rights of citizenship. Women acquire a little of the self-reliance they so much need, in those associations; they learn to transact business; and they gain the power of arranging their ideas, and putting them into words and of talking on subjects of importance and interest. . . .

Every day convinces me more and more of woman's right to the elective franchise, and I would demand no half concession of her rights. If we are to vote at all, let it be for every thing in which, as citizens, we can have an interest. No dealing in half-way measures certainly. . . . I am convinced that the right of franchise secured to woman would enable her to do little to elevate herself, or to produce public good, unless all other political rights were also granted, and she could stand forth man's equal in the eyes of the law and society. . . .

Yours truly,
Mary C. Vaughan.

PLANTING CATHOLIC SCHOOLS
IN NORTH AMERICA

Born in 1824, Josephine Friess received the name Mary Caroline when she became a novice of the Poor School Sisters of Notre Dame in Bavaria at the age of eighteen. In 1847 she was one of four School Sisters who traveled to the United States under the sponsorship of King Ludwig (Louis) as missionaries to German immigrants. She was named American Vicar to the Superior General in 1850, when she established the order's American mother house in Milwaukee, the capital of German immigrant culture. In the following letter, written originally in German, she reported to her sponsors in Germany on the progress of the American missions.

Milwaukee, Wisconsin, April, 1858.
To the Esteemed Director, Louis Mission Society.

A decade has passed since our congregation was transplanted to America—a decade during which we poor religious have received many and great benefits through the kindness and influence of the Director of the Louis Mission Society.

The tiny mustard seed planted by our universally loved Mother General, Mary Teresa of Jesus, warmed by the rays of divine grace and supported by the continual influx of generous donations from Europe, is growing into a fruitful tree. The seed has also been moistened by the waters of adversity and trials, especially such trials as arise from local conditions. To foster and preserve the spirit of our congregation, the voluntary renunciation of one's own will, in a land where the spirit of independence prevails in every phase of life, is indeed difficult. How much more difficult to mould daughters of this country into true religious! Those who are called must needs have will power, and require a longer time of preparation to grasp and adopt the spirit of the congregation. Some of those who enter our candidature return to the world chiefly because in early childhood they were not trained to obedience, submission, and self-renunciation. Add to these deplorable conditions the diversity of nationalities among these young girls who are here to be moulded according to one spirit and one religious rule in order to comply with the demands of our congregation and Holy Church, whose object is to form them into missionary sisters. Theirs is the self-imposed task to strive for perfection and to labor assiduously for the salvation of the children in-

"Mother Caroline's Report to the Louis Mission Society," in *Mother Caroline and the School Sisters of Notre Dame* (Milwaukee: School Sisters of Notre Dame, 1928), pp. 121–26.

trusted to their care. Truly a holy and strenuous work, which requires manlike firmness and indomitable patience and prudence.

To maintain her own position, a School Sister must frequently use her influence indirectly only, and must do so more on account of the attitude of the parents who resent a fancied invasion of their authority, than from any cause presented by the children themselves. If the teacher is firm and persistent such persons regard her as domineering and despotic and her labor among them will be unproductive. Compulsion and 'must' may not be used. What can not be achieved by kindness is unattainable, at least in the average case. All must be accomplished through love and patience. Love of God must be the religious teacher's sole motive, otherwise she may grow weary of her work and completely dissatisfied in her holy vocation.

From what I have written, your Reverence may gain some knowledge of the hardships which we meet in our labors, but with the assistance of divine grace we shall in future endeavor to bear them bravely as we have done in the past.

The growth of our congregation may be seen from the following statistics: In the course of the past year we received an increase of twenty candidates, twenty-four novices, and eleven professed sisters. Four new missions were founded. Of these the first was St. Anthony's Orphanage which shelters seventy-five orphans and was opened in Baltimore, April, 1857; the second was St. Joseph's Orphanage in New Orleans with one hundred and twenty poor children who have lost their parents. In December, we assumed charge of a parochial school in Watertown, Wisconsin, in the Diocese of Milwaukee. Watertown is a recently established city of rapid growth with a population of eight thousand inhabitants. This mission was founded on the third of December, Feast of St. Francis Xavier, and has been placed under his patronage.

The people of Kenosha were rejoiced by the advent among them in January, 1858, of a band of School Sisters who had come to teach their children. The mission was opened in honor of the Most Holy Trinity. The little convent, a frame building, is in the center of a garden on a beautiful site near the shore of Lake Michigan.

These four new missions as well as those of earlier foundation, are blessed by heaven and are prospering. A singular mark of the protection of Divine Providence has been granted to our sisters in New Orleans. Thus far not one of them has been attacked by the diseases peculiar to the South. This immunity is unusual for Northeners. Though intense the heat—the sisters frequently are obliged to change their coiffure three or four times a day—mosquitoes have been a source of still greater sufferings. Gnats and other insects are also troublesome. The class-rooms are less frequented by these unwelcome visitors; otherwise it would be difficult for the sisters to teach, or the pupils to learn.

There are many opportunities to practice mortification. One is constantly bathed in perspiration and tortured by thirst. During class hours several intermissions must be granted to the pupils mainly for the purpose of permitting them a drink of cool water or a little refreshing fruit.

The public examinations were conducted during the excessively warm month of August. These were the first held by our sisters in New Orleans, and thanks be to God, they gave general satisfaction. As is the case in our other schools, so here, too, the number of pupils is steadily increasing. The total number is now not far from seven thousand. What rejoicing throughout eternity, when this great band of children and their teachers will be reunited in Heaven!

On the whole, the children's conduct and progress are satisfactory; but it is lamentable that the majority of our pupils leave school at the age of twelve years. Thus they are withdrawn from the vigilant eye of their teachers just at the age when they are beset by the greatest dangers. Highly susceptible as they have been to good influences, so are they also, in the same degree, to the evil to which a wicked world entices them on all sides.

Alas! how careless, vain and coquettish is youth! And when added to these qualities, heresy and unbelief take root in their hearts the majority are, it would seem, hopelessly lost. Many of the German girls are poor and even at an early age must work for others. Usually they find employment only among non-Catholics. From these they receive kind, gentle treatment; they perceive only refined manners, love of fashion, conveniences and a good table. They have all that they can desire for their bodily welfare and are well paid for their services. They gradually grow indifferent to religion, neglect to attend church services and to receive the sacraments, and before they are aware of it, they have become what their master and their mistress are—unbelievers, or apostates. Exteriorly they appear as ladies, wear hoop skirts, loll in rocking and easy chairs, and finally become ashamed of their German language and ancestry.

For many years the Christian training and education received in childhood may seem to have been lost. But in reality, experience has demonstrated that these had been relegated to the background by youthful giddiness and excessive desire for the enjoyments of life. When by some sudden occurrence which has been directed by an ever watchful Providence, the consciences of these girls are awakened, with renewed zeal they endeavor to work out their salvation. Often a mission preached in some parish causes such blessed conversions.

More than ever before, our young girls are now applying themselves to needlework. In this way they avoid idleness and all its pernicious consequences. Encouraged by our sisters, they knit their own shawls, hoods, stockings and scarfs; they sew many articles of clothing, and mend and darn quite deftly. Crocheting has made great strides in our schools. Even little girls save their pennies to buy linen thread with which they busily crochet lace for altar cloths, communion cloths, albs and surplices. They take great pride in seeing their work used in the churches.

They also show themselves kind to the poor. During Advent and Lent many children save their spending money, denying themselves candy and cakes, in order to buy clothes for the poor at Christmas time.

For more than a year there has been a business depression throughout the country. There has been also a great drop in prices for farm products. The sisters on our country missions rarely see money, and must be satisfied if instead they receive food. Our boarding schools, music, art and needlework departments are all suffering in consequence of the scarcity of funds, hence there are only a few pupils in some places. The sisters on the missions can save little for the Mother House.

This will suffice to give you a picture of our poor and needy conditions. How much longer the financial depression will endure God alone knows. We have even been obliged to postpone the acceptance of candidates whose monetary conditions have been affected by the state of the country. In our extreme distress we rely on God's help and also humbly implore the esteemed Director of the Louis Mission Society to send us alms. We promise to continue to pray daily with our pupils for you and for all our benefactors across the sea.

May heaven hear our ardent prayers and bestow richest blessings on you all as a reward for the generous gifts you have sent and which we have spent solely in helping to spread the knowledge of the Faith. This is our only ambition, as it is also the purpose of your society. I am overwhelmed with emotion when I consider the wonderful achievements of this benevolent society. Churches, convents and schools in the New World proclaim to all, the blessing that rests on every mite sacrificed in faithful and loving attachment to Holy Church.

Thousands owe to you the preservation of their Faith, and their Christian education—the highest blessings for time and eternity which were made possible only by the institutions established and supported by your generous donations.

And we, Poor School Sisters! Each one of us was sorely in need of her share in this support for the extension of her congregation, for the education to fit her for the duties of her vocation, and for the attainment of her beautiful and exalted ideal. By this she has attained her highest spiritual goal—she has become a Spouse of Christ and a missionary. Keen appreciation of these inestimable benefits inspires in us true love and gratitude towards our benefactors, and has indeed, erected in our hearts an imperishable monument to their munificence.

We regard it a most sacred obligation to continue our prayers for the society. I feel unbounded confidence in the prayers of little children for with them the Holy Spirit unites His supplications to the Heavenly Father.

These poor little ones! It makes one's heart ache to see them abandoned by their own parents and given to us, nay, forced upon us. We have recently had such a case. An infant nine months old, not yet baptized, was brought here by a poor but honest mother—a person devoid of faith and hope. She asked us to keep her child. Truly, at such moments, a religious forgets her own dire wants! I could not refuse, for is it not of such that we read in Scripture, 'Father and mother have abandoned me, but the Lord hath taken me up?' With these little children our house receives a special blessing, sufficient remuneration for our work.

SINCE WE CAME TO AMERICA

Although studies of immigration to the United States often focus on south-ern and eastern Europeans who settled in urban areas, before 1890 the majority of immigrants came from northern Europe and the British Isles and became farmers. These three letters were written in Norwegian by three different immigrant women to family members in Norway.

JANNICKE SÆHLE TO JOHANNES SÆHLE

Koshkonong Prairie, September 28, 1847

Dear Brother:

We sailed in the morning at seven o'clock, with fair wind and weather, and we had lost sight of the shores of our dear fatherland by half-past three, when the pilot left us. I remained on deck until six o'clock in the evening, but as the wind was sharp and cold I was not able to stay there any longer, but had to go down to the hold, where general vomiting had been going on for a long time. And after five minutes my turn came, also, to contribute my share to the Atlantic Ocean. . . .

On May 20 we left our good ship "Juno," with its brave crew, who said goodbye to us with a three-times-repeated hurrah. The captain accompa-nied us on board a steamer which was to carry us to Albany. He took us about to see things. It was like a complete house four stories high, and very elegantly furnished, with beautiful rugs everywhere. He now parted from us with the best wishes. Captain Bendixen treated us more like relatives than like passengers. He was very entertaining and was courte-ous in every respect.

The later journey was good beyond expectation. Things went merrily on the railroads. Once in a while the passengers, when we neared some of the noteworthy sights that we rushed past on the trip, would stick their heads out of the windows so that they might see everything, but one after the other of them had the misfortune to see his straw hat go flying away with the wind caused by the speed of the train.

On the third of June, after we had passed several cities which for lack of space I cannot tell about, we reached Milwaukee, where we remained three days. We left Milwaukee on the seventh and came to Koshkonong on the ninth. Torjersen, after having made the acquaintance here of a

Theodore C. Blegen, ed. and trans., "Immigrant Women and the American Frontier," in *Studies and Records of the Norwegian-American Historical Society* 5 (1930), pp. 18–29. Reprinted by permission of the Norwegian-American Historical Association.

worthy family named Homstad, from Namsen, who settled here last year and found this land the best after long travels, has now bought a little farm of forty acres of land, with a fairly livable log house and a wheat field of four and a half acres. This has brought him forty-five barrels of winter wheat, in addition to potatoes, beans, peas, more than a hundred heads of cabbage, cucumbers, onions in tremendous amounts, and many other kinds [of vegetables]. For this farm he paid $250, and with the farm followed respectfully four pigs.

After having lived here and having been in good health the whole time, I left on the sixteenth of August for Madison, the capital of Wisconsin, which is situated twenty-two miles from here. There I have worked at a hotel for five weeks, doing washing and ironing; and I enjoy the best treatment, though I cannot speak with the people. I have food and drink in abundance. A breakfast here consists of chicken, mutton, beef, or pork, warm or cold wheat bread, butter, white cheese, eggs, or small pancakes, the best coffee, tea, cream, and sugar. For dinner the best courses are served. Supper is eaten at six o'clock, with warm biscuits, and several kinds of cold wheat bread, cold meats, bacon, cakes, preserved apples, plums, and berries, which are eaten with cream, and tea and coffee—and my greatest regret here is to see the superabundance of food, much of which has to be thrown to the chickens and the swine, when I think of my dear ones in Bergen, who like so many others must at this time lack the necessaries of life.

I have received a dollar a week for the first five weeks, and hereafter shall have $1.25, and if I can stand it through the whole winter I shall get a dollar and a half a week, and I shall not have to do the washing, for I did not think I was strong enough for this work. Mrs. Morison has also asked me to remain in her service as long as she, or I, live, as she is going to leave the tavern next year and live a more quiet life with her husband and daughter, and there I also could live more peacefully and have a room by myself, and I really believe that so far as she is concerned I could enter upon this arrangement, provided such a decision is God's will for me. . . .

Do not forget to thank God, on my behalf, who has guided me so well. I cannot thank Him enough myself.

Jannicke

HENRIETTA JESSEN TO ELEONORE AND "DOREA" WILLIAMSIN

Milwaukee, February 20, 1850

My dear Sisters Dorea and Norea:

Fate has indeed separated me from my native land and all that was dear to me there, but it is not denied me to pour forth my feelings upon this paper. My dear sisters, it was a bitter cup for me to drink, to leave a dear mother and sisters and to part forever in this life, though living. Only the thought of the coming world was my consolation; there I shall see you all. Of the emigrants from Arendal, I think, probably none went on board with a heavier heart than I, and thanks be to the Lord who gave me strength to carry out this step, which I hope will be for my own and my children's best in the future. So I hope that time will heal the wound, but up to the present I cannot deny that homesickness gnaws at me hard. When I think, however, that there will be a better livelihood for us here than in poor Norway, I reconcile myself to it and thank God, who protected me and mine over the ocean's waves and led us to a fruitful land, where God's blessings are daily before our eyes.

. . . Since we came to America neither my children nor I have been sick abed a day, for which God is to be thanked, who strengthens my body and my poor soul. I have not had so pleasant a winter as I might have had. My husband fell ill in the middle of September and had to keep to his bed until eight days before Christmas. Then he began to sit up a little and now he is up most of the day, but he is so weak that he cannot think of beginning to work for two months and perhaps not then. The doctor calls the sickness dysentery. Yes, my poor Peder has suffered much in this sickness. The doctor gave up all hope of his life and we only waited for God's hour, but at twelve o'clock one night his pulse changed and the doctor said that now it was possible that he would overcome the sickness, but he said that it would be very stubborn and [the recovery] slow. That sickness I can never forget. Think, in one terrible day and night my husband lost eight pots of blood, that was the night before he was near death, and I was alone with him and my children. But afterwards there were a few of the Norwegians who were so kind as to help me for a time watching over him, the one relieving the other. For seven weeks I was not out of my clothes. From these lines you will see that I have experienced a little in America; but now that the worst is over, I thank the almighty Father from my innermost heart, who has cared for us and met our daily needs. We have lacked nothing. Good food and drink we have had daily. I believe I may say that even if I had been in my own native town I would hardly have received the help I have had here and I receive two dollars a week (that is, in goods). I will not speak of my own kind family, what they would have done for me, but I mean the public. There are four Norwegian families quite near where we live who have been very sympathetic with me in my misfortune and have proved their faith by their works; they have given me both money and articles for the house. Among these four families there is a man named Samuel Gabrielsen, who has been like a rare good brother to me. I will not say how much that kind man has given us, for he has told me that I should not tell anyone. "I give to you now because I know that it will be a help to you, but I do not give to be praised." He knows my brother-in-law well; in fact, Gabrielsen says that Williamsin is the best man he knows in the world and all the Norwegians whom I talk with say the same. . . .

The winter here in America is just as long as in Norway and much colder, but the nights are not so long. At Christmas time we had light until five o'clock in the afternoon. Ask Margaret to tell Peder Mekelsen that I advise him to go to New York and from there by canal boat to Buffalo and then by steamboat here to Milwaukee. Nels Klaapene, the sail maker, lives here in the vicinity; his wife's name is Ingebaar. I am writing with a pen and the paper says stop. And now in conclusion I ask God's blessing upon you all. God guard you from all evil in your peaceful homes. A thousand greetings to you, Norea, with your husband and children, and you, Dorea, with your husband and children, from me, my husband, and my children.

Your devoted sister,
Henrietta Jessen

GURI ENDRESON TO RELATIVES

Harrison P. O., Monongalia Co., Minnesota,
December 2, 1866

Dear Daughter and your husband and children, and my beloved Mother:

I have received your letter of April fourteenth, this year, and I send you herewith my heartiest thanks for it, for it gives me great happiness to hear from you and to know that you are alive, well, and in general thriving. I must also report briefly to you how things have been going with me recently, though I must ask you to forgive me for not having told you earlier about my fate. I do not seem to have been able to do so much as to write to you, because during the time when the savages raged so fearfully here I was not able to think about anything except being murdered, with my whole family, by these terrible heathen. But God be praised, I escaped with my life, unharmed by them, and my four daughters also came through the danger unscathed. Guri and Britha were carried off by the wild Indians, but they got a chance the next day to make their escape; when the savages gave them permission to go home to get some food, these young girls made use of the opportunity to flee and thus they got away alive, and on the third day after they had been taken, some

Americans came along who found them on a large plain or prairie and brought them to people. I myself wandered aimlessly around on my land with my youngest daughter and I had to look on while they shot my precious husband dead, and in my sight my dear son Ole was shot through the shoulder. But he got well again from this wound and lived a little more than a year and then was taken sick and died. We also found my oldest son Endre shot dead, but I did not see the firing of this death shot. For two days and nights I hovered about here with my little daughter, between fear and hope and almost crazy, before I found my wounded son and a couple of other persons, unhurt, who helped us to get away to a place of greater security. To be an eyewitness to these things and to see many others wounded and killed was almost too much for a poor woman; but, God be thanked, I kept my life and my sanity, though all my movable property was torn away and stolen. But this would have been nothing if only I could have had my loved husband and children—but what shall I say? God permitted it to happen thus, and I had to accept my heavy fate and thank Him for having spared my life and those of some of my dear children.

I must also let you know that my daughter Gjærtru has land, which they received from the government under a law that has been passed, called in our language "the Homestead law," and for a quarter section of land they have to pay sixteen dollars, and after they have lived there five years they receive a deed and complete possession of the property and can sell it if they want to or keep it if they want to. She lives about twenty-four American miles from here and is doing well. My daughter Guri is away in house service for an American about a hundred miles from here; she has been there working for the same man for four years; she is in good health and is doing well; I visited her recently, but for a long time I knew nothing about her, whether she was alive or not.

My other two daughters, Britha and Anna, are at home with me, are in health, and are thriving here. I must also remark that it was four years on the twenty-first of last August since I had to flee from my dear home, and since that time I have not been on my land, as it is only a sad sight because at the spot where I had a happy home, there are now only ruins and remains left as reminders of the terrible Indians. Still I moved up here to the neighborhood again this summer. A number of families have moved back here again so that we hope after a while to make conditions pleasant once more. Yet the atrocities of the Indians are and will be fresh in memory; they have now been driven beyond the boundaries of the state and we hope that they never will be allowed to come here again. I am now staying at the home of Sjur Anderson, two and a half miles from my home. I must also tell you how much I had before I was ruined in this way. I had seventeen head of cattle, eight sheep, eight pigs, and a number of chickens; now I have six head of cattle, four sheep, one pig; five of my cattle stayed on my land until February, 1863, and lived on some hay and stacks of wheat on the land; and I received compensation from the government for my cattle and other movable property that I lost. Of the six cattle that I now have three are milk cows and of these I have sold butter, the summer's product, a little over two hundred and thirty pounds; I sold this last month and got sixty-six dollars for it. In general I may say that one or another has advised me to sell my land, but I would rather keep it for a time yet, in the hope that some of my people might come and use it; it is difficult to get such good land again, and if you, my dear daughter, would come here, you could buy it and use it and then it would not be necessary to let it fall into the hands of strangers. And now in closing I must send my very warm greetings to my unforgetable dear mother, my dearest daughter and her husband and children, and in general to all my relatives, acquaintances, and friends. And may the Lord by his grace bend, direct, and govern our hearts so that we sometime with gladness may assemble with God in the eternal mansions where there will be no more partings, no sorrows, no more trials, but everlasting joy and gladness, and contentment in beholding God's face. If this be the goal for all our endeavors through the sorrows and cares of this life, then through his grace we may hope for a blessed life hereafter, for Jesus sake.

Always your devoted
Guri Olsdatter

IRON TEETH (MAH-I-TI-WO-NEE-NI) REMEMBERS THE CHEYENNE REMOVAL

This account by Thomas B. Marquis is a reconstruction of interviews conducted in 1926 with a ninety-two-year-old Cheyenne woman named Mah-i-Ti-Wo-Nee-Ni, or Iron Teeth. In her discussions with Marquis, Iron Teeth described Indian resistance to the United States reservation policy from the 1860s through the 1880s, including the forced removal of the Cheyennes from the northern plains in 1877 and their long march home in 1878. Three of her five children died in the return. Iron Teeth's father was Cheyenne, her mother Sioux; in this account, many individuals are identified by both their Cheyenne and their Sioux names.

. . . The Cheyennes and the Sioux had a big fight with soldiers when I was about 32 years old. We were camped during that winter up toward the head of Tongue River. There was much cold weather and deep snow. We considered that the Indians owned all of the lands in this region. But the white people kept coming into it or through it, killing our grain and using up the grass at the best places for camping. Some soldiers built a fort in the Powder River country. One day my husband and other Cheyennes who had been away came back to our camp and told us that the Sioux and Cheyennes had killed a hundred of the soldiers at the fort. We built a big bonfire and had a general celebration.

A few years after that peace was made between the whites and the Cheyennes and Sioux. Our tribes were to have a permanent home in our favorite Black Hills country. We were promised that all white people would be kept away from us there. But after we had been there a few years, General Custer and his soldiers came there and found gold. Many white people crowded in, wanting to get the gold. Our young men wanted to fight these whites, but there were too many of them coming. Soldiers came and told us we would have to move to another part of the country and let the white people have this land where the gold was. This action of the soldiers made bad hearts in many of the Cheyennes and Sioux. They said it was no use to settle on any new lands because the white people would come there also and drive us out. The most angered ones went out to the old hunting grounds lying between the Powder and Bighorn Rivers.

Thomas B. Marquis, *The Cheyennes of Montana*, ed. Thomas D. Weist (Algonac, Mich.: Reference Publications, 1978), pp. 68–78. The editors are grateful to Bethel Saler for bringing this document to their attention.

My husband and I took our family to the Red Cloud Agency, known to us as the White River Agency, where all Cheyennes had been told to go. He was in bad humor because of our having been driven from our Black Hills home country, but he thought it was best to do whatever the white people ordered us to do. In a year or two we heard that many white soldiers were going out into our old western hunting grounds to fight the Indians there and make them come back to the new reservations in Dakota. Later, in the middle of that summer, we heard that all of the soldiers had been killed in a great battle at the Little Bighorn River.

When we were told of the great victory by the Indians, my husband said we should now go to the Montana lands, to join our people there. With many others, we left Dakota and found the Cheyennes. The tribe traveled together during much of the remainder of that summer, hunting along the Powder, Tongue and Rosebud Rivers. My husband was busy killing buffalo, antelope, deer, and other animals, and I was busy tanning skins and storing up meat and berries for use during the winter. We stayed with the main tribal band led by our favorite Old Man Chief, Morning Star, or Dull Knife. When the leaves fell from the trees and the grass died, the tribal camp was made on a small stream flowing into the upper part of Powder River, almost in the Bighorn Mountains. Our men did not want to fight. They wanted to keep entirely away from all white people, wanted to be left alone so they might get food and skins to provide for their families. They said that nobody would trouble us in this place so far away from other people.

But we were not allowed to live in peace. When the snow had fallen deep, a great band of soldiers came. They rode right into our camp and shot women and children as well as men. Crows, Pawnees, Shoshonis, some Arapahoes, and other Indians were with them. We who could do so ran away, leaving our warm lodges and the rich stores of food. As our family was going out from camp, my husband and our older son kept behind and fought off the soldiers. My husband had a horse, but he was leading it as he walked, so he might shoot better when afoot. I saw him fall, and his horse went away from him. I wanted to go back to him, but my two sons made me go on away with my three daughters. From the hilltops we Cheyennes looked back and saw all of our lodges and everything in them being burned into nothing but smoke and ashes.

We wallowed through the mountain snow for several days. Most of us were afoot. We had no lodges, only a few blankets, and there was only a little dry meat among us. Some died of wounds, many froze to death. We came down from the mountains to the valley of the Tongue River and followed down this stream. After 11 days of traveling, we found a camp of Oglala Sioux. They fed us and gave us shelter. But the remainder of that winter was a hard one for all of us.

When spring came, all of the Cheyennes surrendered to soldiers or went back to the Dakota agencies. I was afraid of all white men soldiers. It seemed to me they represented the most extreme cruelty. They had just killed my husband and burned our whole village. There was in my mind a clear recollection of a time, 12 years before this, when they had killed and scalped many of our women and children in a peaceable camp near Mexico. At that time, I had seen a friend of mine, a woman, crawling along on the ground, shot, scalped, crazy, but not yet dead. After that I always thought of her when I saw white men soldiers.

In Dakota, we Northern Cheyennes were told that we must go to Oklahoma, to live there on a reservation with the Southern Cheyennes. None of us wanted to go there. We liked best the northern country. But one of our chiefs, Red Sash, or Standing Elk, made friends with the white men soldier chiefs by lying to them and telling them we were willing to go. My two sons then said it was the only thing our family could do. I suppose all of the other Cheyennes felt the same way. . . .

In Oklahoma we all got sick with chills and fever. When we were not sick, we were hungry. We had been promised food until we could plant corn and wait for it to grow, but much of the time we had no food. Our men asked for their guns to be given back to them, so they might kill game, but the guns were kept from them. Sometimes a few of them would take their bows and arrows and slip away to get buffalo or other meat, but soldiers would go after them and make them come back to the agency. The bows and arrows were used at times for killing cattle belonging to white men. Any time this happened, the whole tribe was punished. The punishment would be the giving of less food to us, and we would be kept still closer to the agency. We had many deaths from both the fever sickness and starvation. We talked among ourselves about the good climate and the plentiful game in our old northern country hunting lands.

After about a year, Little Wolf and Morning Star, our principal Old Man Chiefs, told the agent: "We are going back to the North."

The agent replied: "Soldiers will follow you and kill you."

My two sons joined the band determined to leave there. I and my three daughters followed them. I think that, altogether, there were about 500 Cheyennes in this band. The white soldiers chased us. They came from every direction. Some of the Indians went back as soon as the bullets began to fly. But my older son kept saying that we should go on toward the North unless we were killed, that it was better to be killed than to go back and die slowly.

Only one buffalo, a calf, was killed by our men during the long flight back to the old home country. A few cattle belonging to white people were killed. Our chiefs told the young men not to do this, but our people were very hungry and no other food could be found. I have heard it said they killed some white people not soldiers. If they did, it must have been white people who started the fight. At that time all of us were trying to stay entirely away from all other people, so we could travel without interruption.

Chills and fever kept me sick along the way. We had no lodges. At night, when we could make any kind of camp, my daughter helped me at making willow branch shelters. Day after day, through more than a month, I kept my youngest daughter strapped to my body, in front of me, on my horse. I led another horse carrying the next-youngest daughter. The oldest daughter managed her own mount. The two sons always stayed behind, to help watch for soliders. . . .

We dodged the soldiers during most of our long journey. But always they were near to us, trying to catch us. Our young men fought them off in seven different battles. At each fight, some of our people were killed, women and children the same as men. I do not know how many of our grown-up people were killed. But I know that more than 60 of our children were gone when we got to the Dakota country. . . .

Morning Star said we should be contented, now that we were on our own land. He took us to Fort Robinson, where we surrendered to the soldiers. They took from us all our horses and whatever guns they could find among us. They said then that we must go back to the South, but our men told them it was better to die by bullets. After a few weeks of arguing, our men were put into a prison house. We women and children were told we might go to the agency. Some of them went there, but most of us went into the prison with the men. In one room, about 30 feet square, were 43 men, 29 women and 20 or 30 children.

"Now are you willing to go back to the South?" the soldier chiefs asked us.

Nobody answered them. The quantity of food given to us became less and less every day, until they gave us none at all. Then they quit bringing water to us. Eleven days we had no food except the few mouthfuls of dry meat some of the women had kept in their packs. Three days we had no water.

Guns had been kept hidden in the clothing of some of the women. One day, a woman accidentally dropped a six-shooter on the floor. Soldiers came and searched us again, taking whatever weapons they could find. But we kept five six-shooters, with some cartridges for them. I had one in the breast of my dress. We hid all of these under a loose board in the floor. My family blanket was spread over this board.

The men decided to break out of this jail. The women were willing. It was considered that some of us, perhaps many of us, would be killed. But it was hoped that many would escape and get away to join other Indians somewhere. Women cut up robes to make extra moccasins. I made extra pairs for myself and my three children. We piled our small packs by the two windows and the one door, or each woman held her own pack ready at hand. The plan was to break out just after the soldiers had gone to bed for the night. I gave my son the six-shooter I had. He was my oldest child, then 22 years of age.

After the night bugle sounded, my son smashed a window with the gun I had given him. Others broke the other window and tore down the door. We all jumped out. My son took the younger of the two daughters upon his back. The older daughter and I each carried a small pack. It was expected the soldiers would be asleep, except the few guards. But bands of them came hurrying to shoot at us. One of them fired a gun almost at my face, but I was not harmed. It was bright moonlight and several inches of snow covered the ground. For a short distance all of the Indians followed one broken trail toward the river, but soon we had to scatter. My son with the little girl on his back ran off in one direction, while the other daughter and I went in another direction. We had no agreed plan for meeting again.

I and the daughter with me found a cave and crawled into it. We did not know what had become of the son and his little sister. A man named Crooked Nose also came into our cave. We could hear lots of shooting. The next day we still heard shots, but not so many. Each day after that there was some further firing of guns. We stayed in the cave seven nights and almost seven days. More snow kept falling, it was very cold, but we were afraid to build a fire. We nibbled at my small store of dry meat and ate snow for water. Each day we could hear the horses and voices of soldiers searching for Indians. Finally, a Captain found our tracks where we had gone out of and back into the cave. He called to us. I crept out. He promised to treat us well if we would go with him. He and his soldiers then took us back to Fort Robinson. . . .

I was afraid to ask anybody about my son and the little daughter, as my asking might inform the soldiers of them. But I kept watching for them among the Indians there. After a while the little girl came to me. I asked her about her brother. It appeared she did not hear me, so I asked again. This time she burst out crying. Then I knew he had been killed. She told me how it had been done. That night, they had hidden in a deep pit. The next morning, some soldiers had come near to them. The brother had said to her: "Lie down, and I will cover you with leaves and dirt. Then I will climb out and fight the soldiers. They will kill me, but they will think I am the only one here, and they will go away after I am dead. When they are gone, you can come out and hunt for our mother." The next day she came out, but the soldiers caught her. . . .

A day or two later all of us were again put into the prison house. Our number was now only about half what it had been. . . .

We expected then that the soldiers would come at once into the prison and shoot all of us. But they did not. Instead, a few days later we were taken to Pine Ridge Agency. There we were put among the Oglala Sioux. Little Wolf and his small band, who had separated from us in coming from Oklahoma, went to Fort Keogh and then were put upon lands by Tongue River, in Montana. Other Cheyennes were with us in association with the Oglalas on Pine Ridge Reservation. Finally, after 12 years, all of us were brought together on this Tongue River Reservation.

THE GREAT INDIGNATION MEETING

In 1870, Utah Territory became the second federal constituency to enfranchise women (Wyoming Territory had granted woman suffrage in 1869). At the moment when Utah women gained the vote, however, some Utah men stood in danger of losing it, for that same year the United States Congress debated a bill that would have deprived men who practiced polygamy of most of the rights of citizenship. In 1852, Joseph Smith, the founder of the Church of Jesus Christ of Latter-day Saints, had publicly pronounced the church's practice of "plural" (or "celestial") marriage. Smith did not teach that plural marriage was necessary for salvation, but rather that it would gain the men and women who practiced it entry into the highest orders of eternal life. Although the bill introduced by Rep. Shelby Cullom of Illinois and debated in 1870 did not become law, Congress succeeded in disenfranchising polygamous men in Utah in 1882 and took the ballot away from Utah women in 1887.

GREAT INDIGNATION MEETING OF THE LADIES OF SALT LAKE CITY, TO PROTEST AGAINST THE PASSAGE OF CULLOM'S BILL

Notwithstanding the inclemancy of the weather, the Tabernacle was densely packed with ladies of all ages—old, young, and middle aged. On the motion of Sister Eliza R. Snow, Mrs. Sarah N. Kimball (President of the Female Relief Society of the 15th ward) was elected president of the Meeting. . . .

E. R. Snow

. . . My sisters, we have met to-day to manifest our views and feelings concerning the oppressive policy exercised towards us by our Republican Government. Aside from all local and personal feelings, to me it is a source of deep regret that the standard of American liberty should have so far swayed from its original towering position as to have given rise to circumstances which not only rendered such a meeting opportune but absolutely necessary.

. . . Shall we—ought we to be silent when every right of citizenship—every vestige of civil and religious liberty is at stake? When our husbands and sons—our fathers and brothers are threatened, being either restrained in their obedience to the commands of God, or incarcerated year

"Great Indignation Meeting . . . ," Salt Lake City (Utah) *Deseret Evening News,* January 14 and 15, 1870.

after year in the dreary confines of a prison, will it be thought presumptuous for us to speak? Are not our interests one with our brethren? Ladies, this subject as deeply interests us as them. In the kingdom of God woman has no interests separate from those of man—all are mutual.

Our enemies pretend that in Utah woman is held in a state of vassalage—that she does not act from choice, but by coercion—that we would even prefer life elsewhere were it possible for us to make our escape. What nonsense! We all know that if we wished, we could leave any time—either to go singly or we could rise *en masse*, and there is no power here that could or would ever wish to prevent us.

I will now ask this intelligent assembly of ladies: Do you know of any place on the face of the earth, where woman has more liberty, and where she enjoys such high and glorious privileges as she does here, as a Latter-day Saint? "No!" The very idea of women here in a state of slavery is a burlesque on good common sense. The history of this people with a very little reflection, would instruct outsiders on this point,—it would show at once that the part which woman has acted in it could never have been performed against her will. Amid the many distressing scenes through which we have passed, the privations and hardships consequent on our expulsion from State to State, and our location in an isolated, barren wilderness, the women in this Church have performed and suffered what could never have been borne and accomplished by slaves.

And now, after all that has transpired, can our opponents expect us to look on with silent indifference and see every vestige of that liberty, for which many of our patriotic grandsires fought and bled, that they might bequeath to us, their children, the precious boon of national freedom, wrested from our grasp? If so, they will learn their mistake, we are ready to inform them. They must be very dull in estimating the energy of female character, who can persuade themselves that women, who, for the sake of their religion, left their homes, crossed the plains with handcarts, or, as many had previously done, drove ox, mule and horse teams from Nauvoo and from other points when their husbands and sons went at their country's call, to fight her battles in Mexico; yes, that very country which had refused us protection, and from which we were then struggling to make our escape I say, those who think that such women and the daughters of such women do not possess too much energy of character to remain passive and mute under existing circumstances, are "reckoning bills without their host." To suppose that we should not be aroused when our brethren are threatened with fines and imprisonment for their faith, and obedience to the laws of God, is an insult to our womanly natures.

Were we the stupid, degraded, heart-broken beings that we have been represented, silence might better become us; but, as women of God—women filling high and responsible positions—performing sacred duties—women who stand not as dictators, but as counselors to their husbands, and who, in the purest, noblest sense of refined womanhood, being truly their helpmates; we not only speak because we have the right, but justice and humanity demand that we should.

Instead of being lorded over by tyrannical husbands, we, the ladies of Utah, are already in possession of a privilege which many intelligent and high aiming ladies in the States are earnestly seeking i.e. the right to vote. Although as yet we have not been admitted to the common ballot box, to us the right of suffrage is extended in matters of far greater importance. This we say truthfully not boastingly; and we may say farther, that if those sensitive persons who profess to pity the condition of the women of Utah, will secure unto us those rights and privileges which a just and equitable administration of the laws of the Constitution of the United States guarantees to every loyal citizen, they may reserve their sympathy for objects more appreciative.

Harriet Cook Young.

In rising to address this meeting, delicacy prompts me to explain the chief motives which have dictated our present action. We, the ladies of Salt Lake City, have assembled here today—not for the purpose of assuming any particular political power, nor to claim any special prerogative which may, or may not belong to our sex; but to express our indignation at the unhallowed efforts of men, who, regardless of every principle of manhood, justice, and constitutional liberty, would force upon a religious community, by a direct issue, either the curse of apostasy or the bitter alternative of fire and sword. Surely the instinct of self-preservation, the love of liberty and happiness, and the right to worship God are dear to our sex as well as to the other, and when these most sacred of all rights are thus wickedly assailed, it becomes absolutely our duty to defend them.

The mission of the Latter-day Saints is to reform abuses which have for ages corrupted the world, and to establish an era of peace and righteousness. The Most High is the founder of this mission, and in order to its establishment, His providences have so shaped the world's history, that, on this continent, blest above all other lands, a free and enlightened Government has been instituted, guaranteeing to all, social, political, and religious liberty. The Constitution of our country is therefore hallowed to us, and we view with a jealous eye every infringement upon its great principles, and demand, in the sacred name of liberty, that the miscreant, who would trample it under his feet, by depriving a hundred thousand American citizens of every vestige of liberty, should be anathematized throughout the length and breadth of the land as a traitor to God and his country.

It is not strange that among the bigoted and the corrupt such a man and such a measure should have originated; but it will be strange indeed, if such a measure find favor with the honorable and high minded men who wield the destinies of the nation. Let this seal of ruin be attached to the archives of our country and terrible must be the results. Woe will wait upon her steps, and sorrow and desolation will stalk through the land; peace and liberty will seek another clime, while anarchy, lawlessness and bloody strife hold high carnival amid the general wreck. God forbid that wicked men be permitted to force such an issue upon the nation!

It is true that a corrupt press, and an equally corrupt priestcraft are leagued against us—that they have pandered to the ignorance of the masses and vilified our institution to that degree, that it has become popular to believe that the Latter-day Saints are unworthy to live; but it is also true that there are many, very many right thinking men who are not without influence in the nation, and to such do we now solemnly and earnestly appeal. Let the United voice of this assembly give the lie to the popular clamour that the women of Utah are oppressed and held in bondage. Let the world know that the women of Utah prefer virtue to vice, and the home of an honorable wife to the gilded pageantry of fashionable temples of sin. Transitory allurements, glaring to the senses as the flame is to the moth, but short lived and cruel in their results possess no charms for us. Every woman in Utah may have her husband, the husband of her choice. Here we are taught not to destroy our children, but to preserve them, for they, reared in the path of virtue, and trained to righteousness, constitute our true glory.

It is with no wish to accuse our sisters who are not of our faith, but we are dealing with facts as they exist. Wherever monogamy reigns, adultery, prostitution, free-love and foeticide, directly or indirectly, are its concomitants. It is not enough to say that the virtuous and the high-minded frown upon these evils, we believe they do, but frowning does not cure them, it does not even check their rapid growth; either the remedy is too weak or the disease is too strong. The women of Utah comprehend this and they see in the principle of a plurality of wives, the only safeguard against adultery, prostitution, free-love, and the reckless waste of pre-natal life practiced throughout the land.

It is as co-workers in the great mission of universal reform, not only in our own behalf, but also, by precept and example to aid in the emancipation of our sex generally, that we accept in our heart of hearts, what we know to be a divine commandment; and here, and now, boldly and publicly, we do assert our right, not only to believe in this holy commandment, but to practice what we believe.

While these are our views, every attempt to force that obnoxious measure upon us must of necessity, be an attempt to coerce us in our religious and moral convictions, against which did we not most solemnly protest, we would be unworthy the name of American women. . . .

Phoebe Woodruf

Ladies of Utah, as I have been called upon to express my views upon the important subject; which has called us together this day, I will say that I am happy to be one of your number in this association. I am proud that I am a citizen of Utah, and a member of the Church of Jesus Christ of Latter-day Saints. I have been a member of this Church for thirty-six years, and had the privilege of living in the days of the Prophet Joseph and heard his teachings for many years. He ever counseled us to honor, obey, and maintain the principles of our noble Constitution, for which our fathers fought, and many of them sacrificed their lives to establish. President Brigham Young has always taught the same principle. This glorious legacy of our fathers, the Constitution of the United States, guarantees unto all citizens of this great Republic the right to worship God according to the dictates of their own consciences, as it expressly says, "Congress shall make no laws respecting an establishment of religion or prohibiting the free exercise thereof." Cullom's bill is in direct violation of this declaration of the Constitution, and, I think it is our duty to do all in our power by our voices and influence to thwart the passage of this bill, which commits a violent outrage upon our rights, and the rights of our fathers, husbands and sons; and whatever may be the final result of the action of Congress in passing or enforcing oppressive laws for the sake of our religion, upon the noble men who have subdued these deserts, it is our duty to stand by them and support them by our faith, prayers, and works through every dark hour unto the end, and trust in the God of Abraham, Isaac and Jacob to defend us, and all who are called to suffer for keeping the commandments of God. Shall we as wives and mothers sit still and see our husbands, and sons, whom we know are obeying the highest behest of heaven, suffer for their religion without exerting ourselves to the extent of our power for their deliverance? No! verily, no!! God has revealed unto us the law of the Patriarchal order of marriage and commanded us to obey it. We are sealed to our husbands for time and eternity, that we may dwell with them and our children in the world to come, which guarantees unto us the greatest blessing for which we are created. If the rulers of our nation will so far depart from the spirit and the letter of our glorious Constitution as to deprive our Prophets, Apostles and Elders of citizenship, and imprison them for obeying this law, let them grant us this our last request, to make their prisons large enough to hold their wives, for where they go we will go also. . . .

PART V

SLAVERY, WAR,
AND EMANCIPATION

JAMES CURRY'S MOTHER

This account by James Curry, an escaped slave, was told to (and much later published by) Elizabeth Buffum Chace, a wealthy Quaker matron whose home in Valley Falls, Rhode Island, was a station on the Underground Railroad aiding slaves to escape to Canada.

"I was born in Person County, North Carolina. My master's name was Moses Chambers. My mother was the daughter of a white man and a slave woman. She, with her brother, were given, when little children, to my master's mother, soon after her marriage, by her father. Their new master and mistress were both drunkards, and possessed very little property besides these two slaves. My mother was treated very cruelly. O! I cannot tell you how dreadful her treatment was while she was a young girl. It is not proper to be written; but the treatment of females in slavery is very dreadful.

"When she was about fifteen years old, she attempted to run away. She got about fifteen miles, and stopped at the house of a poor white woman, with the intention of staying there four weeks, until her brother, who had a wife near there, came down to see her, which he did once in four weeks. She could not bear to go farther without hearing from her mother, and giving her intelligence of herself. She also wished to procure herself some clothes, as she was very destitute. At the end of three weeks, there came in a white man, who knew and arrested her, and returned her to her master. She soon afterwards married a slave in the neighborhood.

"Her mistress did not provide her with clothes, and her husband obtained for her a wheel, which she kept in her hut, for the purpose of spinning in the night, after her day's work for her cruel mistress was done. This her mistress endeavored to prevent, by keeping her spinning in the house until twelve or one o'clock at night. But she would then go home, and, fixing her wheel in a place made in the floor to prevent it making a noise, she would spin for herself, in order that she might be decently clad in the daytime. Her treatment continued so bad, that she, with her sister Ann, who was the slave of her mistress's sister, resolved to run away again. Her sister had a husband, who concluded to go too; and then my mother informed her husband, and they all four started together.

"Not knowing any better, they went directly south. After travelling two or three nights, Ann's husband thought they could travel safely by day,

Malcolm R. Lovell, ed., *Two Quaker Sisters* (New York: Liveright, 1937), pp. 136–46. Reprinted by permission of the publisher.

and so they walked on in the morning. They had got but a little way, when they met a white man, who stopped and asked them, 'Are you travellers?' They answered, 'Yes, sir.' 'Are you free?' 'Yes, sir.' 'Have you free papers?' 'Yes, sir.' (They got some person to furnish them before they started.) 'Well,' said he, 'go back to the next village, and we will have them examined.' So he took them before a magistrate, who examined the papers and said, 'These won't do.' He then said to the girls, 'Girls, we don't doubt that *you* are free, and if you choose, you may go on; but these boys you have stolen from their masters, and they must go to jail.' At that time, before the laws against emancipation were passed, bright mulattoes, such as these girls were, would be allowed to pass along the road unmolested, but now they could not. The girls, being unwilling to part with their husbands, went to jail with them, and being advertised, their masters came after them in a few days. This ended my mother's running away. Having young children soon, it tied her to slavery.

"Two or three years after this, she was separated from her husband by the removal of her master to the south. The separation of the slaves in this way is little thought of. A few masters regard their union as sacred, but where one does, a hundred care nothing about it. I knew a member of a Methodist church, who was making up a drove of slaves to send by his two sons to Alabama. He had one girl, whom he intended to send in this drove, whose husband belonged to another man. While preparing to depart, one of his sons said to him, 'It is wrong thus to separate man and wife.' The father raved at him, in great fury, saying, 'Do you talk to me about *a nigger's wife?*' The drove was sent off, and in two or three months, the other son wrote to his father, that he who had thus compassionated the negro's sufferings was dead, and before he returned, his mother died also.

"My uncle learned the hatter's trade, and being very smart, he supported his drunken master and mistress. He used to make hats, and then go off and sell them, and return the money to his master. But they spent so much that they got in debt, and were obliged to sell the slaves, who were purchased by their son, Moses Chambers. After this, my mother was married to a free colored man, named Peter Burnet, who was my father. When they had been married about two years, he travelled south with a white man, as his servant, who sold him into slavery, and she never saw him again. After a few years, she married a slave belonging to her master, and has since had six children. She gave to each of her children two names, but we were called by only one. It is not common for slaves to have more than one name, but my mother was a proud-spirited woman, and she gave her children two. She was a very good and tender mother.

She never made a public profession of religion, but she always tried to do right, and taught her children to know right from wrong. When I was a little child, she taught me to know my Maker, and that we should all die, and if we were good, we should be happy. . . .

"My mother was cook in the house for about twenty-two years. She cooked for from twenty-five to thirty-five, taking the family and the slaves together. The slaves ate in the kitchen. After my mistress's death, my mother was the only woman kept in the house. She took care of my master's children, some of whom were then quite small, and brought them up. One of the most trying scenes I ever passed through, when I would have laid down my life to protect her if I had dared, was this: after she had raised my master's children, one of his daughters, a young girl, came into the kitchen one day, and for some trifle about the dinner, she struck my mother, who pushed her away, and she fell on the floor. Her father was not at home. When he came, which was while the slaves were eating in the kitchen, she told him about it. He came down, called my mother out, and with a hickory rod, he beat her fifteen or twenty strokes, and then called his daughter and told her to take her satisfaction of her, and she did beat her until she was satisfied. O! it was dreadful, to see the girl whom my poor mother had taken care of from her childhood, thus beating her, and I must stand there, and did not dare to crook my finger in her defence.

"My mother's labor was very hard. She would go to the house in the morning, take her pail upon her head, and go away to the cow-pen, and milk fourteen cows. She then put on the bread for the family breakfast, and got the cream ready for churning, and set a little child to churn it, she having the care of from ten to fifteen children, whose mothers worked in the field. After clearing away the family breakfast, she got breakfast for the slaves; which consisted of warm corn bread and buttermilk, and was taken at twelve o'clock. In the meantime, she had beds to make, rooms to sweep, and many other duties. Then she cooked the family dinner, which was simply plain meat, vegetables and bread. Then the slaves' dinner was to be ready at from eight to nine o'clock in the evening. It consisted of corn bread, or potatoes, and the meat which remained of the master's dinner, or one herring apiece. At night she had the cows to milk again. There was little ceremony about the master's supper, unless there was company. This was her work day by day. Then in the course of the week, she had the washing and ironing to do for her master's family, who, however, were clothed very simply, and for her husband, seven children and herself.

"She would not get through to go to her log cabin until nine or ten o'clock at night. She would then be so tired, that she could scarcely stand; but she would find one boy with his knee out, and another with his elbow out, a patch wanting here, and a stitch there, and she would sit down by her lightwood fire, and sew and sleep alternately, often till the light began to streak in the east; and then lying down, she would catch a nap, and hasten to the toil of the day. Among the slave children were three little orphans, whose mothers, at their death, committed them to the care of my mother. One of them was a babe. She took them and treated them as her own. The master took no care about them. She always took a share of the cloth she had provided for her own children, to cover these little friendless ones. She would sometimes ask the master to procure them some clothes, but he would curse them and refuse to do it. We would sometimes tell her, that we would let the master clothe them, for she had enough to do for her own children. She replied, 'Their master will not clothe them, and I cannot see them go naked; I have children and I do not know where their lot may be cast; I may die and leave them, and I desire to do by these little orphans, as I should wish mine to be done by.'

VIRGINIA LADIES' PETITION TO
ELIMINATE SLAVERY

This petition was composed and sent to the Virginia General Assembly in 1832, just after Nat Turner's Rebellion, a slave uprising in Southampton County that left nearly sixty members of slaveholding families dead before it was ended by the militia. White revenge followed immediately, in the form of random killings of scores of blacks and the hanging of twenty slaves for participation. The rebellion caused a reassessment of slavery by many Virginians, including the 215 women who sent this petition to the legislature.

MEMORIAL OF THE LADIES OF AUGUSTA TO THE GENERAL ASSEMBLY OF VIRGINIA PRAYING THE ADOPTION OF SOME MEASURE FOR THE SPEEDY EXTIRPATION OF SLAVERY FROM THE COMMONWEALTH

Signed by 215 Ladies

[in a different hand] January 19th 1832 ref'd to select comm'ee

To the Hon. the General Assembly of the State of Virginia, [this] memorial of the subscribing females of the county of Augusta humbly represents that although it be unexampled in our beloved State, that females should interfere in its political concerns, and although we feel all the timidity incident to our sex in taking this step, yet we hold our right to do so to be unquestionable, and feel ourselves irresistably impelled to the exercise of that right by the most potent considerations and the perilous circumstances which surround us. We pretend not to conceal from you, our fathers and brothers, our protectors by your investment with the political power of the land, the fears which agitate our bosoms, and the dangers which await us, as revealed by recent tragical deeds. Our fears, we admit, are great, but we do not concede that they are the effects of blind & unreflecting cowardice; we do not concede that they spring from the superstitious timidity of our sex. Alas! we are indeed timid, but we appeal to your manly reason, to your more mature wisdom to attest the justice & propriety of our fears, when we call to your recollection the late slaughter of our sisters & their little ones, in certain parts of our land, & the strong probability that that slaughter was but a partial execu-

Petition, Inhabitants of Augusta County, January 19, 1832, Legislative Petitions, General Assembly, Legislative Department, Archives and Records Division, Library of Virginia, Richmond, Va. The editors are indebted to Elizabeth Varon for locating and providing a copy of this document.

tion of a widely projected scheme of carnage. We know not, we cannot know the night, nor the unguarded moment, by day or by night, which is pregnant with our destruction, & that of our husbands, & brothers, & sisters, & children; but we do know that we are, at every moment, exposed to the means of our own excision, & of all that is dear to us in life. The bloody monster which threatens us is warmed & cherished in our own hearths. O hear our prayer, & remove it, yes protectors of our persons, ye guardians of our peace!

Tell us not of the labors & hardships which we shall endure when our bond-servants shall be removed from us. They have no terrors for us. Those labors & hardships cannot be greater, or so great as those we now endure in providing for & ruling the faithless beings who are subjected to us. Or were they greater, still they are, in our esteem, less than the small dust in the balance, compared with the burden of our fears and our dangers. But what have we to fear, from these causes, more than females of other countries? Are they of the east, & of the west, of England, of France, more "cumbered with much serving" than we are? Are they less enlightened, or less accomplished? However we may be flattered, we will not be argued out of our senses, & persuaded into a belief which is contradicted by experience, & the testimony of sober facts. Many, very many of our sisters & brothers have fled to other lands, from the evils which we experience: and they send us back the evidences of their contentment & prosperity. They lament not their labors & hardships, but exult in their deliverance from servitude to their quondam slaves: And we, too, would fly—we, too, would exult in similar deliverance, were our destiny not otherwise ordered than it is. That destiny is in your hands, & we implore your high agency in ordering it for the best. We would enjoy such exultation on our native soil. Do not slight our importunities. Do not disregard our fears. Our destiny is identified with yours. If we perish, alas! what will become of you & your offspring?

We are not political economists, but our domestic employments, our engagements in rearing up the children of our husbands & brothers, our intimate concern with the interests & prosperity of society, we presume, cannot but inform us of the great & elementary principles of that important science. Indeed it is impossible that that science can have any other basis than the principles which are constantly developing themselves to us in our domestic relations. What is a nation but a family on a large scale? Our fears teach us to reflect & reason. And our reflections & reasonings have taught us that the peace of our homes, the welfare of society, the prosperity of future generations call aloud & imperiously for some decisive & efficient measure—and that measure cannot, we believe, be efficient, or of much benefit, if it have not for its ultimate object, the extinction of slavery, from amongst us. Without, therefore, entering upon a detail of facts & arguments, we implore you by the urgency of our fears, by the love we bear you as our fathers & brothers, by our anxieties for the little ones around us, by our estimate of domestic & public weal, by present danger, by the prospects of the future, by our female virtues, by the patriotism which flows in & animates our bosoms, by our prayers to Almighty GOD, not to let the power with which you are invested lie dormant, but that you exert it for the deliverance of yourselves, of us, of the children of the land, of future ages, from the direst curse which can befal a people. Signalize your legislation by this mighty deed. This we pray: and in duty will ever pray.

AN APPEAL TO THE WOMEN OF THE NOMINALLY FREE STATES, BY ANGELINA GRIMKÉ

Angelina Grimké (1805–1879) took the same path as her older sister Sarah away from her native South Carolina, to the North, to Quakerism, abolitionism, and women's rights. She became publicly identified with the antislavery cause when William Lloyd Garrison printed a letter she had written to his abolitionist newspaper, the Liberator, *in 1835. Her background as a white Southerner and her deep commitment to women's moral equality with men gave her abolitionist views a unique dynamism, and she became a sought-after lecturer. After composing her antislavery* Appeal to the Christian Women of the South *in 1836, she addressed the following appeal to Northern women. Her outspokenness against racism as well as slavery was not typical of white abolitionist women who had grown up in the North.*

. . . [In] a country where women are degraded and brutalized, and where their exposed persons bleed under the lash—where they are sold in the shambles of "negro brokers"—robbed of their hard earnings—torn from their husbands, and forcibly plundered of their virtue and their offspring; surely in *such* a country, it is very natural that *women* should wish to know "the reason *why*"—especially when these outrages of blood and nameless horror are practiced in violation of the principles of our national Bill of Rights and the Preamble of our Constitution. We do not, then, and cannot concede the position, that because this is a *political subject* women ought to fold their hands in idleness, and close their eyes and ears to the "horrible things" that are practiced in our land. The denial of our duty to act, is a bold denial of our right to act; and if we have no right to act, then may *we* well be termed "the white slaves of the North"— for, like our brethren in bonds, we must seal our lips in silence and despair. . . .

Slavery exerts a most deadly influence over the morals of our country, not only over that portion of it where it actually exists as "a domestic institution," but like the miasma of some pestilential pool, it spreads its desolating influence far beyond its own boundaries. Who does not know that licentiousness is a crying sin at the North as well as at the South? and who does not admit that the manners of the South in this respect

Angelina Grimké, *An Appeal to the Women of the Nominally Free States,* 2d ed., issued by an Antislavery Convention of American Women (Boston: Isaac Knapp, 1838), pp. 13–16, 19–23, 49–53, 60–61.

have had a wide and destructive influence on Northern character? Can crime be fashionable and common in one part of the Union and unrebuked by the other without corrupting the very heart's blood of the nation, and lowering the standard of morality everywhere? Can Northern men go down to the well-watered plains of the South to make their fortunes, without bowing themselves in the house of Rimmon and drinking the waters of that river of pollution which rolls over the plain of Sodom and Gomorrah? Do they return uncontaminated to their homes, or does not many and many a Northerner dig the grave of his virtue in the Admahs and Zeboims of our Southern States. And can our theological and academic institutions be opened to the sons of the planter without endangering the purity of the morals of our own sons, by associations with men who regard the robbery of the poor as no crime, and oppression as no wrong? Impossible! . . .

But this is not all; our people have erected a false standard by which to judge men's character. Because in the slaveholding States colored men are plundered and kept in abject ignorance, are treated with disdain and scorn, so here, too, in profound deference to the South, we refuse to eat, or ride, or walk, or associate, or open our institutions of learning, or even our zoological institutions to people of color, unless they visit them in the capacity of *servants,* of menials in humble attendance upon the Anglo-American. Who ever heard of a more wicked absurdity in a Republican country?

Have Northern women, then, nothing to do with slavery, when its demoralizing influence is polluting their domestic circles and blasting the fair character of *their* sons and brothers? Nothing to do with slavery when *their* domestics are often dragged by the merciless kidnapper from the hearth of their nurseries and the arms of their little ones? Nothing to do with slavery when Northern women are chained and driven like criminals, and incarcerated in the great prison-house of the South? Nothing to do with slavery? . . .

We have hitherto addressed you more as moral and responsible beings, than in the distinctive character of women; we have appealed to you on the broad ground of *human rights* and human responsibilities, rather than on that of your peculiar duties as women. We have pursued this course of argument designedly, because, in order to prove that you have any duties to perform, it is necessary first to establish the principle of moral being—for all our rights and all our duties grow out of this principle. *All moral beings have essentially the same rights and the same duties,* whether they be male or female. . . .

WOMEN THE VICTIMS OF SLAVERY

Out of the millions of slaves who have been stolen from Africa, a very great number must have been women who were torn from the arms of their fathers and husbands, brothers and children, and subjected to all the horrors of the middle passage and the still greater sufferings of slavery in a foreign land. Multitudes of these were cast upon our inhospitable shores; some of them now toil out a life of bondage, "one hour of which is fraught with more misery than ages of that" which our fathers rose in rebellion to oppose. But the great mass of female slaves in the southern States are the descendants of these hapless strangers; 1,000,000 of them now wear the iron yoke of slavery in this land of boasted liberty and law. They are our country women—*they are our sisters;* and to us, as women, they have a right to look for sympathy with their sorrows, and effort and prayer for their rescue. Upon those of us especially who have named the name of Christ, they have peculiar claims, and claims which *we must answer, or we shall incur a heavy load of guilt.* . . .

WOMEN ARE SLAVEHOLDERS

Multitudes of the Southern women hold men, women and children as *property. They* are pampered in luxury, and nursed in the school of tyranny; *they* sway the iron rod of power, and *they* rob the laborer of his hire. Immortal beings tremble at *their* nod, and bow in abject submission at *their* word, and under the cowskin too often wielded by *their* own delicate hands. Women at the South hold *their own sisters* and brothers in bondage. Start not at this dreadful assertion—we speak that which some of us do know—we testify that which some of us have seen. Such facts ought to be known, that the women of the North may understand *their* duties, and be incited to perform *them.*

Southern families often present the most disgusting scenes of dissension, in which the mistress acts a part derogatory to her own character as a woman. . . .

[T]here are *female tyrants* too, who are prompt to lay their complaints of misconduct before their husbands, brothers and sons, and to urge them to commit acts of violence against their helpless slaves. Others still more cruel, place the lash in the hands of some trusty domestic, and stand by whilst he lays the heavy strokes upon the unresisting victim, deaf to the cries for mercy which rend the air, or rather the more enraged at such appeals, which are only answered by the Southern lady with the prompt command of "give her more for that." This work of chastisement is often performed by a brother, or other relative of the poor sufferer, which circumstance stings like an adder the very heart of the slave while her body writhes under the lash. Other mistresses who cannot bear that their delicate ears should be pained by the screams of the poor sufferers, write an order to the master of the Charleston workhouse, or the New Orleans calaboose, where they are most cruelly stretched in order to render the stroke of the whip or the blow of the paddle more certain to produce cuts and wounds which cause the blood to flow at every stroke. And let it be remembered that these poor creatures are often *women* who are most indecently divested of their clothing and exposed to the gaze of the executioner of a *woman's* command.

What then, our beloved sisters, must be the effects of such a system upon the domestic character of the white females? Can a corrupt tree bring forth good fruit? Can such despotism mould the character of the Southern woman to gentleness and love? or may we not fairly conclude that all that suavity, for which slaveholding ladies are so conspicuous, is in many instances the paint and the varnish of hypocrisy, the fashionable polish of a heartless superficiality?

But it is not the character alone of the mistress that is deeply injured by the possession and exercise of such despotic power, nor is it the degradation and suffering to which the slave is continually subject; but another important consideration is, that in consequence of the dreadful state of morals at the South, the wife and the daughter sometimes find their homes a scene of the most mortifying, heart-rending preference of the degraded domestic, or the colored daughter of the head of the family. There are, alas, too many families, of which the contentions of Abraham's household is a fair example. But we forbear to lift the veil of private life any higher; let these few hints suffice to give you some idea of what is daily passing *behind* that curtain which has been so carefully drawn before the scenes of domestic life in Christian America.

THE COLORED WOMEN OF THE NORTH ARE OPPRESSED

[Another] reason we would urge for the interference of northern women with the system of slavery is, that in consequence of the odium which the degradation of slavery has attached to *color* even in the free States, our *colored sisters* are dreadfully oppressed here. Our seminaries of learning are closed to them, they are almost entirely banished from our lecture rooms, and even in the house of God they are separated from their white brethren and sisters as though we were afraid to come in contact with a colored skin. . . .

Here, then, are some of the bitter fruits of that inveterate prejudice which the vast proportion of northern women are cherishing towards their colored sisters; and let us remember that every one of us who denies the sinfulness of this prejudice, . . . is awfully guilty in the sight of Him who is no respecter of persons. . . .

But our colored sisters are oppressed in other ways. As they walk the streets of our cities, they are continually liable to be insulted with the vulgar epithet of "nigger"; no matter how respectable or wealthy, they cannot visit the Zoological Institute of New-York except in the capacity of nurses or servants—no matter how worthy, they cannot gain admittance into or receive assistance from any of the charities of this city. In Philadelphia, they are cast out of our Widow's Asylum, and their children are refused admittance to the House of Refuge, the Orphan's House and the Infant School connected with the Alms-House, though into these are gathered the very offscouring of our population. These are only specimens of that soul-crushing influence from which the colored women of the north are daily suffering. Then, again, some of them have been robbed of their husbands and children by the heartless kidnapper, and others have themselves been dragged into slavery. If they attempt to travel, they are exposed to great indignities and great inconveniences. Instances have been known of their actually dying in consequence of the exposure to which they were subjected on board of our steamboats. No money could purchase the use of a berth for a delicate female because she had a colored skin. Prejudice, then, degrades and fetters the minds, persecutes and murders the bodies of our free colored sisters. Shall *we* be silent at such a time as this? . . .

Much may be done, too, by sympathizing with our oppressed colored sisters, who are suffering in our very midst. Extend to them the right hand of fellowship on the broad principles of humanity and Christianity, treat them as *equals,* visit them as *equals,* invite them to co-operate with you in Anti-Slavery and Temperance and Moral Reform Societies—in Maternal Associations and Prayer Meetings and Reading Companies. . . .

Multitudes of instances will continually occur in which you will have the opportunity of *identifying yourselves with this injured class* of our fellow-beings: embrace these opportunities at all times and in all places, in the true nobility of our great Exemplar, who was ever found among the *poor and the despised,* elevating and blessing them with his counsels and presence. In this way, and this alone, will you be enabled to subdue that deep-rooted prejudice which is doing the work of oppression in the free States to a most dreadful extent.

When this demon has been cast out of your own hearts, when *you* can recognize the colored woman as a WOMAN—*then* will you be prepared to send out an appeal to our Southern sisters, entreating them to "go and do likewise."

NARRATIVES OF ESCAPED SLAVES

Accounts of slave life by men and women who managed to escape from bondage in the South were the first form of African American literature to be published and a principal tool of the antislavery movement. Abolitionist Benjamin Drew, a Bostonian who traveled to Canada in 1855 to collect the stories of black refugees from slavery, recorded a series of narratives, including these.

MRS. JAMES SEWARD

The slaves want to get away bad enough. They are not contented with their situation.

I am from the eastern shore of Maryland. I never belonged but to one master; he was very bad indeed. I was never sent to school, nor allowed to go to church. They were afraid we would have more sense than they. I have a father there, three sisters, and a brother. My father is quite an old man, and he is used very badly. Many a time he has been kept at work a whole long summer day without sufficient food. A sister of mine has been punished by his taking away her clothes and locking them up, because she used to run when master whipped her. He kept her at work with only what she could pick up to tie on her for decency. He took away her child which had just begun to walk, and gave it to another woman,—but she went and got it afterward. He had a large farm eight miles from home. Four servants were kept at the house. My master could not manage to whip my sister when she was strong. He waited until she was confined, and the second week after her confinement he said, "Now I can handle you, now you are weak." She ran from him, however, and had to go through water, and was sick in consequence.

I was beaten at one time over the head by my master, until the blood ran from my mouth and nose: then he tied me up in the garret, with my hands over my head,—then he brought me down and put me in a little cupboard, where I had to sit cramped up, part of the evening, all night, and until between four and five o'clock, next day, without any food. The cupboard was near a fire, and I thought I should suffocate.

My brother was whipped on one occasion until his back was as raw as a piece of beef, and before it got well, master whipped him again. His back was an awful sight.

Benjamin Drew, ed., *A Northside View of Slavery: The Refugee, or the Narratives of Fugitive Slaves in Canada, Related by Themselves* (Boston: John P. Jowett, 1856), pp. 41–44, 50–51, 138, 140–41, 224–27.

We were all afraid of master: when I saw him coming, my heart would jump up into my mouth, as if I had seen a serpent.

I have been wanting to come away for eight years back. I waited for Jim Seward to get ready. Jim had promised to take me away and marry me. Our master would allow no marriages on the farm. When Jim had got ready, he let me know,—he brought to me two suits of clothes—men's clothes—which he had bought on purpose for me. I put on both suits to keep me warm. We eluded pursuit and reached Canada in safety.

MRS. NANCY HOWARD

I was born in Anne Arundel county, Maryland,—was brought up in Baltimore. After my escape, I lived in Lynn, Mass., seven years, but I left there through fear of being carried back, owing to the fugitive slave law. I have lived in St. Catharines less than a year.

The way I got away was,—my mistress was sick, and went into the country for her health. I went to stay with her cousin. After a month, my mistress was sent back to the city to her cousin's, and I waited on her. My daughter had been off three years. A friend said to me,—"Now is your chance to get off." At last I concluded to go,—the friend supplying me with money. I was asked no questions on the way north.

My idea of slavery is, that it is one of the blackest, the wickedest things that ever were in the world. When you tell them the truth, they whip you to make you lie. I have taken more lashes for this, than for any other thing, because I would not lie.

One day I set the table, and forgot to put on the carving-fork—the knife was there. I went to the table to put on a plate. My master said,—"Where is the fork?" I told him "I forgot it." He says,—"You d——d black b——, I'll forget you!"—at the same time hitting me on the head with the carving-knife. The blood spurted out,—you can see. [Here the woman removed her turban and showed a circular cicatrice denuded of hair, about an inch in diameter, on the top of her head.] My mistress took me into the kitchen and put on camphor, but she could not stop the bleeding. A doctor was sent for. He came, but asked no questions. I was frequently punished with raw hides,—was hit with tongs and poker and any thing. I used when I went out, to look up at the sky, and say, "Blessed Lord, oh, do take me out of this!" It seemed to me I could not bear another lick. I can't forget it. I sometimes dream that I am pursued, and when I wake, I am scared almost to death.

HENRY GOWENS

I have had a wide experience of the evils of slavery, in my own person, and have an extensive knowledge of the horrors of slavery, in all their length and breadth, having witnessed them in Old Virginia, North Carolina, New Virginia, Tennessee, Alabama, and Mississippi. I belonged in the State of Virginia, and am, I suppose, about forty years old. . . .

About the first of Gen. Jackson's Presidency, my master employed an overseer, named Kimball, over one hundred and thirty slaves, in Lauderdale Co., Alabama. This Kimball was one of the most cruel men I ever saw. . . .

In the picking cotton season, Mr. K. would punish the women in the severest manner, because they did not pick cotton fast enough. He would thrust their heads into a cotton basket. What I say now would scarcely be believed only among those who are in that neighborhood, because it looks too cruel for any one to do or to believe, if they had no experience of such things or had not seen the like,—they would not dare lift up their heads, as perhaps he would punish them twice as much. Then he would throw clothes up over their heads and the basket, and flog them as hard as he could with a rugged lash, cutting their flesh terribly, till the blood ran to their heels. Sometimes they would from the torment lift their heads, when he would perhaps give them a third more than he otherwise would; and this without reference to any particular condition they might be in at the time. The men he would generally place across a log, tie their hands together, and their feet together, and put a rail through under the log with the ends between their feet and hands; and in this condition, which is itself painful, he would apply the lash. Sometimes, to cramp down the mind of the husband, he would compel him to assist in the punishment of his wife. Who will tell of the good of slavery? I would rather be a brute in the field, than to endure what my people have to endure, what they have endured in many parts of the slave-holding States.

There was one religious old woman, Aunt Dinah,—very pious: all believed she was, even my master. She used to take care of the infants at the quarters while the mothers were out at work. At noon, the mothers would come home to nurse their children, unless they were too far off—then the infants were carried to them. Aunt Dinah, knowing how cruelly the women were treated, at last, when the master was absent, picked up courage to go to the mistress and complain of the dealings of the overseer. My mistress belonged to the Presbyterian Church; Aunt Dinah to the Baptist. The mistress then began to my master about the cruelty on the place, without disclosing how she got her information. I do not think the master would have interfered, were it not that the mistress also told him of the overseer's intimacy with some of the female slaves. She being a well-bred lady, the master had to take some notice of the management. He told the overseer to change his mode of punishing the women; to slip their clothes down from their shoulders, and punish them on their backs. No interference was ever made except in this one instance.

The overseer had one child by a slave woman. I left the child there a slave. At the expiration of a year Kimball left. Three months after, or thereabouts, he was hanged in Raleigh, N.C., for the murder of his stepfather. The slaves were rejoiced at his being hung, and thought he ought to have been hung before he came there to be overseer.

MRS. JOHN LITTLE

I was born in Petersburg, Va. When very young, I was taken to Montgomery county. My old master died there, and I remember that all the people were sold. My father and mother were sold together about one mile from me. After a year, they were sold a great distance, and I saw them no more. My mother came to me before she went away, and said, "Good by, be a good girl; I never expect to see you any more."

Then I belonged to Mr. T—— N——, the son of my old master. He was pretty good, but his wife, my mistress, beat me like sixty. Here are three scars on my right hand and arm, and one on my forehead, all from wounds inflicted with a broken china plate. My cousin, a man, broke the plate in two pieces, and she said, "Let me see that plate." I handed up the pieces to her, and she threw them down on me: they cut four gashes, and I bled like a butcher. One piece cut into the sinew of the thumb, and made a great knot permanently. The wound had to be sewed up. This long scar over my right eye, was from a blow with a stick of wood. One day she knocked me lifeless with a pair of tongs,—when I came to, she was holding me up, through fright. Some of the neighbors said to her, "Why don't you learn Eliza to sew?" She answered, "I only want to learn her to do my housework, that's all." I can tell figures when I see them, but cannot read or write.

I belonged to them until I got married at the age of sixteen, to Mr. John Little, of Jackson. My master sold me for debt,—he was a man that would drink, and he had to sell me. I was sold to F—— T——, a planter and slave-trader, who soon after, at my persuasion, bought Mr. Little.

I was employed in hoeing cotton, a new employment: my hands were badly blistered. "Oh, you must be a great lady," said the overseer, "can't handle the hoe without blistering your hands!" I told him I could not help it. My hands got hard, but I could not stand the sun. The hot sun made me so sick I could not work, and, John says if I had not come away, they would surely have sold me again. There was one weakly woman named Susan, who could not stand the work, and she was sold to Mississippi, away from her husband and son. That's one way of taking care of the sick and weak. That's the way the planters do with a weakly, sickly "nigger."—they say "he's a dead expense to 'em," and put him off as soon as they can. After Susan was carried off, her husband went to see her: when he came back he received two hundred blows with the paddle.

I staid with T—— more than a year. A little before I came away, I heard that master was going to give my husband three hundred blows with the paddle. He came home one night with an axe on his shoulder, tired with chopping timber. I had his clothes all packed up, for I knew he would have to go. He came hungry, calculating on his supper,—I told him what was going. I never heard him curse before—he cursed then. Said he, "If any man, white or black, lays his hand on me to-night, I'll put this axe clear through him—clear through him": and he would have done it, and I would not have tried to hinder him. But there was a visitor at the house, and no one came: he ran away. Next morning, the overseer came for him. The master asked where he was; I could have told him, but would not. My husband came back no more.

When we had made arrangements for leaving, a slave told of us. Not long after, master called to me, "Come here, my girl, come here." I went to him: he tied me by the wrist with a rope. He said, "Oh, my girl, I don't blame you,—you are young, and don't know; it's that d——d infernal son of a ——; if I had him here, I'd blow a ball through him this minute." But he was deceived about it: I had put John up to hurrying off.

Then master stood at the great house door, at a loss what to do. There he had Willis, who was to have run away with us, and the man who betrayed us. At last he took us all off about half a mile to a swamp, where old A—— need not hear us as he was going to meeting, it being Sunday. He whipped Willis to make him tell where we were going. Willis said, "Ohio State." "What do you want to be free for? G—— d—— you, what do you know about freedom? Who was going with you?" "Only Jack." "G—— d—— Jack to h——, and you too." While they were whipping Willis, he said, "Oh, master, I'll never run away." "I didn't ask you about that, you d—— son of a ——, you." Then they tried to make him tell about a slave girl who had put her child aside: but he knew nothing about that. As soon as they had done whipping him, they put a plough clavis about his ankle to which they attached a chain which was secured about his neck with a horse-lock.

Then they took a rheumatic boy, who had stopped with us, whom I had charged not to tell. They whipped him with the paddle, but he said he was ignorant of it: he bore the whipping, and never betrayed us. Then they questioned him about the girl and the child, as if that boy could know anything about it! Then came my turn; they whipped me in the same way they did the men. Oh, those slaveholders are a brutish set of people,—the master made a remark to the overseer about my shape. Before striking me, master questioned me about the girl. I denied all knowledge of the affair. I only knew that she had been with child, and that now she was not, but I did not tell them even that. I was ashamed of my situation, they remarking upon me. I had been brought up in the house, and was not used to such coarseness. Then he (master) asked, "Where is Jack?" "I don't know." Said he, "Give her h——, R——." That was his common word. Then they struck me several blows with the paddle. I kept on telling them it was of no use to whip me, as I knew nothing to tell them. No irons were ready for me, and I was put under a guard,—but I was too cunning for him, and joined my husband.

SARAH PARKER REMOND ON AMERICAN SLAVERY

A well-educated free black woman born about 1815 in Salem, Massachu-
setts, Sarah Remond became an influential abolitionist in the 1850s, as
did her brother Charles L. Remond. She spoke frequently under the aus-
pices of the American Anti-Slavery Society. During 1859 and 1860 she
went overseas and lectured in Scotland, Ireland, and England on the aboli-
tion of slavery, and was very well received by curious and appreciative
crowds. The following is an account of one of her lectures in London.

Miss Sarah P. Remond, a lady of colour from the United States of America,
last evening delivered a lecture on American Slavery, to a highly respectable audience, in the Music Hall, Store-street, Bedford-square. The lecturer was introduced by Mr. L. A. Chamerovzow, who said that, as
Secretary of the British and Foreign Anti-Slavery Society, he had much
pleasure in bespeaking for Miss Remond the kind attention of the meeting. His acquaintance with her had been short, but her reputation for zeal
and labour in the anti-slavery cause had been known to him for years.
The lady's brother was a delegate to the World's Anti-Slavery Convention
in 1840, and was well remembered for the eloquence he displayed on
that occasion. . . .

Miss Remond then rose, and said she was the representative in the first
place of four millions of human beings held in slavery in a land boasting
of its freedom—of 400,000 persons of colour nominally free, but treated
worse than criminals. She was the representative also of that body of
abolitionists in the United States, reproachfully called Garrisonians; an
epithet, however, which she deemed it an honour to appropriate. What
was the crime of the millions thus enslaved? The head and front of their
offending was the colour of their skin. She did not represent the politics
of the country, nor even the religious sentiment of the country, for that
had been corrupted by the influence of slavery. She pleaded especially on
behalf of her own sex. Words were inadequate to express the depth of the
infamy into which they were plunged by the cruelty and licentiousness
of their brutal masters. If English women and English wives knew the
unspeakable horrors to which their sex were exposed on southern plantations, they would freight every westward gale with the voice of their
moral indignation, and demand for the black woman the protection and
rights enjoyed by the white. It was a dark and evil hour when the first

"An Account of Miss Remond's Lecture," *Anti-Slavery Advocate* (London) 2, no. 31 (July 1, 1859), pp. 251–52.

slave-ship landed its unhallowed cargo on the soil of Virginia. But it was a still darker one when the patriots of the revolution compromised their principles, and incorporated slavery in the federal constitution. There was this immeasurable difference between the condition of the poorer English woman and that of the slave woman—that their persons were free and their progeny their own; while the slave woman was the victim of the heartless lust of her master, and the children whom she bore were his property. The situation of the free coloured population was also one of deep degradation. They were expelled from railway cars and steamboats, and excluded, even in the house of God, from the privileges common to other worshippers. Miss Remond then traced the career of Mr. Garrison from the year 1833 to the present time, and recounted in a touching manner the perils to which he had been exposed, the sacrifices he had made, and the progress which had been effected by his unwearied labours during the last quarter of a century. She had listened with indignation a few nights before to the statement that the slaves were happy and contented. If so, why had more than 40,000 fled to the free soil of Canada, and were ready to sell their lives in defence of the sovereignty of Queen Victoria? The lecturer read an affecting account of the sale by auction of a woman who was recommended on account of her being indistinguishable by complexion from the white race, for her unsullied virtue, her personal beauty, and her elevated piety, and who, for these reasons, brought a high price that she might become the mistress of some depraved monster. The lecturer paid a high tribute to Mr. Wendell Philipps, who, with Mr. Garrison, had been traduced by the person whose assertions she already noticed, and concluded by pointing out the value to the American anti-slavery cause of those expressions of sympathy which it was in the power of the people of England to send across the Atlantic, which would greatly cheer the hearts of those engaged in the great struggle now going on, and tend greatly to advance the cause of negro emancipation.

Miss Remond was listened to with great attention and much apparent interest, and sat down midst great applause.

A SLAVE WRITES TO HER FORMER MISTRESS

This rare letter written by a slave tells a story of forced migration and family breakup.

Georgia Bullock Co.   August 29[?] 1857

My Loving Miss Patsey I have long bin wishing to imbrace this presant and pleasant opertunity of unfolding my Plans and fealings Since I was constrained to leav my Long Loved home and friends which I cannot never gave my Self the Least Promis of returning to. I am well and injoying good health and has ever Since I Left Randolph. When I Left Randoph I went to Rockingham and Stad there five weaks and then I left there and went to Richmon Virginia to be Sold and I stade there three days and was bought by a man by the name of Groover and brought to Georgia and he kept me about Nine months and he being a trader Sold me to a man by the Name of Rimes and he Sold me to a man by the Name of Lester and he has owned me four years and Says that he will keep me til death Siparates us without Some of my old north Caroliner friends wants to buy me again. My Dear Mistress I cannot tell my fealings nor how bad I wish to See you and old Boss and Miss Rahol and her brother. I do not [k]now which I want to See the worst Miss Rahol or mother. I have though[t] that I wanted to See mother but never befour did I [k]no[w] what it was to want to See a parent and could not. I wish you to gave my love to old Boss, Miss Rahol and Bailum and gave my manafold love to mother brothers and Sister and pleas to tell them to Right to me So I may here from them if I cannot See them and also I wish you to right to me and Right me all the nuse. I do want to [k]now whether old Boss is Still Living on now and all the rest of them and I want to [k]now whether Bailum is married or no. I wish to [k]now what has Ever become of my Presus little girl. I left her in goldsborough with Mr. Walker and I have not herd from her Since and Walker Said that he was going to carry her to Rockingham and give her to his Sister and I want to [k]no[w] whether he did or no as I do wish to See her very mutch and Boss Says he wishes to [k]now whether he will Sell her or now and the least that can buy her and that he wishes a answer as Soon as he can get one as I wish him to buy her and my Boss being a man of Reason and fealing wishes to grant my trubled breast that mutch gratification and wishes to [k]now whether

Violet to Patsey Padison, August 29[?], 1857, Joseph Allred Papers, Special Collections Library, Duke University. The editors are indebted to Joan Cashin for locating and providing a copy of this document.

he will Sell her or now. So I must come to a close by Enscribing my Self your long loved and well wishing play mate as a Sarvant until death. Vilet   Sister of Georgia

To Miss Patsey Padison of North Carolina

My Bosses Name is James B. Lester and if you Should think anuff of me to right me which I do beg the favor of you as a Servant direct your letter to Millars, Bullock County Georgia. Pleas to right me. So fare you well in love.

LOUISA MCCORD ON ENFRANCHISEMENT OF WOMAN

Louisa McCord, daughter of planter and statesman Langdon Cheves, was born into the elite of South Carolina in 1810. Well educated—an intellectual, indeed, with a particular passion for political economy—she remained single until the age of thirty. With her husband David McCord, a lawyer, she lived near South Carolina College, in Columbia, and became the mother of three children. She utterly rejected Northern woman's rights principles and was an avid defender of the antebellum Southern way of life. In this essay, which was published in the prestigious Southern Quarterly Review *(over her initials only), she responded to the published proceedings of the third woman's rights convention, held in Worcester, Massachusetts, in 1851, and to a favorable review of the convention's proceedings that had appeared in the English* Westminster Review. *(Note: "Cuffee" was a common name for a male slave.)*

A true woman, fulfilling a woman's duties, (and do not let our masculine readers suppose that we would *confine* these to shirt-making, pudding-mixing, and other such household gear, nor yet even to the adornment of her own fair person,) a high-minded, intellectual woman, disdaining not her position, nor, because the world calls it humble, seeking to put aside God's and Nature's law, to *her* pleasure; an earnest woman, striving, as all earnest minds *can* strive, to do and to work, even as the Almighty laws of Nature teach her that God would have her to do and to work, is, perhaps, the highest personification of Christian self-denial, love and charity, which the world can see. God, who has made every creature to its place, has, perhaps, not given to woman the most enviable position in his creation, but a most clearly defined position he *has* given her. Let her object, then, be to raise herself *in* that position. *Out* of it, there is only failure and degradation. . . .

Woman's condition certainly admits of improvement, (but when have the strong forgotten to oppress the weak?) but never can any amelioration result from the guidance of her prophets in this present move. Here, as in all other improvements, the good must be brought about by working with, not against—by seconding, not opposing—Nature's laws. Woman, seeking as a woman, may raise her position,—seeking as a man, we repeat, she but degrades it. Every thing contrary to Nature, is abhorrent to Nature, and the mental aberrations of woman, which we are now discuss-

L. S. M., "Enfranchisement of Woman," *Southern Quarterly Review,* n.s., 5, no. 10 (April 1852), pp. 322–41.

ing, excite at once pity and disgust, like those revolting physical deformities which the eye turns from with involuntary loathing, even while the hand of charity is extended to relieve them. We are no undervaluer of woman; rather we profess ourselves her advocate. Her mission is, to our seeming, even nobler than man's, and she is, in the true fulfilment of that mission, certainly the higher being. . . . Woman's duty, woman's nature, is to love, to sway by love; to govern by love, to teach by love, to civilize by love! . . . Pure and holy, self-devoted and suffering, woman's love is the breath of that God of love, who, loving and pitying, has bid *her* learn to love and to suffer, implanting in her bosom the one single comfort that she is the watching spirit, the guardian angel of those she loves. We say not that all women are thus; we say not that most women are thus. Alas! no; for thus would man's vices be shamed from existence, and the world become perfect. But we do say, that such is the type of woman, such her moral formation, such her perfection, and in so far as she comes not up to this perfection, she falls short of the model type of her nature. . . . *Fulfil* thy destiny; *oppose* it not. Herein lies thy track. Keep it. Nature's sign-posts are within thee, and it were well for thee to learn to read them. . . . Woman, *cherish thy mission.* Fling thyself not from the high pedestal whereon God has placed thee. Cast not from thee thy moral strength— for, lo! what then art thou! Wretchedly crawling to thy shame, thy physical weakness trampled under foot by a brutal master, behold thee, thou proud mother of earth, to what art thou sunk! . . .

What first do these reformers ask? "Admission in law and in fact, to equality in all rights, political, civil and social, with the male citizens of the community." "Women are entitled to the right of suffrage, and to be considered eligible to office." "Civil and political rights acknowledge no sex, and therefore the word 'male' should be struck from every state constitution." "A co-equal share in the formation and administration of laws,—municipal, state and national,—through legislative assemblies, courts and executive offices." Then follows the memorable quotation from the "memorable document" about all men being created free and equal, the ladies arguing, with some reason, that "men" here, certainly stands for human beings, thereby prove their right at least equal to Cuffee's. . . .

But, their reasoning in all this? for they have an argument. First, then, as we have just seen, they claim that the distinctions of *sex and colour are accidental and irrelevant to all questions of government.* This is certainly clinching the argument, and that by an assumption which is so extremely illogical, that we are forced to say, if this reforming sisterhood can advance no better ground for their pretensions, it shows them ill-fitted for the reins of state which they propose taking in hand. . . . Sex and colour are severally so essential to the being of a woman and a negro, that it is impossible to imagine the existence of either, without these distinctive marks. . . .

If beings are created to different ends, it is impossible to consider in them the point of equality or inequality, except in so far as their differences are of a kind to still allow them to be cast in the same category. As, for instance, the man, as animal, is superior to the beast, whose subordinate intellect makes him, as co-labourer of the soil, or as rival candidate for its benefits, inferior to man. The white man is, for the same reason, superior to the negro. The woman, classed as man, must also be inferior, if only (we waive for the moment the question of intellect) because she is inferior in corporeal strength. A female-man must necessarily be inferior to a male-man, so long as the latter has the power to knock her down. In womanhood is her strength and her triumph. Class both as woman, and the man again becomes the inferior, inasmuch as he is incapable of fulfilling her functions. A male woman could as ill assume the place and duties of womanhood, as a female-man could those of manhood. Each is strong in his own nature. They are neither inferior, nor superior, nor equal. They are different. The air has its uses, and the fire has its uses, but these are neither equal nor unequal—they are different. . . . God has made it so, and reason, instinct and experience teach us its uses. Woman, Nature teaches you yours. . . .

We, of the conservatives, who judge of the uses of things by their aptitudes, can read woman's duties anywhere better than in an election crowd, scuffling with Cuffee for a vote. Imagine the lovely Miss Caroline, the fascinating Miss Martha, elbowing Sambo for the stump! All being equals, and no respect for persons to be expected, the natural conclusion is, that Miss Caroline or Martha, being indisputably (even the Worcester conventionalists allow that) corporeally weaker than Sambo, would be thrust into the mud. "Hello da! Miss Caroline git two teet knock out, and Miss Marta hab a black eye and bloody nose!" "Well, wha' faw I stop fa dat? Ebery man must help hisself. I git de stump anyhow, and so, fellow-citizens, Sambo will show how Miss Marta desarve what she git." Or, let us suppose them hoisted through this dirty work. The member is chaired—some fair lady, some Mrs. or Miss Paulina Davis, who, we see, figures as President of the last convention, or one of her vices, Angelina Grimké Weld, or Lucretia Mott—let us imagine the gentle Paulina, Angelina, or Lucretia fairly pitted, in the Senate, against Mr. Foote, for instance, or Mr. Benton, or the valourous Houston, or any other mere patriot, whom luck and electioneering have foisted there. We do not doubt their feminine power, in the war of words—and again we beg to defer a little the question of intellect—but are the ladies ready for a boxing match? Such things happen sometimes; and though it is not impossible that the fair Paulina, Angelina and Lucretia might have the courage to face a pistol, have they the strength to resist a blow? . . .

The fact, that women have been queens and regents, and filled well these positions, as cited by the reviewer in the cases of Elizabeth, Isabella, Maria Theresa, Catharine of Russia, Blanche, etc., proves that woman, as a woman and a monarch—with the double difference, that the habits of the civilized world accord to these positions—has had the intellect to fill the position well; but it does not prove, and rather goes to disprove, her power of struggling with the masses. As woman and queen, doubly isolated from those masses, she kept her position, simply because of such isolation—because, supported by the laws and habits of society, none dared insult or resist her. But, suppose those laws and habits abrogated, what would have become of the virago, Elizabeth, when she gave the lordly Essex a blow on the ear? If ever it should happen to the fair Paulina, Angelina or Lucretia to try, under the new *regime*, a similar experiment on any of their male coadjutors or opponents, it is rather probable that they may receive, upon the subject of aptitudes and uses, a somewhat striking lesson. . . . Joan of Arc, (decidedly the most remarkable of heroines, and, strange to say, not cited by the reviewer,) was a wonderful woman; great as a woman; a phenomenon in her way, certainly, but still a woman-phenomenon. Her deeds were unusual for woman, but, nevertheless, done as a woman, and claiming, for their sanction, not the rights and habits of manhood, but divine inspiration. She never levelled herself to man, or, so doing, must have sunk to the rank of the coarse *femmes de la Halle* of the French revolution. Such, too, would of necessity be the case with the man-woman that our conventionists would manufacture. Deprived of all which has hitherto, in separating her from man, wrapped her, as it were, in a veil of deity; naked of all those observances and distinctions which have been, if not always her efficient, still her only shield; turned out upon the waste common of existence, with no distinctive mark but corporeal weakness; she becomes the inevitable victim of brutal strength. . . . Man is corporeally stronger than woman, and because he, in the unjust use of his strength, has frequently, habitually, (we will allow her the full use of her argument,) even invariably, oppressed and misused woman, how does she propose to correct the abuse? Strangely, by pitting woman against man, in a direct state of antagonism; by throwing them into the arena together, stripped for the strife; by saying to the man, this woman is a man like yourself, your equal and similar, possessing all rights which you possess, and (of course she must allow) possessing none others. In such a strife, what becomes of corporeal weakness? . . . Woman throws away her strength, when she *brings herself down* to man's level. She throws away that moral strength, that shadow of divinity, which nature has given her to keep man's ferocity in curb. Grant her to be his equal, and instantly she sinks to his inferior, which, as yet, we maintain she has never been. . . .

As regards the question of intellect, it is a most difficult one to argue. We are ourselves inclined to believe that the difference of intellect in the sexes exists, as we have said, rather in kind than degree. There is much talk of the difference of education and rearing bestowed upon individuals of either sex, and we think too much stress is laid upon it. Education, no doubt, influences the intellect in each individual case; but it is as logically certain, that intellect, in its kind and degree, influences education *en masse;*—that is to say, Thomas, the individual man, may be better suited to woman's duties, than Betty, the individual woman, and *vice versa.* Thomas might make a capital child's nurse, in which Betty succeeds but badly; while Betty might be quite competent to beat Thomas hollow in a stump oration; and yet we have a fair right to argue, that Thomas and Betty are but individual exceptions to a general rule, which general rule is plainly indicated by the universal practice of mankind. The fact that such relative positions of the sexes, and such habits of mind, have existed, more or less modified, in all ages of the world, and under all systems of government, goes far to prove that these are the impulses of instinct and teachings of Nature. It is certainly a little hard upon Mrs. Betty to be forced from occupations for which she feels herself particularly well qualified, and to make way for Mr. Thomas, who, although particularly *ill*-qualified for them, will be certain to assert his right; but laws cannot be made for exceptional cases, and if Mrs. Betty has good sense, as well as talent, she will let the former curb the latter; she will teach her woman-intellect to curb her man-intellect, and will make herself the stronger woman thereby. The fact that less effort has been made to teach woman certain things, is a strong argument that she has (taking her as a class) less aptitude for being taught those certain things. It is difficult to chain down mind by any habit or any teaching, and if woman's intellect had the same turn as man's, it is most unlikely that so many myriads should have passed away and "made no sign." . . .

We have already endeavoured to prove that, whatever the intellect of woman, it would have no influence in altering the relative position of the sexes; we now go farther, and maintain that the nature of her intellect confirms this position. The higher her intellect, the better is she suited to fulfil that heaviest task of life which makes her the "martyr to the pang without the palm." If she suffers,—what is this but the fate of every higher grade of humanity, which rises in suffering as it rises in dignity? for, is not all intellect suffering?

We have, throughout this article, made no reference to the biblical argument, because, with those who receive it, it is too well known and too decisive to need farther comment. To those who reject it, it is of course no argument. We have endeavoured to prove that common sense, quite independently of revelation, marks the place of woman, and that while the Scriptures confirm, they are by no means necessary to decide the question. . . .

Let woman make herself free, in the true sense of the word, by the working out of her mission. "Liberty is duty, not license;" and woman is freest when she is the truest woman; when she finds the fewest difficulties in the way of conforming herself to her nature. . . . Life's devoted martyr she may be—man's ministering angel she may be; but, for heaven's sake, mesdames, the conventionists,—not Cuffee's rival candidate for the Presidency!

L. S. M.

UNION WOMEN IN WARTIME

So various were the impacts of the Civil War that it is almost impossible to generalize about them usefully. These three examples of the experiences of Union women, one a widow whose son was in the army, the second a former slave in Kentucky (a Union state), the third a working wife and mother, suggest the range of consequences of the war mobilization for women.

MARY HERRICK

The Civil War brought Northern women into newly immediate relation to the federal government. Tens of thousands of women wrote to President Lincoln or Secretary of War Edwin Stanton to discover their husbands' or sons' whereabouts or to request their release from military service. Among the letter writers was the outspoken Mary Herrick, of New York state.

E. M. Stanton   Nunda, [N.Y.] May 30, 1863
Secretary of War.

I am a widow my Son is in the army vollenteered last august to fill up the 33 went as a nine months man was promised to be discharged when the time of the regiment was out my husband has been dead 15 years and George B. Herrick of the 33 was all the child I ever had so I am left all alone I have a small plase and dont want to be taxed to death. that is I don't want the copperhead collecter to take what lidle I have for taxes. he threatened to sell my things for the vollenteer tax because I am poor and did not have the money as soon a he wanted it. My son George B. Herrick is a printer by trade inlisted in Rochestr was well aquainted with Col. Tayler before the war broke out. George B. Herrick my son paid one hundred and fifty dollars of his heard earnings towards *this war* before he inlisted I did not think him well anough to go but he was better when he went south 5 years ago and I consented to let him go and he has done as much as eney in his department being *Agitants cleark*! Mr Stanton and Lincan and co that is what they call you dont you think you and the President could find *some means* to Protect those of us that have given all we had towards this war but a plase to stay. I would like to keep a plase to stay if possible. if I dont have eney thing but bread and water! by good

Letters Received, 1863, Enlisted Branch, Adjutant General's papers, box 22, RG 94, National Archives. The editors are grateful to Rachel Filene Seidman for locating and providing a copy of this document.

rights you should pass a law to exempt such as I am from heavey taxes as you have money so plenty you could verrey easy make me a donation of one hundred and fiftey dollars and then I can have something to pay the extrey taxes with. it is unjust and cruel to tax a poor woman to death *you* have plentey of simpathy for the slaves and I think slavery is an abomination in the sight of god. that is one reason why I don't want to be a slave to this *war*! eney reffrences you want you can have Mr. Morey of the dayley Union is aquainted with Georg he has worked in there office. Doct Chaffee of Springfield Massachusetts is likewise aquainted and George is a member of the Typographical union.

With Respect, Mary W. Herrick

Nunda, Jun 13, 1863

Sir I received yours of the 8 on the 11 and enclosed was 6 sheets of a sercler [circular] in pamphlet form; and as the letter had bin opened I did not [k]now as I received all that you enclosed: thanks maney thanks for your reply as I did [not] expect eney: I was somewhat surprised to find an answer and more so to find that the envelope had been opened and I think in the office here and I am afraid the Post master done it himself; I think a *woman* has all the rights of a *free* american sitisen and I want the uneion as it was without *slaverey*: I dont want one state or stripe less in that dear old flag that has floated over me ever since I was born in this land of the brave and this *contrey of the free*: my son is a firm suporter of the war gave all he had and then went himself: and has done more than some that was in perfect health when they arrived in dixey: hoping *not to live if the uneion* is to be *severed*: hoping this cruel rebellion may soon be *crushed out*. if I was a man I would fight to *crush it*, but my son think it is no plase for me eaven as nurse in the hospitals. but I can pray for peace once more to fold her blessed wings around us and return each son to his dessolate mother.

With Respect, . . . Mrs. Mary W. Herrick, Livingston c[ou]n[ty]

CLARISSA BURDETT

Four slaveholding states—Kentucky, Missouri, Maryland, and Delaware—did not join the Confederacy and remained under Union control during the war. Slaveowners in these border areas were especially angry when their former slaves joined the Union army, and often took out their resentments on the women who stayed home, as in the case of Clarissa Burdett.

Camp Nelson Ky   27th of March 1865

Personally appeared before me J M Kelley Notary Public in and for the County of Jessamine State of Kentucky Clarissa Burdett a woman of color who being duly sworn according to law doth despose and say

I am a married woman and have four children. My husband Elijah Burdett is a soldier in the 12" U.S.C.H. Arty. I and my children belonged to Smith Alford Garrard County Ky. When my husband enlisted my master beat me over the head with an axe handle saying as he did so that he beat me for letting Ely Burdett go off. He bruised my head so that I could not lay it against a pillow without the greatest pain. Last week my niece who lived with me went to Camp Nelson. This made my master very angry and last monday March 20" 1865 he asked me where the girl had gone. I could not tell him[.] He then whipped me over the head and said he would give me two hundred lashes if I did not get the girl back before the next day. On Wednesday last March 22" he said that he had not time to beat me on Tuesday but now he had time and he would give it to me. He then tied my hands threw the rope over a joist stripped me entirely naked and gave me about three hundred lashes. I cried out. He then caught me by the throat and almost choked me then continued to lash me with switches until my back was all cut up. The marks of the switches are now very visible and my back is still very sore. My master was a very cruel man and strongly sympathizes with the rebels. He went with the Rebel General Bragg when the latter retreated from the State. He took me and my children to Beans Station and send the parents and two sisters of my niece to Knoxville where he sold them. After he whipped me on Wednesday last he said he would give me until next morning to bring the girl back, and if I did not get her back by that time he would give me as much more. I knew that I would be whipped so I ran away. My master frequently said that he would be jailed before one of his niggers woulg go to Camp. I therefore knew he would not permit any of my children to come with me. So when I ran away I had to leave my children with my master. I have four children there at present and I want to get them but I cannot go there for them knowing that master who would whip me would not let any of my children go nor would he suffer me to get away

her
(Signed) Clarissa   Burdett
mark

Affidavit of Clarissa Burdett, March 27, 1865, filed with H-8 1865, Registered Letters Received, ser. 3379, TN Asst. Comr., RG 105, National Archives. Published in *Freedom: A Documentary History of Emancipation, 1861–1867*, series 1, vol. 1, *The Destruction of Slavery*, ed. Ira Berlin et al. (New York: Cambridge University Press, 1985), pp. 615–16, and reprinted with the permission of Cambridge University Press.

JULIA UNDERHILL

Disowned by her parents in Maine when she married a local schoolteacher, Julia Frances Rundlett Underhill (1841?–1864) moved with her husband to Menasha, Wisconsin, where she gave birth to two daughters. After her husband enlisted in the Union army and was sent south, she went to live in Massachusetts, where two sympathetic aunts cared for her children while she disguised herself as a boy in order to obtain decent employment. How many women took such a course it is impossible to say, but Underhill's letters to her husband suggest how difficult it was for a lone woman to support her children and remain "free from insult." Her identity was discovered by a doctor as she lay dying of fever in a boardinghouse near the iron works where she was employed; her husband learned of her death while awaiting discharge in an army hospital.

Menasha April 8th 1864

My Dear Leemon.

I wrote to you day before yesterday and today I send the questions you wanted I hope you will get them all right. we are well and getting along well, the babys read and spell and do their mischief and talk about their papa; most every day they want a needle and thread to make you a shirt or some other kind of garment. I tell you they *work buisy* when they work for you. In one of your last letters you wanted to know how folks treated me. Everybody treates me with respect. I dont think I have got an enemy in Menasha. without is some of the [parties?] that have insulted me and I give them *hell every time*. 2 or 3 days ago a man met me in the street and said he would like to get aquainted with me (I had never seen him before). I said *"Sir if you have nothing better to do you had better enlist. I dont wish to get aquainted with you, you are too impudent*. this was all I said. I tell you he *looked vinegar* at me. There is a good many such fellows here. every time I go out there is a set of loafers standing around that must eat up every woman with their eyes. But there is a good many good folks here, there is no danger but what any *soldier* woman can get help as long as she tries to do what is right, and carries herself streight, but let her get a *bad name*, and *decent folks wont help her*, for the last 3 weeks they have been clearing out the bad houses here in Menasha. One family named Jordan came back after they had been driven away and they took out a fire engine and threw water untill they came out of the house, and then they tore the house down, good enough for them.

Julia Underhill to Leemon Underhill, April 8 and July 26, 1864, Underhill Papers, Minnesota Historical Society, St. Paul, Minn.

Your letters come more regular than they did, though they dont come so quick when they are sent by the way of New York. I shall be glad when I get to mass[achusetts] I am tired of living alone, though I never should want to leave here, if Pet had been true to you, and staid a part of the time with me. yesterday I saw a man that was born and brought up in the place where Aunt Hannah lives and that Mr Hunt that I have written about came from Maine, is aquainted with some of my fathers family though he dont know my father. I am not afraid my aunts will get tired of me I will make my children mind and try and do the best I can of course I shall have to pay my way as they have to work for all they have, but I wont have any rent to pay and I wont have to buy any wood. Aunts Hannah and Mary have a house and barn and a cow and 11 acres of land (I believe it is 11 acres if I remember rightly) so I will have plenty of chance to work in their garden which will suit me much better than living in town and staying in the house all of the time, in the country I can go out doors without being *stared to death*. damn a city or village to live in I am *tired, tired* of it, I think when you come back from the war my aunts will want us to live with them always, the man from the place said North Leaverett was a quiet place, write often and dont forget your babys and your

Julia

Lainsborough July 26th 1864

My Dear Leemon,

I have not recieved a letter from you for two weeks. I am still away from home at work. I hear from the babys every week and my aunt Hannah puts all of my letters that come to their P[ost] Office in a large envelope and send them to me. the babys are well and getting along first rate. in my last letter I sent you my likeness I hope you will get it. don't I make quite a good looking boy. *I have got a good* place to work and am *my employer's pet boy.* I get the easiest jobs allways. rainy days and sundays I am learning a trade to run a stationary engine. it generally take 3 years to learn the trade. my employer says he thinks I will be a good engineer in three months, then I can get 75 dollars per month and board. I am verry lonesome but I must beer it; times are so hard that I must work in this way to support the babys. there is a verry severe drouth most all over northern states. there will be about 2/3 the usual grain raised it will be verry hard times. I hope the war will end this fall so you can come home. try and get your discharge. in one of your last letters you say I write as though I was doing something unpleasant. I love you as much as I ever did. but of course my stile of living would make some difference in my letters. I wonder what you will say to me after you get these letters. I hope you will not be angry with me. it is the easiest way to support myself and now I am free from insult. my employer says I am the smartest best boy he ever saw. there is 10 or 12 men works here. last Saturday a man was turned off for ill treating me. I think my position working as I do a thousand times more honorable than to sell my honor and if I get found out it will be an honor to me.

I left the place where I worked when I wrote to you last. I had to work to many hours and I found a better man to work for and easier work, better board. if you do not object, I think I shall work here until you come back from the war. I can go home once a month. I wish you was here. it is an iron factory where I work where they make pig iron. they don't put me into any dangerous places or give me disagreeable work. A colledge student works here who will teaches me evenings this winter. sunday my employer told me that he thought I would make a *mark in the world*, and that *boys like me* were scarce. he is a verry particular man and I am steady, use *no rough language*, am *strictly temperate* and this suits him. I *appear happy* and contented, *but Leemon I am so lonesome.* I can tell now how you feel away from all, but I must 'tis necessary. times are so hard cotton sheeting is $1.00 per yard. everything according—Gold $2.55.

Don't think any more that I don't *Love you* or doubt me again. I *could not forget you or cease to love you as long as you were true to me.* I shall feel verry impatient untill I get an answer to these letters. I wonder what you will say to me. I shall write every sunday. I am verry buissy.

Write often and *don't forget me*,

Ever your own J——

GERTRUDE CLANTON THOMAS'S CIVIL WAR DIARY

Gertrude Clanton (1834–1907), a daughter of Southern privilege, became a belle of Augusta, Georgia, and married a local Princeton graduate, Jefferson Thomas, in 1852. Since the labor of the household was taken care of by slaves, she had time to keep an extraordinary journal from 1848 to 1889. In 1864 she was the mother of four children (Turner Clanton, eleven; Mary Belle, six; Jefferson Davis, three; and Cora Lou, one) and was again pregnant.

Monday, July 4, 1864   . . . Today is the fourth day of July. I had forgotten it until this morning. One of our waggon tires ran off while we were moving and all the blacksmith's shops were shut up when we sent to have it mended. It is warm, so very warm! This is a very disagreeable house to live in—cold, exceedingly cold in winter and hot, excessively hot in summer. I enjoyed the spring very well but none of my surroundings are congenial to my taste. I think I am luxurious in my taste. . . . Were I a refugee I could more willingly submit to the annoyance of an uncomfortable house but there is a great scarcity of houses to rent. I expect I annoy Mr Thomas by my frequent allusions to this subject so hereafter my journal I think I shall tell you when anything worries me for you know it is almost impossible for me not to have someone to talk to. I wish I had a book with a key to it in which I could write what I feel. . . .

I don't think Mr Thomas understands or is interested in my struggles and trials. He listens sometimes when my "Heart unfolds its leaves" and I read to him some of its pages. Listens, but that is all.

Thursday, July 28, 1864   . . . On Monday forenoon Cora, Lila Thomas Mamie and I went round to the 3d Georgia Hospital to carry a lunch to the sick men. We found all the rooms crowded but gave the lunch we had to the patients in St Paul's ward. All of the cots were occupied most of the men suffering with diarrhea and intermittent fever—A young man by the name of Rainwater and one by the name of Dennard, the latter from lower Georgia were the only two we conversed much with. Everything appeared as comfortable as it was possible for a Hospital to be—In

The Secret Eye: The Journal of Ella Gertrude Clanton Thomas, 1848–1889, ed. Virginia Ingraham Burr (Chapel Hill: University of North Carolina Press, 1990), pp. 226–30, 235–39, 257–58, 260, 264–65, 272–73, 275. Copyright © 1990 by Virginia Ingraham Burr and Gertrude Despeaux. Reprinted by permission of the editor and publisher.

the afternoon there was a call in the papers for the ladies to meet at the Catholic Church to render some assistance. Riding there Mamie and I found a state of destitution such as I had read of but never imagined before. Laying on the floor upon beds hastily filled with straw were wounded men, wounded in every manner. Some with their arms and legs cut off, others with flesh wounds, two men in a dying state, another poor fellow with the ever present thought of home mingling in his delirium as he sits up and gathering his coarse shoes proceeds to put them on saying "I am going home, I have a furlough to go home." Soothingly I spoke to him and smoothing his coat his only pillow I persuaded him to lay down. Near the door lay a man singularly ugly at best but almost horrible with the accumulation of dirt consequent upon having travelled upon the cars. All those men had been brought down from the hospital in Greensboro [Georgia] the people fearing a raid. One of the men named Jones on the right hand side of the church was dying. A crowd of ladies were standing around him. One of them asked him if he wished anything. "Nothing" the man replied "except to be prepared to die." During the night the summons came for him, his soul was required of him.

The next morning visiting the church, in the vestibule or piazzi of the church I saw something covered up but did not know what it was until told that the dead man was there. He was resting on a soiled straw bed covered with a common blue blanket with the flies swarming over it. A gentleman (Mr Milligan I think, and by the way the only one who was there paying them any attention) lifted the blanket from off his face remarking "that it was very much such a face as Stonewall Jackson's." There lay the man around whom had clustered all the endearing associations of home. A mother—a wife—a sister had loved him. Perhaps now around the family altar a group of children pray "please bring Pa home safe and well," happily unconscious how he died. God grant they never may know! A crowd of children and servants were around him at times, all privileged to lift the blanket from his careworn but intellectual face—and there he lay unknown & uncared for, prepared for the hasty burial which awaited him. For the weary soul I could not weep but for those who loved him my heart went out in yearning sympathy as the tears (which I was ashamed should be seen) coursed rapidly down my cheek—I don't know where that man's family lives but if I did what could I write them. I could tell them that he was dead but I would not have them know how he died. . . .

Tuesday, July 12, 1864   This morning I rose with the expectation of going in town. I had rested badly last night and was feeling very dull this morning. Our well was out of order having just been operated upon. A large number of clothes had to be washed and other domestic annoyances conspired to make me cross. Mr Thomas concluded he felt so badly he would not go. I started late. . . . [T]he carriage passed a poor woman and her little boy carrying berries into town. Both were barefooted. I passed them but then told Daniel to stop and invited them to ride with me. With an apology for her bare feet she accepted the offer. As I listened to her simple story, her husband in the hospital in Richmond, one brother killed and the other not heard from, she just from the poor house, having moved yesterday and this morning starting out with berries to sell—As I listened I felt ashamed that the little trials of life should so affect me. I bought her basket of fruit leaving her with a bright smile of contentment upon her face and then rode to the cemetery. Entering the enclosure I knelt by Pa's grave and there besought God's guidance for the future. . . .

A large number of Yankee prisoners were at Allen's station as we came up. Some of the officers were good looking men with beards neatly trimmed and dressed clean but the privates! Such an outlandish set of men I have seldom seen. They were in box cars, some of them with their pants rolled high above the knees, shirt bosoms open to the waist, hair matted, shirts torn across the backs and presenting a repulsive appearance altogether. Yet I cannot have the vindictive feelings I hear expressed. A Fallen captive foe cannot be the object of such feelings. It is for the triumphant foe—when he attempts to lord it over me and mine that I shall reserve my indignant and righteous rage. . . .

Saturday, September 17, 1864   . . . How I do wish this war was over. I wish to breathe free. I feel pent up, confined—cramped and shall I confess it am reminded of that Italian story of *The Iron Shroud* where daily—daily hourly and momently the room contracts, the victim meanwhile utterly impotent to avert the impending doom. Never have I so fully realised the feeble hold upon this world's goods as I do now. I don't think I have ever enjoyed that peculiarly charming season the Indian Summer more than I have during the past few weeks. Looking up the three Avenues and at the Goats Cows and Horses so quietly walking about, listening at the cooing of Pigions, the chirping of the different fowls in the yard—I imagine this contrasted with men clad in Yankee uniform rudely violating the privacy of my home. I imagine the booming of Yankee cannon and the clash of Yankee sabres and I ask myself how soon shall this thing be?? Nor does it require an imaginative mind to foretell such an event but the last page of my Journal must bear no such cowardly record.

I have sometimes doubted on the subject of slavery. I have seen so many of its evils chief among which is the terribly demoralising influence upon our men and boys but of late I have become convinced the Negro *as a race* is better off with us as he has been than if he were made free, but I am by no means so sure that we would not gain by his having his freedom given him. I grant that I am not so philanthropic as to be willing voluntarily to give all we own for the sake of the principle, but I do think that if we had the same invested in something else as a means of support I would willingly, nay gladly, have the responsibility of them taken off my shoulders. . . .

Thursday, September 22, 1864   Was it ominous that I should find my pen split when I took it up to write tonight? In these troublous times how superstitious we become. Shall I dare hope that this new Journal which I am commencing will record Peace, an independent Southern Confederacy? Truly the skies are gloomy and the heavy storm appears ready to discharge its thunders in our very midst. Yet how calm, how indifferent we are—we laugh, we smile, we talk, we jest, just as tho no enemy were at our door. And yet the idea has several times suggested itself to me that someday I would have to aid in earning my own support. We have made no arrangement whatever for such a contingency. Gold has increased in value and we have *not a dollar*—and yet I am hopeful of the success of our cause, the ultimate success of our Confederacy, while I do not think it improbable that *we* will lose our fortunes before that final success is achieved. . . .

Friday, September 23, 1864   . . . But as to the doctrine of slavery altho I have read very few abolition books (*Uncle Tom's Cabin* making most impression) nor have I read many pro slavery books—yet the idea has gradually become more and more fixed in my mind that the institution of slavery is not right—but I am reading a new book, *Nellie Norton*, by the Rev E W Warren which I hope will convince me that it is right— Owning a large number of slaves as we do I might be asked why do I not free them? This if I could, I would not do, but if Mr Thomas would sell them to a man who would look after their temporal and spiritual interest I would gladly do so. Those house servants we have if Mr Thomas would agree to it I would pay regular wages but this is a subject upon which I do not like to think and taking my stand upon the moral view of the subject, I can but think that to hold men and women in perpetual bondage is wrong—During my comparatively short life, spent wholly under Southern skies, I have known of and heard too much of its demoralizing influence to consider the institution a blessing— . . .

Wednesday, March 29, 1865 . . . At times I feel as if I was drifting on, on, ever onward to be at last dashed against some rock and I shut my eyes and almost wish it was over, the shock encountered and I prepared to know what destiny awaits me. I am tired, oh so tired of this war. I want to breathe free. I feel the restraint of the blockade and as port after port becomes blockaded, I feel shut up, pent up and am irresistibly reminded of the old story of the iron shroud contracting more and more each hour, each moment.

. . . I have seen poverty staring me in the face when I expected Sherman in Augusta and our planting interest was destroyed and God knows there was nothing attractive in the gaunt picture presented. But even then I nerved myself and was prepared to do something if I could—I believe it was the sitting still and doing nothing which unnerved me more than anything else. I looked forward and asked myself, what can I do? Nothing, except teach school and if I left Augusta nothing to support me with my little ones—If I remained, the doubt as to wether I could procure a school unless compelled to take the oath—and a new idea just now presents itself to my mind. I wonder if I would not be compelled to teach the young and perhaps old ideas of the Negroes how to shoot.* I'm sure if their ideas were as contrary as the mind of the teacher would be, the shoots would be decidedly twisted.

Monday, May 1, 1865 What a first of May. It had not occurred to me until I commenced to write—Today I have witnessed what I am sorry shall prove our last experience as a Confederate Nation—A riot has taken place in Augusta—an event often dreaded but never experienced before! Soon after breakfast I heard that the soldiers were breaking open the stores on Broad Street and helping themselves—Immediately after I saw numbers of men walking rapidly, some running with large bags bundles and &c upon their shoulders—The bell just now tolls for one oclock. When another 1st of May rolls around, the bell which for so long a time has tolled to remind us to pray for the soldiers and alas by so many of us has been neglected—will toll no more—God help us. As an independent nation we will not exist—The bright dream of Southern independence has not been realised—The war is over and again we become a part of the United States—how united will depend alone upon treatment we receive from the hands of the North. It will prove to their interest to be very discreet for the South will prove a smouldering volcano requiring but

*A reference to James Thomson's well-known poem, "The Seasons" (1726–30): "Delightful task! to rear the tender thought,/To teach the young idea how to shoot."-Ed.

little to again burst forth. Treated as members of one family—a band of brothers, *in time* we may have a common interest—but pressed too hard upon, our property taken from us—a desperate people having nothing to lose, the South may again revolt. . . .

Monday, May 8, 1865 . . . Hereafter I shall put my Journal in a safe place for I intend to express myself fearlessly and candidly upon all points. Last week was the turning point, the crisis with me. "The flood which taken at the tide" would have led to feelings of union brotherhood and kindly feeling—*Today I am more intensely opposed* to the *North* than at any period of the war—We have been imposed upon—led to believe that terms of Treaty had been agreed upon which would secure to us a lasting and honourable peace. The treaty entered into between [Generals] Sherman and Johnston, the Northern President refuses to ratify—Now that we have surrendered—are in a great degree powerless we can count with certainty upon nothing. Our Negroes will be freed our lands confiscated and imagination cannot tell what is in store for us but thank God I have an increased degree of faith—a faith which causes me to feel that all this will be for our good.

Mr T appeared cast down, utterly spirit broken yesterday when the news first reached him and when I would hint at a brighter sky would mock at such anticipations—This morning while packing the camphor chest I planned a school for next winter and was astonished at the bouyancy of temperament which would permit me to indulge in anticipations founded upon such a plan, but I cannot say "Why art thou cast down oh my soul?" for indeed I am not cast down. On the contrary I am not the person to permit pecuniary loss to afflict me as long as I have health and energy. As to the emancipation of the Negroes, while there is of course a natural dislike to the loss of so much property in my inmost soul I cannot regret it—I always felt that there was a great responsibility—It is in some degree a great relief to have this feeling removed. For the Negroes I know that I have the kindest possible feeling—For the Yankees who deprive us of them I have no use whatever.

Monday, May 29, 1865 Out of all our old house servants not one remains except Patsey and a little boy Frank. We have one of our servants Uncle Jim to take Daniel's place as driver and butler and a much more efficient person he proves to be. Nancy has been cooking since Tamah left. On last Wednesday I hired a woman to do the washing. Thursday I expected Nancy to iron but she was sick. In the same way she was sick the week before when there was ironing to do. I said nothing but told

Patsey to get breakfast. After it was over I assisted her in wiping the breakfast dishes, a thing I never remember to have done more than once or twice in my life. I then thoroughly cleaned up the sitting room and parlour. . . . Immediately after breakfast as I was writing by the window Turner directed my attention to Nancy with her two children, Hannah and Jessy, going out of the gate. I told him to enquire "where she was going." She had expected to leave with flying colours but was compelled to tell a falsehood for she replied "I will be back directly." I knew at once that she was taking "french leave" and was not surprised when I went into her room sometime afterwards to find that all her things had been removed. I was again engaged in housework most of the morning. . . .

Belmont, Monday, June 12, 1865   I must confess to you my journal that I do most heartily dispise Yankees, Negroes and everything connected with them. The theme has been sung in my hearing until it is a perfect abomination—I positively instinctively shut my ears when I hear the hated subject mentioned and right gladly would I be willing never to place my eyes upon another as long as I live. Everything is entirely re-versed. I feel no interest in them whatever and hope I never will— . . .

A FREEDWOMAN BEFORE THE SOUTHERN
CLAIMS COMMISSION

*When the Union army under General Sherman came marching through
South Carolina, North Carolina, and Georgia in the spring of 1865, it
brought freedom to many slaves but also—differentiating little between
the property of enemy Confederates and of slaves—routed many blacks
from their homes and commandeered the property that they had managed
to guard during the war. In 1871 the federal government set up the Southern Claims Commission to hear requests for compensation for property
taken by the Union army. Former slaves such as Nancy Johnson and her
husband were required to present detailed information to prove their ownership of the goods for which they asked compensation. (The questions
generating the responses presented here have not been preserved.)*

[Savannah March 22, 1873]

General Interrogatories by Special Com'r—My name is Nancy Johnson. I
was born in Ga. I was a slave and became free when the army came here.
My master was David Baggs. I live in Canoochie Creek The claimant is
my husband. He was a good Union man during the war. He liked to have
lost his life by standing up for the Union party. He was threatened heavy.
There was a Yankee prisoner that got away & came to our house at night;
we kept him hid in my house a whole day. He sat in my room. White
people didn't visit our house then. My husband slipped him over to a
man named Joel Hodges & he conveyed him off so that he got home. I
saw the man at the time of the raid & I knew him. He said that he tried
to keep them from burning my house but he couldn't keep them from
taking everything we had. I was sorry for them though a heap. The white
people came hunting this man that we kept over night; my old master
sent one of his own grandsons & he said if he found it that they must
put my husband to death, & I had to tell a story to save life. My old
master would have had him killed   He was bitter. This was my master
David Baggs. I told him that I had seen nothing of him. I did this to save
my husbands life. Some of the rebel soldiers deserted & came to our
house & we fed them. They were opposed to the war & didn't own
slaves & said they would die rather than fight. Those who were poor

Testimony of Nancy Johnson, claim of Boson Johnson, Liberty Co., Georgia case files, Approved
Claims, ser. 732, Southern Claims Commission, 3d Auditor, RG 217 [I-5], National Archives.
Published in *Freedom: A Documentary History of Emancipation, 1861–1867*, series 1, vol. 1, *The
Destruction of Slavery*, ed. Ira Berlin et al. (New York: Cambridge University Press, 1985), pp.
150–54, and reprinted with the permission of Cambridge University Press.

white people, who didn't own slaves were some of them Union people. I befriended them because they were on our side. I don't know that he ever did any thing more for the Union; we were way back in the country, but his heart was right & so was mine. I was served mighty mean before the Yankees came here. I was nearly frostbitten: my old Missus made me weave to make clothes for the soldiers till 12 o'clock at night & I was so tired & my own clothes I had to spin over night. She never gave me so much as a bonnet. I had to work hard for the rebels until the very last day when they took us. The old man came to me then & said if you won't go away & will work for us we will work for you; I told him if the other colored people were going to be free that I wanted to be. I went away & then came back & my old Missus asked me if I came back to behave myself & do her work & I told her no that I came to do my own work. I went to my own house & in the morning my old master came to me & asked me if I wouldn't go and milk the cows: I told him that my Missus had driven me off—well said he you go and do it—then my Mistress came out again & asked me if I came back to work for her like a "*nigger*"—I told her no that I was free & she said be off then & called me a stinking bitch. I afterwards wove 40 yds. of dress goods for her that she promised to pay me for; but she never paid me a cent for it. I have asked her for it several times. I have been hard up to live but thank God, I am spared yet. I quit then only did a few jobs for her but she never did anything for me except give me a meal of victuals, you see I was hard up then, I was well to do before the war.

Second Set of Interrogatories by Spec'l Com'r.

1   I was present when this property was taken.

2   I saw it taken.

3   They said that they didn't believe what I had belonged to me & I told them that I would swear that it belonged to me. I had tried to hide things. They found our meat, it was hid under the house & they took a crop of rice. They took it out & I had some cloth under the house too & the dishes & two fine bed-quilts. They took them out. These were all my own labor & night labor. They took the bole of cloth under the house and the next morning they came back with it made into pantaloons. They were starved & naked almost. It was Jan & cold, They were on their way from Savannah. They took all my husbands clothes, except what he had on his back.

4   These things were taken from David Bagg's place in Liberty County. The Yankees took them. I should think there were thousands of them. I could not count them. They were about a day & a night

5   There were present my family, myself & husband & this man Jack Walker. He is way out in Tatnal Co. & we can't get him here

6   There were what we called officers there. I don't know whether they ordered the property taken. I put a pot on and made a pie & they took it to carry out to the head men. I went back where the officers camped & got my oven that I cooked it in back again. They must have ordered them or else they could not have gone so far & they right there. They said that they stood in need of them. They said that we ought not to care what they took for we would get it all back again; that they were obliged to have something to eat. They were mighty fine looking men.

7   They took the mare out of the stable; they took the bacon under the house, the corn was taken out of the crib, & the rice & the lard. Some of the chickens they shot & some they run down; they shot the hogs.

8   They took it by hand   the camp was close by my house.

9   They carried it to their camps; they had lots of wagons there.

10   They took it to eat, bless you: I saw them eating it right there in my house. They were nearly starved.

11   I told one of the officers that we would starve & they said no that we would get it all back again come & go along with us; but I wouldn't go because the old man had my youngest child hid away in Tatnal Co: he took her away because she knew where the gold was hid & he didn't want her to tell. My boy was sent out to the swamp to watch the wagons of provisions & the soldiers took the wagons & the boy, & I never saw him anymore. He was 14 yrs. old. I could have got the child back but I was afraid my master would kill him; he said that he would & I knew that he would or else make his children do it: he made his sons kill 2 men big tall men like you. The Lord forgive them for the way they have treated me. The child could not help them from taking the horses. He said that Henry (my boy) hallooed for the sake of having the Yankees find him; but the Yankees asked him where he was going & he didn't know they were soldiers & he told them that he was going to Master's mules.

12   I didn't ask for any receipt.

13   It was taken in the day time, not secretly.

14   When they took this property, the army was encamped. Some got there before the camps were up. Some was hung up in the house. Some people told us that if we let some hang up they wouldn't touch the rest, but they did, they were close by. They commenced taking when they first came. They staid there two nights. I heard a heap of shooting, but I

don't think that they killed anybody. I didn't know any of the officers or quartermasters.

15   This horse was as fine a creature as ever was & the pork &c were in good order.

16   *Item No. 1.*   I don't know how old the mare was. I know she was young. She was medium sized. She was in nice order, we kept a good creature. My husband bought it when it was a colt, about 2 years old. I think he had been using it a year & a little better. Colored people when they would work always had something for themselves, after working for their masters. I most forgot whether he paid cash or swapped cows. He worked & earned money, after he had done his masters work. They bridled & carried her off; I think they jumped right on her back

Item No. 2.   We had 7 hogs & we killed them right there. It was pickled away in the barrel: Some was done hung up to smoke, but we took it down & put it into the barrels to keep them from getting it. He raised the hogs. He bought a sow and raised his own pork & that is the way he got this. He did his tasks & after that he worked for himself & he got some money & bought the hogs and then they increased. He worked Sundays too; and that was for ourselves. He always was a hardworking man. I could not tell how much these would weigh; they were monstrous hogs, they were a big breed of hogs. We had them up feeding. The others were some two years old, & some more. It took two men to help hang them up. This was the meat from 7 hogs.

Item No. 3.   I had half a barrel of lard. It was in gourds, that would hold half a bushel a piece. We had this hid in the crib. This was lard from the hogs.

Item No. 4   I could not tell exactly how much corn there was but there was a right smart. We had 4 or 5 bushels ground up into meal & they took all the corn besides. They carried it off in bags and my children's undershirts, tied them like bags & filled them up. My husband made baskets and they toted some off in that way. They toted some off in fanners & big blue tubs.

Item No. 5.   I don't know exactly how much rice there was; but we made a good deal. They toted it off in bundles, threshed out—It was taken in the sheaf   They fed their horses on it. I saw the horses eating it as I passed there. They took my tubs, kettles &c. I didn't get anything back but an oven.

Item No. 7.   We had 11 hogs. They were 2 or 3 years old. They were in pretty good order. We were intending to fatten them right next year— they killed them right there.

Item No. 8.   I had 30 or 40 head of chickens. They took the last one.

They shot them. This property all belonged to me and my husband. None of it belonged to Mr. Baggs   I swore to the men so, but they wouldn't believe I could have such things. My girl had a changable silk dress & all had [talanas?] & they took them all—It didn't look like a Yankee person would be so mean. But they said if they didn't take them the whites here would & they did take some of my things from their camps after they left.

her
Nancy   ×   Johnson
mark

THE RACE PROBLEM—AN AUTOBIOGRAPHY

Nearly forty years after the abolition of slavery, African American women in the South faced continuous harassment, insult, and discrimination. The following account, published anonymously in a northern journal in 1904, comes from one of the more fortunate southern black women. Well educated and the daughter of a store owner, she grew up relatively protected, never having had to work in a white person's home.

There is no sacrifice I would not make, no hardship I would not undergo rather than allow my daughters to go in service where they would be thrown constantly in contact with Southern white men, for they consider the colored girl their special prey.

It is commonly said that no girl or woman receives a certain kind of insult unless she invites it. That does not apply to a colored girl and woman in the South. The color of her face alone is sufficient invitation to the Southern white man—these same men who profess horror that a white gentleman can entertain a colored one at his table. Out of sight of their own women they are willing and anxious to entertain colored women in various ways. Few colored girls reach the age of sixteen without receiving advances from them—maybe from a young "upstart," and often from a man old enough to be their father, a white haired veteran of sin. Yes, and men high in position, whose wives and daughters are leaders of society. I have had a clerk in a store hold my hand as I gave him the money for some purchase and utter some vile request; a shoe man to take liberties, a man in a crowd to place his hands on my person, others to follow me to my very door, a school director to assure me a position if I did his bidding.

It is true these particular men never insulted me but once; but there are others. I might write more along this line and worse things—how a white man of high standing will systematically set out to entrap a colored girl—but my identification would be assured in some quarters. My husband was also educated in an American Missionary Association school (God bless the name!), and after graduating took a course in medicine in another school. He has practiced medicine now for over ten years. By most frugal living and strict economy he saved enough to buy for a home a house of four rooms, which has since been increased to eight. Since our marriage we have bought and paid for two other places, which we rent.

"The Race Problem—An Autobiography by a Southern Colored Woman," *Independent* 56 (March 17, 1904), pp. 586–89.

My husband's collections average one hundred dollars a month. We have an iron-bound rule that we must save at least fifty dollars a month. Some months we lay by more, but never less. We do not find this very hard to do with the rent from our places, and as I do all of my work except the washing and ironing.

We have three children, two old enough for school. I try to be a good and useful neighbor and friend to those who will allow me. I would be contented and happy if I, an American citizen, could say as Axel Jarlson (the Swedish emigrant, whose story appeared in THE INDEPENDENT of January 8th, 1903) says, "There are no aristocrats to push him down and say that he is not worthy because his father was poor." There are "aristocrats" to push me and mine down and say we are not worthy because we are colored. The Chinaman, Lee Chew, ends his article in THE INDEPENDENT of February 19th, 1903, by saying, "Under the circumstances how can I call this my home, and how can any one blame me if I take my money and go back to my village in China?"

Happy Chinaman! Fortunate Lee Chew! You can go back to your village and enjoy your money. This is my village, my home, yet am I an outcast. See what an outcast! Not long since I visited a Southern city where the "Jim Crow" car law is enforced. I did not know of this law, and on boarding an electric car took the most convenient seat. The conductor yelled, "What do you mean? Niggers don't sit with white folks down here. You must have come from 'way up yonder. I'm not Roosevelt. We don't sit with niggers, much less eat with them."

I was astonished and said, "I am a stranger and did not know of your law." His answer was: "Well, no back talk now; that's what I'm here for—to tell niggers their places when they don't know them."

Every white man, woman and child was in a titter of laughter by this time at what they considered the conductor's wit.

These Southern men and women, who pride themselves on their fine sense of feeling, had no feeling for my embarrassment and unmerited insult, and when I asked the conductor to stop the car that I might get off, one woman said in a loud voice, "These niggers get more impudent every day; she doesn't want to sit where she belongs."

No one of them thought that I was embarrassed, wounded and outraged by the loud, brutal talk of the conductor and the sneering, contemptuous expressions on their own faces. They considered me "impudent" when I only wanted to be alone that I might conquer my emotion. I was nervous and blinded by tears of mortification which will account for my second insult on this same day.

I walked downtown to attend to some business and had to take an elevator in an office building. I stood waiting for the elevator, and when the others, all of whom were white, got in I made a move to go in also, and the boy shut the cage door in my face. I thought the elevator was too crowded and waited; the same thing happened the second time. I would have walked up, but I was going to the fifth story, and my long walk downtown had tired me. The third time the elevator came down the boy pointed to a sign and said, "I guess you can't read; but niggers don't ride in this elevator; we're white folks here, we are. Go to the back and you'll find an elevator for freight and niggers."

The occupants of the elevator also enjoyed themselves at my expense. This second insult in one day seemed more than I could bear. I could transact no business in my frame of mind, so I slowly took the long walk back to the suburbs of the city, where I was stopping.

My feelings were doubly crushed and in my heart, I fear, I rebelled not only against man but God. I have been humiliated and insulted often, but I never get used to it; it is new each time, and stings and hurts more and more.

The very first humiliation I received I remember very distinctly to this day. It was when I was very young. A little girl playmate said to me: "I like to come over to your house to play, we have such good times, and your ma has such good preserves; but don't you tell my ma I eat over here. My ma says you all are nice, clean folks and she'd rather live by you than the white people we moved away from; for you don't borrow things. I know she would whip me if I ate with you, tho, because you are colored, you know."

I was very angry and forgot she was my guest, but told her to go home and bring my ma's sugar home her ma borrowed, and the rice they were always wanting a cup of.

After she had gone home I threw myself upon the ground and cried, for I liked the little girl, and until then I did not know that being "colored" made a difference. I am not sure I knew anything about "colored." I was very young and I know now I had been shielded from all unpleasantness.

My mother found me in tears and I asked her why was I colored, and couldn't little girls eat with me and let their mothers know it.

My mother got the whole story from me, but she couldn't satisfy me with her explanation—or, rather, lack of explanation. The little girl came often to play with me after that and we were little friends again, but we never had any more play dinners. I could not reconcile the fact that she and her people could borrow and eat our rice in their own house and not sit at my table and eat my mother's good, sweet preserves.

The second shock I received was horrible to me at the time. I had not gotten used to real horrible things then. The history of Christian men selling helpless men and women's children to far distant States was unknown to me; a number of men burning another chained to a post an impossibility, the whipping of a grown woman by a strong man unthought of. I was only a child, but I remember to this day what a shock I received. A young colored woman of a lovely disposition and character had just died. She was a teacher in the Sunday school I attended—a self-sacrificing, noble young woman who had been loved by many. Her coffin, room, hall, and even the porch of her house were filled with flowers sent by her friends. There were lovely designs sent by the more prosperous and simple bouquets made by untrained, childish hands. I was on my way with my own last offering of love, when I was met by quite a number of white boys and girls. A girl of about fifteen years said to me, "More flowers for that dead nigger? I never saw such a to-do made over a dead nigger before. Why, there must be thousands of roses alone in that house. I've been standing out here for hours and there has been a continual stream of niggers carrying flowers, and beautiful ones, too, and what makes me madder than anything else, those Yankee teachers carried flowers, too!" I, a little girl, with my heart full of sadness for the death of my friend, could make no answer to these big, heartless boys and girls, who threw stones after me as I ran from them.

When I reached home I could not talk for emotion. My mother was astonished when I found voice to tell her I was not crying because of the death of Miss W., but because I could not do something, anything, to avenge the insult to her dead body. I remember the strongest feeling I had was one of revenge. I wanted even to kill that particular girl or do something to hurt her. I was unhappy for days. I was told that they were heartless, but that I was even worse, and that Miss W. would be the first to condemn me could she speak.

That one encounter made a deep impression on my childish heart; it has been with me throughout the years. I have known real horrors since, but none left a greater impression on me.

My mother used to tell me if I were a good little girl everybody would love me, and if I always used nice manners it would make others show the same to me.

I believed that literally until I entered school, when the many encounters I had with white boys and girls going to and from school made me seriously doubt that goodness and manners were needed in this world. The white children I knew grew meaner as they grew older—more capable of saying things that cut and wound.

I was often told by white children whose parents rented houses: "You think you are white because your folks own their own home; but you ain't, you're a nigger just the same, and my pa says if he had his rights he would own niggers like you, and your home, too."

A child's feelings are easily wounded, and day after day I carried a sad heart. To-day I carry a sad heart on account of my children. What is to become of them? The Southern whites dislike more and more the educated colored man. They hate the intelligent colored man who is accumulating something. The respectable, intelligent colored people are "carefully unknown"; their good traits and virtues are never mentioned. On the other hand, the ignorant and vicious are carefully known and all of their traits cried aloud.

In the natural order of things our children will be better educated than we, they will have our acccumulations and their own. With the added dislike and hatred of the white man, I shudder to think of the outcome.

In this part of the country, where the Golden Rule is obsolete, the commandment, "Love thy neighbor as thyself" is forgotten; anything is possible.

I dread to see my children grow. I know not their fate. Where the white girl has one temptation, mine will have many. Where the white boy has every opportunity and protection, mine will have few opportunities and no protection. It does not matter how good or wise my children may be, they are colored. When I have said that, all is said. Everything is forgiven in the South but color.

PART VI

HEALTH, MEDICINE,
AND SEXUALITY

ON FEMALE HEALTH IN AMERICA

Catharine Beecher's **Letters to the People on Health and Happiness** *(1855) presented her own assessment of American women's health and included information from health reformers such as Mrs. R. B. Gleason, who had practiced medicine for ten years at the Elmira Water-Cure establishment. The "Water-Cure," which achieved some popularity in the mid-nineteenth century, especially among women, involved visiting mineral springs and wrapping hot and cold water packs around the body to remedy a variety of ills.*

STATISTICS OF FEMALE HEALTH

During my extensive tours in all portions of the Free States, I was brought into most intimate communion, not only with my widely-diffused circle of relatives, but with very many of my former pupils who had become wives and mothers. From such, I learned the secret domestic history both of those I visited and of many of their intimate friends. And oh! what heartaches were the result of these years of quiet observation of the experience of my sex in domestic life. How many young hearts have revealed the fact, that what they had been trained to imagine the highest earthly felicity, was but the beginning of care, disappointment, and sorrow, and often led to the extremity of mental and physical suffering. Why was it that I was so often told that "young girls little imagined what was before them when they entered married life"? Why did I so often find those united to the most congenial and most devoted husbands expressing the hope that their daughters would never marry? For years these were my quiet, painful conjectures.

But the more I traveled, and the more I resided in health establishments, the more the conviction was pressed on my attention that there was a terrible decay of female health all over the land, and that this evil was bringing with it an incredible extent of individual, domestic, and social suffering, that was increasing in a most alarming ratio. At last, certain developments led me to take decided measures to obtain some reliable statistics on the subject. During my travels the last year I have sought all practicable methods of obtaining information, and finally adopted this course with most of the married ladies whom I met, either

Catharine Beecher, *Letters to the People on Health and Happiness* (New York: Harper & Bros., 1855), pp. 121–23, 129–30, and note 1, pp. 7–11.

on my journeys or at the various health establishments at which I stopped.

I requested each lady first to write the *initials* of *ten* of the married ladies with whom she was best acquainted in her place of residence. Then she was requested to write at each name, her impressions as to the health of each lady. In this way, during the past year, I obtained statistics from about two hundred different places in almost all of the Free States. . . .

It must be remembered, that in regard to those marked as "sickly," "delicate," or "feeble," there can be no mistake, the knowledge being in all cases *positive,* while those marked as "well" may have ailments that are not known. For multitudes of American women, with their strict notions of propriety, and their patient and energetic spirit, often are performing every duty entirely silent as to any suffering or infirmities they may be enduring. . . . [Here the statistics are entered, showing the large majority to be either delicate or sickly.]

I will now add my own personal observation. First, in my own family connection: I have nine married sisters and sisters-in-law, all of them either delicate or invalids, except two. I have fourteen married female cousins, and not one of them but is either delicate, often ailing, or an invalid. In my wide circle of friends and acquaintance all over the land out of my family circle, the same impression is made. In Boston I can not remember but one married female friend who is perfectly healthy. In Hartford, Conn., I can think of only one. In New Haven, but one. In Brooklyn, N.Y, but one. In New York city, but one. In Cincinnati, but one. In Buffalo, Cleveland, Chicago, Milwaukee, Detroit, those whom I have visited are either delicate or invalids. I am not able to recall, in my immense circle of friends and acquaintance all over the Union, so many as *ten* married ladies born in this century and country, who are perfectly sound, healthy, and vigorous. Not that I believe there are not more than this among the friends with whom I have associated, but among all whom I can bring to mind of whose health I have any accurate knowledge, I can not find this number of entirely sound and healthy women.

Another thing has greatly added to the impression of my own observations, and that is the manner in which my inquiries have been met. In a majority of cases, when I have asked for the number of perfectly healthy women in a given place, the first impulsive answer has been "not one." . . . During the past year I made my usual inquiry of the wife of a Methodist clergyman, who resided in a small country-town in New York. Her reply was, "There are no healthy women where I live, and my husband says he would travel a great many miles for the pleasure of finding one."

In another case I conversed with a Baptist clergyman and his wife, in

Ohio, and their united testimony gave this result in three places where his parishioners were chiefly of the industrial class. They selected at random ten families best known in each place:

Worcester, Ohio: Women in perfect health, two. In medium health, one. *Invalids, seven.*

Norwalk, Ohio: Women perfectly healthy, one, but doubtfully so. Medium, none. *Invalids, nine.*

Cleveland, Ohio: Women in perfect health, one. Medium health, two. *Invalids, seven.*

In traveling at the West the past winter, I repeatedly conversed with drivers and others among the laboring class on this subject, and always heard such remarks as these: "Well! it is strange how sickly the women are getting!" "Our women-folks don't have such health as they used to do!" . . .

COMMUNICATION FROM MRS. R. B. GLEASON

The pelvic organs are subject to a great variety of displacements, and of functional and organic diseases. And yet they all have so many symptoms in common, that it requires not only good anatomical, pathological, and physiological knowledge, but close and well-cultivated diagnostic powers to decide *which* organ is diseased, and *how* it is diseased. For example, sometimes a displacement of the uterus will cause a sense of weight, dragging, and throbbing, accompanied by pain in the back and in front of the hips. But inflammation, ulceration, and induration of this organ will produce precisely the same results; and sometimes *mere nervous debility* in these parts will induce these symptoms, especially when the imagination is excited in reference to the subject. It also is often the case that extreme prolapsus occurs *in which there is no pain at all.* . . .

It has become a very common notion, that when any local displacement of the pelvic organs occur, a woman must cease to use her arms, cease to exercise vigorously, and keep herself on the bed much of her time. All which, in most cases, is exactly the three things which she ought not to do. And thus it is that, when from want of fresh air and exercise, and from the many pernicious practices that debilitate the female constitution, the pelivc organs indicate debility, and these nerves begin to ache, immediately a harness is put on for local support, and the bed becomes the constant resort. And thus the muscular debility and nervous irritability are increased. And yet, all that is needed is fresh air, exercise, simple diet, and *proper* mental occupation. . . .

It is probable that thousands of women who are suffering from pain in the back and pelvic evils, and who either will soon be invalids or imagine themselves so, could be relieved entirely by obeying these directions:

1. Wash the whole person on rising in cool water. Dress loosely, and let *all* the weight of clothing rest on the shoulders.
2. Sleep in a well-ventilated room; exercise the muscles a great deal, especially those of the arms and trunk, taking care to lie down and rest as soon as fatigue is felt.
3. Take a sitting-bath ten minutes at a time, in the middle of the forenoon and afternoon, with water at 85, reducing it gradually each day till at 60. Let the water reach above the hip, and while bathing rub and press the abdomen *upward*.

Wear a wet double girdle by night around the lower part of the body. Make it one-third of a yard wide; wring it well, and when on, cover it with double cotton flannel. If pain and weakness are felt, wear it by day also, adding clothing enough to prevent chilliness.

My heart aches when I see how the mass of women, by ignorance and by blind bondage to custom and fashion, bring on themselves pangs innumerable and premature old age. Many a blooming bride at twenty, finds herself, at thirty, wrinkled and care-worn; unhappy as a wife, unreasonable as a mother, and almost useless as a citizen. While some have inherited too much physical depravity to be preserved by any methods in good health, the majority have been most miserably spendthrift in using up their vital powers, thus rendering the joy of their married life as evanescent as the morning cloud. Many a wife who, but for her physical condition, would have been happy in her social relation, says to me, with a sigh, "I ought never to have been married, for my life is one prolonged agony. I could endure it myself alone, but the thought that I am, from year to year, becoming the mother of those who are to partake of and perpetuate the misery that I endure, makes me so wretched that I am well-nigh distracted." . . .

The young miss who wickedly wastes her health, and receives with an indifferent toss of the head all cautions in regard to health, little dreams of the bitter tears she will shed when it is too late for repentance to avail. The prospective husband may take great care to protect the fair but frail one of his choice; he may in after years fondly cherish the wife of his youth when she aches constantly and fades prematurely; still he has no helpmate—no one to double life's joys or lighten life's labors for him. Some sick women grow selfish and forget that, in a partnership such as theirs, others suffer when they suffer. Every true husband has but half a life who has a sick wife.

A few days since a gentleman living with his third wife, whom he had just placed under my care, said, "There is nothing that I have so much desired as a companion *in good health*; but it is what I have seldom enjoyed in all my married life." Then, with a sigh, he rose, and walked quickly to and fro in his spacious parlors, saying, "my home is again shaded by sickness and sorrow, and my last hope of domestic joy is blighted." His elegant residence and political honors could give him no enjoyment while his wife was an invalid.

A young husband, in thriving business, of naturally a hopeful heart, presents the case of his wife, and asks, "Can she ever be well? Will she ever have her former hopeful, loving, patient spirit?" Then the tears gathered as he said, "We used to be happy, but now, when I come from business, she can only tell of her suffering, and reproach me because I do not try more to relieve her." Then he added, by way of self-defense, "I do try to nurse her, and tend baby when I can be spared from business; I get the best help I can, but nothing satisfies—*she is so nervous!*" The wife, I found, had been brought up elegantly but indolently, and so neither body nor spirit were developed sufficiently to bear healthfully the changes which maternity induces.

There are no class of infirmities more likely to induce irritabilty of temper and depression of spirit than those that affect the pelvic organs. A husband, whose wife had spent some months with us as a patient, said afterward that he should consider her stay there the best investment he ever made, even if there had been no other improvement in his wife than the change in her temper.

LUCY THURSTON'S SURGICAL OPERATION

This rare description of a nineteenth-century mastectomy comes from Lucy Thurston, who with her husband, Asa, was a missionary in Hawaii from 1820 until her death in 1876. Sixty years old at the time of the operation, Thurston lived another twenty-one years. Thurston describes her ordeal in an 1855 letter to her daughter Mary.

I have hitherto forborne to write respecting the surgical operation I experienced in September, from an expectation that you would be with us so soon. That is now given up; so I proceed to give a circumstantial account of those days of peculiar discipline. At the end of the General Meeting in June your father returned to Kailua, leaving me at Honolulu, in Mr. Taylor's family, under Dr. Ford's care. Dr. Hillebrand was called in counsel. During the latter part of August they decided on the use of the knife. Mr. Thurston was sent for to come down according to agreement should such be the result. I requested him to bring certain things which I wished, in case I no more returned to Kailua. Tremendous gales of wind were now experienced. One vessel was wrecked within sight of Kailua. Another, on her way there, nearly foundered, and returned only to be condemned. In vain we looked for another conveyance. Meantime, the tumor was rapidly altering. It had nearly approached the surface, exhibiting a dark spot. Should it become an open ulcer, the whole system would become vitiated with its malignity. Asa said he should take no responsibility of waiting the arrival of his father. Persis felt the same. Saturday P.M., the doctors met in consultation, and advised an immediate operation. The next Tuesday (12th of September), ten o'clock A.M., was the hour fixed upon. In classifying, the Dr. placed this among "capital operations." Both doctors advised not to take chloroform because of my having had the paralysis. I was glad they allowed me the use of my senses. Persis offered me her parlor, and Asa his own new bridal room for the occasion. But I preferred the retirement and quietude of the grass-thatched cottage. Thomas, with all his effects moved out of it into a room a few steps off. The house was thoroughly cleaned and prettily fitted up. One lady said it seemed as though it had been got up by magic. Monday, just at night, Dr. Ford called to see that all was in readiness. There were two lounges trimmed,

Lucy G. Thurston, *Life and Times of Mrs. Lucy G. Thurston, Wife of Rev. Asa Thurston, Pioneer Missionary to the Sandwich Islands, Gathered from Letters and Journals Extending Over a Period of More than Fifty Years, Selected and Arranged by Herself* (Ann Arbor, Mich.: S. C. Andrews, 1882), pp. 168–75. The editors are indebted to Dana Robert for alerting them to the existence of this document.

one with white, the other with rose-colored mosquito netting. There was a reclining Chinese chair, a table for the instruments, a wash-stand with wash bowls, sponges, and pails of water. There was a frame with two dozen towels, and a table of choice stimulants and restoratives. One more table with the Bible and hymn book.

That night I spent in the house alone for the first time. The family had all retired for the night. In the still hour of darkness, I long walked back and forth in the capacious door-yard. Depraved, diseased, helpless, I yielded myself up entirely to the will, the wisdom, and the strength of the Holy One. At peace with myself, with earth, and with heaven, I calmly laid my head upon my pillow and slept refreshingly. A bright day opened upon us. My feelings were natural, cheerful, elevated. I took the Lord at his own word: "As the day is, so shall thy strength be." There with an unwavering heart, I leaned for strength and support. Before dressing for the occasion, I took care to call on Ellen, who had then an infant a week old by her side. It was a cheerful call, made in a common manner, she not being acquainted with the movements of the day. I then prepared myself for the professional call. Dr. Judd was early on the ground. I went with him to Asa's room, where with Asa and Sarah we sat and conversed till other medical men rode up. Dr. Judd rose to go out. I did the same. Asa said: "You had better not go, you are not wanted yet." I replied: "I wish to be among the first on the ground, to prevent its coming butt end first." On reaching my room, Dr. Ford was there. He introduced me to Dr. Hoffman of Honolulu, and to Dr. Brayton of an American Naval ship, then in port. The instruments were then laid out upon the table. Strings were prepared for tying arteries. Needles threaded for sewing up the wound. Adhesive plasters were cut into strips, bandages produced, and the Chinese chair placed by them in the front double door. Everything was now in readiness, save the arrival of one physician. All stood around the house or in the piazza. Dr. Ford, on whom devolved the responsibility, paced the door-yard. I stood in the house with others, making remarks on passing occurrences. At length I was invited to sit. I replied: "As I shall be called to lie a good while, I had rather now stand." Dr. Brayton, as he afterwards said, to his *utter astonishment* found that the lady to be operated on was standing in their midst.

Dr. Hillebrand arrived. It was a signal for action. Persis and I stepped behind a curtain. I threw off my cap and dressing gown, and appeared with a white flowing skirt, with the white bordered shawl purchased in 1818, thrown over my shoulders. I took my seat in the chair. Persis and Asa stood at my right side; Persis to hand me restoratives; Asa to use his strength, if self-control were wanting. Dr. Judd stood at my left elbow for the same reason; my shawl was thrown off, exhibiting my left arm, breast and side, perfectly bare. Dr. Ford showed me how I must hold back my left arm to the greatest possible extent, with my hand taking a firm hold of the arm of my chair: with my right hand, I took hold of the right arm, with my feet I pressed against the foot of the chair. Thus instructed, and everything in readiness, Dr. Ford looked me full in the face, and with great firmness asked: "Have you made up your mind to have it cut out?" "Yes, sir." "Are you ready now?" "Yes, sir; but let me know when you begin, that I may be able to bear it. Have you your knife in that hand now?" He opened his hand that I might see it, saying, "I am going to begin now." Then came a gash long and deep, first on one side of my breast, then on the other. Deep sickness seized me, and deprived me of my breakfast. This was followed by extreme faintness. My sufferings were no longer local. There was a general feeling of agony throughout the whole system. I felt, every inch of me, as though flesh was failing. During the whole operation, I was enabled to have entire self control over my person, and over my voice. Persis and Asa were devotedly employed in sustaining me with the use of cordials, ammonia, bathing my temples, &c. I myself fully intended to have seen the thing done. But on recollection, every glimpse I happened to have, was the doctor's right hand completely covered with blood, up to the very wrist. He afterwards told me, that at one time the blood from an artery flew into his eyes, so that he could not see. It was nearly an hour and a half that I was beneath his hand, in cutting out the entire breast, in cutting out the glands beneath the arm, in tying the arteries, in absorbing the blood, in sewing up the wound, in putting on the adhesive plasters, and in applying the bandage.

The views and feelings of that hour are now vivid to my recollection. It was during the cutting process that I began to talk. The feeling that I had reached a different point from those by whom I was surrounded, inspired me with freedom. It was thus that I expressed myself. "It has been a great trial to my feelings that Mr. Thurston is not here. But it is not necessary. So many friends, and Jesus Christ besides. His left hand is underneath my head, His right hand sustains and embraces me. I am willing to suffer. I am willing to die. I am not afraid of death. I am not afraid of hell. I anticipate a blessed immortality. Tell Mr. Thurston my peace flows like a river.

> "Upward I lift mine eyes.
>   From God is all my aid:
> The God that built the skies,
>   And earth and nature made.

> God is the tower
>> To which I fly;
>> His grace is nigh
>> In every hour."

God disciplines me, but He does it with a gentle hand. At one time I said, "I know you will bear with me." Asa replied, "I think it is you that have to bear from us."

The doctor, after removing the entire breast, said to me, "I want to cut yet more, round under your arm." I replied, "Do just what you want to do, only tell me when, so that I can bear it." One said the wound had the appearance of being more than a foot long. Eleven arteries were taken up. After a beginning had been made in sewing it up, Persis said: "Mother, the doctor makes as nice a seam as you ever made in your life." "Tell me, Persis, when he is going to put in the needle, so that I can bear it." "Now—now—now," &c. "Yes, tell me. That is a good girl." Ten stitches were taken, two punctures at every stitch, one on either side. When the whole work was done, Dr. Ford and Asa removed my chair to the back side of the room, and laid me on the lounge. Dr. Brayton came to my side, and taking me by the hand said: "There is not one in a thousand who would have borne it as you have done."

Up to this time, everything is fresh to my recollection. Of that afternoon and night, I only remember that the pain in the wound was intense and unremitting, and that I felt willing to be just in the circumstances in which I was placed. I am told that Dr. Ford visited me once in the afternoon, and once in the night, that Persis and Asa took care of me, that it seemed as if I suffered nearly as much as during the operation, and that my wound was constantly wet with cold water. I have since told Persis, that "I thought they kept me well drugged with paregoric." He replied, "We did not give you a drop." "Why then do I not remember what took place?" "Because you had so little life about you." By morning light the pain had ceased. Surgeons would understand the expression, that the wound healed by a "union of the first intention."

The morning again brought to my mind a recollection of events. I was lying on my lounge, feeble and helpless. I opened my eyes and saw the light of day. Asa was crossing the room bearing a Bible before him. He sat down near my couch, read a portion, and then prayed.

For several days, I had long sinking turns of several hours. Thursday night, the third of suffering, Thomas rode nearly two miles to the village for the Dr., once in the fore part of the evening, again at eleven. At both times he came. At two o'clock he unexpectedly made his third call that night. It was at his second call that he said to Persis: "In the morning make your mother some chicken soup. She has starved long enough." (They had been afraid of fever.) Persis immediately aroused Thomas, had a chicken caught, a fire made, and a soup under way that same midnight hour. The next day, Friday, I was somewhat revived by the use of wine and soup. In the afternoon, your father arrived. It was the first time since the operation, that I felt as if I had life enough to endure the emotion of seeing him. He left Kailua the same day the operation was performed. A vessel was passing in sight of Kailua. He rowed out in a canoe and was received on board. Hitherto, Persis, Asa and Thomas, had been my only nurses both by day and by night. The doctor gave directions that no one enter the room, but those that took care of me.

For weeks my debility was so great, that I was fed with a teaspoon, like an infant. Many dangers were apprehended. During one day, I saw a duplicate of every person and every thing that my eye beheld. Thus it was, sixteen years before, when I had the paralysis. Three weeks after the operation, your father for the first time, very slowly raised me to the angle of 45 degrees. It seemed as if it would have taken away my sense. It was about this time that I perceptibly improved from day to day, so much so, that in four weeks from my confinement, I was lifted into a carriage. Then I rode with your father almost every day. As he was away from his field of labor, and without any family responsibilities, he was entirely devoted to me. It was of great importance to me, that he was at liberty and in readiness ever to read simple interesting matter to me, to enliven and to cheer, so that time never passed heavily. After remaining with me six weeks, he returned to Kailua, leaving me with the physician and with our children.

In a few weeks, Mother, Mr. Taylor, Persis, Thomas, Lucy, Mary, and George bade farewell to Asa and Sarah, and to little Robert, their black-eyed baby boy. Together we passed over the rough channels up to the old homestead. Then, your father instead of eating his solitary meals, had his family board enlarged for the accommodation of three generations.

And here is again your mother, engaged in life's duties, and life's war-fare. Fare thee well. Be one with us in knowledge, sympathy, and love, though we see thee not, and when sickness prostrates, we feel not thy hand upon our brow.

⌁

THE MURDERS OF MARRIAGE,
BY MARY GOVE NICHOLS

Restive in the bonds of a deplorable marriage, which brought her one child and several miscarriages, Mary Gove (1810–1884) began giving classes and public lectures on female physiology to women in and near Boston in the late 1830s. In 1842 she published her Lectures to Ladies on Anatomy and Physiology *and left her husband to embark on a health reform career; by 1845 she was conducting a water-cure boardinghouse in New York City and socializing with utopian communitarians and artists. After she met and married Thomas Low Nichols in 1848, the couple opened a number of short-lived health establishments. When they wrote this selection, they advocated complete freedom for the individual, including the right of a woman to choose the father of her child.*

People are constantly asking the question, What would become of children if married persons were allowed to separate? *Let me tell conservatism that nine-tenths of the children that now burden the world would never be born.* Couples are held together by their own prejudices and the pressure of public opinion till a child is born. This child belongs to the father, and he wants a housekeeper and a nurse for it; he wants some one to reputably supply the amative want; perhaps the woman may be attractive to him—besides, the whole social mechanism holds this couple as in a vice together. The wife may have an utter indifference to the husband, or a loathing and abhorrence of him; but she must bear more children as a condition of support, and for the privilege of keeping the babe of her love in her bosom—of having something to fill her poor, desolate heart, and compensate her for a life of impurity which her spirit revolts against, till its oft violated instincts are unable to distinguish good from evil. . . .

The general idea and feeling, whether we know it or not, is that woman is property. She has no right to herself if she is married. Nine-tenths of the children born in marriage are not desired by the mother, often not by the father, though it is a great blessing that great love is born with them. Women have not, as a universal fact, the passion that asks the sexual indulgence. Vast numbers of the women of civilization have neither the sexual nor maternal passion. All women want love and support. They do not want to bear children, or to be harlots for this love or this support.

T. L. Nichols, M.D., and Mrs. Mary S. Gove Nichols, *Marriage: Its History, Character and Results; Its Sanctities, and Its Profanities; Its Science and Its Facts* (New York: T. L. Nichols, 1854), pp. 200–202, 215–16, 223–24, 228–30, 240–42, 244–45.

In marriage as it at present exists, the instinct against bearing children and against submitting to the amative embrace, is almost as general as the love for infants after they are born. The obliteration of the maternal and sexual instincts in woman is a terrible pathological fact. It has not been defined by theologians, physicians, or political economists. People know no more its meaning than they know the meaning of purity in woman.

A healthy and loving woman is impelled to material union as surely, often as strongly, as man. Would it not be great injustice in our Heavenly Father to so constitute woman as to suffer the pangs of childbirth with no enjoyment of the union that gives her a babe. The truth is that healthy nerves give pleasure in the ultimates of love with no respect to sex; and the same exhausted and diseased nerves, that deny to woman the pleasures of love, give her the dreadful pangs of childbirth.

The apathy of the sexual instinct in woman is caused by the enslaved and unhealthy condition in which she lives. Many inherit from mothers, who are victims in unloving marriage, the diseased amativeness that makes them early subject to masturbation; and this habit destroys the health of the nervous system. Others inherit an apathetic state that does not impel them to any material union. Healthy and loving women are destroyed by being made bond-women, having no spontaneity, and bearing children more rapidly than they ought, and in unhealthy condition. . . .

People talk of the sanctity of marriage. Is there any sanctity where there is force on the one side, and fear on the other? And yet men have no faith in themselves, and less than none in women. They say, "We must keep to such a state as this for fear we should fall into something worse." The perpetuation of hate, discord, and impurity in children, is the lowest and worst that I can conceive for our human race. . . .

Because I speak of the false and evil, I am by no means unconscious of the good and true. There is much love and consequent sanctity in our marriages; but there are sad mistakes, and horrible, adulterous unions. When marriage becomes what it must be in a true freedom, *union in love*, it will be divinely beautiful. When it is a bargain, a sacrifice, made from other motives than affection, and, besides, is indissoluble, it is shocking to all true moral sense. When we consider love as alone sanctifying the union of the sexes, then we see the necessity of divorce, to prevent people living in adultery, who have married without love, or who have ceased to love after marriage. . . .

The hereditary evils to children born in a sensual and unloving marriage are everywhere visible. They are written in every lineament of the

Present,—sensuality, sickness, suffering, weakness, imbecility, or outrageous crime. I speak what I know, and testify what I have seen in a long and varied medical practice, when I assert that masturbation in children, and every evil of sensuality, spring from the polluted hot-bed of a sensual and unloving marriage, where woman is subjected to a destroying sensualism during pregnancy and lactation. I have been consulted by mothers for children born without love, where the mother was subjected to intercourse during pregnancy. The children seemed incurable masturbators, and though with good intellect and much clear perception, and delicacy, and modesty, it was often a work of time, and much labor and care to cure them. I have also known cases where subsequent children, born in a second marriage which was loving and healthful, had no such tendency. They were pure from birth, as the first were impure. . . .

Another instance of this kind, though not so aggravated in its character, nor attended with like results, is revived in my memory. A lady of the finest intellect, most devoted piety, great fascination and charm of manner and qualities, but delicate and weak in health, was loved and sought in marriage by a truly great man; one of the best our present age has had the good fortune to produce. This lady was from an early age a victim of diseased amativeness in the form of solitary vice. Her standard of purity was that unconsciously adopted by the Church and the world, that a woman should be "chaste as ice";* that there should be no attraction felt by her, or, at least, manifested for the masculine principle; that all such attraction derogates from feminine purity and propriety. This lady, as hundreds of others have done, brought her disease and false virtue to me. She told me that she felt herself pure, that God had delivered her from all temptation to a sensual life. That though she loved her husband most tenderly, she had never the slightest sensual attraction toward him. He was a man of great strength, and delicacy, and beauty of character; she said though not delivered by God from the temptation to amative indulgence, he still respected her slightest wish, and was as separate from her, as if not her husband, and yet perfectly faithful to the bond of marriage.

She gave him great credit for his forbearance toward her, and his self government, but lamented very sincerely his temptations to a sensual life. In the early years of her marriage she had several times miscarried, prov-

*I remember a distinguished Physiologist once boasted to me that his wife was "chaste as ice." The poor creature was so destroyed by amative disease, that the uterus was nearly or quite cancerous, and the marital union was of course a terror and a curse to her, in such a situation. The comfort the husband found in such condition was, that his wife was "chaste as ice"—that she would never be tainted by the breath of scandal—that she was a woman of undoubted piety and purity. Purity!! Pah!

ing that she had no right to be a mother, for she was placed in the best conditions for bearing her children, and yet was not able to nourish the foetus above three or four months. She told me the story with self righteous complacency, and yet she was full of sorrow for her husband. Whilst she talked, I silently took the measure of my auditor and patient. Could she understand me? Would she confess that she was a victim to masturbation? Could she know how false, diseased, and impure she was, and could she be made to see that her noble and self sacrificing husband was a true, pure and natural human being. I mentally answered my own questions in the affirmative.

"My dear," said I, "you are very sick and weak. Your nervous system is drained of its life. It is not natural, or true, for woman to be without the amative passion. It is a great wrong in her nature when she is deprived of the wish and power for amative pleasure. She is diseased, and this disease has a cause." "What is the cause?" said she, thoughtfully. "Atony of the nervous system from birth, or a diseased amativeness that causes solitary vice, and thus results in the same atonic condition which is termed virtue and purity in woman." I talked on in this way—she bowed her beautiful head in tears and deep humiliation. So sudden and woman-like was her perception, that she saw her life of falseness, her whole inheritance of evil, and all the injustice she had done her husband at a glance. . . .

The slavery, and consequent unsanctified sensuality of the present and past, have debased and degraded the world's idea of material union, until their thought is as impure as their deed. The human mind must be redeemed from this impurity and disgust, and love is the only redemption. The law of life and of growth, of all good, is—We must be free to act, so long as we do not unjustly interfere with the well-being of others.

When a conservator of public morals, such as Horace Greeley, regards with horror the assertion that woman has the right to choose the father of her child, the fact proves much—alas! how much. It proves the low estate from which woman has just begun to emerge. She is degraded by law and custom even lower than the beasts which perish; and if one asserts her right to any ownership of herself, so-called moralists, and philosophers reject the thought with horror. Is there no sacredness left in this man's heart? Does he wish to be the father of babes when the mother has no choice, when she would come loathing to his arms, feeling that the union scarred her soul for eternity, and with the thought of murder in her mind rather than bear the babe thus forced upon her? Is this Mr. Greeley's morality when he says, "I utterly abhor what you term the right of a woman to choose the father of her child"? Alas for woman if men are not better than this creed! They are, and they are not. The best are enslaved by law, custom and organization, and go on murdering frail wives, not daring to think of any escape from the necessity, not even when their material wants are healthful and legitimate, and a wife utterly unfit to be a wife or a mother. I have no doubt that Mr. Greeley has at times the conception of what love and purity are, and what they would do for the world in pure births; but the bondage of public opinion, and his own nature is upon him. He has not leisure or ability to comprehend a world's want, and he only asks that mankind be saved from a worse estate than their miserable present; and the only means of salvation he sees is law, binding people to an outward decency, if possible, whilst their internal life is a foul, rotting ulcer—and if their children live they perpetuate the sad state of their parents. Thus the world is filled with disease, misery, crime and premature death. . . .

I clip an illustration from yesterday's paper:

"CHILD SUPPOSED TO BE MURDERED BY ITS MOTHER.—On Thursday a servant girl living at the house of S. T. Wright, Esq., West Morrissiania, who was pregnant, was suspected by some of the family of intending to use foul means to dispose of her infant when born. They followed her; finding she was likely to be detected, she drew a knife she had in her hand across the child's throat, but in her hurry she did not strike the throat, but nearly cut off its jaw, then throwing it down the sink, left it. The alarm was immediately spread, and the neighbors, throwing off the building, discovered the child already dead. An investigation was held by Coroner Johnson, which resulted in the arrest of the inhuman mother."—*Tribune*.

"If a black mother or slave at the south had committed such a crime, we should have been told that it was to save the child from the horrors of slavery, and another 'Uncle Tom's Cabin' would be written. But black mothers do not commit such follies, and the crime is too common among our white servants to meet more than a passing notice."—*Day Book*.

Here is a crime, committed under one oppressive institution, made a sort of indirect apology for another institution which is nearly parallel in its evils. The servant girl, who is the horror of almost all who read of her crime, may have a more natural and loving heart than many who shudder at her sin. She may have been utterly maddened by her terrible conditions, and therefore irresponsible. . . . And who caused the crime and the punishment? Who but a society steeped in murder and adultery? for at this same time I had a lady patient, the wife of a man worth half a million, who confessed to me that she had six times had abortion procured, and by her family physician, too. "I could not bear children to such a brute," were her words of excuse.

Again the question occurs, What is to become of children if married people are allowed to separate? The answer again is what becomes of them now?

I believe that the number of children murdered in marriage before birth, is as much greater than by unmarried women, as the proportion of children born in marriage, is greater than the number of illegitimate offspring. Society asks, What is to become of children that women are forced to bear? Society provides prisons for them, and the death penalty now. Might it not be well to leave women the liberty to choose whether they will bear children to be hung, or not?

TESTIMONY AS TO THE INSANITY
OF ELIZABETH PACKARD

Elizabeth Ware Packard, born in 1816, was the daughter and wife of conservative Protestant ministers. In the 1850s she began to gravitate toward liberal religious doctrines. When she disregarded her husband's repeated demands that she stop expounding her views to adult Sunday school classes, he had her committed to the state insane asylum in Jacksonville, Illinois, where she spent three years. The hearing represented in this document was held in 1864 to rule on Packard's complaint that after her release from the Jacksonville Asylum her husband had kept her a virtual prisoner in their home. The court found Packard sane. She spent much of the rest of her life lobbying for laws to ensure the personal liberties of married women and their rights over their children.

STATE OF ILLINOIS,

KANKAKEE COUNTY.

To the Honorable CHARLES R. STARR, *Judge of the 20th judicial circuit in the State of Illinois.*

William Haslet, Daniel Beedy, Zalmon Hanford, and Joseph Younglove, of said county, on behalf of Elizabeth P. W. Packard, wife of Theophilus Packard, of said county, respectfully represent unto your Honor, that said Elizabeth P. W. Packard, is unlawfully restrained of her liberty, at Manteno, in the county of Kankakee, by her husband, the Rev. Theophilus Packard, being forcibly confined and imprisoned in a close room of the dwelling-house of her said husband, for a long time, to wit, for the space of six weeks, her said husband refusing to let her visit her neighbors and refusing her neighbors to visit her; that they believe her said husband is about to forcibly convey her from out the State; that they believe there is no just cause or ground for restraining said wife of her liberty; that they believe that said wife is a mild and amiable woman. And they are advised and believe, that said husband cruelly abuses and misuses said wife, by depriving her of her winter's clothing, this cold and inclement weather, and that there is no necessity for such cruelty on the part of said husband to said wife; and they are advised and believe, that said wife desires to come to Kankakee City, to make application to your Honor for a writ of *habeus corpus,* to liberate herself from said confinement or imprisonment, and that said husband refused and refuses to allow said wife to come to

Mrs. E. P. W. Packard, *Modern Persecution, or Married Woman's Liabilities, as Demonstrated by the Action of the Illinois Legislature,* vol. 2 (Hartford, 1875), pp. 25–26, 30–33, 34–38.

Kankakee City for said purpose; and that these petitioners make application for a writ of *habeus corpus* in her behalf, at her request. These petitioners therefore pray that a writ of *habeus corpus* may forthwith issue, commanding said Theophilus Packard to produce the body of said wife, before your Honor, according to law, and that said wife may be discharged from said imprisonment. (Signed), WILLIAM HASLET. DANIEL BEEDY. ZALMON HANFORD. J. YOUNGLOVE. . . .

J. W. BROWN, being sworn, said:

I am a physician; live in this city; have no extensive acquaintance with Mrs. Packard. Saw her three or four weeks ago. I examined her as to her sanity or insanity. I was requested to make a visit, and had an extended conference with her; I spent some three hours with her. I had no difficulty in arriving at the conclusion, in my mind, that she was insane.

Cross-examination.—I visited her by request of Mr. Packard, at her house. The children were in and out of the room; no one else was present. I concealed my object in visiting her. She asked me if I was a physician, and I told her no; that I was an agent, selling sewing machines, and had come there to sell her one.

The first subject we conversed about was sewing machines. She showed no sign of insanity on that subject.

The next subject discussed, was the social condition of the female sex. She exhibited no special marks of insanity on that subject, although she had many ideas quite at variance with mine, on the subject.

The subject of politics was introduced. She spoke of the condition of the North and the South. She illustrated her difficulties with Mr. Packard, by the difficulties between the North and the South. She said the South was wrong, and was waging war for two wicked purposes: first, to overthrow a good government, and second, to establish a despotism on the inhuman principle of human slavery. But that the North, having right on their side, would prevail. So Mr. Packard was opposing her, to overthrow free thought in woman; that the despotism of man may prevail over the wife; but that she had right and truth on her side, and that she would prevail. During this conversation I did not fully conclude that she was insane.

I brought up the subject of religion. We discussed the subject for a long time, and then I had not the slightest difficulty in concluding that she was hopelessly insane.

Question. Dr., what particular idea did she advance on the subject of religion that led you to the conclusion that she was hopelessly insane?

Answer. She advanced many of them. I formed my opinion not so much on any one idea advanced, as upon her whole conversation. She then said that she was the 'Personification of the Holy Ghost.' I did not know what she meant by that.

Ques. Was not this the idea conveyed to you in that conversation: That there are three attributes of the Deity—the Father, the Son, and the Holy Ghost? Now, did she not say, that the attributes of the Father were represented in mankind, in man; that the attributes of the Holy Ghost were represented in woman; and that the Son was the fruit of these two attributes of the Deity?

Ans. Well, I am not sure but that was the idea conveyed, though I did not fully get her idea at the time.

Ques. Was not that a new idea to you in theology?

Ans. It was.

Ques. Are you much of a theologian?

Ans. No.

Ques. Then because the idea was a novel one to you, you pronounced her insane.

Ans. Well, I pronounced her insane on that and other things that exhibited themselves in this conversation.

Ques. Did she not show more familiarity with the subject of religion and the questions of theology, than you had with these subjects?

Ans. I do not pretend much knowledge on these subjects.

Ques. What else did she say or do there, that showed marks of insanity?

Ans. She claimed to be better than her husband—that she was right—and that he was wrong—and that all she did was good, and all he did was bad—that she was farther advanced than other people, and more nearly perfection. She found fault particularly that Mr. Packard would not discuss their points of difference on religion in an open, manly way, instead of going around and denouncing her as crazy to her friends and to the church.

She had a great aversion to being called insane. Before I got through the conversation she exhibited a great dislike to me, and almost treated me in a contemptuous manner. She appeared quite lady-like. She had a great reverence for God, and a regard for religious and pious people. . . .

ABIJAH DOLE, sworn, and says:

I know Mrs. Packard; have known her twenty-five or thirty years. I am her brother-in-law. Lived in Manteno seven years. Mrs. Packard has lived there six years. I have been sent for several times by her and Mr. Packard, and found her in an excited state of mind. I was there frequently; we were very familiar. One morning early, I was sent for; she was in the west room; she was in her night clothes. She took me by the hand and led me to the bed. Libby was lying in bed, moaning and moving her head. Mrs.

Packard now spoke and said, 'How pure we are.' 'I am one of the children of heaven; Libby is one of the branches.' 'The woman shall bruise the serpent's head.' She called Mr. Packard a devil. She said, Brother Dole, these are serious matters. If Brother Haslet will help me, we will crush the body. She said Christ had come into the world to save men, and that she had come to save woman. Her hair was disheveled. Her face looked wild. This was over three years ago.

I was there again one morning after this. She came to me. She pitied me for marrying my wife, who is a sister to Mr. Packard; said, I might find an agreeable companion. She said if she had cultivated amativeness, she would have made a more agreeable companion. She took me to another room and talked about going away; this was in June, before they took her to the State Hospital. She sent for me again; she was in the east room; she was very cordial. She wanted me to intercede for Theophilus, who was at Marshall, Michigan; she wanted him to stay there, and it was thought not advisable for him to stay. We wished him to come away, but did not tell her the reasons. He was with a Swedenborgian.

After this I was called there once in the night. She said she could not live with Mr. Packard, and she thought she had better go away. One time she was in the Bible-class. The question came up in regard to Moses smiting the Egyptian; she thought Moses had acted too hasty, but that all things worked for the glory of God. I requested her to keep quiet, and she agreed to do it.

I have had no conversation with Mrs. Packard since her return from the Hospital; she will not talk with me because she thinks I think she is insane. Her brother came to see her; he said he had not seen her for four or five years. I tried to have Mrs. Packard talk with him, and she would not have anything to do with him because he said she was a crazy woman. She generally was in the kitchen when I was there, overseeing her household affairs.

I was Superintendent of the Sabbath School. One Sabbath, just at the close of the school, I was behind the desk, and almost like a vision she appeared before me, and requested to deliver or read an address to the school. I was much surprised; I felt so bad, I did not know what to do. (At this juncture the witness became very much affected, and choked up so that he could not proceed, and cried so loud that he could be heard in any part of the court-room. When he became calm, he went on and said,) I was willing to gratify her all I could, for I knew she was crazy, but I did not want to take the responsibility myself, so I put it to a vote of the school, if she should be allowed to read it. She was allowed to read it. It occupied ten or fifteen minutes in reading.

I cannot state any of the particulars of that paper. It bore evidence of her insanity. She went on and condemned the church, all in all, and the individuals composing the church, because they did not agree with her. She looked very wild and very much excited. She seemed to be insane. She came to church one morning just as services commenced, and wished to have the church act upon her letter withdrawing from the church immediately. Mr. Packard was in the pulpit. She wanted to know if Brother Dole and Brother Merrick were in the church, and wanted them to have it acted upon. This was three years ago, just before she was taken away to the hospital.

Cross-examined.—I supposed when I first went into the room that her influence over the child had caused the child to become deranged. The child was ten years old. I believed that she had exerted some mesmeric or other influence over the child, that caused it to moan and toss its head. The child had been sick with brain fever; I learned that after I got there. I suppose the mother had considerable anxiety over the child; I suppose she had been watching over the child all night, and that would tend to excite her. The child got well. It was sick several days after this; it was lying on the bed moaning and tossing its head; the mother did not appear to be alarmed. Mr. Packard was not with her; she was all alone; she did not say that Mr. Packard did not show proper care for the sick child. I suppose she thought Libby would die.

Her ideas on religion did not agree with mine, nor with my view of the Bible.

I knew Mr. Packard thought her insane, and did not want her to discuss these questions in the Sabbath School. I knew he had opposed her more or less. This letter to the church was for the purpose of asking for a letter from church.

Question. Was it an indication of insanity that she wanted to leave the Presbyterian Church?

Answer. I think it strange that she should ask for letters from the church. She would not leave the church unless she was insane.

I am a member of the church—I believe the church is right. I believe everything the church does is right. I believe everything in the Bible.

Ques. Do you believe literally that Jonah was swallowed by a whale, and remained in its belly three days, and was then cast up?

Ans. I do.

Ques. Do you believe literally that Elijah went direct up to Heaven in a chariot of fire—that the chariot had wheels, and seats, and was drawn by horses?

Ans. I do—for with God all things are possible.
Ques. Do you believe Mrs. Packard was insane, and is insane?
Ans. I do.

ABORTION IN NEW YORK

Prior to the 1840s, abortion before "quickening" (when the first fetal movements are felt, in the fourth or fifth month of pregnancy) was not a crime in the United States, and abortionists such as Madame Restell (the nameless "Madam" below) advertised and practiced openly. If a woman died undergoing an abortion, however, the person operating on her was liable for murder. Physicians and journalists began a successful antiabortion crusade about mid-century. By the 1880s, both state laws and the federal Comstock Law (which prohibited advertising or sending "obscene" material through the mails) had made abortion illegal. The following selection comes from a genre of urban exposé writing popular throughout the century. The practice of abortion was not limited to cities, however.

On the 26th of August, 1871, at three o'clock in the afternoon, a truck drove up to the baggage-room of the Hudson River Railway depot, in Thirtieth street, and deposited on the sidewalk a large, common-looking travelling trunk. The driver, with the assistance of a boy hanging about the depot, carried the trunk into the baggage-room, and at this instant a woman of middle age, and poorly attired, entered the room, presented a ticket to Chicago, which she had just purchased, and asked to have the trunk checked to that place. The check was given her, and she took her departure. The baggage-master, half an hour later, in attempting to remove the trunk to the platform from which it was to be transferred to the baggage-car, discovered a very offensive odor arising from it. His suspicions were at once aroused, and he communicated them to the superintendent of the baggage-room, who caused the trunk to be removed to an old shed close by and opened. As the lid was raised a terrible sight was revealed. The trunk contained the dead body of a young woman, fully grown, and the limbs were compressed into its narrow space in the most appalling manner. The discovery was at once communicated to the police, and the body was soon after removed to the Morgue, where an inquest was held upon it.

The woman had been young and beautiful, and evidently a person of refinement, and the post mortem examination, which was made as speedily as possible, revealed the fact that she had been murdered in the effort to produce an abortion upon her. The case was at once placed in the hands of the detectives, and full details of the horrible affair were laid

James D. McCabe, *Lights and Shadows of New York Life; Or, the Sights and Sensations of the Great City* (Philadelphia: National Publishing Company, 1872), pp. 618–30.

before the public in the daily press. The efforts to discover the murderer were unusually successful. Little by little the truth came out. . . . [Dr. Jacob] Rosenzweig was arrested on suspicion, and committed to the Tombs to await the result of the inquest. The body was subsequently identified by an acquaintance of the dead woman, as that of Miss Alice Bowlsby, of Patterson, New Jersey. A further search of Rosenzweig's premises resulted in the finding of a handkerchief marked with the dead woman's name, and other evidence was brought to light all making it too plain for doubt that Alice Bowlsby had died from the effects of an abortion produced upon her by Jacob Rosenzweig. The wretch was tried for his offence, convicted, and sentenced to seven years of hard labor in the penitentiary.

This affair produced a profound impression not only upon the city, but upon the whole country, and drew the attention of the public so strongly to the subject of abortion as a trade, that there is reason to believe that some steps will be taken to check the horrible traffic.

Bad as Rosenzweig was, he was but one of a set who are so numerous in the city that they constitute one of the many distinct classes of vile men and women who infest it.

The readers of certain of the city newspapers are familiar with the advertisements of these people, such as the following:

A LADIES' PHYSICIAN, Dr. ——, Professor of Midwifery, over 20 years' successful practice in this city, guarantees certain relief to ladies, with or without medicine, at one interview. Unfortunates please call. Relief certain. Residence, ——. Elegant rooms for ladies requiring nursing.

IMPORTANT TO FEMALES, Dr. and Madame —— (25 years' practice) guarantee certain relief to married ladies, with or without medicine, at one interview. Patients from a distance provided with nursing, board, etc. Electricity scientifically applied.

A CURE FOR LADIES immediately. Madame ——'s Female Antidote. The only reliable medicine that can be procured; certain to have the desired effect in twenty-four hours, without any injurious results.

SURE CURE FOR LADIES in trouble. No injuroius medicines or instruments used. Consultation and advice free.

These are genuine advertisements, taken from a daily journal of great wealth and influence, which every morning finds its way into hundreds of families. . . .

A recent writer thus describes these wretches and their mode of operations:

"Under the head of abortionists, it must be understood there are different classes. First, there is the one whose advertisements, under the head of 'Dr.,' are conspicuous in almost every paper which will print them. . . .

"These men, some of them at least, are received into fashionable society, not because of their gentlemanly or engaging manners, nor even yet on account of their money, but from the fact that they exercise a certain amount of influence and are possessed of a vast deal of audacity. They are cognizant of many a family secret that comes under the jurisdiction of their peculiar vocation; and this fact enables them successfully, if they like, to dare these parties to treat them any other than respectfully. There is a skeleton in every house, a secret in every family; and too often the doctor, midwife, and accoucheur have to be treated publicly, socially, and pecuniarily in accordance with this fact. . . .

"Next come the female abortionists, who in some cases transact a larger and more profitable business than the doctors. There are several reasons for this, the principal of which is, that a female would, under the peculiar circumstances in which she is placed, reveal her condition to one of her own sex rather than to a man. The number of female abortionists in New York City is a disgrace and a ridicule upon the laws for the prevention of such inhuman proceedings. True, the majority of them are of the poorer class, but there are many who are literally rolling in wealth, the result of their illegal and unnatural pursuits. The names of many could be mentioned. One, however, will be sufficient, and, although she has been the most successful of her contemporaries, yet her card is a good criterion for the rest of her class. Her name, Madame ——, is well known, and needs no comment. Most of the better and most successful of her kind are in the habit of receiving no less than one hundred or one hundred and fifty dollars for each case, and often as much as five hundred or one thousand dollars. The less successful of the female abortionists, whose practice or business is limited, to some extent, through lack of funds to advertise the same, are content with considerably less sums for their services. . . .

"The female abortionists in New York are mostly of foreign birth or extraction, and have generally risen to their present position from being first-class nurses—in Germany, especially, there being medicine schools or colleges in which they graduate after a course of probably six or nine months' study as nurses. . . .

The principal, and indeed the only object of these wretches is to extort money from their victims. They have no interest in their "patients," either scientific or humane, as is shown by the readiness with which they consent to risk the lives of the poor creatures in their hands, and the rapacity with which they drain their money from them.

Perhaps the reader may ask, "Why, then, do women seek these wretches, instead of applying to educated physicians?" The answer is plain. Educated physicians are, as a rule, men of honor and humanity as well as skill. They know that to produce an abortion at any stage of pregnancy is to commit murder by destroying the child, and they also know that such an act, if it does not endanger the mother's life at the time, will doom her to great future suffering and disease, and probably to a painful death at the "turn of life." Therefore, as men of honor and good citizens, as well as lovers of science, they refuse to prostitute their profession and stain their souls with crime. . . .

In this city there are over twenty of these wretches plying their trade, and advertising it in the public prints. How well they succeed we have already shown, and in order to make it evident how great are their profits, we quote the following description of one of the most notorious female abortionists:

"By common consent, as well as by reason of her peculiar calling, Madam ——, of Fifth avenue, is styled 'The wickedest woman in New York.' According to her advertisement in the papers and the City Directory, she calls herself a 'female physician and professor of midwifery.'

"Madam —— is about fifty-five years of age, is a short, plump, vulgar-looking woman, with dark, piercing eyes and jet-black hair. Once she was handsome, but possesses now no traces of her former beauty. She looks like an upstart or 'shoddy' female, but not particularly wicked or heartless. She commenced business about twenty years ago. Her establishment at that time was in C—— street, and for some time she was but little known. About four years after she had begun business an event occurred which rendered her one of the most notorious women of the city. A young woman died who had been under her treatment, and Madam —— was arrested. She was tried before one of the courts, and her trial became a sensation for many days. The papers were filled with the testimony in the case, and the arguments of the leading counsel were given in full. All sorts of accounts, too, were furnished as to the history of the accused, the evil of abortion, and the necessity of adopting stricter laws in regard to it. . . .

"Madam —— had already made considerable money from her improper trade, and it was rumored at the time that she purchased a verdict of 'Not Guilty' for one hundred thousand dollars. It was a big price to pay, but she regained her liberty, and, what was more, made money by the large investment. Her trial proved to be an immense advertisement for her, and shortly afterward she removed from C—— street, purchasing a large mansion on Fifth avenue, not far from the Central Park. In that house she has lived from that time to the present, and says she intends to remain there until her death. . . ."

[D]ay after day in this great city this terrible slaughter of innocent beings goes on, and it will go on until the law makes the publication of the advertisements of these wretches, and the practice of their arts and the sale of their drugs, criminal offences.

It must not be supposed, however, that the best customers of the vendors of medicines for producing miscarriage and abortion are those who seek to hide their shame. It is a terrible fact that here, as in many other parts of the country, the crime of destroying their unborn offspring is repeatedly practised by married women in the secresy of domestic life. These buy largely of the drugs and pills sold by the professional abortionists. New York is bad enough in this respect, but the crime is not confined to it. It is an appalling truth that so many American wives are practicers of the horrible sin of "prevention" that in certain sections of our country, the native population is either stationary or is dying out. So common is the practice, that the Roman Catholic Archbishop of Baltimore and the Episcopal Bishop of Western New York, felt themselves called upon, a year or two ago, to publicly warn their people of the awful nature of it.

It is fashionable here, as elsewhere, not to have more than one, two, or three children. Men and women tell their friends every day that they do not mean to increase their families. They do mean, however, to enjoy the blessings of the married state, and to avoid its responsibilities. There is scarcely a physician in the city who is not applied to almost daily by persons of good position for advice as to the best means of preventing conception. The physicians of New York are men of honor, and they not only refuse to comply with the request, but warn the applicants for advice as to the true moral and physical nature of the course they are seeking to adopt. Yet this warning does not turn them from their purpose. Failing to secure the assistance of scientific men, they seek the advice, and purchase the drugs, of the wretches whose trade is child murder. The evil grows greater every year. These wretches send their drugs all over the country, and "the American race is dying out." In 1865, there were 780,931 families in the State of New York. Of these, 196,802 families had no children, 148,208 families had but one child each, 140,572 families had but two children each, and 107,342 families had but three children each. In nearly one-fourth of all the families there was not a child, and in 592,924 families, or more than three-fourths of all in the State, there was only a small fraction over one child to each family. Only about one child to each mother in the State reaches maturity. The New England States show even a worse state of affairs.

Is it a wonder, then, that Madame —— and her associates grow rich?

A FOX WOMAN COMES OF AGE

This account of menarche comes from the life story of a Fox (Mesquakie) woman, whose name was withheld by agreement. The story was recorded in syllabary by tribal member Harry Lincoln in 1918, then published in this English translation by anthropologist Truman Michelson, an expert in Algonquian linguistics. Michelson's numerous studies of the Fox emphasized the subtle changes in their language, folklore, and religion resulting from centuries of war, land loss, and interaction with native and European-American neighbors. The Mesquakie inhabited the Great Lakes region upon first European contact, but by the early twentieth century their largest settlement was near Tama, Iowa.

And then I was thirteen years old. "Now is the time when you must watch yourself: at last you are nearly a young woman. Do not forget this which I tell you. You might ruin your brothers if you are not careful. The state of being a young woman is evil. The manitous hate it. If any one is blessed by a manitou, if he eats with a young woman he is then hated by the one who blessed him and the (manitou) ceases to think of him. That is why it is told us, 'be careful' and why we are told about it beforehand. At the time when you are a young woman, whenever you become a young woman, you are to hide yourself. Do not come into your wickiup. That is what you are to do." She frightened me when she told me.

Lo, sure enough when I was thirteen and a half years old, I was told, "Go get some wood and carry it on your back." It was nearly noon when I started out. When I was walking along somewhere, I noticed something strange about myself. I was terribly frightened at being in that condition. I did not know how I became that way. "This must be the thing about which I was cautioned when I was told," I thought.

I went and laid down in the middle of the thick forest there. I was crying, as I was frightened. It was almost the middle of summer after we had done our hoeing. After a while my mother got tired of waiting for me. She came to seek me. Soon she found me. I was then crying hard.

"Come, stop crying. It's just the way with us women. We have been made to be that way. Nothing will happen to you. You will have gotten over this now in the warm weather. Had it happened to you in winter you would have had a hard time. You would be cold when you bathed as

"The Autobiography of a Fox Indian Woman," ed. and trans. Truman Michelson, *40th Annual Report of the Bureau of American Ethnology to the Secretary of the Smithsonian Institution, 1918–19* (Washington, D.C.: Government Printing Office, 1925), pp. 303–9.

you would have to jump into the water four times. That is the way it is when we first have it. Now, to-day, as it is warm weather, you may swim as slowly as you like when you swim," I was told. "Lie covered up. Do not try to look around. I shall go and make (a wickiup) for you," I was told.

I was suffering very much there in the midst of the brush. And it was very hot.

It was in the evening when I was told, "At last I have come for you. I have built (a place) for you to live in. Cover your face. Do not think of looking any place." I was brought there to the small wickiup. And I was shut off by twigs all around. There was brush piled up so that I could not see through it. There was only a little space where I lived to cook outside. My grandmother must have made it a size so that there was only room for us to lie down in.

"I shall fetch your grandmother to be here with you," my mother told me. It was another old woman. As a matter of fact the reason she was brought there was for to give me instructions. I did not eat all day long. The next day I was told, "We shall fetch things for you to use in cooking." I was not hungry as I was frightened. The next day my grandmother went to eat. It was only as long as she (took) when she went to eat that I was alone, but I was afraid. In the evening I was brought little buckets to cook with, any little thing to eat, water and wood. Then for the first time I cooked.

And my grandmother would keep on giving me instructions there, telling me how to lead a good life. She really was a very old woman. Surely she must have spoken the truth in what she had been saying to me. "My grandchild," she would say to me, "soon I shall tell you how to live an upright life. To-day you see how old I am. I did exactly what I was told. I tried and thought how to live an upright life. Surely I have reached an old age," she told me. "That is the way you should do, if you listen to me as I instruct you. Now as for your mother, I began giving her instructions before she was grown up, every time I saw her. Because she was my relative is why I gave her instructions, although she was well treated by her father's sister by whom she was reared. That is why she knows how to make things which belong to the work of us women. If you observe the way your mother makes anything, you would do well, my grandchild. And this. As many of us as entered young womanhood, fasted. It was very many days: some fasted ten days, some four, five, every kind of way. To-day, to be sure, things are changing. When I was a young woman I fasted eight days. We always fasted until we were grown up," my grandmother told me.

My mother only came to fetch me water and little sticks of wood so that I might kindle a fire when I cooked. And we made strings. That is what we did.

"Do not touch your hair: it might all come off. And do not eat sweet things. And if what tastes sour is eaten, one's teeth will come out. It is owing to that saying that we are afraid to eat sweet things," my grandmother told me. She always gave me good advice from time to time. "Well, there is another thing. Now the men will think you are mature as you have become a young woman, and they will be desirous of courting you. If you do not go around bashfully, for a long time they will not have the audacity to court you. When there is a dance, when there are many boys saying all sorts of funny things, if you do not notice it, they will be afraid of you for a very long time. If you laugh over their words, they will consider you as naught. They will begin bothering you right away. If you are immoral your brothers will be ashamed, and your mother's brothers. If you live quietly they will be proud. They will love you. If you are only always making something in the same place where you live, they will always give you something whenever they get it. And your brothers will believe you when you say anything to them. When one lives quietly the men folks love one. And there is another thing. Some of the girls of our generation are immoral. If one goes around all the time with those who are immoral, they would get one in the habit of being so, as long as one has not much intelligence. Do not go around with the immoral ones, my grandchild," my grandmother told me. "And this. You are to treat any aged person well. He (she) is thought of by the manitou: because he (she) has conducted his (her) life carefully is why he (she) reached an old age. Do not talk about anyone. Do not lie. Do not steal. If you practice stealing, you will be wretched. Do not (be stingy) with a possession of which you are fond. (If you are stingy) you will not get anything. If you are generous you will (always) get something. Moreover, do not go around and speak crossly toward anyone. You must be equally kind to (every) old person. That, my grandchild, is a good way to do," my grandmother said to me. She was indeed always instructing me what to do.

Soon I had lived there ten days. "Well, at last you may go and take a bath," my mother said to me. We started to the river. "Take off your waist," I was told. After I had taken it off I leaped into the water. Then, "I am going to peck you with something sharp," I was told. I was pecked all over. "And now on your lower part," I was told. "Only use your skirt as a breechcloth," is what I was told. I was also pecked on my thighs. "It will be that you will not menstruate much if the blood flows plentifully," I was told. I was made to suffer very much. I put on other garments. I threw away those which I had formerly been wearing around. And then for the first time I looked around to see. And again I had to cook alone for myself outside for ten days. After ten days I again went to bathe. And then for the first time I began to eat indoors with (the others).

I told my mother, "My grandmother has always been instructing me what I should do," I said to her. She laughed. "That is why I went after her, so she would instruct you thoroughly in what is right. 'She might listen to her,' is what I thought of you."

And I began to be told to make something more than ever. Moreover, when she made a basket, she said to me, "You (make one)." I would make a tiny basket. Later on the ones which I made were large ones. And then I was fifteen years old.

THE WORKING GIRLS OF BOSTON

This 1884 report, published by the Massachusetts Bureau of Statistics of Labor, was the result of an investigation into the "moral, sanitary, physical and economical conditions" of women working in jobs other than domestic service. The conclusions were based on the personal histories of 1,032 of the 20,000 "working girls" in Boston.

SANITARY SURROUNDINGS AT HOME

. . . In numerous cases . . . girls were found living for the sake of economy in very limited quarters, which could not be conducive to good sanitary conditions. In some instances, girls were found living in small attic rooms, lighted and ventilated by the skylight only; the furnishings generally consisted of a small single bed, bureau and chair, with no wardrobe, except one curtained in the corner. In other cases, girls were forced to content themselves with small side rooms without a chance for a fire, which in some cases was sadly needed. One girl had a small side room in the third story of a respectable house, but said she could not expect much more at the present cost of living; still others were reported as living together with other members of the family in a tenement of one back room and side bedroom; another, as one of 18 families in a single building with hardly the necessary articles of furniture; another, occupying the third story of a house which seemed the poorest on the street. On the other hand, girls were found living in large rooms, quite well and sometimes handsomely furnished, in some instances with side rooms adjoining, not perhaps because they could really afford such quarters, but because they preferred to economize in other ways, in order to have some of the comforts, in look at least, of home.

In a few cases where girls reported their health as being poor, or not good, they also complained of the poor board provided, as well as of the unpleasant surroundings at home; one girl made the statement that her home was pleasant and healthy, but to the agent of the bureau the reverse seemed to be the case, for the hall was dirty, the floor covered with a worn-out rag carpet while the air was filled with disagreeable odors; the girl appeared to be in poor health, untidily dressed, and dirty. Another was found living in the upper story of a cheap tenement house, directly in the rear of a kerosene factory having a tall chimney that constantly

Carroll Wright, "The Working Girls of Boston," in the 15th *Annual Report of the Massachusetts Bureau of Statistics of Labor, for 1884,* reprint ed. (Boston, 1889), pp. 64–66, 69–75.

puffed out thick black smoke, which together with the offensive smell of the kerosene, forced the occupants always to keep the kitchen windows closed. In another case, one of the girls said that she spent all her spare time and Sundays with her sister in another part of the city, as her home was very unpleasant and uncomfortable; she also said the Board of Health had visited the house last year and recommended many alterations, but she did not know whether they were attended to or not. Another girl was found living in four small rooms as one of a family of 12, in a house located very near a stable and having bad drainage. One other girl complained of the odor from the waterclosets in the halls, and said it was anything but agreeable.

In a house where a considerable number of girls are cared for, it was found that there was no elevator in the building, and some of the girls were obliged to go up five flights of stairs to reach their rooms, two or three girls being placed in each room; the upper story of the building was without heat, and in winter was said to be like an ice house; radiators are placed at the ends of halls, and transoms open into the rooms, but these have no particular effect on the temperature of the rooms and there are no other ways of heating; extra charge is made for rooms heated directly by the register and even then such rooms are not always to be obtained, they being generally occupied, and there being but a few of them. . . .

EFFECT OF WORK ON HEALTH

Long hours, and being obliged to stand all day, are very generally advanced as the principal reasons for any lack or loss of health occasioned by the work of the girls. The nature of the work is mentioned as a cause for decline, which together with the other causes described will be found to be prevalent in all the various branches of their work.

Feather sorters, cotton sorters, and workers on any material which in its nature is apt to give off a "dust," complain of the disagreeable if not actually injurious effect on the health of persons so employed.

Taking the question by industries and occupations in detail, we find in "Personal Service," that the restaurant employés generally complain of long hours, no dinner hour to speak of, and the great strain upon them from being busy all day on their feet. They all complain of a low state of health, and are pretty much tired out on reaching home. . . .

In "Trade," a bookkeeper was found who had ruined her eyes, by bringing her books home nights and working until twelve and one o'clock. Among the saleswomen, "standing all day" is generally reported as being very trying on their health and strength. In one store, no stools are provided, the girls being obliged to go to one end of the store to sit down.

. . . A good many saleswomen consider their work very hard, and that it has a bad effect on their health; in one instance, a girl says she has paid out over $500 in doctor's bills during the past few years. In one store, it is very unsatisfactory in this respect; no talking is allowed, only half enough time is given for dinner, and being obliged to walk home at night, the girl is completely exhausted; on Saturday she brings dinner and supper. . . .

In bakeries the strain of long hours and standing is especially felt by the salesgirls, while in other branches of business the health of many girls is so poor as to necessitate long rests, one girl being out a year on this account. Another girl in poor health was obliged to leave her work, while one other reports that it is not possible for her to work the year round, as she could not stand the strain, not being at all strong. A girl, who had worked in one place for three years, was obliged to leave on account of poor health, being completely run down from badly ventilated workrooms, and obliged to take an eight months' rest; she worked a week when not able, but left to save her life. She says she has to work almost to death to make fair compensation (now $12 per week).

Under "Manufactures," in *Bookbinderies* and in the manufacture of *Brushes,* girls complain of their health being run down on account of work, or from over-work. In *Boots and shoes,* the work is very hard, the girls being obliged to be on their feet all day, and in cases where they have to walk any great distance to their homes they become very tired at night.

In the manufacture of *Buttons,* the girls say the work is rather dangerous, as they are liable to get their fingers jammed under the punch, or caught in the die when it comes down to press the parts of the button together. A man (although not a surgeon) is provided to dress wounds three times for each individual without charge; afterwards, the person injured must pay all expenses. There are 35 machines in use, and accidents are of very frequent occurrence. . . .

In making *Paper boxes,* the girls are obliged to stand, a practice they think is very injurious. The coloring matter in materials used in the construction and covering of boxes is considered dangerous to health by some, one girl being at home sick three months from blood poisoning caused by work. . . .

In the *Clothing* business, the general testimony is that the work is very hard, and is the cause of a great deal of sickness among the working girls so employed. The tax on the strength is very great, and it would seem that unless a girl is strong and robust, the work soon proves too severe for her, and if followed thereafter results disastrously. The running of heavy sewing machines by foot power soon breaks down a girl's health, as several girls have testified. One girl says that steam was introduced six month's ago to her great satisfaction, as she thinks foot power machines too severe for female operators. The girls think all the machines should be run by steam.

Other girls object to standing so much, and say that being on their feet all day and then walking to their homes makes them very tired at night.

The effect of the work on the health of the working girls engaged in tailoring is very apparent from their testimony. A girl who used to bring her work home, says she overtaxed her strength and is now sick. Others tell the same story, and say that overwork, and the desire to do more than strength would allow, has very seriously affected their health, in one case, the overstraining of the nerves causing deafness, while another girl says, "overwork, cold dinners, and constant application, has brought on chronic rheumatism." . . .

In one or two cases, the girls report that the sewing has affected the eyes, compelling the use of glasses at all times and blue glasses on the street.

Under *Food preparations,* a girl engaged in salt packing is troubled with asthma and bronchitis; she was told at the hospital that the salt would eat into her lungs, as they are diseased; she would leave, if she could find other work.

In the manufacture of confectionery, on account of hot temperatures of rooms, etc., the work is not considered healthy. Some of the girls say work is very severe, they being on their feet all day, while others are out sick, being run down from work.

In the cleaning and packing of fish, the girls say that the fishermen put cayenne pepper and saltpetre on the fish, and girls in handling get their hands and fingers blistered, and often the outside skin taken off; the effect being the same as though they were obliged to keep their hands in a strong caustic solution. One girl says she has tried rubber gloves, but without success. Another girl (a fish packer) says in consequence of the steam necessary to be used the atmosphere is very damp. She says other girls are obliged to stand in cold water all day, having their hands exposed to cold water, and when one was questioned as to what shop she worked in, she answered, "they're not shops, they're working stalls where we are." The same complaint as to standing all day is noticed in this branch of business.

In *Type foundries,* the workroom is always filled with a fine lead dust, caused by "rubbing"; in some shops, this is quite perceptible when standing at one end of the room. . . .

In *Straw goods,* the girls very generally speak of the unhealthy nature of their business. In working on dyed braids, especially green, there is, according to the testimony of one girl, a very fine dust which produces a hacking which is almost constant, and to persons of consumptive tendencies, very injurious. Girls are advised by physicians in such cases to abandon the work. . . . Some throat or lung trouble is very prevalent among the girls working on straw, and the hacking cough peculiar to the business is well-nigh universal. A great many girls are said to die of consumption, while many are often subject to severe cases of sickness, the direct result of work. . . .

The individual testimony regarding shops and their surroundings, and the effect of work upon health, has been given, as nearly as possible, in the language of the person interviewed. This testimony is that of the few, the great majority being in good health and in good surroundings.

It is in evidence from other sources that in a few stores, and in some of considerable size, the water-closet accommodations are very deficient, in one instance 60 women being obliged to use one closet. The evil effect of waiting for the use of a closet common to so large a number is apparent. Many of these women are constantly under the care of physicians for some disease growing out of the condition or things described. . . .

SEX IN EDUCATION, BY DR. EDWARD H. CLARKE

In the decades just after the Civil War, institutions of higher learning multiplied and educational opportunities for women became much more numerous and varied. Just as coeducation was becoming the dominant form for women's higher education, the prominent physician and Harvard professor Edward H. Clarke dropped his bombshell, Sex in Education; or, A Fair Chance for Girls *(1873). The book sparked a vigorous debate on the health consequences of women's higher education.*

It is idle to say that what is right for man is wrong for woman. Pure reason, abstract right and wrong, have nothing to do with sex: they neither recognize nor know it. They teach that what is right or wrong for man is equally right and wrong for woman. Both sexes are bound by the same code of morals; both are amenable to the same divine law. Both have a right to do the best they can; or, to speak more justly, both should feel the duty, and have the opportunity, to do their best. Each must justify its existence by becoming a complete development of manhood and womanhood; and each should refuse whatever limits or dwarfs that development.

The problem of woman's sphere, to use the modern phrase, is not to be solved by applying to it abstract principles of right and wrong. Its solution must be obtained from physiology, not from ethics or metaphysics. . . .

The *quaestio vexata* of woman's sphere will be decided by her organization. This limits her power, and reveals her divinely-appointed tasks, just as man's organization limits his power, and reveals his work. In the development of the organization is to be found the way of strength and power for both sexes. Limitation or abortion of development leads both to weakness and failure.

Neither is there any such thing as inferiority or superiority in this matter. Man is not superior to woman, nor woman to man. The relation of the sexes is one of equality, not of better and worse, or of higher and lower. By this it is not intended to say that the sexes are the same. They are different, widely different from each other, and so different that each can do, in certain directions, what the other cannot; and in other directions, where both can do the same things, one sex, as a rule, can do them better than the other; and in still other matters they seem to be so nearly

Edward H. Clarke, *Sex in Education; or, A Fair Chance for Girls* (2d printing, Boston: Osgood & Co., 1875), pp. 11–14, 125–34.

alike, that they can interchange labor without perceptible difference. All this is so well known, that it would be useless to refer to it, were it not that much of the discussion of the irrepressible woman-question, and many of the efforts for bettering her education and widening her sphere, seem to ignore any difference of the sexes; seem to treat her as if she were identical with man, and to be trained in precisely the same way; as if her organization, and consequently her function, were masculine, not feminine. . . . Our girls' schools, whether public or private, have imposed upon their pupils a boy's regimen; and it is now proposed, in some quarters, to carry this principle still farther, by burdening girls, after they leave school, with a quadrennium of masculine college regimen. . . .

This is grounded upon the supposition that sustained regularity of action and attendance may be as safely required of a girl as of a boy; that there is no physical necessity for periodically relieving her from walking, standing, reciting, or studying; that the chapel-bell may call her, as well as him, to a daily morning walk, with a standing prayer at the end of it, regardless of the danger that such exercises, by deranging the tides of her organization, may add to her piety at the expense of her blood; that she may work her brain over mathematics, botany, chemistry, German, and the like, with equal and sustained force on every day of the month, and so safely divert blood from the reproductive apparatus to the head; in short, that she, like her brother, develops health and strength, blood and nerve, intellect and life, by a regular, uninterrupted, and sustained course of work. All this is not justified, either by experience or physiology. . . . Girls lose health, strength, blood, and nerve, by a regimen that ignores the periodical tides and reproductive apparatus of their organization.

Appropriate education of the two sexes, carried as far as possible, is a consummation most devoutly to be desired; identical education of the two sexes is a crime before God and humanity, that physiology protests against, and that experience weeps over. . . . Because a gardener has nursed an acorn till it grew into an oak, they would have him cradle a grape in the same soil and way, and make it a vine. . . . The sustained regimen, regular recitation, erect posture, daily walk, persistent exercise, and unintermitted labor that toughens a boy, and makes a man of him, can only be partially applied to a girl. The regimen of intermittance, periodicity of exercise and rest, work three-fourths of each month, and remission, if not abstinence, the other fourth, physiological interchange of the erect and reclining posture, care of the reproductive system that is the cradle of the race, all this, that toughens a girl and makes a woman of her, will emasculate a lad. A combination of the two methods of education, a compromise between them, would probably yield an average result, excluding the best of both. It would give a fair chance neither to a boy nor a girl. Of all compromises, such a physiological one is the worst. It cultivates mediocrity, and cheats the future of its rightful legacy of lofty manhood and womanhood. It emasculates boys, stunts girls; makes semi-eunuchs of one sex, and agenes of the other.

The error which has led to the identical education of the two sexes, and which prophecies their identical co-education in colleges and universities, is not confined to technical education. It permeates society. It is found in the home, the workshop, the factory, and in all the ramifications of social life. The identity of boys and girls, of men and women, is practically asserted out of the school as much as in it, and it is theoretically proclaimed from the pulpit and the rostrum. Woman seems to be looking up to man and his development, as the goal and ideal of womanhood. The new gospel of female development glorifies what she possesses in common with him, and tramples under her feet, as a source of weakness and badge of inferiority, the mechanism and functions peculiar to herself. In consequence of this wide-spread error, largely the result of physiological ignorance, girls are almost universally trained in masculine methods of living and working as well as of studying. The notion is practically found everywhere, that boys and girls are one, and that the boys make the one. Girls, young ladies, to use the polite phrase, who are about leaving or have left school for society, dissipation, or self-culture, rarely permit any of Nature's periodical demands to interfere with their morning calls, or evening promenades, or midnight dancing, or sober study. Even the home draws the sacred mantle of modesty so closely over the reproductive function as not only to cover but to smother it. Sisters imitate brothers in persistent work at all times. Female clerks in stores strive to emulate the males by unremitting labor, seeking to develop feminine force by masculine methods. Female operatives of all sorts, in factories and elsewhere, labor in the same way; and, when the day is done, are as likely to dance half the night, regardless of any pressure upon them of a peculiar function, as their fashionable sisters in the polite world. All unite in pushing the hateful thing out of sight and out of mind; and all are punished by similar weakness, degeneration, and disease.

There are two reasons why female operatives of all sorts are likely to suffer less, and actually do suffer less, from such persistent work, than female students; why Jane in the factory can work more steadily with the loom, than Jane in college with the dictionary; why the girl who makes the bed can safely work more steadily the whole year through, than her little mistress of sixteen who goes to school. The first reason is, that the female operative, of whatever sort, has, as a rule, passed through the first critical epoch of woman's life: she has got fairly by it. In her case, as a rule, unfortunately there are too many exceptions to it, the catamenia have been established; the function is in good running order; the reproductive apparatus—the engine within an engine—has been constructed, and she will not be called upon to furnish force for building it again. The female student, on the contrary, has got these tasks before her, and must perform them while getting her education; for the period of female sexual development coincides with the educational period. . . .

The second reason why female operatives are less likely to suffer, and actually do suffer less, than school-girls, from persistent work straight through the year, is because the former work their brains less. To use the language of Herbert Spencer, "That antagonism between body and brain which we see in those, who, pushing brain-activity to an extreme, enfeeble their bodies," does not often exist in female operatives, any more than in male. On the contrary, they belong to the class of those who, in the words of the same author, by "pushing bodily activity to an extreme, make their brains inert." Hence they have stronger bodies, a reproductive apparatus more normally constructed, and a catamenial function less readily disturbed by effort, than their student sisters, who are not only younger than they, but are trained to push "brain-activity to an extreme." Give girls a fair chance for physical development at school, and they will be able in after life, with reasonable care of themselves, to answer the demands that may be made upon them.

DR. MARY PUTNAM JACOBI ON
FEMALE INVALIDISM

After earning her M.D. degree in 1864 from the Female Medical College of Pennsylvania, Mary Putnam Jacobi (1842–1906) pursued further medical training in Paris and returned to the United States in 1871 to become the nation's leading woman physician. Successful in private practice, she also published more than a hundred scientific papers, including an 1876 commentary on issues raised by Dr. Edward Clarke, which won her Harvard's Boylston Prize. A staunch defender of women's career choices and a suffragist, she showed her generation's distance from Catharine Beecher in this analysis of the underlying reasons for women's ill health.

In the first place, it seems to me that this entire question [of female invalidism] needs to be dealt with on a much larger scale, and from a more anthropologic standpoint than is usually the case. Impairment of reproductive function through disease, or imperfect development of the reproductive organs, is a race fact of the greatest importance; and much evidently depends on quite a combination of conditions. To assume, as good old Miss Beecher did, that all the troubles connected with reproductive organs can be explained by the habit of wearing many petticoats, is to rely upon a most superficial and inadequate explanation. Miss Beecher suggested, as a remedy for the evil, a hoop skirt, which actually and by independent agency came into fashion a few years later; but I doubt, if it greatly changed the conditions Miss Beecher was considering.

In the most general sense, and apart from specific infections and mechanical injury, utero-ovarian disease is evidently traceable to imperfect development; and it cannot be denied that this is alarmingly prevalent among American, and especially among New England girls. But I think it is putting the cart before the horse to assert that this imperfect development of the reproductive organs and corresponding nerve centres, is due to over-stimulus, over-education of the intellectual centres. . . .

I believe it is also true that the imperfect development of reproductive organs, nerve centres, and correlatively of sexual instincts, is one reason that the intellectual life of women, and the cerebral cortex, has in the present generation become more active. To suppose that cerebral activity

Dr. Mary Putnam Jacobi to Dr. Edes, a letter on female invalidism (1895), in *Mary Putnam Jacobi, M.D.: Pathfinder in Medicine,* ed. the Women's Medical Association of New York City (New York and London: G. P. Putnam's Sons, 1925), pp. 478, 480–82. Reprinted by permission of the Women's Medical Association. Copyright 1925 by the Women's Medical Association.

could dwarf sexual activity (which is often alleged) is absurd, or rather, though theoretically conceivable, is in contradiction with known facts. The one fact, now noted by ethnologists, that sexual passion is far more highly developed among highly civilized people than among savages, shows that normally the two poles of existence develop *pari passu* and not in antagonism to each other. Detailed proof could easily be furnished were it necessary.

But until now, women have not held a normal position as complete human beings; their mental activity, though often considerable has been spontaneous, untrained, unsubjected to systematic educational drill. I think the flagging of reproductive activities, due to temporary impairment of race vitality, has facilitated this extraordinary new departure in the *régime* of the race, whereby the sex whose brain has been hitherto neglected, is to-day educated, stimulated, often unfortunately forced.

But because this new departure is a race innovation, it undoubtedly involves difficulties and dangers, risks a certain dislocation of organic adjustment, which can only be gradually triumphed over. It requires the most careful study of individual cases, and recollection of three facts. First, that the girls already in possession of the most active, responsive and readily educatable brains, may be essentially deficient in general organic force, and especially as manifested in the reproductive organs, hence unprovided with the undercurrent of sexual strength which is needed to healthfully support cerebral activities. Second, that the other girls—and there are to-day not a few of this class—who are not only mentally active but seem physically sound and strong, may not have the final reproductive strength; their menstrual life is healthy, but they may either break down in child-bearing or have delicate children. Third, that the reproductive imperfection in question may show itself at first by no more tangible symptoms than more incapacity for love or marriage, or fantastic perversity of sentiment in regard to these fundamental interests, this incapacity frequently involving or determining social situations that react most disastrously upon the health of the "highly strung" individual.

With all these race and constitutional complications, when educational systems are adopted which not only ignore such general considerations but violate the most elementary principles of ordinary hygiene; when brains which are not only immature but female, and whose stock of inherited capacity for trained work has all been derived from the parent of the opposite sex; when such brains are submitted to an often illogical cramming; when food is inadequate and exercise absolutely neglected; when hours of work are imposed which no adult woman would bear, and few men; when all this work is carried on under the stimulus of high-pressure competition, emulation, vanity, sometimes fear; when hundreds of girls are shut up together in the exciting atmosphere of a college life, so that their nerves are mutually reacting on each other,—under all these circumstances it is not at all wonderful that towards the close of adolescence so many girls exhibit constitutional debility and uterine disease.

It must, however, be noted, and contrary to what might theoretically be expected, that the influence of superior education, although occasionally seeming to be detrimental, is far less so than any other observed agency. Where there is to be trouble, this is always distinctly foreshadowed at or before the ages of sixteen, seventeen, eighteen, when the college education begins. My own statistics, as collected in the essay on "Rest in Menstruation," and also those which have since been collected by college alumnae, all show that the least ill-health is found among the women who have been most highly educated. Of course, the fact partly shows that only healthy girls complete their course and graduate; others fall away earlier. At all events, the college-bred women are still so much in the minority that the general statistics are hardly affected by them; yet physicians often write as if these constituted the mass of nervous invalids.

But the list of causes of the special invalidism of the century is not yet ended. Every city physician who has also seen country people must have noticed that while mechanical injuries from childbirth are rather more common among country people, their influence is apt to remain limited to mechanical discomfort. But a much less degree of injury in city women excites, or is liable to excite, a protean swarm of nervous disorders. The French comment emphatically on this contrast between the Parisian and peasant women. Evidently this implies more delicately strung nervous organization, in more unstable equilibrium, as more developed among the inhabitants of cities, or specifically among the women who have been freed from manual labor. I think Tolstoi is quite right in asserting that such freedom is a curse to the "upper classes."

If the excessive drudgery of New England ancestors under unfavorable conditions weakened the constitution of their descendants, the excessive luxury of these descendants is certainly a second cause of weakness. I am not speaking now of coarse and unreasonable luxury, but of the refined and delicate ease of life and sensibility in which so many thousands now contrive to live—up to a certain point an advantage and a grace, beyond this a dangerous effeminacy. In manual drudgery, or in Puritan asceticism, there are dangers from exhaustion, depression, or gloom; but there is at least a discipline, an enforced stoicism, which is of immense value in bearing toil, trouble or shock. To-day stoicism has vanished from education, as asceticism from creeds; it is considered natural and almost laudable to break down under all conceivable varieties of strain—a winter dissipation, a houseful of servants, a quarrel with a female friend, not to speak of more legitimate reasons.

Women who expect to go to bed every menstrual period expect to collapse if by chance they find themselves on their feet for a few hours during such a crisis. Constantly considering their nerves, urged to consider them by well-intentioned but short-sighted advisers, they pretty soon become nothing but bundles of nerves. They suffer from lack of the wholesome neglect to which their grandmothers were habitually consigned; too much attention is paid to women as objects, while yet they remain in too many cases insufficiently prepared to act as independent subjects. A healthy objectivity is one of the greatest desiderata for modern women. To knock the nonsense out of them, to direct attention from self, to substitute a cosmic horizon for that of their own feelings, who does not know the importance of this for thousands of hysterical women? and equally the impossibility of attaining it?

I think, finally, it is in the increased attention paid to women, and especially in their new function as lucrative patients, scarcely imagined a hundred years ago, that we find explanation of much ill-health among women, freshly discovered to-day, but which always existed, and which is often due to conditions arising among men, and not therefore new. Shattered nervous systems are inherited by girls from the alcoholism of the fathers; gonorrhea contracted by wives from husbands; sterility due to licentiousness in which the innocent woman may have no share; enforced celibacy due to bad social arrangements; occasionally, though less and less frequently, childbirths too close together; certainly all these causes of ill-health to women have existed for centuries. I think the peculiarity of the present time is that now attention is being drawn to the special effects produced upon women by these general causes.

EFFEMINATE MEN, MASCULINE WOMEN

At the turn of the twentieth century, many doctors argued that what would come to be called homosexuality was better understood as sexual "inversion." Instead of focusing on the gender of an individual's sexual partner, they defined sexual "inversion" as consisting in adopting the expected behavior of the other sex. Doctors increasingly viewed "inversion" as a problem requiring medical intervention.

Weak physiological traits, like moral traits, can be increased or decreased by education, training, and example. Environment plays a most active and powerful rôle in this development. The child born of parents in the prime of physiological life, each one having strong sex characteristics, is apt to show these characteristics in its development and growth, regardless of environment and education. But not so the unfortunate child born of unstable parents; of those who have assumed the responsibility of parentage when life is on the wane, or whose physical or mental activities have been in channels far removed from anticipation and thoughts of married life. Such parents belong to the physiologically degenerate class. They forget that the tendency is, in all animal life, to degenerate rather than improve. This goes on, generation after generation, unless care is exercised to introduce improved blood on one side or the other.

When a child demonstrates in its acts and tastes an indifference to the natural preference and inclination of its sex, it should be strictly confined to the companionship of that sex. Its education should be along the same lines, and every encouragement given it to develop its normal attributes. An indifferent boy who grows up an effeminate man should be allowed to share the ridicule and contempt thrust upon him with his parents, the mother being given the major part. This same mother, who shields her son from physical harm, will bring him up in the nursery with embroidery; take the poor creature, dressed up in linens and velvet, to exhibit him to female admirers; shift him off to the nursery of her hostess, where he is left to dress dolls and have his hair curled by the female attendants, and sit down to a make-believe tea party with his little girl playmates.

He grows up psychically unsexed, detested by the vigorous male, utilized as a willing servitor by the society woman, and sternly admonished by a true father if he finds him dancing attendance with all his mincing

William Lee Howard, M.D., "Effeminate Men and Masculine Women," *New York Medical Journal* 71 (May 5, 1900), pp. 686–87. The editors are grateful to George Chauncey for help in locating this document.

manners upon a daughter. The female with masculine ambition is always amusing and often pitiable; but the attenuated, weak-voiced neuter, the effeminate male: pity him, but blame his mother for the false training, and give scorn to the father for his indifference. Even the woman, when she meets such a man, should passionately and involuntarily exclaim: "O! surgit amari aliquid."

The female possessed of masculine ideas of independence; the viragint who would sit in the public highways and lift up her pseudo-virile voice, proclaiming her sole right to decide questions of war or religion, or the value of celibacy and the curse of woman's impurity, and that disgusting antisocial being, the female sexual pervert, are simply different degrees of the same class—degenerates. These unsightly and subnormal beings are the victims of poor mating. When a woman neglects her maternal instincts, when her sentiment and dainty feminine characteristics are boldly and ostentatiously kept submerged, we can see an antisocial creature more amusing than dangerous. When such a woman marries, which she often does for the privileges derived from attaching Mrs. to her name, the husband is certain to be one she can rule, govern, and cause to follow her in voice and action. Should this female be unfortunate enough to become a mother, she ceases to be merely amusing, and is an antisocial being. She is then a menace to civilization, a producer of nonentities, the mother of mental and physical monstrosities who exist as a class of true degenerates until disgusted Nature, no longer tolerant of the woman who would be a man, or the man who would be a woman, allows them to shrink unto death.

The female who prefers the laboratory to the nursery; the mother quick with child who spends her mornings at the club, discussing "social statics," visiting the saloons and tenements in the afternoon, distributing, with an innocence in strange contrast to her assumptions, political tracts asking the denizens to vote her ticket, is a sad form of degeneracy. Such females are true degenerates, because they are unphysiological in their physical incompleteness. The progeny of such human misfits are perverts, moral or psychical. Their prenatal life has been influenced by the very antithesis of what the real woman would surround her expected child with. The child born of the "new woman" is to be pitied. If it could be taken away from its environments, kept from the misguidance of an unwilling mother, nurtured, tutored, and directed along the sex line Nature has struggled to give it, often would the child be true to its latent normal instincts and grow to respected womanhood or manhood. Unfortunate it is that this development does not take place. The weak, plastic, developing cells of the brain are twisted, distorted, and a perverted psychic growth promoted by the false examples and teachings of a discontented mother. These are the conditions which have been prolific in producing the antisocial "new woman" and the disgusting effeminate male, both typical examples of the physiological degenerate.

It is this class that clamors for "higher education" for the woman; that crowds public halls, shouting for the freedom of woman and demanding all the prerogative of the man. It is these female androids who are insulated in the dark umbrage of ignorance and delusion regarding their negative nature, who are faddist, 'ism'-ites, and mental roamers. Ideally mobile, they go from the laboratory to the convent, ever restless, continuously discontented, morbidly majestic at periods, hysterically forcible at times. They form sects and societies regardless of sense or science.

They demonstrate their early perverted mental growth by their present lack of reasoning powers. They form the victims of shrewder degenerates. They claim to know more about the science of medicine without study than the men who have devoted their lives to that science. They walk broadcast, superciliously flaunting our health laws and hygienic regulations in the faces of the assumed intelligent masses, and shout their incomprehensible jargon and blasphemous voicings from the portals of their money-making mosques.

THE STORY OF AUNT EASTER

Long after childbirth became a medical event for city dwellers, African American midwives in the rural South regularly delivered black and white babies and earned local respect for their skills in herbal medicine. Easter Sudie Campbell, the daughter of slaves, practiced in Hopkinville, Kentucky; she was about seventy-two years old when she was interviewed under the auspices of the Federal Writers' Project of the Works Progress Administration (WPA) in the 1930s. The WPA interviewer's cultural distance from the Southern midwife is suggested by the clumsy "dialect" imposed on the oral record. By the 1930s, ideas such as Aunt Easter's about ghosts and prenatal "marking" were often scorned as superstitious by formally educated people of both races but had not disappeared, especially among rural folk.

Aunt Easter as she is called has followed the profession of a mid-wife for forty years. She is still active and works at present among the negros of Hopkinsville.

"Yes, sho, I make my own medicines, humph, dat aint no trouble. I cans cure scrofula wid burdock root and one half spoon of citrate of potash. Jes make a tea of burdock root en add the citrate of potash to hit. Sasafras is food foh de stomach en cleans yer out good. I'se uses yeller percoon root foh de sore eyes.

"Wen I stayed wid Mrs. Porter her chaps would break out mighty bad wid sores in de fall of de year and I'se told Mrs. Porter I'se could core dat so I'se got me some elder berries en made pies out of hit en made her chaps eat hit on dey war soon cored.

"If twont foh de white folks I sho would hev a hard time. My man he jes wen erway en I haint neber seed him ergin en I'se had five chilluns en do white folks hev heped me all dese years. Dese trifling niggers dey wont hepe dey own kind of folks. If youse got de tooth ache I make a poultice of scrape irish pertatoes en puts hit on de jaw on de side de tooth is aching en dat sho takes de fever out of de tooth. I'se blows terbacco smoke in de ear en dat stops de ear ache.

"Wen I goes on her baby case I jest let nature hev hits way. I'se alays teas de baby de first thing I does is ter blow my breath in de baby's muff en I spanks it jes a little so hit will cry den I gives hit warm catnip tea so

"Story of Easter Sudie Campbell," in *The American Slave: A Composite Autobiography*, vol. 16, ed. George Rawick (Westport, Conn.: Greenwood, 1972), pp. 90–93. Copyright © 1972 by Greenwood Press. Reprinted by permission of Greenwood Publishing Group, Inc., Westport, Conn.

if hit is gwine ter hev de hivos dey will break out on hit. I alays hev my own catnip en sheep balls foh sum cases need one kind of tea en sum ernother. I give sink field tea ter foh de colic. Hit is jes good fuh young baby's stomach. I'se been granning foh nigh unter forty year en I'se only lost two babies, dat war born erlive. One of dese war de white man's fault, dis bably war born wid de jaundice en I tolds dis white man ter go ter de store en git me sum calomel en he says, 'whoeber heard of givin a baby sech truck', an so dat baby dies.

"Of course youse can ted wheder the baby is gwine ter be a boy er girl fore tis born. If de mother carries dat child more on de left en high up dat baby will be a boy en if she carries hit more ter de middle dat will be a girl. Mothers oughter be more careful while carrying dar chillums not ter git scared of enthing foh dey will sho mark dar babies wid turrible ugly things. I knows once a young wooman war expecting en she goes black-berry hunting en er bull cow wid long horns got after her en she was so scairt dat she threw her hands ober her head en wen dat baby boy war born he hed to nubs on his head jes like horns beginning ter grow so I'se hed her call her doctor en dey cuts dem off. One white woman I'se waited on like hot choclate en she alays wanted more she neber hed nuff of dat stuff en one day she spills sum on her laig en it jes splotched en burned her en wen dat gal war born she hed a big brown spot on her laig jes like her Mammy's scar frum de burn. Now you see I noes yer ken mark de babies.

"Dar war a colored wooman once I'se waited on dat hed to help de white folks kill hogs en she neber did like hog liver but de white folks told her ter take one home en fix hit foh her supper. Well she picked dat thing up en started off wid hit en hit made her feel creepy all ober en dat night her baby war born a gal child en de print of er big hog-liver war standing out all ober one side of her face. Dat side of her face is all blue er purplish en jes the shape of a liver. En hits still dar.

"I'se grannied ober three hundred chilluns en I noes wat I'se talking about. . . .

"Wen my Pappy kum home from de war, he war on de "Govmint" side he brung a pistol back wid him dat shot a ball dey hed caps on hit en used dese in de war. De Ku Klux cum after him one night en he got three of dem wid his pistol, nobody eber knowed who got dose Kluxes.

"Ghosts—

"Sho dar is ghosts. One night es I war going home from work de tallest man I eber seed followed me wid de prettiest white shirt on en den he passed me, en waited at de corner I war a feeling creepy en wanter run but jes couldn't git my laigs ter move en wen I'se git ter de corner war he war I said 'Good Ebening' en I seed him plain es day en he did not speak en jes disappeared right fore my eyes. . . .

"Once I hed a dream I knowed I ner bout saw hit. I alays did cook ebery night er pot er beans on de fire foh de chilluns ter eat next day while I war at work en Lizzie my daughter uster git up in de night en git her some beans en eat dem en dis dream war so real dat I couldn't tell if hit war Lizzie er no but dis wooman jes glided by my bed en went afore de fire en stood dar den she jes went twixt my bed en went by de wall. I jes knowed wen I woke up dat my child was sick dat lived erway from home en wanted my son ter take me ter see her. He said he would go hisself en see so he wen en wen he come back he had a headache en fore morning dat nigger war dead. So you see dat war de sign of de dream. I war jes warned in de dream en didn't hev sense nuff ter know hit."

PART VII

WOMEN'S WORK
IN AN INDUSTRIAL AGE

HAVE BEEN BUSY ALL DAY

Antoinette Porter King started keeping a diary at the age of thirty, when she and a number of her extended family moved from Whitewater, Wisconsin, to southern Minnesota. The group included her husband (William), their three children (Willie, Nellie, and Selah), her two brothers (Rob and Lib, who was married to her husband's sister), her husband's two brothers and sister Eliza, and assorted spouses and children. Among the first white settlers to make land claims in Jackson Township, the family had been farming in Minnesota for six years when Antoinette made the following entries in 1872. Although she sometimes recorded washing or ironing, in general she focused on events that broke her daily routine of cooking, baking, cleaning, and farm chores.

July [1872]

Tues 2nd   Have been busy all day. I have so much to do before the 4th. Have got to go to town again & it is so very warm. Shower last night.

Wed 3rd   Nearly tired to death. Washing, baking, ironing & so many things to do. Mr & Mrs Strong called. Went to town. E & I came home alone. Wm staid to the Lodge.

Thurs 4th   Rather cool but very pleasant all day. Had quite a Celebration. Everything passed off quite pleasantly. Mrs Brownell, Eliza & I, Wm Johnson, Strong, & Loop sung. The pieces selected were Fling out the Joyfull Banner, Hail Our Country, Natal Morn, The Flag of our Union & America. Went to Mr Baldwins to tea. Willie hurt his eye with a fire cracker.

Fri 5th   Well the Glorious Fourth is over & I am glad it dont come but once a year. If I have to work so hard everytime I dont think I shall want to go.

Sat 6th   Hard rain this afternoon. Rob breaking. Children at school.

Sun 7th   Quite warm all day. I have been sick all day. I am tired out. Towards eve Wm went over to Petersons & to Alberts. I went with him.

Mon 8th   Rain last night. Very warm today. Wm gone to town to attend to Miners suit. I have been washing & baking for Rob. Mother Kings birthday yesterday. I believe she is 65.

Tues 9th   Very warm all day. Rob & Curtis started for Okabena. I have been sick nearly all day. I worked to hard yesterday. Willie is 15 years old

Antoinette Porter King Papers, diary, Minnesota Historical Society, St. Paul, Minn.

today. Wm has gone over to Tuttles to get a horse to mow with. Cool & pleasant this eve.

Wed 10th   It has been a very warm day. Thermometer 93 degrees about 10 o'clock. Wm mowing for Albert. Moved the stove out today. Have been busy all day scrubbing, whitewashing &c. I am terrible weary. It seems good to have the stove out. Nellie says she feels like work now.

Thurs 11th   It has been warmer still today. Thermometer stood at over a hundred this forenoon. Wm mowing for M. S. The flies have made their appearance & I am sorry. They are such a pest. Last Monday William sold our old Cherry cow to Mr Brooks for $32.00. I guess I shall have to give up making cheese now.

Fri 12th   Wm mowing for himself. Pretty warm yet.

Sat 13th   Wm raking hay. Willie took Tuttles horse home. Rollie came out to see Willie. Rob & Curtis got back from Okabena this eve. Effa came down for her kitten. Appearance of rain. Has been very warm this afternoon. Sent letters to Vie & Lucy.

Sun 14th   A little cooler. Mr & Mrs Brooks here today. Wm & I & Johnnie took them home & then we went down to Alberts after the wagon. Sprinkled a little this afternoon.

Mon 15th   Hard shower this morning. Cooler during the day than usual. Wm went to town for some lumber, oil &c. Wm went to Ulters also for oats. I went with him. Our wheat looks nice.

Tues 16th   Commenced making cheese. Had nearly forgotten how. Quite cool this morning. Wm mowing for Tuttle. Rob breaking.

Wed 17th   Very cold all day. Overcoats quite comfortable. Wm mowing for Rob. Rob breaking. Willie & Selah went to the River for Raspberries. Got about a tablespoonful. It is so cold I have made up a good fire & am writing close by the stove & am none to warm. Wind in the North East.

October
Wed 2nd   Quite pleasant today. M. S. & Eliza have gone to Town. Left the baby with me. I made my tomatoe pickles today. Made some molasses cookies too.

Sat Oct 5th   It has been very pleasant during the week.

Mon 7th   I went up to Heath in the afternoon. I staid & helped Eliza. They have threshers. I am going to help her tomorrow.

Tues 8th   Have been helping E all day. Eliza came up this afternoon. Wm went to the Convention.

Thurs 10th   Very cold today. It froze very hard last night. Willie & the Bowden boys are digging potatoes.

Wed 16th   We are having quite fine weather this fall. Prairie fires running every night. Wm, M. S. & Rob gone to Town.

Sat 19th   It has been a lovely day. Last Wed E Heath & I walked to Town to attend Mrs Walden funeral. Nellie has gone to Lonas to stay all night.

Sun 20th   Pleasant but rather windy. Calls today from Curtis, Lona & Minnie Bratt, E Heath, Mr & Mrs Tuttle. Wm & I & Mr Johnson went up to the Graveyard to select a spot for little Georgie. We are going to move him.

Tues 22nd   I washed. Quite pleasant. Wm plowing. Minnie Bratt called. She has been crocheting a tidy. E. H. called also. While she was here a man came for her to go to the Dr to sit up tonight with his wife. She is very sick. I expect they will send for me tomorrow so I must go to ironing.

Wed 23rd   Mr Smith came for me this afternoon. Wm is plowing. It is quite pleasant.

Fri 25th   Feel somewhat tired. Mr Ashley brought me home last night. Mrs Brownell is dead. Died yesterday about 4 oclock. Poor sufferer is now at rest. How sad to part with friends. The Doctor takes it very hard. I feel so sorry for him.

Sat 26th   A beautiful day. Attended funeral. Mr Johnson, A Strong, Eliza & I sung. Pluma Kimbell played the organ. Sang "Weep not for Me" & several other pieces that the Doctor selected. One was Bonar "A few more years shall roll."

Sun 27th   Cold chilly wind. I went with William to E Heaths.

Mon 28th   Rainy & windy during the day. Rain thunder & lightning tonight.

Tues 29th   Rained all the day & all night.

November
. . . Fri 15th   The third day of snowing & blowing. Very dreary weather.

Sun 17th   Cold as charity.

Tues 19th   Colder still. Rob started for Windom. It was so cold he turned back. He was going for lumber for our house. Albert moved yesterday.

Wed 20th   Quite a fine day. Curtis here sewing.

Thurs 21st   Mr Thompson from Plainview, Minn made [illegible] Grange. Gave a lecture at Jackson & organized a Grange. Quite a number attended both ladies & gentlemen. It is called Jackson Grange—Patrons of Husbandry. Wm was elected Master. Eliza Barney Goddess of Flower Flora. Goddess of grain Ceres—Mrs Brooks. Goddess of fruits Pomona—myself. Hope it will prove a success.

Fri 22nd   William started for Windom for lumber for our house.

Sat 23rd   Quite pleasant. Willie went to town. Curtis called for bread. Eliza came over, caught a Sparerib. Had some for Supper.

Sun 24th   Wm got home from Windom. Pretty cold & some what stormy.

Mon 25th   William & Willie gone down to work on the house. I washed. Went up to Heaths a little while. Quite a pleasant day.

. . .

December

Sun 1st   The first Sunday in our new home. It don't look very homelike yet—but I think it will in a few days. Wm & Willie went out on the town. E Heath called.

Mon 2nd   Storming a little here & pretty hard on the prairie. Glad I don't live on the prairie any more.

Tues 3rd   Somewhat cold but pleasant. Eliza & the children came down. We all went to the Grange in the eve.

Wed 4th   Eliza went home this morning. They all stayed all night. Did not get to bed until most morning. Feel mean & lazy today. Wm went out for the cows &c.

Thurs 5th   Quite pleasant. Thawed considerable. Went calling to Woodwards, McCorts & Thomas.

Fri 6th   Wm started for Winnebago City. I washed.

Sat 7th   Fine & pleasant all day. Wm has had two nice days to travel. I expect him home tomorrow. Wish he would come tonight. The children are all in bed & I must go for the fire is all out & the house is cold. Selah has a bad cold. He keeps coughing. Mr Brooks called this eve & left a copy of the Iowa Homestead. I hear the wind blowing. I do hope it wont storm before William gets back.

Sun 8th   The sun is shining bright but the wind blows cold & I expect it is not very pleasant on the prairie. It is now 3 o'clock in the afternoon. The children have just been popping corn. Willie & Selah are just going out to water the stock. Now I wish William would come. It is a lonesome day to me.

Mon 9th   Last evening Mattie Moore & Mary Thomas called, also Mr B

H Johnson & Rollie. William got home at 4 o'clock in the eve. He had a cold day to travel. Nearly a barrel of apples were taken at the Depot. Father King sent us six barrels of fruit. I like my new shawl ever so much & my hat too. I sent to Vie for them. My shawl is black with fancy stripe. My hat is white straw trimmed with black lace, ribbon, silk, a red velvet flower & black plume. The flower is real pretty. The hat & shawl cost me $10. Vie sent me a calico dress made Polanaise, a light green stripe. It is very pretty & I think it a real nice present. Eliza came down for her things. It is quite cold today. Our horses & Alberts are sick with the Horse disease. I hope it wont prove serious. William went out to the place with the oxen for a load of hay. I made some blankets for the horses this eve. Mr Tuttle called.

Tues 10th   Cloudy & lonesome today. Wm going for a load of hay. Did not go. Rather pleasant. Wm doing some Probate business for Mr & Mrs Ford. Went over town. I went to Mrs McCorts to help her tie a comforter. Nellie is out to Elizas. Went Monday. I wish she would come home. I miss her so. Wm gone to Mr Johnsons. The grangers met there this eve to talk over matters.

Wed 11th   Snowed considerable last night & it is still snowing. It is cloudy & dreary. I must go to work. Isherwood came for milk.

Thurs 12th   Quite pleasant today. My birthday—37 years old. Eliza & Mitchell came down. Had chicken pie for Supper. Had quite a little party, E & M, Albert & Lona, Rob & Minnie Bratt & Mrs E Klock.

Fri 13th   Sun shining brightly but rather cold. Poor old Ponto died this morning. Died of old age I expect. He refused to eat yesterday. Poor old faithful nag. How sorry I am to have him die. He was over 13 years old. How bad Vie will feel when she hears he is dead. I washed.

Sat 14th   Cold blustering & stormy today. I want to iron but my clothes are not dry enough. Mr Brooks here to dinner. Wm went over Town this eve. Awful cold.

Sun 15th   Yesterday Vie was 30 years old. She is getting to be quite an old Maid. Today Minnie Bratt & I went to Quarterly Meeting. It was so cold yesterday that the Elder could not get here. Wm had to go out for some hay today. It is a very cold day.

Fri 20th   A very cold day. Lona & I visited Mrs Young in the eve. We started to go to Singing School but it was so cold we backed out.

Sat 21st   Colder than it was yesterday. Found three of my cans bursted. They were filled with gooseberries.

Mon 23rd   Colder & colder. It has been terrible cold for a few days.

Thermometer 30 below this morning. Yesterday I went to church in the morning. In the eve Wm & I went over to Heaths a little while. Last Thursday Minnie Bratt went calling at Mr Strongs, Mrs Browns & the Dr.

Tues 24th   Awful cold yet. How tired I am of such very cold weather. Last night Mrs Klock, Lona & I went over town. It was very cold. It is Christmas eve. Nellie & Selah are hanging up their stockings in readiness for "old Santa." I am afraid they will not find much. Have been cutting Nellie's waterproof cloak today.

Wed 25th   Christmas day. Not quite as cold as it has been. Snowed some last night. Had a picnic supper over to Lonas. Had quite a pleasant time & a good Supper. In the eve Albert & Lona, Minnie & Rob, Ed & Ella went to Thomas' to the dance. Wm & I concluded not to go. Wm went out on the prairie for a load of hay. M. S. was down yesterday & wanted us to come out there today but it was too cold to go.

Thurs 26th   Considerable warmer. I have been washing. Wm has been working on his sled. Rob treated me to some claret—the first I ever tasted. I want to go out to Elizas real bad. I must write to Vie. I sent a letter to Cousin Louise this week.

Sat 28th   Wm went out for a load of hay. Mr & Mrs Baldwin visited here. Quite a pleasant day. Mr Brooks called.

Sun 29th   Not very cold. Rather misty. Wm & I, Nellie & Johnnie went out to Mr Brooks. Had a sing.

Mon 30th   Rather cold. Wm drawing logs from the old bridge.

Tues 31st   Real pleasant. Went out to Elizas. Had a real good visit.

THE SWEATING SYSTEM, CHARITY, AND ORGANIZATION

At the end of the nineteenth century only about 3 percent of the women employed in industrial occupations were organized into trade unions, and the American Federation of Labor (AFL), founded in 1886, focused its efforts on skilled male laborers, not on women and children in sweatshops. Union advocates such as Ida Van Etten—a woman of independent means who had adopted the cause of workingwomen—attempted to get the recently founded AFL more interested in organizing women, with reports and analyses such as this 1890 speech to the federation's national convention. Van Etten and another union advocate named Eva Valesh succeeded in pushing the AFL's executive board to create a salaried office for a national women's organizer for a few years in the early 1890s.

THE SWEATING SYSTEM

Any review of the condition of women workers, however brief, would be incomplete without an exposition of the "sweating" system—a system which thrives upon the ignorance of the newly-arrived immigrants, the miseries and misfortunes of the very poor and upon the helplessness of women and little children, which pays no regular rate of wages and has no prescribed hours of work.

The "sweater" is only possible under a competitive system of industry. He is the natural outcome of cupidity and the intense desire for large profits and quick returns on the one side and the want, misery, degradation and ignorance of the workers on the other.

Neither capital nor skill are requisite for a sweater, only the heartlessness and cunning of a slave-driver. He is usually one of the workmen who saves enough money to hire a room in a tenement house, buys or rents a few machines, for which he charges his employees three dollars a month, obtains a supply of work for some large manufacturer of cloaks or ready-made clothing, secures his "hands" and begins business.

These "sweater's" dens are always located in the most wretched, overcrowded tenement house districts. He has no scale of wages, but pays the lowest that he can possibly induce his miserable victims to work for. He trades upon the unhappiness and misfortunes of the dwellers in the neighborhood.

Ida M. Van Etten, "The Condition of Women Workers Under the Present Industrial System," an address at the national convention of the American Federation of Labor, Detroit, December 8, 1890, pp. 7–10, 12–14. Published by the American Federation of Labor.

If a woman has a sick husband or children, she becomes a choice bit of speculation to this human shark. He says to her, "I will give you so much." She must take it or see her children starve.

Bad as is the condition of women-workers in factories, that of tenement-house workers is infinitely worse. In the factory, from the mere presence of a number of people, a sort of public opinion is formed which is often powerful enough to deter in some measure the employer from many acts of extreme oppression and injustice. Then, too, they are under the active operations of the factory law, which, however incomplete and badly executed, affords some protection to the workers.

With the present force of factory inspectors it is impossible to reach and properly inspect these dens, hidden away as they are in the cellars and garrets and rear buildings of tenement houses. And even were the force ten times greater than it now is, it would be necessary to have a law compelling the registration of all factories employing three or more persons.

One of the most frightful features of the "sweating" system is the unchecked employment of very young children. In these districts it is no unusual sight to see children of five, six, or even four years, employed all day sewing on buttons, pulling out bastings, or carrying huge piles of work to and from the "sweater's" shop.

A teacher in one of the primary schools on the East Side told me not long since of a little girl in her class who was constantly falling asleep. When she asked her at what time she usually went to bed, to her astonishment the child answered, "One o'clock," and explained that she had to "pull out bastings" until that time. The family were Russians and employed by a "sweater" in the cloak trade.

About three months ago I was able to get together thirty-five coat makers, all of whom worked under the "sweating" system, for the purpose of forming an organization.

Familiar as I was with many of the hardships of the working-women of New York, still what these girls told me, and which I afterwards verified by investigation, was a revelation to me. I found that the *usual* work-day of girls in this trade was from five or six o'clock in the morning until seven, eight, and often in the busy season until ten, o'clock at night; that in the clothing trade there exists an iniquitous system of "task" work which surpasses in cold-blooded cruelty anything I had ever before heard or read of.

The "sweater" in this trade pays so much a day, usually from 50 cents to $1.00, but in order to receive this sum the worker must perform a certain task—so many pieces of work. This task is beyond the ability of any girl to perform in any decent work-day, or at any reasonable degree of swiftness. To do even a portion of it, it is necessary that the girls should begin at five or six o'clock in the morning and work until late at night.

Even with these hours, the girls told me it was the exception when a worker finished her task in a day; but she is not paid for a day until the allotted task is fully completed. So that, even with these inhuman hours and the frightful rate of speed with which these girls worked, one day's work always lapped over upon the next day, and although doing six, and often even seven, days' work of from sixteen to eighteen hours' duration, they rarely received but four days' pay.

And mark the subtle cruelty and cunning of this! There are no hours prescribed. If you ask the "sweater," he will say: "Oh, my girls can come to work if they like at eight o'clock." But the "task" is made so herculean that it is impossible to accomplish it in less than a work-day of from sixteen to eighteen hours. And with the cruel necessity of want driving these young girls on, the "sweater" needs no other slave-driver, no superintendent, no foreman.

The thirty-five girls, many of whom were mere children, resembled in no respect other young girls. They were pale, spiritless, bent, and weary. So young, and yet with all youthful joy and buoyancy crushed out of them by the workings of a social system which systematically allows the weaker to go to the wall!

And, remember, it is not hundreds, but thousands, of women and girls who work under these conditions.

One day last August I visited a tenement-house in Ludlow street, entirely given up to the "sweaters." In every room were crowded together from six to ten men and women, four or five machines, with a cooking-stove at white heat, for the use of the pressers. Women, with white, pinched faces, unkempt hair, dressed in ragged, dirty, "unwomanly rags," were working from sixteen to eighteen hours a day for a pittance of from 50 to 75 cents. No words of mine can picture to you the horror of it—the dirt, the squalor, the food these people eat, the clothes they wear, the beds they sleep in, the air they breathe, and, more pitiful than all, their weary faces, out of which all hope and joy had long since been banished. All make up a scene that would linger in the mind, like Doré's pictures of Dante's "Inferno."

The overcrowding on the East Side must be seen to be appreciated.

In Essex street is a boarding-house frequented by cloak and knee-pants makers. It is on the first floor of an old tumbledown rookery, and comprises a front room, perhaps 16 × 14 feet, two dark bedrooms, one a mere passage-way, and a rear room with one window opening upon a tall brick wall. The family consisted of a man and his wife and six children. They kept eleven boarders in these quarters.

And this is the system we are living under—for let it be borne in mind that the "sweating" system is but the logical carrying out of the principles of the competitive system of industry, the natural result of the control of the means of production for private profit. You see in the "sweating" system the future condition of the working class foreshadowed, unless a radical change is brought about by you in the laws regulating the production and distribution of wealth. . . .

CHARITABLE INSTITUTIONS

So awful has become the condition of working-women in large cities that it has become the shame and disgrace of our times, and so gigantic has the evil become that even the bravest shrink back from undertaking its amelioration. Workingmen, engaged in the work of building up their own trade unions, and with, in many cases, a fancied antagonism of interests existing between the men and women workers in a trade—although I am convinced that men are opposed to women as co-workers only when they become a factor in reducing wages—still, all has contributed to cause the working-man, whose duty it naturally was to teach and train these women in the principles and methods of organized labor, to become passive lookers-on in their struggle for existence.

The result of this inaction on the part of working-men, and the increasing horrors of women's condition, has caused a multitude of palliative and charitable schemes for their relief to spring up in all large cities which still further increases the evils of working-women's condition.

Working-men, by their sturdy independence, achieved chiefly through the power of organization, have placed themselves beyond the ordinary workings of charity. In times of sickness and out of work, the workman turns for relief and help to his trade union, and without loss of self-respect accepts aid from its fund, which he has himself helped to accumulate by his dues and assessments.

But working-women, without the moral and financial support of organization and with the more wretched conditions prevailing, as a result of this lack, have truly become the *victims of charity and philanthropy.* So great has this evil become that I hold that charity should be classed as *one* of the direct causes of the wretched industrial condition of working-women.

Charity has for a long time tried its hand at alleviating the evils of their condition. It has built lodging-houses, Christian Homes, refuges, reformatories, etc., and still the evils go on increasing—nay, these very methods have added a fearful impetus to the causes of the evils.

The evils of charity are both moral and economic. It robs the character of the working-woman of its qualities of self-respect, its moral and intellectual independence and in the place of these sterling virtues implants the seeds of distrust and a cringing, false respect for money and position.

From an economic standpoint the evils are still more serious and far-reaching. Although charity undoubtedly had its origin in the noblest and most unselfish motives of human conduct, it has, in later times, been warped and turned aside from its original and legitimate purpose and become a disturbing element in industrial affairs. In a simpler state of society, its only function was the care and relief of the sick and those disabled by age or accident: but in the nineteenth century it has become the most powerful ally of the competitive system of industry and forms one of the strongest bulwarks of its support and continuance. According to the reports of the Commissioners of Charities the amount expended in public and private charity during the last ten years has enormously increased.

We find charity everywhere supplementing the present industrial system, bolstering it up and making its operations possible; accepting its horrible results as a normal state of things; and instead of bitterly and relentlessly attacking the root of the evil, attempting to plaster up and palliate its *consequences*.

Charity has only succeeded in making it easier for the unscrupulous employers of women to exploit them safely and respectably. By the side of the huge factory, whose owner is growing enormously rich, upon the spoilation of his women workers, it builds the Lodging House or Christian Home, and this enables the manufacturer to pay wages below the living point.

The "sweating" system would in many cases be almost impossible, were it not for the thoughtless charity of innumerable Church Relief, St. Vincent de Paul Societies, etc., etc. . . .

ORGANIZATION

Thus it can readily be seen that women-workers either must become organized and receive not only equal pay for equal work, but also equal opportunities for working, or they will, by degrees, naturally form an inferior class in every trade in which they enter; a class more poorly paid, and who will, in consequence, work longer hours; who will receive less consideration from their employers, and who will be without means of redress, even in those grievances which are most degrading to their womanhood. In this condition they will be a constant menace to wages; they will be used, in case of strikes and lockouts, to supply the places of union men; and, in short, we shall witness the horrible spectacle of workers whose interests are identical being used against each other for the purpose of lowering the general condition of their class.

The bitterness with which employers oppose the organization of women furnishes the best evidence of their present value in supplying them with ignorant, unthinking and consequently cheap laborers.

SPEAK-OUT ON DOMESTIC SERVICE

To wealthy observers who bemoaned the "servant problem" in the latter part of the nineteenth century, it was always a question why working-women seemed to prefer the factory, grim though it was, over the security of domestic service. Helen Campbell, a journalist who investigated the circumstances of workingwomen in the 1880s and wrote moving stories of "prisoners of poverty" unable to support themselves in industrial employments, asked this question about domestic service to workingwomen of her acquaintance.

Our interest lies in discovering what is at the bottom of the objection to domestic service; how far these objections are rational and to be treated with respect, and how they may be obviated. The mistress's point of view we all know. We know, too, her presentation of objections as she fancies she has discovered them. What we do not know is the ground taken by sensible, self-respecting girls, who have chosen trades in preference, and from whom full detail has been obtained as to the reasons for such choice. . . .

In the present case it seems well to take the individual testimony, each girl whose verdict is chosen representing a class, and being really its mouthpiece.

First on the list stands Margaret M——, an American, twenty-three years old, and for five years in a paper-box factory. Seven others nodded their assent, or added a word here and there as she gave her view, two of them Irish-Americans who had had some years in the public schools.

"It's freedom that we want when the day's work is done. I know some nice girls, Bridget's cousins, that make more money and dress better and everything for being in service. They're waitresses, and have Thursday afternoon out and part of every other Sunday. But they're never sure of one minute that's their own when they're in the house. Our day is ten hours long, but when it's done it's done, and we can do what we like with the evenings. That's what I've heard from every nice girl that ever tried service. You're never sure that your soul's your own except when you are out of the house, and I couldn't stand that a day. Women care just as much for freedom as men do. Of course they don't get so much, but I know I'd fight for mine."

"Women are always harder on women than men are," said a fur-sewer,

Helen Campbell, *Prisoners of Poverty* (Boston: Little, Brown, 1900), pp. 222–31.

an intelligent American about thirty. "I got tired of always sitting, and took a place as chambermaid. The work was all right and the wages good, but I'll tell you what I couldn't stand. The cook and the waitress were just common, uneducated Irish, and I had to room with one and stand the personal habits of both, and the way they did at table took all my appetite. I couldn't eat, and began to run down; and at last I gave notice, and told the truth when I was asked why. The lady just looked at me astonished: 'If you take a servant's place, you can't expect to be one of the family,' she said. 'I never asked it,' I said; 'all I ask is a chance at common decency.' 'It will be difficult to find an easier place than this,' she said, and I knew it; but ease one way was hardness another, and she couldn't see that I had any right to complain. That's one trouble in the way. It's the mixing up of things, and mistresses don't think how they would feel in the same place."

Third came an Irish-American whose mother had been cook for years in one family, but who had, after a few months of service, gone into a jute-mill, followed gradually by five sisters.

"I hate the very words 'service' and 'servant,'" she said. "We came to this country to better ourselves, and it's not bettering to have anybody ordering you round."

"But you are ordered in the mill."

"That's different. A man knows what he wants, and doesn't go beyond it; but a woman never knows what she wants, and sort of bosses you everlastingly. If there was such a thing as fixed hours it might be different, but I tell every girl I know, 'Whatever you do, don't go into service. You'll always be prisoners and always looked down on.' You can do things at home for them as belongs to you that somehow it seems different to do for strangers. Anyway, I hate it, and there's plenty like me."

"What I minded," said a gentle, quiet girl, who worked at a stationer's, and who had tried household service for a year,—"what I minded was the awful lonesomeness. I went for general housework, because I knew all about it, and there were only three in the family. I never minded being alone evenings in my own room, for I'm always reading or something, and I don't go out hardly at all, but then I always know I can, and that there is somebody to talk to if I like. But there, except to give orders, they had nothing to do with me. It got to feel sort of crushing at last. I cried myself sick, and at last I gave it up, though I don't mind the work at all. I know there are good places, but the two I tried happened to be about alike, and I shan't try again. There are a good many would feel just the same."

"Oh, nobody need to tell me about poor servants," said an energetic woman of forty, Irish-American, and for years in a shirt factory. "Don't I know the way the hussies'll do, comin' out of a bog maybe, an' not knowing the names even, let alone the use, of half the things in the kitchen, and asking their twelve and fourteen dollars a month? Don't I know it well, an' the shame it is to 'em! but I know plenty o' decent, hard-workin' girls too, that give good satisfaction, an' this is what they say. They say the main trouble is, the mistresses don't know, no more than babies, what a day's work really is. A smart girl keeps on her feet all the time to prove she isn't lazy, for if the mistress finds her sitting down, she thinks there can't be much to do and that she doesn't earn her wages. Then if a girl tries to save herself or is deliberate, they call her slow. They want girls on tap from six in the morning till ten and eleven at night. 'Tisn't fair. And then, if there's a let-up in the work, maybe they give you the baby to see to. I like a nice baby, but I don't like having one turned over to me when I'm fit to drop scrabbling to get through and sit down a bit. I've naught to say for the girls that's breaking things and half doing the work. They're a shameful set, and ought to be put down somehow; but it's a fact that the most I've known in service have been another sort that stayed long in places and hated change. There's many a good place too, but the bad ones outnumber 'em. Women make hard mistresses, and I say again, I'd rather be under a man, that knows what he wants. That's the way with most."

"I don't see why people are surprised that we don't rush into places," said a shop-girl. "Our world may be a very narrow world, and I know it is; but for all that, it's the only one we've got, and right or wrong, we're out of it if we go into service. A teacher or cashier or anybody in a store, no matter if they have got common-sense, doesn't want to associate with servants. Somehow you get a sort of smooch. Young men think and say, for I have heard lots of them, 'Oh, she can't amount to much if she hasn't brains enough to make a living outside of a kitchen!' You're just down once for all if you go into one."

"I don't agree with you at all," said a young teacher who had come with her. "The people that hire you go into kitchens and are not disgraced. What I felt was, for you see I tried it, that they oughtn't to make me go into livery. I was worn out with teaching, and so I concluded to try being a nurse for a while. I found two hard things: one, that I was never free for an hour from the children, for I took meals and all with them, and any mother knows what a rest it is to go quite away from them, even for an hour; and the other was that she wanted me to wear the nurse's cap and apron. She was real good and kind; but when I said, 'Would you like your sister, Miss Louise, to put on cap and apron when she goes out with them?' she got very red, and straightened up. 'It's a very different matter,' she said; 'you must not forget that in accepting a servant's place you accept a servant's limitations.' That finished me. I loved the children, but I said, 'If you have no other thought of what I am to the children than that, I had better go.' I went, and she put a common, uneducated Irish girl in my place. I know a good many who would take nurse's places, and who are sensible enough not to want to push into the family life. But the trouble is that almost every one wants to make a show, and it is more stylish to have the nurse in a cap and apron and so she is ordered into them."

"I've tried it," said one who had been a dressmaker and found her health going from long sitting. "My trouble was, no conscience as to hours; and I believe you'll find that is, at the bottom, one of the chief objections. My first employer was a smart, energetic woman, who had done her own work when she was first married and knew what it meant, or you'd think she might have known. But she had no more thought for me than if I had been a machine. She'd sit in her sitting-room on the second floor and ring for me twenty times a day to do little things, and she wanted me up till eleven to answer the bell, for she had a great deal of company. I had a good room and everything nice, and she gave me a great many things, but I'd have spared them all if only I could have had a little time to myself. I was all worn out, and at last I had to go. There was another reason. I had no place but the kitchen to see my friends. I was thirty years old and as well born and well educated as she, and it didn't seem right. The mistresses think it's all the girls' fault, but I've seen enough to know that women haven't found out what justice means, and that a girl knows it, many a time, better than her employer. Anyway, you couldn't make me try it again."

"My trouble was," said another, who had been in a cotton-mill and gone into the home of one of the mill-owners as chambermaid, "I hadn't any place that I could be alone a minute. We were poor at home, and four of us worked in the mill, but I had a little room all my own, even if it didn't hold much. In that splendid big house the servants' room was over the kitchen,—hot and close in summer, and cold in winter, and four beds in it. We five had to live there together, with only two bureaus and a bit of a closet, and one washstand for all. There was no chance to keep clean or your things in nice order, or anything by yourself, and I gave up. Then I went into a little family and tried general housework, and the mistress taught me a great deal, and was good and kind, only there the kitchen was a dark little place and my room like it, and I hadn't an hour in anything that was pleasant and warm. A mistress might see, you'd think, when a girl was quiet and fond of her home, and treat her different from the kind that destroy everything; but I suppose the truth is, they're worn out with that kind and don't make any difference. It's hard to give up your whole life to somebody else's orders, and always feel as if you was looked at over a wall like; but so it is, and you won't get girls to try it, till somehow or other things are different."

A DOMESTIC PROBLEM

*Abby Morton Diaz, who had lived at the Transcendentalist Brook Farm
Association as a child, became a well-known author of domestic advice
and short stories, especially for children, after the Civil War. An advocate
of many women's causes (including the Women's Educational and Industrial Union in Boston, in which she played a prominent role from 1877 to
1902), she believed in making women's household labor more efficient so
that they might devote more time to their children and to self-improvement.*

I wonder how long it would take to name, just merely to name, all the
duties which fall upon the woman who, to use a common phrase, and a
true one, carries on the family. Suppose we try to count them, one by
one. Doing this will help to give us that clear view of the present state of
things which it is our present object to obtain; though the idea reminds
me of what the children used to say when I was a child, "If you count the
stars you'll drop down dead,"—a saying founded, probably, on the vast-
ness of the undertaking compared with human endurance. It certainly
cannot be called trivial to enumerate the duties to which woman conse-
crates so large a portion of her life, especially when we remember that
into each and all of these duties she has to carry her mind. Where woman's mind must go, woman's mind or man's mind, should not scorn to
follow. So let us make the attempt; and we need not stand upon the order
of our counting, but begin anywhere.

Setting tables; clearing them off; keeping lamps or gas-fixtures in
order; polishing stoves, knives, silverware, tinware, faucets, knobs, &c.;
washing and wiping dishes; taking care of food left at meals; sweeping,
including the grand Friday sweep, the limited daily sweep, and the oft-
recurring dustpan sweep; cleaning paint; washing looking-glasses, windows, window-curtains; canning and preserving fruit; making sauces and
jellies, and "catchups" and pickles; making and baking bread, cake, pies,
puddings; cooking meats and vegetables; keeping in nice order beds, bed-
ding, and bedchambers; arranging furniture, dusting, and "picking up;"
setting forth, at their due times and in due order, the three meals; washing the clothes; ironing, including doing up shirts and other "starched
things;" taking care of the baby, night and day; washing and dressing
children, and regulating their behavior, and making or getting made,

Abby Morton Diaz, *A Domestic Problem: Work and Culture in the Household* (Boston: Osgood &
Co., 1875), pp. 7–16.

their clothing, and seeing that the same is in good repair, in good taste, spotless from dirt, and suited both to the weather and the occasion; doing for herself what her own personal needs require; arranging flowers; entertaining company; nursing the sick; "letting down" and "letting out" to suit the growing ones; patching, darning, knitting, crocheting, braiding, quilting,—but let us remember the warning of the old saying, and forbear in time.

This, however, is only a general enumeration. This is counting the stars by constellations. Examining closely these items: we shall find them made up each of a number of smaller items, and each of these again of items still smaller. What seem homogeneous are heterogeneous; what seem simple are complex. Make a loaf of bread. That has a simple sound, yet the process is complex. First, hops, potatoes, flour, sugar, water, salt, in right proportions for the yeast. The yeast for raising the yeast must be in just the right condition, and added when the mixture is of just the right temperature. In "mixing up" bread, the temperature of the atmosphere must be considered, the temperature of the water, the situation of the dough. The dough must rise quickly, must rise just enough and no more, must be baked in an oven just hot enough and no hotter, and must be "tended" while baking.

Try clearing off tables. Remove food from platters, care for the remnants, see that nothing is wasted, scrape well every plate, arrange in piles, carry out, wash in soap and water, rinse in clear water, polish with dry cloth, set away in their places,—three times a day.

Taking care of the baby frequently implies carrying the child on one arm while working with the other, and this often after nights made sleepless by its "worrying." "I've done many a baking with a child on my hip," said a farmer's wife in my hearing.

But try now the humblest of household duties, one that passes for just nothing at all; try dusting. "Take a cloth, and brush the dust off,"—stated in this general way, how easy a process it seems! The particular interpretation, is that you move, wipe, and replace every article in the room, from the piano down to the tiniest ornament; that you "take a cloth," and go over every inch of accessible surface, including panelling, mop-boards, window frames and sashes, looking-glass frames, picture-frames and cords, gas or lamp fixtures; reaching up, tiptoeing, climbing, stooping, kneeling, taking care that not even in the remotest corner shall appear one inch of undusted surface which any slippered individual, leaning back in his arm-chair can spy out.

These are only a few examples; but a little observation and an exceedingly little experience will show the curious inquirer that there is scarcely one of the apparently simple household operations which cannot be re-solved and re-resolved into minute component parts. Thus dusting, which seems at first to consist of simply a few brushes with a cloth or bunch of feathers, when analyzed once, is found to imply the careful wiping of every article in the room, and of all the woodwork; analyzed again, it implies following the marks of the cabinet-maker's tools in every bit of carving and grooving; analyzed again, introducing a pointed stick under the cloth in turning corners. In fact, the investigator of household duties must do as does a distinguished scientist in analyzing matter,— "continue the process of dividing as long as the parts can be discerned," and then "prolong the vision backward across the boundary of experi-mental evidence." And, if brave enough to attempt to count them, he must bear in mind that what appear to be blank intervals, or blurred, nebulous spaces, are, in reality, filled in with innumerable little duties which, through the glass of observation, may be discerned quite plainly. Let him also bear in mind, that these household duties must be done over and over, and over and over, and as well, each time, as if done to last forever; and, above all, that they every one require mind.

CONDITION OF WOMEN IN RURAL ALABAMA

Sharecropping dominated Southern agriculture in the late nineteenth century. Large cotton plantations once worked by slaves were divided into small farms and leased to individual families at the price of half or more of their crop. Although white sharecroppers outnumbered African Americans, nearly three-quarters of southern blacks worked as sharecroppers. This account was provided by Georgia Washington, an African American graduate of the Hampton Institute in Virginia who worked to spread Hampton's philosophy of racial uplift by founding the People's Village School, a combined social settlement and school in rural Alabama.

For nine years my interest has been centered in building a school on one of the old plantations in Montgomery county, Ala. Most of the seven hundred children who have been reached by the school during that time have come from the surrounding plantations, and the only women with whom I have come in contact have been the mothers of these children. I beg leave then to confine myself to the plantation women of my community at Mt. Meigs Village, Alabama.

Many of these women, born before the war, grew up, married the man picked out for them by master and mistress, and lived on these same old plantations. Large families of children were reared in what is called "Quarters," long distances from the "Big House," in which master and mistress lived. Some of the boys and girls were half grown before ever seeing the face of a white man. The mothers left home with their husbands to work in the fields long before it was day. Women, side by side with the men, cleared new ground, cut down big trees, rolled logs, dug ditches, plowed, hoed, and picked cotton. From those women came the mothers of the present generation.

The mother born on free soil and breathing free air, what is her condition to-day? She is on the same old plantation, perhaps still in the "Quarters." The "Big House," once owned by master and mistress, is now occupied by a dozen or more Negro families. The grandchildren of the original owners of these plantations still hold them and rent the places out to Negroes, taking the crops made for rent and food.

The women are all field hands and still leave home very early for the day's work. At noon each day the women carry home on their backs the

Georgia Washington, "Condition of the Women in the Rural Districts of Alabama: What Is Being Done to Remedy That Condition," *Proceedings of the Hampton Negro Conference*, no. 6 (July 1902) (Hampton, Va.: Hampton Institute Press), pp. 74–77.

wood to cook the dinner, the husband hurries to get under a shady tree and sleep until dinner is ready, then eats and afterward has a smoke. The wife must be ready to go back to the field with him when the noon hour is out. The house was left out of order in the morning, the cooking things scattered about the hearth just as they were used, and the few dishes on the old table are unwashed too. Where the mother takes all the children to the field, the house is locked up and the one window barred, but thanks to the builder the cracks are still there and the air will play through all day.

At dinner no time yet is given to washing dishes or making beds, so after sunset the wife brings wood to cook supper and a light-wood knot to give light. No lamps or oil are used unless some one is sick. Next the woman drags up the cow and milks, brings water for the night, then begins the supper. Perhaps the dishes will get washed for supper. After this nature overcomes the strongest and sleep is sought by all the family, in those same unmade beds or pallets.

Girls grow up in such homes, marry early and in turn make others just like them in which to rear their children. Such a woman is a real drudge, not only for her children, but for her husband, and one of the most surprising things to me is that he grows tired of her and quits, leaving six or eight children to be cared for by the mother.

The mother before the war had no time to rear children, or chance to send them to school or church. She, with the children, belonged to master body and soul. The free woman with the church, school, teachers, preachers and the Bible, what is her excuse for her present condition? This woman too has a large family of children, a worthless husband, a one-roomed log house and no kitchen. The mortgage for food and a few clothes is still made. The wife and children are worked very hard every year to pay it off. Where the family is large they are only half fed and clothed; the mother has to hustle all through the winter, in order to get anything. These people handle very little money; whenever they work by the day or month a written order is given by their employers to some store in the village, and they get their food and their clothing too on this. The great excuse of the mother is that it takes all of her time and money to get food, so she cannot educate the children, but she is trying.

The real condition of the women in the rural districts is beyond my power of description. It is worse than anything I ever heard of. There is hardly any bright side to their lives to be seen, even if we searched with a lighted candle. Within a radius of ten miles from our school, hardly a half-dozen families own their own homes.

What is being done to remedy the present condition of these women?

Perhaps you will be interested to hear of some of the things attempted, and judge for yourself how far they reach the end in view.

At Mt. Meigs, and in fact all over the state, as far as I can learn, are a great many organizations, whose object is to care for the sick members and bury the dead members. Some of these societies number over two hundred members, and one in the city of Montgomery reaches over four hundred. The women outnumber the men in almost every case. Members are cared for by a good doctor when sick. He is paid from their treasury. Whenever a member dies, the whole society turns out in uniform and gives a very nice burying. These societies are kept up by a monthly fee from each member. Our women will always find money to pay these fees. Every thing at home, and even church dues are sacrificed to the societies. The woman who is not a member of one of these is pitied and considered rather out of date.

The Woman's District Association is purely a Baptist church organization, and has for its object the support of Selma University, the great Baptist school of the state. Every loyal Baptist woman is a member and, however poor, is obliged to pay a monthly fee which is given entirely to this one school.

The Southern Federation of Colored Women, of which Mrs B. T. Washington is president, is an organization devoted to the uplifting of women all over the South. This organization is made up of the federations of the several states. The State federation is made up of women's clubs, organized by leading women in both cities and rural districts all over the State. . . .

The club at Mt. Meigs, was made up at first of just the mothers who had children in our school, and as so was called a mothers meeting. It was no easy task to get hold of these women, but I waked up to the fact that time was being wasted on this crowd of children who came to school each day with dirty faces, uncombed hair, ragged clothes, and that in order to get to the bottom of things I must get hold of the mothers. The mothers, on the other hand, wondered what the school-teachers wanted with them. They had never been asked to come to the schoolhouse except at closing exercises, so they decided not to come. But after repeated messages sent by the children from school, six or seven came. We talked things over together, they opened up their hearts to me. This was nine years ago, and we have been friends ever since. I found out that those mothers were dissatisfied themselves and anxious to change things at home and do better, but had no idea how or where to begin. Some of these women looked pretty rough on the outside, but strong mother-hearts beat in their bosoms, and the key-note was struck when they found out that the school was interested in helping their children in more ways than just by the lessons from their books. Their great complaint was poverty, no money to buy clothes, no way to keep those they already had whole and no time to mend or clean up the children before sending them to school in the morning. When I learned more about them I found the home was very scantily supplied with anything. They had no needles or sewing cotton, nor anything with which to mend old clothes. All the little bundles of cloth, sewing cotton, needles etc., that could be spared from our sewing room were given to the mothers for home use. Thus with a little encouragement in the way of learning for the children's sake, these mothers are trying hard, and the children who come now present a much better appearance. The mothers soon learnt how to send the children to bed early in order to wash out and dry by the fire the one set of clothes, so that the little boy with one jacket could keep clean every day. These meetings became a source of information and help. We discussed practical subjects bearing on the home life; such as the care of the children, and of the girl of sixteen; the care of the kitchen and the necessity of keeping it clean, when to wash the dishes, etc. I cannot say that a community of women was changed in one day, but they have tried and many have succeeded in making their homes much better. So many of the homes had no kitchen at all, so the women went to work, cut down the trees, rived the boards and built a queer looking room, but it held a stove and all the cooking things the family owned. On the road from Mt. Meigs to the city of Montgomery are two or three of these home-made kitchens, six by six feet. I know they are kitchens because there is a small stove pipe in the middle of each roof, from which the smoke is pouring out. . . .

The school, with its teachers, brought to the doors of the people of Mt. Meigs village is helping to bring about better things. The church, with its good upright pastor, is doing what it can, but back and beneath all these things is the home. First, in order to have any sort of a home for these mothers and their children, the work system for women must be changed. No woman can be a home-keeper that spends twelve hours of the day in the field. An appeal has been made for a girls' home in connection with our work, where we hope to take twenty-five girls from their homes and train them in the way of house and home-keeping. The only hope for these women and our community lies in the boys and girls who, after being trained, will return to their homes and change things. Right along with the girls the boys must be trained also, since they will be a powerful factor in changing the work system for the women. A few of the young men and women have been sent from Mt. Meigs to Hampton and Tuskegee. We hope to have them back after finishing school, to work at some trade that is needed in our community. We need Tuskegee's and Hampton's idea of work deep rooted in the hearts and minds of these young people in order that when sent back to the South, they may change the old ways of farming, gardening, raising chickens and caring for stock, so that where there is now all desert land, oases may be formed. Then, and not till then will a real change take place in the condition of our women of the rural districts of Alabama.

LEONORA BARRY REPORTS TO THE
KNIGHTS OF LABOR

In the 1880s, the Knights of Labor was the largest labor organization in the nation, including at its height some 500,000 to 750,000 members, probably 50,000 of them women. Both wage-earning women (who typically were excluded from craft unions) and housewives could become members. Women's active role in the Knights can largely be credited to Leonora Barry, the Irish-born widowed mother and hosiery worker who was appointed first director of woman's work in 1886. Although Barry retired from the labor movement upon her remarriage in 1890, she remained active in temperance, woman suffrage, and charity work.

Brothers and sisters in this work, for three years I have labored for and among you with such ability as I possessed, with what success I constitute you my judges. My work has not been confined solely to women and children, but to all of earth's toilers, as I am of the opinion that the time when we could separate the interests of the toiling masses on sex lines is past. Long since, when I became one of the bread-winners of the land, I recognized how much the workingwomen needed enlightenment and assistance to maintain that dignity which by our form of government we are entitled to, and protection from the indignities and injustice heaped upon us, in many instances because of our voiceless, helpless condition, by unprincipled and avaricious men. The many and varied channels of industry into which woman has either forced her way or has been forced, together with the rapid introduction of wage-saving machinery with its facilities for production, has opened a line of competition and strife, greater even among the ranks of women-workers than among men, and in which women suffer much more than men—for many reasons, foremost of which is that, because she is a woman, her natural pride and timidity, coupled with the restrictions of social customs, deter her from making that struggle that can be made by men. Second, because there is such a lack of industrial training among our girls, which throws upon the labor market an army of incompetent women who are compelled to work, but who have little or no practical knowledge of any particular trade or branch of trade to enable them to make the demand that competent labor would be justified in making. If it were possible, I wish that it were not necessary for women to learn any trade but that of domestic

Leonora Barry, "Report of the General Investigator and Director of Woman's Work," *Proceedings of the General Assembly of the Knights of Labor,* 1889, pp. 1–6.

duties, as I believe it was intended that man should be the bread-winner. But as that is impossible under present conditions, I believe women should have every opportunity to become proficient in whatever vocation they choose or find themselves best fitted for. This is a serious question, as those who have the ambition and ability to raise themselves above the hand-to-mouth level are deterred from so doing by the ignorant, the apathetic and the hopeless, who, through long years of dependance, have acquired, as a sort of second nature, the habit of submission and acceptance without question of any terms offered them, with the pessimistic view of life in which they see no ray of hope. Such people cannot be said to live, as living means the enjoyment of nature's gifts, but they simply vegetate like partially petrified creatures. Every effort has been made to perfect and extend the organization of women, but our efforts have not met with the response that the cause deserves, partly because those who have steady employment, fairly good wages and comfortable homes seem to see nothing in organization outside of self-interest, and because they are what they are pleased to term "all right," do not feel it incumbent upon themselves to do anything to assist their less fortunate coworkers. Again, many women are deterred from joining labor organizations by foolish pride, prudish modesty and religious scruples; and a prevailing cause, which applies to all who are in the flush of womanhood, is the hope and expectancy that in the near future marriage will lift them out of the industrial life to the quiet and comfort of a home, foolishly imagining that with marriage their connection with and interest in labor matters end: often finding, however, that their struggle has only begun when they have to go back to the shop and work for two instead of one. All this is the results or effects of the environments and conditions surrounding women in the past and present, and can be removed only by constant agitation and education. But in looking over the events of the past year and realizing the terrible ordeal through which our organization has passed, my only wonder is that so many women have remained faithful through it all. The longer I live the more convinced am I that two qualities—energy and invincible determination—are absolute essentials in the man or woman who would be successful in any work of reform—industrial, social or moral. During the past three years I have met many of this type of humanity, and to the inspiration and encouragement received from them I owe much of the strength that has enabled me to bear the bitter disappointment and humiliation of repeated failures. If my work during the past year meet your approbation, you will have accorded me all I ask in believing that I have endeavored to do my best. . . .

From December 10 to 20 I spoke at different places under jurisdiction

of D.A. [District Assembly] 147, Albany, N.Y. The order there was building up and the prospects were bright. There is one woman's Local, composed of shirtmakers, laundrymakers and different other trades. It is one
of the most active, loyal Locals in the Order, and the brothers of D.A. 147
take pride in assisting the sisters to make it so. 21st and 22d. Spoke in
New London, Conn., where the Local was growing rapidly, many of its
new members being women. . . . 29th. At Harrisburg in the interest of
the Factory Inspection Bill. 30th South Amboy, N.J. where I found the
Local increasing its membership rapidly. February 2. Paterson, N.J. 5th.
Richmond, Va. Men's Local reorganization but the women's Local there
had lapsed. 6th. Manchester, Va. The employes in the cotton-mills of
Manchester were at one time well organized, and through their organization secured a reduction in the hours of labor from twelve to ten, and,
had they continued to keep up their organization, might have remedied
many other evils of which they now complain, such as low wages and
child labor: but, failing to see the importance of doing so, the majority
let go the footing they had secured and left the few, who are capable of
realization to suffer without any near prospect of relief. . . .

It is unnecessary to say more of the condition of Southern working
women than this: They are as much in need of the protection that organization gives and the knowledge acquired by such association as the
women of any other part of the country, where, perhaps, more factories
may be found. Yet the sparsely populated and rich lands of the South,
together with the splendid water facilities, are attracting speculators and
capitalists who desire to invest in productive enterprises, and avenues of
different branches of employment are being daily opened up to the coming toilers of the South making universal and thorough organization all
the more necessary. This does not exist now among either men or
women. Not among the latter, because of the prejudices of old-time customs largely; not among the former, because of the many reasons that
have always separated labor's ranks. . . . Knights of Labor in the South
should make every effort to bring about a shortening of the hours of labor
for woman at least, for all if possible. It is neither just to employer nor
employe to have the cotton manufacturer of Atlanta or the hosiery manufacturer of Macon go into the market with the products of their thirteen-
and-eleven-hour-a-day labor in competition with the products of the ten-
hour-a-day labor of other parts of the country, and this comes even nearer
home, as some of the cotton industries of Atlanta work only ten hours a
day. Also for the establishment of child-labor laws, as it is much easier to
prevent an evil than to kill it after it becomes an established precedent.
Not that children are not employed now—they are in many places; but

not to the extent they will be, if not prevented, as industries spring up all over the country. . . .

April 27 and 28. Spoke in Dayton, Ohio. May 1 and 2. Cincinnati, Ohio. On the afternoon of May 7 I spoke in the interest of working-women before a meeting of the Woman's Christian Temperance Union in Denver, Col. In the evening I visited a leatherworkers' Assembly. . . . Upon my return from Denver, owing to an attack of malaria, I was for several weeks a physical wreck, being unable to do anything except a little local work. On June 28 I went to Danbury, Conn., where I organized a woman's Local of hat-trimmers. On July 15 I addressed a large audience at Lake Bluff, thirty miles north of Chicago, Ill., in the interest of labor. This meeting was held under the auspices of the Lake Bluff Temperance Convocation, but the people who should be interested in everything pertaining to labor's welfare were conspicuous by their absence. . . .

16th and 17th. Meetings in Norwich, Conn. 19th. New Britain, Conn. 21st and 22d. Bristol. 23d. Naugatuck. Twenty of our members drove over to this meeting from Waterbury, a distance of five miles, while hundreds of the people living within sight of the hall either staid at home or fell over each other in their efforts to secure seats at a 10-cent show that was running in the town. My experience has been that there are many places where it is time and money wasted to send Lecturers, as many minds are incapable of absorbing either the purpose or the subject, and, owing to their past and present environments and limited opportunities, can grasp only that which presents something bordering on novelty or variety. . . . To meet this unhappy contingency I would recommend . . . we distribute . . . leaflet and pamphlet literature. By this means we may reach and interest many who now through prejudice or want of interest would not come to hear a Lecturer. I would also urge upon our members the particular necessity of energetic and immediate action for the purpose of preventing the further growth of the social evil along the Pacific coast, which is the outcome of the unlicensed and unrestricted immorality of the Chinese of that locality. Every day tales of horror come to me of the traffic in woman's virtue, resulting from and traceable to the baleful influence of Chinese opium joints and gambling hells. This reference to the social evil reminds me of something that I would be derelict in my duty did I not refer to cases which come to my knowledge frequently in which men use the power which their positions as employes, superintendents or foremen give them to debauch girls in their employ whose employment is dependent on their good-will. It seems to me that our Order should use its influence everywhere to have laws passed for the protection of women against this wrong. It should be made a criminal offense for a man holding any position which gives him power over women to make in any way improper advances to them.

While considerable prominence is given in statistical reports concerning working-women, to the question of their morality and immorality, my experience has been that they, considering their environments, are no more in need of investigation in this respect than women in higher walks of life; and when cases of immorality are found, if an investigation as to the cause were made and an exposé of the facts and partners in guilt were given more prominence, it would have a tendency to stop the action of those who now feel they can cover up their part in the matter, while their unhappy victims are left to bear it all. . . .

Brother Knights of Labor, bend all your energies to organization. Organized effort by the majority means success. With only a minority it means defeat, hopelessness and despair. Let intelligence and justice encircle our every action until the great mass of earth's toilers be brought into the greatest and noblest of all conditions—the brotherhood and sisterhood of humanity—where an injury to one will be the concern of all.

RESCUED CHINESE PROSTITUTES TESTIFY AT THE INDUSTRIAL COMMISSION

Although Chinese men were actively recruited as laborers on the transcontinental railroad (completed in 1869), anti-Chinese sentiment ballooned among Americans soon afterward, producing federal laws of 1882, 1892, 1902, and 1904 that virtually closed immigration from China and left the sex ratio among Chinese in the United States drastically skewed toward men. Both prostitutes and Chinese laborers were specifically denied admission, but federal officers feared illegal immigration and conducted frequent investigations. For this 1901 report by the U.S. Industrial Commission, the government solicited testimony from Chinese women who had been "saved" from prostitution by Donaldina Cameron, matron of the Presbyterian Chinese Mission Home in San Francisco. Cameron's work was similar to that of moral reformers in the 1840s, except that it was cross-cultural. Her cause drew energy from the analogy between forced prostitution and slavery in an era when racial slavery had been decisively rejected.

VOLUNTARY STATEMENT OF LEE YOW CHUN.

Presbyterian Mission Home, *January 17, 1898.*
My name is Lee Yow Chun. I am a native of the Sha Tow village, in the district of Ho Nam, opposite the city of Canton. I have never before been in the United States. I am 16 years old. I reported my age as 20 upon my arrival; that my name was Lee Choy Wan, and that my birthplace was San Francisco. Because we were poor my parents removed to Hongkong, where they could get better wages. My father, whose name was Lee Tsun, died in Hongkong when I was 13. After father's death mother continued to work as a household servant. At Hongkong we lived on Kow Yu Fong street. My mother's name is Lum Ah Mui. She is 40 this year. She worked on Kwok Lun street, No. 31. This is where she was working up to my leaving Hongkong. Mother told me one day that a go-between had been to see her on behalf of a wealthy Chinese merchant living in San Francisco, who wanted a wife from China; that she wanted me to go out and take a walk, so that I could be viewed by the go-between, that she could make her report. I did what I was bid, though I knew that mother told me this with some misgiving, as she had declined the offer once and

U.S. Industrial Commission, *Report,* vol. 15 (Washington, D.C.: Government Printing Office, 1901), pp. 773–75, 783–85.

would decline again but for her good nature and her poverty. The go-between having made her a present of $380 as coming from my intended husband, mother said she consented to take so little because I could only marry that merchant as a concubine and also that in 2 or 3 years I could come back to pay her a visit. About a week after, toward evening of the 3d of the 11th month (November 25, 1897), a man whom I had never seen before nor since, and whose name even I do not know, came to our house and took me to a house on a street next to Kwok Lung street. In this house were several women who said they had been to the United States. My mother wanted to accompany me to that house, and I wanted her to go along too, but the man said since we had to part anyway we might as well part then, so that I would not feel so bad when the time came to go on board. So we parted then and there.

When this man had me in that house he took me to a room, after my hair had been dressed, and with no other in the room brought a piece of paper out of which he taught me certain things I was to say when questioned by the customs officer in San Francisco. When he told me what to say in answer to their question "What is your father's name?" I said, "What does that mean. My father has been dead some years." He said, "We have to do that, as that is the law in California. You can not go there to get married unless you follow my instructions." I then listened until he got through with a list of questions and answers. After I had learned my lesson dinner was served, and about 8 o'clock in the evening I was taken down to the water front, where a little boat was in waiting. I was taken on this little boat and the boat people rowed me out alongside steamer *China,* where we passed the night. At 4 o'clock in the morning, when it was yet dark, I was told to go quietly over to the *China.* Shortly after the *China* started for California. I found 8 other girls on board, with 3 more after we left Shanghai. As I was told that my landing depended upon my remembering my story, I went over it every day from the day we started, at times singing it as we would a song, though often weeping as I sang, whenever I thought of mother and of home.

The Chinaman in Hongkong let me have the paper to learn the story from, telling me that when I got its contents well committed to memory I was to throw the paper overboard. The paper was about 18 inches long. I saw that the other girls each had a story to learn also. A day after our arrival at San Francisco we were questioned by the customs officers. I answered as I was told to do by that man in Hongkong. Three or four days after I was told someone was inquiring for me. He pointed to himself and said very hurriedly: "Take a good look at me, so that you can recognize me afterwards as your father." No sooner had he said this than he hurried off to go. I called after him, saying "I could not recognize a person as my father upon seeing him so short a time." He then came back and stood by the vessel a little longer. A pit-marked woman accompanied him. This woman I soon found to be a procuress. This, together with a caution that my mother gave me, as well as some things that the sailors were good enough to tell me, convinced me that all was not right. Several times I told the customs officers, through one of the male passengers as interpreter, that I did not want to be landed. Another girl was of the same mind as myself. Somehow the importers of the girls found out that we did not want to be landed, and some of them came down to frighten us, saying we would be imprisoned at least 5 months before being sent back, and then we could only go as far as Japan, when we would be taken possession of again. This did not swerve us from the course we decided on. When word came from the collector that I could land, not being able to do anything else I fell in a lump on the floor and cried loudly, saying I did not want to be landed by those people; that I would jump into the sea rather than be taken by them. Somehow the fact I cried reached the ears of the official interpreter, who came with another officer and quieted me. Soon after they returned and said the collector had allowed me to go to a rescue home and there to remain until the next returning boat to China.

I am now in that home, happy and contented, enjoying the prospect of soon being restored to my mother.

STATEMENT OF CHUN HO, RESCUED SLAVE GIRL, AT PRESBYTERIAN CHINESE RESCUE HOME, MISS CAMERON, MATRON, TO UNITED STATES COMMISSIONER OF IMMIGRATION HART H. NORTH, AT SAN FRANCISCO, CAL., SEPTEMBER 17, 1898.

[Questions put by Commissioner North and answered by Chun Ho, through Interpreter J. E. Gardner.]

When Chun Ho is told that a statement is wanted from her on this matter she bursts into tears and says it always makes her cry to think of the ill-treatment she suffered at the hands of the highbinders before she was rescued by the mission.

Q. How old are you?—A. 24.

Q. Where were you born?—A. At Ng Jow, in the province of Kwong Si, the province adjoining that of Kwong Tung.

Q. How did you happen to come to the United States?—A. When I was 19 years old, the mistress No. 3 of a noted procurer by the name of Gwan Lung, who lives in San Francisco, went back to Canton, where my mother happened to be living with me at that time, and gave me glowing accounts of life in California. She painted that life so beautifully that I was seized with an inclination to go there and try my fortune, mother taking $200 Mexican and consenting to my going. I arrived in this country, together with 6 other girls brought by this woman, on the 22d of June, 1893. We all came on fraudulent certificates; the color of those certificates was reddish. (In those days there was such a certificate used, usually known in the customs service as "Red certificates," but they have since been abolished.—J.E.G.) I was told to assume a name to correspond with the name in the fraudulent certificate that was given to me, and I was landed as "Ah Fook." The age in the certificate was 28, and I was told to report my age as 28, which was very much above my true age at the time. The certificate called for a scar on the right temple. As it happened I had no scar. This woman told me to burn my right temple until there should be a mark. The burning was done, but by the time I had arrived in this city the burn had about healed up. The judge had some doubt as to the genuineness of the certificate, and as to my being the party who was entitled to it. I was kept in jail for a few days, but although the burn had healed up, there was some slight mark on my left temple and the judge gave me the benefit of the doubt and I was landed. I was told to claim that I was a married woman; that my husband's name was a Mr. Tsoy, merchant in San Francisco. He was then said to have been a member of the firm of Gum Pun Kee, that was then on Sacramento street, to the best of my recollection. I was also told to claim that my parents were in San Francisco. I was told that if I stuck to those claims I could be landed, and I was landed. The parties interested in my coming over were Quan Lum, his No. 3 mistress, and a noted procurer by the name of May Seen. While I was in jail pending the writ of habeas corpus, these people came frequently to coach me.

When I was first landed I was taken to one of May Seen's houses that were kept by respectable families. They always do that first. From time to time parties came to May Seen's house to see me and to bargain with May Seen as to what price I should be sold at. At the end of two months after my arrival, a Chinaman by the name of Kwan Kay, a highbinder and one who owned some of these houses, came with his woman, Shing Yee, and bought me for $1,950 gold. They gave me a written promise that in four years I should be free. At the end of two years, after taking all my earnings in the meantime, they said I could be redeemed if anyone would pay the sum of $2,100.

I paid my first owners hardly less than $290 a month for the two years; then I was sold for $2,100 to another highbinder by the name of Tsoy

Lung Bo. I was in Tsoy Lung Bo's house for about a year when he wanted to take me into the country. I had to promise that I would go, but in the meantime I took steps to get into the Rescue Home, and before he was able to take me to the country the matron of the Rescue Home came with the police and had me rescued. That was about a year ago, and I am still in the home, but I understand Tsoy Lung Bo has ever since, from time to time, been demanding from me the amount he paid for me, threatening to kill me if I should not pay it before going home to China or leaving the mission. Highbinder after highbinder, through men in his employ or members of his own clique, have been going backward and forward in the vicinity of the home, threatening me and saying it would be much better for me to return to this man; that if I valued life at all to go right back, as the matron of the home could not always protect me. I have an aunt living near the home and sometimes I have visited her, thinking they would not know; but they soon found out, and even threatened my aunt, saying that if she would persist in keeping me, if any harm came to her they would not be responsible. These men stood on the street and called these things out to me at the windows.

Q. What steps did you take to be rescued?—A. I had a friend who took pity on me, and it was he who told the matron, and the matron got three police officers. It was by appointment that we met a short distance from the house. I had to pretend that I was going out to the nearest store to make a little purchase, and on the way the police met me, as it were, and took me to the home.

Q. Tell us what kind of treatment you received during your stay in either one of these two places?—A. My owners were never satisfied, no matter how much money I made. When they were angered in any way, they would vent their anger upon me, which they would also do upon the other girls. When they saw that the matrons of the different rescue homes were very much on the alert, they very often removed us from the houses of ill-repute to family dwellings when they wanted to punish us, so that anyone passing by could not hear our cries very well. Those who frequent those places say that they could not report any ill-treatment; I was often punished in that way. The instruments used were wooden clubs and sometimes anything they could lay their hands on; and one time I was threatened with a pistol held at me.

The work of removing myself and the other girls from where we were to family places where we were punished, was done by members of the highbinder societies. That was a part of their work, for which they receive pay. . . .

Q. Have you ever seen a girl killed for any reason?—A. Yes; I saw one after she had been killed by a highbinder. This highbinder wanted money from her; she either did not have it or put him off, but because she did not pay the money he wanted she was shot by him. I saw her after she had been shot. This last murder took place on Church alley. I also know of three other women that have been killed by highbinders. Two of these were shot and one stabbed to death. As a rule, the murderers of girls forced to lead that life are never brought to justice, because no one would dare to testify against the murderers, who are highbinders.

Miss Cameron here produces a photograph of Chun Ho, taken in the costume usually worn by the girls in these houses, and makes the following statement in regard to the persecution of Chun Ho by the highbinders within the past two weeks:

Chun Ho left the home to pay her aunt a short visit, not more than a couple of blocks from this house. Two or three days after she had been at her aunt's house a Chinaman came here and asked us to go down to the aunt's house, saying that there was a great deal of trouble. We went and found that her former owner had the day before sent a highbinder up to tell her that she must either pay him over $1,000 or else go back and work it out by living that life, and she had sent the highbinder back with a message that she would neither pay the money nor would she go back to that life.

The next evening the owner appeared himself and demanded an interview with her, and the uncle with whom she was staying was afraid to refuse and let him in. He asked Chun Ho if she intended to pay back the price, or if she would go back to him and work it out. She said that she would not do either—that she belonged to the mission now and that the mission ladies would not let her do so. He said that she was not in the mission now and that he would make a great deal of trouble for her if she did not go back. So then she sent up word for one of us to come down.

We went and asked him if it were true that he had been threatening her, and he said that he had lost a great deal of money, over $1,000, by her running into the mission and getting away from him, and now he had come to get it back in some way.

We threatened him with the law and ordered him to leave the house, and so he left. She returned to the mission.

In a few days this man called a meeting of his highbinder society (not being present himself, as he was afraid of being present), but he sent several of the highbinders to her uncle's place of business and forced him to go to the meeting. And there they told him that he would either have to make Chun Ho, his niece, go back to this man's house and work out her own freedom, or else he himself would have to pay over $1,000 for her ransom. He refused to do either, and said that he would appeal to the law and have them arrested if they made him any more trouble; but they still continue to send him threatening messages and to follow her when she goes out on the street to such an extent that, although she is now visiting her aunt, she feels for her own safety she will have to return to the mission.

JANE ADDAMS ON IDLE DAUGHTERS AND WORKING MOTHERS

Jane Addams (1860–1935) decided to establish the first social settlement house in the United States while she was on a trip to Europe in the late 1880s, after her graduation from college and an eight-year period of illness, indecision, and depression. Her work at Hull House in Chicago became a model for many other college graduates. In these two selections from her autobiography (written in midlife) she recalls her decision to found Hull House and shares her observations of working-class mothers. Addams believed that by providing educated women with meaningful work, settlements benefited them as much as their working-class neighbors—one instance, in her view, of the reciprocal dependence of the social classes.

THE SNARE OF PREPARATION

I gradually reached a conviction that the first generation of college women had taken their learning too quickly, had departed too suddenly from the active, emotional life led by their grandmothers and great-grandmothers; that the contemporary education of young women had developed too exclusively the power of acquiring knowledge and of merely receiving impressions; that somewhere in the process of "being educated" they had lost that simple and almost automatic response to the human appeal, that old healthful reaction resulting in activity from the mere presence of suffering or of helplessness; that they are so sheltered and pampered they have no chance even to make "the great refusal."

In the German and French *pensions,* which twenty-five years ago were crowded with American mothers and their daughters who had crossed the seas in search of culture, one often found the mother making real connection with the life about her, using her inadequate German with great fluency, gayly measuring the enormous sheets or exchanging recipes with the German Hausfrau, visiting impartially the nearest kindergarten and market, making an atmosphere of her own, hearty and genuine as far as it went, in the house and on the street. On the other hand, her daughter was critical and uncertain of her linguistic acquirements, and only at ease when in the familiar receptive attitude afforded by the art gallery and the opera house. In the latter she was swayed and moved,

Jane Addams, *Twenty Years at Hull House* (New York: Macmillan, 1911), pp. 71–75, 77, 85–86, 167–75.

appreciative of the power and charm of the music, intelligent as to the legend and poetry of the plot, finding use for her trained and developed powers as she sat "being cultivated" in the familiar atmosphere of the classroom which had, as it were, become sublimated and romanticized.

I remember a happy busy mother who, complacent with the knowledge that her daughter daily devoted four hours to her music, looked up from her knitting to say, "If I had had your opportunities when I was young, my dear, I should have been a very happy girl. I always had musical talent, but such training as I had, foolish little songs and waltzes and not time for half an hour's practice a day."

The mother did not dream of the sting her words left and that the sensitive girl appreciated only too well that her opportunities were fine and unusual, but she also knew that in spite of some facility and much good teaching she had no genuine talent and never would fulfill the expectations of her friends. She looked back upon her mother's girlhood with positive envy because it was so full of happy industry and extenuating obstacles, with undisturbed opportunity to believe that her talents were unusual. The girl looked wistfully at her mother, but had not the courage to cry out what was in her heart: "I might believe I had unusual talent if I did not know what good music was; I might enjoy half an hour's practice a day if I were busy and happy the rest of the time. You do not know what life means when all the difficulties are removed! I am simply smothered and sickened with advantages. It is like eating a sweet dessert the first thing in the morning."

This, then, was the difficulty, this sweet dessert in the morning, and the assumption that the sheltered, educated girl has nothing to do with the bitter poverty and the social maladjustment which is all about her, and which, after all, cannot be concealed, for it breaks through poetry and literature in a burning tide which overwhelms her; it peers at her in the form of heavy-laden market women and underpaid street laborers, gibing her with a sense of her uselessness.

I recall one snowy morning in Saxe-Coburg, looking from the window of our little hotel upon the town square, that we saw crossing and recrossing it a single file of women with semicircular heavy wooden tanks fastened upon their backs. They were carrying in this primitive fashion to a remote cooling room these tanks filled with a hot brew incident to one stage of beer making. The women were bent forward, not only under the weight which they were bearing, but because the tanks were so high that it would have been impossible for them to have lifted their heads. Their faces and hands, reddened in the cold morning air, showed clearly the white scars where they had previously been scalded by the hot stuff which splashed if they stumbled ever so little on their way. Stung into action by one of those sudden indignations against cruel conditions which at times fill the young with unexpected energy, I found myself across the square, in company with mine host, interviewing the phlegmatic owner of the brewery who received us with exasperating indifference, or rather received me, for the innkeeper mysteriously slunk away as soon as the great magnate of the town began to speak. I went back to a breakfast for which I had lost my appetite, as I had for Gray's "Life of Prince Albert" and his wonderful tutor, Baron Stockmar, which I had been reading late the night before. . . .

It is hard to tell just when the very simple plan which afterward developed into the Settlement began to form itself in my mind. It may have been even before I went to Europe for the second time, but I gradually became convinced that it would be a good thing to rent a house in a part of the city where many primitive and actual needs are found, in which young women who had been given over too exclusively to study, might restore a balance of activity along traditional lines and learn of life from life itself; where they might try out some of the things they had been taught and put truth to "the ultimate test of the conduct it dictates or inspires.". . .

PROBLEMS OF POVERTY

We early learned to know the children of hard-driven mothers who went out to work all day, sometimes leaving the little things in the casual care of a neighbor, but often locking them into their tenement rooms. The first three crippled children we encountered in the neighborhood had all been injured while their mothers were at work: one had fallen out of a third-story window, another had been burned, and the third had a curved spine due to the fact that for three years he had been tied all day long to the leg of the kitchen table, only released at noon by his older brother who hastily ran in from a neighboring factory to share his lunch with him. When the hot weather came the restless children could not brook the confinement of the stuffy rooms, and, as it was not considered safe to leave the doors open because of sneak thieves, many of the children were locked out. During our first summer an increasing number of these poor little mites would wander into the cool hallway of Hull-House. We kept them there and fed them at noon, in return for which we were sometimes offered a hot penny which had been held in a tight little fist "ever since mother left this morning, to buy something to eat with." Out of kindergarten hours our little guests noisily enjoyed the hospitality of our bedrooms under the so-called care of any resident who volunteered to keep an eye on them, but later they were moved into a neighboring apartment under more systematic supervision.

Hull-House was thus committed to a day nursery which we sustained for sixteen years first in a little cottage on a side street and then in a building designed for its use called the Children's House. It is now carried on by the United Charities of Chicago in a finely equipped building on our block, where the immigrant mothers are cared for as well as the children, and where they are taught the things which will make life in America more possible. Our early day nursery brought us into natural relations with the poorest women of the neighborhood, many of whom were bearing the burden of dissolute and incompetent husbands in addition to the support of their children. Some of them presented an impressive manifestation of that miracle of affection which outlives abuse, neglect, and crime,—the affection which cannot be plucked from the heart where it has lived, although it may serve only to torture and torment. "Has your husband come back?" you inquire of Mrs. S., whom you have known for eight years as an overworked woman bringing her three delicate children every morning to the nursery; she is bent under the double burden of earning the money which supports them and giving them the tender care which alone keeps them alive. The oldest two children have at last gone to work, and Mrs. S. has allowed herself the luxury of staying at home two days a week. And now the worthless husband is back again—the "gentlemanly gambler" type who, through all vicissitudes, manages to present a white shirtfront and a gold watch to the world, but who is dissolute, idle and extravagant. You dread to think how much his presence will increase the drain upon the family exchequer, and you know that he stayed away until he was certain that the children were old enough to earn money for his luxuries. Mrs. S. does not pretend to take his return lightly, but she replies in all seriousness and simplicity, "You know my feeling for him has never changed. You may think me foolish, but I was always proud of his good looks and educated appearance. I was lonely and homesick during those eight years when the children were little and needed so much doctoring, but I could never bring myself to feel hard toward him, and I used to pray the good Lord to keep him from harm and bring him back to us; so, of course, I'm thankful now." She passes on with a dignity which gives one a new sense of the security of affection.

I recall a similar case of a woman who had supported her three children for five years, during which time her dissolute husband constantly demanded money for drink and kept her perpetually worried and intimidated. One Saturday, before the "blessed Easter," he came back from a long debauch, ragged and filthy, but in a state of lachrymose repentance. The poor wife received him as a returned prodigal, believed that his remorse would prove lasting, and felt sure that if she and the children went to church with him on Easter Sunday and he could be induced to take the pledge before the priest, all their troubles would be ended. After hours of vigorous effort and the expenditure of all her savings, he finally sat on the front doorstep the morning of Easter Sunday, bathed, shaved and arrayed in a fine new suit of clothes. She left him sitting there in the reluctant spring sunshine while she finished washing and dressing the children. When she finally opened the front door with the three shining children that they might all set forth together, the returned prodigal had disappeared, and was not seen again until midnight, when he came back in a glorious state of intoxication from the proceeds of his pawned clothes and clad once more in the dingiest attire. She took him in without comment, only to begin again the wretched cycle. There were of course instances of the criminal husband as well as of the merely vicious. I recall one woman who, during seven years, never missed a visiting day at the penitentiary when she might see her husband, and whose little children in the nursery proudly reported the messages from father with no notion that he was in disgrace, so absolutely did they reflect the gallant spirit of their mother. . . .

While one was filled with admiration for these heroic women, something was also to be said for some of the husbands, for the sorry men who, for one reason or another, had failed in the struggle of life. Sometimes this failure was purely economic and the men were competent to give the children, whom they were not able to support, the care and guidance and even education which were of the highest value. Only a few months ago I met upon the street one of the early nursery mothers who for five years had been living in another part of the city, and in response to my query as to the welfare of her five children, she bitterly replied, "All of them except Mary have been arrested at one time or another, thank you." In reply to my remark that I thought her husband had always had such admirable control over them, she burst out, "That has been the whole trouble. I got tired taking care of him and didn't believe that his laziness was all due to his health, as he said, so I left him and said that I would support the children, but not him. From that minute the trouble with the four boys began. I never knew what they were doing, and after every sort of a scrape I finally put Jack and the twins into institutions where I pay for them. Joe has gone to work at last, but with a disgraceful record behind him. I tell you I ain't so sure that because a woman can make big money that she can be both father and mother to her children."

As I walked on, I could but wonder in which particular we are most stupid—to judge a man's worth so solely by his wage-earning capacity that a good wife feels justified in leaving him, or in holding fast to that wretched delusion that a woman can both support and nurture her children.

One of the most piteous revelations of the futility of the latter attempt came to me through the mother of "Goosie," as the children for years called a little boy who, because he was brought to the nursery wrapped up in his mother's shawl, always had his hair filled with the down and small feathers from the feather brush factory where she worked. One March morning, Goosie's mother was hanging out the washing on a shed roof before she left for the factory. Five-year-old Goosie was trotting at her heels handing her clothespins, when he was suddenly blown off the roof by the high wind into the alley below. His neck was broken by the fall, and as he lay piteous and limp on a pile of frozen refuse, his mother cheerily called him to "climb up again," so confident do overworked mothers become that their children cannot get hurt. After the funeral, as the poor mother sat in the nursery postponing the moment when she must go back to her empty rooms, I asked her, in a futile effort to be of comfort, if there was anything more we could do for her. The overworked, sorrow-stricken woman looked up and replied, "If you could give me my wages for tomorrow, I would not go to work in the factory at all. I would like to stay at home all day and hold the baby. Goosie was always asking me to take him and I never had any time." This statement revealed the condition of many nursery mothers who are obliged to forego the joys and solaces which belong to even the most poverty-stricken. The long hours of factory labor necessary for earning the support of a child leave no time for the tender care and caressing which may enrich the life of the most piteous baby.

With all of the efforts made by modern society to nurture and educate the young, how stupid it is to permit the mothers of young children to spend themselves in the coarser work of the world! It is curiously inconsistent that with the emphasis which this generation has placed upon the mother and upon the prolongation of infancy, we constantly allow the waste of this most precious material. I cannot recall without indignation a recent experience. I was detained late one evening in an office building by a prolonged committee meeting of the Board of Education. As I came out at eleven o'clock, I met in the corridor of the fourteenth floor a woman whom I knew, on her knees scrubbing the marble tiling. As she straightened up to greet me, she seemed so wet from her feet up to her chin, that I hastily inquired the cause. Her reply was that she left home at five o'clock every night and had no opportunity for six hours to nurse her baby. Her mother's milk mingled with the very water with which she scrubbed the floors until she should return at midnight, heated and exhausted, to feed her screaming child with what remained within her breasts.

WOMEN'S EVOLUTION
FROM ECONOMIC DEPENDENCE

*Among women's rights advocates at the turn of the century, Charlotte
Perkins Gilman (1860–1935) stood out. Her thoroughgoing analysis of
women's economic dependence on men took her beyond reliance on the
vote as a remedy for women's inferior position. In numerous books, articles, stories, poems, and speeches beginning in the mid-1890s, she criti-
cized the "sexuo-economic" relation holding women in thrall to men and
expounded her view of the progressive evolution of society which would
require women to free themselves. Her book* Women and Economics
(1898) had an international impact.

Fortunately, the laws of social evolution do not wait for our recognition
or acceptance: they go straight on. And this greater and more important
change than the world has ever seen, this slow emergence of the long-
subverted human female to full racial equality, has been going on about
us full long enough to be observed. . . .

The change in education is in large part a cause of this, and progres-
sively a consequence. Day by day the bars go down. More and more the
field lies open for the mind of women to glean all it can, and it has
responded most eagerly. Not only our pupils, but our teachers, are mainly
women. And the clearness and strength of the brain of the woman prove
continually the injustice of the clamorous contempt long poured upon
what was scornfully called "the female mind." There is no female mind.
The brain is not an organ of sex. As well speak of a female liver.

Woman's progress in the arts and sciences, and trades and professions,
is steady; but it is most unwise to claim from these relative advances the
superiority of women to men, or even their equality, in these fields. What
is more to the purpose and easily to be shown is the superiority of the
women of to-day to those of earlier times, the immense new development
of racial qualities in the sex. . . .

No sociological change equal in importance to this clearly marked improvement of an entire sex has ever taken place in one century. Under it
all, the *crux* of the whole matter, goes on the one great change, that of
the economic relation. This follows perfectly natural lines. Just as the
development of machinery constantly lowers the importance of mere

Charlotte Perkins Gilman, *Women and Economics: A Study of the Economic Relations Between Men
and Women as a Factor in Social Evolution,* 6th ed. (Boston: Small Maynard and Co., 1913 [orig.
1898]), pp. 146, 149, 151–56, 210–11, 213, 215–16, 220, 223.

brute strength of body and raises that of mental power and skill, so the pressure of industrial conditions demands an ever-higher specialization, and tends to break up that relic of the patriarchal age,—the family as an economic unit.

Women have been led under pressure of necessity into a most reluctant entrance upon fields of economic activity. The sluggish and greedy disposition bred of long ages of dependence has by no means welcomed the change. Most women still work only as they "have to," until they can marry and "be supported." Men, too, liking the power that goes with money, and the poor quality of gratitude and affection bought with it, resent and oppose the change; but all this disturbs very little the course of social progress.

A truer spirit is the increasing desire of young girls to be independent, to have a career of their own, at least for a while, and the growing objection of countless wives to the pitiful asking for money, to the beggary of their position. . . .

For a while the introduction of machinery which took away from the home so many industries deprived woman of any importance as an economic factor; but presently she arose, and followed her lost wheel and loom to their new place, the mill. To-day there is hardly an industry in the land in which some women are not found. Everywhere throughout America are women workers outside the unpaid labor of the home, the last census giving three million of them. This is so patent a fact, and makes itself felt in so many ways by so many persons, that it is frequently and widely discussed. Without here going into its immediate advantages or disadvantages from an industrial point of view, it is merely instanced as an undeniable proof of the radical change in the economic position of women that is advancing upon us. She is assuming new relations from year to year before our eyes; but we, seeing all social facts from a personal point of view, have failed to appreciate the nature of the change.

Consider, too, the altered family relation which attends this movement. Entirely aside from the strained relation in marriage, the other branches of family life feel the strange new forces, and respond to them. "When I was a girl," sighs the gray-haired mother, "we sisters all sat and sewed while mother read to us. Now every one of my daughters has a different club!" She sighs, be it observed. We invariably object to changed conditions in those departments of life where we have established ethical values. For all the daughters to sew while the mother read aloud to them was esteemed right; and, therefore, the radiating diffusion of daughters among clubs is esteemed wrong,—a danger to home life. In the period of the common sewing and reading the women so assembled were closely

allied in industrial and intellectual development as well as in family relationship. They all could do the same work, and liked to do it. They all
could read the same book, and liked to read it. (And reading, half a
century ago, was still considered half a virtue and the other half a fine
art.) Hence the ease with which this group of women entered upon their
common work and common pleasure.

The growing individualization of democratic life brings inevitable
change to our daughters as well as to our sons. Girls do not all like to
sew, many do not know how. Now to sit sewing together, instead of being
a harmonizing process, would generate different degrees of restlessness,
of distaste, and of nervous irritation. And, as to the reading aloud, it is
not so easy now to choose a book that a well-educated family of modern
girls and their mother would all enjoy together. As the race become more
specialized, more differentiated, the simple lines of relation in family life
draw with less force, and the more complex lines of relation in social life
draw with more force; and this is a perfectly natural and desirable process
for women as well as for men.

It may be suggested, in passing, that one of the causes of "Americanitis"
is this increasing nervous strain in family relation, acting especially upon
woman. As she becomes more individualized, she suffers more from the
primitive and undifferentiated conditions of the family life of earlier
times. What "a wife" and "a mother" was supposed to find perfectly suitable, this newly specialized wife and mother, who is also a personality,
finds clumsy and ill-fitting,—a mitten where she wants a glove. The home
cares and industries, still undeveloped, give no play for her increasing
specialization. Where the embryonic combination of cook-nurse-laun-
dress-chambermaid-housekeeper-waitress-governess was content to be
"jack of all trades" and mistress of none, the woman who is able to be
one of these things perfectly, and by so much less able to be all the others,
suffers doubly from not being able to do what she wants to do, and from
being forced to do what she does not want to do. To the delicately differentiated modern brain the jar and shock of changing from trade to trade
a dozen times a day is a distinct injury, a waste of nervous force. With
the larger socialization of the woman of to-day, the fitness for and accom-
panying desire for wider combinations, more general interest, more organized methods of work for larger ends, she feels more and more heavily
the intensely personal limits of the more primitive home duties, interests,
methods. And this pain and strain must increase with the advance of
women until the new functional power makes to itself organic expression, and the belated home industries are elevated and organized, like the
other necessary labors of modern life. . . .

Is our present method of home life, based on the economic dependence of woman in the sex-relation, the best calculated to maintain the individual in health and happiness, and develope in him the higher social faculties? The individual is not maintained in health and happiness,—that is visible to all; and how little he is developed in social relation is shown in the jarring irregularity and wastefulness of our present economic system.

Economic independence for women necessarily involves a change in the home and family relation. But, if that change is for the advantage of individual and race, we need not fear it. It does not involve a change in the marriage relation except in withdrawing the element of economic dependence, nor in the relation of mother to child save to improve it. But it does involve the exercise of human faculty in women, in social service and exchange rather than in domestic service solely. This will of course require the introduction of some other form of living than that which now obtains. It will render impossible the present method of feeding the world by means of millions of private servants, and bringing up children by the same hand.

It is a melancholy fact that the vast majority of our children are reared and trained by domestic servants,—generally their mothers, to be sure, but domestic servants by trade. To become a producer, a factor in the economic activities of the world, must perforce interfere with woman's present status as a private servant. House mistress she may still be, in the sense of owning and ordering her home, but housekeeper or house-servant she may not be—and be anything else. Her position as mother will alter, too. Mother in the sense of bearer and rearer of noble children she will be, as the closest and dearest, the one most honored and best loved; but mother in the sense of exclusive individual nursery-maid and nursery-governess she may not be—and be anything else. . . .

Marriage and "the family" are two institutions, not one, as is commonly supposed. We confuse the natural result of marriage in children, common to all forms of sex-union, with the family,—a purely social phenomenon. Marriage is a form of sex-union recognized and sanctioned by society. It is a relation between two or more persons, according to the custom of the country, and involves mutual obligations. Although made by us an economic relation, it is not essentially so, and will exist in much higher fulfilment after the economic phase is outgrown.

The family is a social group, an entity, a little state. It holds an important place in the evolution of society quite aside from its connection with marriage. There was a time when the family was the highest form of social relation,—when to the minds of pastoral, patriarchal tribes there was no conception so large as "my country," no State, no nation. . . .

The family is a decreasing survival of the earliest grouping known to man. Marriage is an increasing development of high social life, not fully evolved. So far from being identical with the family, it improves and strengthens in inverse ratio to the family. . . .

Marriage has risen and developed in social importance as the family has sunk and decreased. . . . Marriage is not perfect unless it is between class equals. There is no equality in class between those who do their share in the world's work in the largest, newest, highest ways and those who do theirs in the smallest, oldest, lowest ways.

Granting squarely that it is the business of women to make the home life of the world true, healthful, and beautiful, the economically dependent woman does not do this, and never can. The economically independent woman can and will. . . . A noble home life is the product of a noble social life. The home does not produce the virtues needed in society. But society does produce the virtues needed in such homes as we desire today. The members of the freest, most highly civilized and individualized nations, make the most delightful members of the home and family. The members of the closest and most highly venerated homes do not necessarily make the most delightful members of society.

PART VIII

NEW WOMEN,
NEW WORLDS

FRANCES WILLARD HERALDS
"THE DAWN OF WOMAN'S DAY"

As president of the Woman's Christian Temperance Union (WCTU) from 1879 to 1898, Frances Willard (1839–1898) built a powerful organization dedicated to reforming society according to the values of Protestant women. Under her leadership, the WCTU advocated prohibition, woman suffrage, social purity, peace, and arbitration, as well as a host of social and political reforms. Willard summarized her vision of women's political and moral role in this 1888 address to the Chicago Woman's League, which she also served as president.

Mother-love works magic for humanity, but organized mother-love works miracles. Mother-hearted women are called to be the saviors of the race. I speak it reverently, as a loyal worshiper of Him who said, "Mother, behold thy Son."

We all know that organization is the one great thought of Nature. It is the difference between chaos and order; it is the incessant occupation of God. But, next to God, the greatest organizer on this earth is the mother. She who sends forth from the sanctuary of her own being a little child has organized a great spiritual world, and set it moving in the orbit of unchanging law. Hence woman, by her organism, is the greatest organizer ever organized by our beneficent Creator.

But, in the nature of the case, the mother, patiently preoccupied in deeds of love for those about her, has been slowest of all to reflect on her own innate powers and has not until recently so much as dreamed of the resistless force of the world's aggregated motherhood. When I was graduated from college in 1859 there was not on the face of the earth, I venture to say,—certainly there was not in my native land, the most progressive land of all,—a national society of women. We worked on in weakness and seclusion, in loneliness and isolation. But we learned at last the gracious secret that has transformed the world for men and made them masters. We learned the mighty difference between the wide, open hand with individual fingers impotent because separate, and the condensed, constructive, organized power of those fingers when combined. We learned that floating timbers on the sea are not more futile as compared with the same timbers when organized into a ship than are solitary

Frances Willard, "The Dawn of Woman's Day," *Our Day: A Record and Review of Current Reform* 2, no. 11 (November 1888), pp. 345–60. The editors are grateful to Carolyn De Swarte Gifford for locating and providing a copy of this document.

human beings as compared with the same persons when organized and instructed, unified and equipped in societies and guilds. The mighty work done to mitigate the horrors of our Civil War first revealed to us and to our brothers the latent power of the nation's womanhood; next came the holy zeal of the Women's Foreign Missionary Societies; then the heavenly enthusiasm of the Woman's Temperance Crusade, with its marvelous sequel, the Woman's Christian Temperance Unions; then the beautiful younger sister, the Woman's Home Missionary Society, while the Women's Christian Association and Congress, the women's clubs, the industrial and educational unions, relief corps, protective agency, the mighty labor movement, and the countless societies for local help to the sick, the friendless, and the poor abundantly testify to that *esprit de corps* which we women have at last acquired and are now so sure to utilize for purposes of blessings vastly wider, more pervasive, and more varied than we could at first have dared to undertake or dreamed of compassing.

From this time on the world will have in it no active, organic force so strong for its uplifting as its organized mother-hearts. You will notice the breadth of my generalization. I do not say "all mothers," because all women who are technically mothers are not "mother-hearted," while many a woman is so, from whom the criss-cross currents of the world have withheld her holiest crown. . . .

It has required more than a generation of training within the sheltering circle of a church, where most of us have had our schooling in organized endeavor, to prepare us for so large a thought as was launched at Washington, D.C., last spring in the International Council. . . .

It is the unanimous voice of this council that all institutions of learning, and of professional instruction, including schools of theology, law, and medicine, should, in the interest of humanity, be as freely opened to women as to men; that opportunities for industrial training should be as generally and liberally provided for one sex as for the other. The representatives of organized womanhood in this council will steadily demand that in all avocations in which both men and women engage equal wages shall be paid for equal work; and, finally, that an enlightened society should adopt, as the only adequate expression of the high civilization which is its office to establish and maintain, an identical standard of personal purity and morality for men and women.

The general declaration of the National Council of the United States as well as of the World's Council was as follows:—

We women, sincerely believing that the best good of our homes and nation will be advanced by our own greater unity of thought, sympathy, and purpose, and that an organized movement of women will best conserve the highest good of the family and the state, do hereby band ourselves together in a confederation of workers committed to the overthrow of all forms of ignorance and injustice and to the application of the Golden Rule to society, custom, and law. This council is organized in the interest of no one propaganda, and has no power over its auxiliaries beyond that of suggestion and sympathy; therefore no society voting to become auxiliary to this council shall thereby render itself liable to be interfered with in respect to its complete organic unity, independence, and methods of work, or be committed to any principle or method of any other society, or to any utterance or act of the council itself, beyond compliance with the terms of this constitution.

No sooner was this new thought launched on the seething waves of journalism than good women everywhere began to say to one another: "If unification is strength in the national movements of women, why not in the States, and why not in each city, town, and village? If, as the 'Council Women' said in their preamble, such an organization 'will incalculably increase the world's sum total of womanly courage, efficiency, and *esprit de corps,* widen our horizon, correct the tendency to an exaggerated impression of the value of one's own work as compared with that of others, and put the wisdom and experience of each at the service of all,' then let us all have councils, local and state, and let us have them speedily."

Here in Chicago seventy societies have already responded to the call and fifty-seven have allied themselves with the new movement. In Kansas a state woman's council was organized, as I suppose, this week, and another will be in Ohio the 11th of this month. I have never known a movement among women so enthusiastic and spontaneous. The time for it has fully come; the clock of God has struck the hour, and the best manhood of the manliest nation reaches out a brother's hand of help to us as we move forward bearing woman's white flag of peace, inscribed, "For Home and for Humanity."

This is the latest outgrowth of that gospel which raises woman up and with her lifts toward Heaven the world.

Let us think for a little while about the results to be expected from this movement. Naturally they will be twofold: First, the reflex influence of such association upon the members themselves. For instance: Here is a woman devoted to self-culture. She learns, not to put aside her Plato, but to alternate its study with that of Helen Campbell's "Prisoners of Poverty" and to divide her time at the art gallery with her visits to the white slaves.

Here is a woman who is so devoted to the Waifs' Mission that she takes no time for books. Her association with the self-culturist leads her to ask for "Emerson's Essays" at the Public Library, and perhaps to advance so far beyond her former horizon as to join a Robert Browning club. Here is a home missionary woman devoted to the Bohemians, not of journalism, but of Pilsen on the *Nord Seit*. She is assigned to duty with a foreign missionary woman, and from association with her discovers that electricity and steel have shrunk the world till it is hardly bigger than an orange, that the Bohemian beyond the sea needs looking after just as badly as his brother on this side, while the zenanas of India and the Congo atrocities in Africa become so vivid in recital as to seem knocking for relief at her door. Meanwhile the foreign missionary woman at her side makes the useful discovery that the telescope of observation by which she was wont to bring the distant near can be adjusted as a microscope, magnifying to her perceptions the tenement-house horrors of her own city. Here is a temperance woman who solemnly believed prohibition was the be-all of the republic's hopes and the end-all of its sorrows; but the Knight of Labor woman at her elbow convinced her that economic conditions enter into that colossal problem and prevailed on her to read Edward Bellamy's wonderful book, entitled "Looking Backward," while the working woman graciously accepted in return a copy of the platform of the Prohibition party, which appeared to be quite edifying reading. Here again is a Republican woman placed alongside a Democratic woman, and as true yoke-fellows they go on a legal embassy from the Woman's to the City Council, and whatever their opinion of their respective parties may be, from what they there perceive, they will be pretty sure to gain from one another a more hopeful view of those two great marching armies of civilization, whose guns are ballots and whose bullets are ideas.

Here is a Protestant woman who thinks there is no good in Catholics, never was, and never will be, but she is placed on the Public Library Committee with a communicant of the Cathedral, and finds her "so much like other folks" that she would really have supposed her to be a devout Presbyterian, while the Catholic sister comes into kindly fellowship with her Baptist committeewoman, and will never again believe but that Protestants are really reputable people and quite likely to be saved.

Thus in a thousand ways the blessed education into a tolerant spirit goes swiftly on; the cobwebs of ignorance are brushed away; the rusty chains of prejudice are filed in two, and sectarianism is replaced by sisterly love; meanwhile the horizon of the heart is widened because the outlook of the brain is elevated, and into the lonesome little coves, inlets, and bays flow the strong, healthful tides of life's cosmopolitan sea.

But this is only the beginning. These women in council will not be theorists—they will be above all else practitioners in that word's widest sense. They will have no use for any philosophy of life that cannot be translated in terms of good works as well as of good will. Their deeds will all be "deeds of weekday holiness, nor will they ever chance to learn that aught is easier than to bless." In the wide realm of human misery they will have one guiding star and that is JUSTICE. Wherever there is a sister more down-trodden than any other, more helpless and forgotten, there by the law of spiritual gravitation they will delight to invest the weight of their power and the momentum of their united enthusiasm. . . .

Society and government are two circles which interplay like rainbows round a fountain, and that fountain is the home. Women in league or council will bring their united power to bear wherever in the operation of an unjust law, whether it be of custom or of legislation, any woman is defrauded of her right. Let us picture them in action: The Municipal Council is in session; but the Board of Directors of the Woman's Council is in session also; it represents not some single, isolated, and comparatively uninfluential society, but the united forces of Chicago's organized womanhood. We want an ordinance giving better protection to shop and factory girls; providing more carefully for their physical health, comfort, and convenience, guarding them so far as possible from moral disaster and disease. Through our office secretary we have sent out petitions to every woman's society in the city asking for this ordinance and pledging its enforcement by means of women inspectors from our own number who will serve without fee or reward. The petitions come back signed by tens of thousands. All reputable employers are with us in this effort, and the wage-workers of the city are well pleased to have our help, hence the voting majority that makes and unmakes city councils is on our side.

Thus panoplied with the power of organization of numbers or a majority among the voters, and, best of all, pleading a cause that tends toward human brotherhood, the Women's Council goes before the City Council and wins the day. But without the law-enforcer back of the law, it is like a rusty sword in a still more rusty scabbard. Already the working-girls of Chicago have much more law upon their side than is utilized for their defense. But there has been no eye to pity, and no hand to save. Now you are here, the women whose opulent and forceful lives have been from a thousand springs of opportunity and blessing; you are here with the arrest of thought in your brains and the enthusiasm of humanity in your hearts; let us bring the solid weight and total momentum of Chicago's organized womanhood to bear upon the problem of a better and a happier life for working-girls. For one I promise, overwhelmed with cares and duties as I am, to give one afternoon in the week as an inspector to see that the laws we have and mean to get for these women are carried into execution. Nor do I see anything generous about the offer. It will help me as much as it can possibly help those to whom I minister. . . . And we, going straight to those who need our help, shall learn a thousand ways of helping that we do not yet dream of now, while the public sentiment we can arouse and educate will wonderfully hasten the better day. We must be willing to go forward upon this untried pathway just a step at a time. The whole question of tenement-house misery will open before us, and we shall yet find remedies; the unutterable problem of Chicago's haunts of infamy will be understood and studied as it has not been before; the right of working women to one day in seven for rest; the people's right to outlaw the liquor saloon as well as the gambling saloon—these and cognate forms of philanthropy will claim our courage and devotion.

Think for a moment of all this upon a larger scale. When each village, town, and city of our State shall have its league or council of good women, they can do for their localities what we hope to do for ours. . . . A law for the better protection of women; for raising the age of consent; for the teaching of hygiene in all grades of the public schools, with especial reference to stimulants and narcotics; for compulsory education; also for appropriations in aid of the industrial school for girls and other institutions to which our philanthropic women are devoted—we must together strive for these.

Locally, a Woman's League should, in the interest of that mothering which is the central idea of our new movement, seek to secure for women admission to all school committees, library associations, and boards intrusted with the care of the defective, dependent, and delinquent classes; all professional and business associations; all colleges and professional schools that have not yet set before us an open door of ingress: and each local league should have the power to call in the united influence of its own state league or of the National Council if its own influence did not suffice.

In the development of this movement I am confident that it will impart to women such a sense of strength and courage that their corporate self-respect will so increase that such theatrical bills as we now see displayed will not be permitted for an hour without our potent protest; and the exhibition of women's forms and faces in the saloons and cigar stores, which women's self-respect will never let them enter, and the disgraceful literature now for sale on so many public newsstands, will not be tolerated by the womanhood of any town or city. . . .

Dear friend, you know the story of Androcles and the lion; how the poor animal came limping out of the forest, knowing the gentleness of Androcles and unable longer to endure the pain of the sharp thorn it carried. To me that lion is a figure of humanity in its rough strength and staggering misery as it turns toward mother-hearted women for relief. I wish that we might have as a seal and emblem of our society the picture of a woman healing a lion's hurt. You know, as the sequel of the story, that when, long afterward, Androcles was condemned to fight with a lion in the arena, it proved to be his former friend who received him with every demonstration of tenderness and loyalty.

Let us work on with the HUMAN rather than the WOMAN question as our deepest motive, and in the individual no less than the collective struggle of our lives we shall discover friends where foes were feared.

MARY CHURCH TERRELL GREETS THE NATIONAL CONGRESS OF MOTHERS

Elected first president of the National Association of Colored Women in 1896, Mary Church Terrell (1863–1954) was one of the most distinguished African American leaders of her era. When she delivered this message to the National Congress of Mothers (whose members were mainly white women), Terrell had borne four children, three of whom died within a few days of birth. She attributed their deaths to the inferior medical care they received in a segregated hospital in Washington, D.C.

The National Association of Colored Women felicitates the National Congress of Mothers upon the success it has already achieved, upon the good it has already accomplished, and expresses through me the hope that its past is an earnest of its future. The Association which I represent is the only national organization which colored women have. We therefore feel that a great responsibility is resting upon us, and are putting forth every possible effort to discharge our duty worthily. Into the homes of our people we go preaching he gospel of cleanliness, and morality, cultivation of the mind and the dignity of labor. We feel keenly the need of an enlightened motherhood and make Mothers' meetings a special feature of our work. We know that as the present generation of children are guided aright or are misguided, so will the next generation of men and women stand or fall in their duty to their country, to their race and to themselves. We believe in the saving grace of the kindergarten and are bending all our energies toward establishing as many as possible. Classes in domestic science are formed by some of our clubs and they are getting good results.

We teach our children to be honest and industrious, to cultivate their minds, to become skilled workmen, to be energetic and then to be hopeful. It is easy enough to impress upon them the necessity of being honest and industrious, of cultivating their minds and becoming skilled workmen but did it ever occur to you, Mothers of the Congress how difficult a thing it is for colored women to inspire their children with hope or offer them an incentive for their best endeavor under the existing conditions of things in this country?

As the mother of the dominant race looks into the innocent face of her babe, her heart thrills not only with happiness in the present, but also with joyful anticipation of the future. For well she knows that honor,

Mary Church Terrell, "Greetings from the National Association of Colored Women," *National Association Notes* 2 (March 1899), p. 1.

wealth, fame and greatness in any vocation he may choose, are all his, if he but possess the ability and determination to secure them. She knows that if it is in him to be great, all the exterior circumstances which can help him to the goal of his ambition, the laws of his country, public opinion of his countrymen and manifold opportunities are his without the making—From his birth he is a King in his own right and is no suppliant for justice. Contrast, if you will, the feelings of hope and joy which thrill the heart of the white mothers with those which stir the soul of her colored sister. Put yourselves for one minute in her place, (you could not endure the strain longer) and imagine, if you can, how you would feel if situated similarly—As a mother of the weaker race clasps to her bosom the babe which she loves as fondly as you do yours, her heart cannot thrill with joyful anticipations of the future. For before her child she sees the thorny path of prejudice and proscription which his little feet must tread—She knows that no matter how great his ability, or how lofty his ambition, there are comparatively few avocations in which any one of his race may hope to succeed—She knows that no matter how skilful his hand, how honest his heart, or how great his need, trade unions will close their doors in his face and make his struggle for existence desperate indeed—So rough does the way of her infant appear to many a poor black mother that instead of thrilling with the joy which you feel, as you clasp your little ones to your breast, she trembles with apprehension and despair—

This picture, Mothers of the Congress, is not overdrawn, and a moment's reflection upon the subject, which I have touched so lightly will enable you to supply much that I have been obliged to omit. May I not ask you then, that when you teach your children the lofty principles which this Congress represents, you will make a special effort to train them to be just and broad enough to judge men and women by their intrinsic merit, rather than by the adventitious circumstances of race, or color or creed? You will teach them, I am sure, that when they grow to be men and women, if they deliberately prevent their fellow creatures from earning an honest living, by closing the doors of trade against them, and shutting them out of employment, that the Father of all men will hold them responsible for the crimes which are the result of their injustice and for the human wrecks which the ruthless crushing of hope and ambition always makes.

In the name of the children of my race, Mothers of the National Congress, I come, asking you to do all in your power by word and deed to give them the opportunities which you desire for your own. In the name of justice and humanity, in the name of the helplessness and innocence of childhood, black childhood as well as white childhood, I ask you to do all in your power, both by precept and example, to make the future of the children of my race as bright and as promising as should be that of every child born on this American soil.

To you I come as to the court of last appeal. It is the women of the country who mould public opinion. And when they say that trades and avocations shall not be closed against men and women on account of race or color, then the day of prejudice and proscription will darken dawn no more.

CATHOLICS DEBATE THE WOMAN QUESTION

In 1893 a Congress of Catholic Women was held as part of the World's Columbian Exhibition in Chicago. The Catholic World brought its fruits to readers by publishing a "roundtable conference," which included the two papers reprinted here. The congress resulted in the founding of the Catholic Women's League, with Alice Timmons Toomy as its president. Katherine Conway, the author of the second paper—a defense of the traditional vocations of marriage and monasticism for Catholic women—was herself a successful writer, journalist, and editor who lived as a single professional woman all her life.

THERE IS A PUBLIC SPHERE FOR CATHOLIC WOMEN.

Alice Timmons Toomy.

The Catholic Women's Congress held in Chicago, May 18, gave an outline sketch of the work of Catholic women, beginning with a paper on "The Elevation of Womanhood through the Veneration of the Blessed Virgin;" and closing with the life-work of Margaret Haughery, of New Orleans, the only woman in America to whom the public have raised a statue.

The enthusiasm awakened by this congress drew a large body of Catholic women together, who organized a National League for work on the lines of education, philanthropy, and "the home and its needs"— education to promote the spread of Catholic truth and reading circles, etc.; philanthropy to include temperance, the formation of day nurseries and free kindergartens, protective and employment agencies for women, and clubs and homes for working-girls; the "home and its needs" to comprehend the solution of the domestic service question, as well as plans to unite the interests and tastes of the different members of the family. Each active member of the league registers under some one branch of work according to her special attraction. The underlying idea of the league is that Catholic women realize that there is a duty devolving on them to help the needy on lines which our religious cannot reach, even were they not already so sadly overworked. Tens of thousands of our ablest Catholic women are working with the W.C.T.U. and other non-Catholic philanthropies, because they find no organization in their own church as a field for their activities. Every Catholic woman who has had much association

"The Woman Question Among Catholics: A Roundtable Conference," *Catholic World* 57 (1893), pp. 674–77, 681–84.

outside the church is frequently met with the question, Why don't you Catholics take care of your own poor, and not leave so much work for other churches to do for you? The truth is that ours is the church of the poor, and manifold as is the charity work of the religious and the benevolent societies, a vast amount has to go undone because there is no one to attend to it. It seems safe to compute that fully one-half our church members are among the needy, one-tenth of our members are wealthy, and the remaining forty per cent. are well to do. The occupations of the very wealthy seem so all-engrossing that the care of the needy seems to fall naturally on the well-to-do, who are happily not so far removed from the poor in condition as to be insensible to their wants. Mankind has repeated the "Our Father" for well-nigh two thousand years, and yet the great body of humanity seems only now waking up to the fact that "*our* Father" implies a common brotherhood; that "no man liveth to himself alone"; that we are our brothers' keepers. Surely then, in the face of these great facts, it can only be through misapprehension of terms that the question is asked "Is there a public sphere for Catholic women?" As well ask "Is there a public sphere for the religious?" since who is so public as the man or woman who gives his whole life, with all its powers, for the good of humanity? It cannot be that the estimate of the Catholic woman is so poor that it is supposed that her love of home, her sense of duty and womanly instincts will suffer by her taking counsel with a body of women for a few hours every week as to the best methods of improving the condition of her fellow-women? Catholic women enter into the gaieties, and even the follies, of society. Many lose more money and time for dress and fashion than would be consumed by works of philanthropy. Yet no alarm seems to be taken as to the danger to womanliness in this sphere! . . .

However wise or pious a woman may be, she meets with daily problems for which no literature offers solution, but from which the light of other women's experience may clear away the difficulty. The great power of the age is organization, and nowhere is it more needed than among Catholic women, whose consciences and hearts are so keenly alive to evils that individuals find themselves powerless to overcome. The proof that the Catholic Women's League is needed is shown by the daily applications for affiliation, and for an organizer to go to other cities and establish branches.

Miss Eliza Allen Starr, ever zealous in good works, writes of the "Catholic Women's National League": "This compassionate work, to which woman seems called by her very nature, if left to individuals is likely to be desultory; its continuity depending upon family and personal circumstances; whereas an organization takes the work along through summer and winter, sickness and health, convenience and inconvenience, the one who has dropped out of line under some pressure of necessity takes up work again, with a feeling of gratitude that all has been going on well in spite of her shortcomings. Our educational charities providing Catholic instruction for our veriest little ones, by taking them from under the feet of laboring mothers in their small rooms and giving them an intelligent use of their hands, so as to prepare them for industrial occupations in every grade for which they may prove to have a capacity—these free kindergartens become nurseries for good mechanics and citizens, for skilled needle-women of all kinds, with whom a taste for beautiful forms and harmonious colors may be a fortune; in every case raising the grade of labor by the superior intelligence with which it is pursued. The mercifulness of these day nurseries is only appreciated by those who realize what it is for a poor mother to leave her unweaned babe all day in the care of her other mere infants, in order to eke out the father's wages in behalf of their increasing family. The day nursery takes care of her baby; the kindergarten gives occupation to her restless boys and girls; and after a hard day's work she returns with a heart and step lightened by finding her children fresher and sweeter for the kindly influences around them all day." Then, again, providing homes for Catholic self-supporting girls has immense importance. In the midst of a life necessarily cut loose from family and friends, this home preserves a Catholic atmosphere—Catholic habits and traditions, establishing a standard of Catholic opinion on all matters instead of a worldly one. One word for our name, "National League." Thus named because we live under the rule of a league of grand States, and under such rule hand should touch hand, shoulder touch shoulder, from Maine to Louisiana, from the Atlantic to the Pacific; thus adding to the natural force of individual activity a momentum which will be equal, we trust, to the ever-increasing demands upon our sympathies; while upon occasion we shall be found to possess a standing army ready to throw itself into the work suggested by any emergency. Volumes might be written to show the true relation of Catholic women to humanity; but surely enough has been said to answer the question, "Is there a Public Sphere for Catholic Women?"

WOMAN HAS NO VOCATION TO PUBLIC LIFE.

Katherine E. Conway.

To the writer it seems settled beyond question that woman, as woman, can have no vocation to public life. Vocation implies a need to be filled, and full competence to fill it on the part of the one called. Woman, being after man and from man, does not represent humanity in the full and complete sense that man does. It cannot be necessary, nor even useful, that she should try to do what she cannot do. . . .

The vocation of the overwhelming majority of women is to wifehood and motherhood; and their bodily and mental sensitiveness and timidity, and the fixed aversion, or at least indifference, of most of them to public work, are safeguards raised by God's own hand about the sanctuary of life.

We Catholics recognize for women another and higher vocation, to which but a small number are called. But the instinct against publicity, so strong in the woman of the home, is intensified in the woman of the convent. Natural love moves the normal woman to self-sacrifice, almost to self-effacement. She is proud to surrender her name, to merge her identity in that of her husband. Supernatural love acts on the lines of nature and the nun gladly sinks her individuality in her order, her membership in which is the sign of her special and exclusive union with the Divine.

The territory between the home and the convent is small, and the Catholic women within it are ordinarily there in the fulfilment of some very evident filial or sisterly duty—another manifestation, indeed, of the sacrificial spirit of normal Christian womanhood.

But, it is at once objected, women have filled and do fill certain public places with credit, and the Catholic Church herself in the persons of such women—to quote from best-known examples—as Catherine of Siena, and Joan of Arc, and Isabella of Castile, has furnished the strongest possible arguments to the modern American pleaders for the free admission of women into public life.

The writer realizes the force of these examples as fully as do the most ardent advocates of "the emancipation of women"; but they bear for her in a different direction.

While believing that woman, as woman, has no public sphere, she believes also that the woman as an intelligence, a rational creature, responsible for her own deeds and free to choose her own state of life, may be or do what she can; and that some women by virtue, not of their womanhood, but of their strong individualities, marked ability, and the demands of unusual environment, may have a special call to some public duty.

But these things having been at all times granted by the Catholic Church, one marvels to hear the "woman question" raised among Catholic women. What doors, indeed, has she closed on intelligence and ability as manifested by women but the doors of the sanctuary and the pulpit? and here the ecclesiastical law but emphasizes the Divine law against women as priests and preachers. Women may have free scope in philosophy and theology, law, medicine, letters, the liberal arts, the trades and industries, as students and teachers; their own ability and opportunity alone determining their limitations. When Novella d'Andrea was teacher of canon law, and Maria Agnesi professor of mathematics, and other women professors of anatomy and Greek in the Papal University of Bologna—to say nothing of women students in the same institution— there was very slight esteem for women as souls or intelligences either in old England or New England.

The state, not the church, has ruled on the question of women in government and politics.

With this liberal attitude on the part of the church, the Catholic woman in public life has still remained the exception. Catholic women have still, as a rule, made early marriages and been the joyful mothers of many children; or have followed an early vocation to the cloister. Their intellectual force has ordinarily been expended in the training of their own children; or, in the nun's case, in the training of the future congenial wives of intelligent men. . . .

The indifference of Catholic women of every grade of intelligence and education to woman suffrage, and the disinclination of the most of them to identify themselves with the public work of organized women in its recent manifestations of "Woman's Congresses," "Woman's Days," etc., furnish a strong argument against women in public life. For the Catholic woman is the normal woman.

But what of the effect of the higher education of woman? The notion that it will materially affect the situation seems to be based on the false assumption that it is a movement apart. Said the scholarly Bishop of Peoria, the Right Rev. John Lancaster Spalding: "The higher education of the priest is the highest education of man." May we not further say: the higher education of man involves also the higher education of woman?

This higher education—we use the word education in its fullest sense—will produce not a more abundant yield of women publicists; but of noble, intelligent, and virtuous women for the home and social life.

In all this "woman question" the partisans of alleged progress seem to forget one foundation fact: that, as between men and women, it is not so much a question of greater or less, or better or worse, as a question of different.

Neither are they satisfied to let the exceptional remain "the index of the possible." They want to make it the index of the ordinary.

~

MARY LEASE, PROPHET OF THE FARMERS' ALLIANCE

Reflecting their position on the family farm, women played a significant role in the agrarian protest movement of the 1880s and 1890s. Whole families participated in the social activities of the Farmers' Alliance, and women may have made up as much as one-quarter of Alliance membership. Many Populists endorsed temperance and woman suffrage. Women's influence declined, however, as Populist strategy evolved from an emphasis on social and economic cooperatives to the creation of a third political party, calling for government ownership of railroads and banks, a graduated income tax, and "free silver." One of the Populist movement's most charismatic orators was Mary E. Lease, best known today for her remark that farmers should raise "less corn and more hell." She delivered the following speech in 1891 to the national convention of the Woman's Christian Temperance Union.

MADAME PRESIDENT AND FELLOW-CITIZENS:—If God were to give me my choice to live in any age of the world that has flown, or in any age of the world yet to be. I would say, O God, let me live here and now, in this day and age of the world's history. For we are living in a grand and wonderful time—a time when old ideas, traditions and customs have broken loose from their moorings and are hopelessly adrift on the great shoreless, boundless sea of human thought—a time when the gray old world begins to dimly comprehend that there is no difference between the brain of an intelligent woman and the brain of an intelligent man; no difference between the soul-power or brain-power that nerved the arm of Charlotte Corday to deeds of heroic patriotism and the soul-power or brain-power that swayed old John Brown behind his death dealing barricade at Ossawattomie. We are living in an age of thought. The mighty dynamite of thought is upheaving the social and political structure and stirring the hearts of men from centre to circumference. Men, women and children are in commotion, discussing the mighty problems of the day. The agricultural classes, loyal and patriotic, slow to act and slow to think, are to day thinking for themselves; and their thought has crystallized into action. Organization is the key note to a mighty movement among the masses which is the protest of the patient burden-bearers of the nation against years of economic and political superstition.

"Mrs. Mary Elizabeth Lease: The Kansas Prophet of the Farmers' Alliance . . . The Exact Text of her Famous Washington Speech . . . ," *Journal of the Knights of Labor,* April 2, 1891. The editors are indebted to Michael Goldberg for locating and providing a copy of this document.

The mightiest movement the world has known in two thousand years, which is sending out the gladdest message to oppressed humanity that the world has heard since John the Baptist came preaching in the wilderness that the world's Redeemer was coming to relieve the world's misery. We witness to-day the most stupendous and wonderful uprising of the common people that the world has known since Peter the Hermit led the armies of the East to battle against the Saracens in the Holy Land.

The movement among the masses to-day is an echo of the life of Jesus of Nazareth, an honest endeavor on the part of the people to put into practical operation the basic principles of Christianity: "Whatsoever ye would that men should do unto you, do ye even so unto them."

In an organization founded upon the eternal principles of truth and right, based upon the broad and philanthropic principle, "Injury to one is the concern of all," having for its motto, "Exact justice to all, special privileges to none,"—the farmers and laborers could not well exclude their mothers, wives and daughters, the patient burden-bearers of the home, who had been their faithful companions, their tried friends and trusted counselors through long, weary years of poverty and toil. Hence the doors of the Farmers' Alliance were thrown open wide to the women of the land. They were invited into full membership, with all the privileges of promotion; actually recognized and treated as human beings. And not only the mothers, wives and daughters, but "the sisters, the cousins and the aunts," availed themselves of their newly-offered liberties, till we find at the present time upward of a half-million women in the Alliance, who, because of their loyalty to home and loved ones and their intuitive and inherent sense of justice, are investigating the condition of the country, studying the great social, economic and political problems, fully realizing that the political arena is the only place where the mighty problems of to-day and to-morrow can be satisfactorily fought and settled, and amply qualified to go hand-in-hand with fathers, husbands, sons and brothers to the polls and register their opinion against legalized robbery and corporate wrong.

George Eliot tells us that "much that we are and have is due to the unhistoric acts of those who in life were ungarlanded and in death sleep in unvisited tombs." So to the women of the Alliance, who bravely trudged twice a week to the bleak country school-house, literally burning midnight oil as they studied with their loved ones the economic and political problems, and helped them devise methods by which the shackles of industrial slavery might be broken, and the authors of the nation's liberties, the creators of the nation's wealth and greatness, might be made free and prosperous—to these women, unknown and uncrowned, belongs the honor of defeating for re-election to the United States Senate that man who for eighteen years has signally failed to represent his constituents, and who during that time has never once identified himself with any legislation for the oppressed and overburdened people.

Three years ago this man Ingalls made a speech on woman suffrage at Abilene, Kan., in which he took occasion to speak in the most ignorant and vicious manner of women, declaring that "a woman could not and should not vote because she was a woman." Why? She was a woman, and that was enough; the subject was too delicate for further discussion.

But we treasured up these things in our hearts, and then his famous, or, rather, infamous, interview in a New York paper appeared, in which he declared that: "It is lawful to hire Hessians to kill, to mutilate, to destroy. Success is the object to be attained; the decalogue and the golden rule have no place in a political campaign; the world has outgrown its Christ and needs a new one." This man said the law-abiding, God-fearing women must no longer be permitted to misrepresent us. So we worked and waited for his defeat. And the cyclone, the political Johnstown, that overtook the enemies of the people's rights last November, proves what a mighty factor the women of the Alliance have been in the political affairs of the nation.

I overheard yesterday morning at the hotel breakfast table a conversation between two gentlemen in regard to Ingalls. "I consider his defeat," said the first speaker, "to be a national calamity." "Your reasons," said the second. "Why, he is such a brilliantly smart man," he replied. "True," said the other; "but he must needs be a smart man to be the consummate rascal he has proven himself to be." And I thought as I heard the remarks, "Our opinion is also shared by men." You wonder, perhaps, at the zeal and enthusiasm of the Western women in this reform movement. Let me tell you why they are interested. Turn to your old school-maps and books of a quarter of a century ago, and you will find that what is now the teeming and fruitful West was then known as the Treeless Plain, the Great American Desert. To this sterile and remote region, infested by savage beasts and still more savage men, the women of the New England States, the women of the cultured East, came with husbands, sons and brothers to help them build up a home upon the broad and vernal prairies of the West. We came with the roses of health on our cheek, the light of hope in our eyes, the fires of youth and hope burning in our hearts. We left the old familiar paths, the associations of home and the friends of childhood. We left schools and churches—all that made life dear—and turned our faces toward the setting sun. We endured hardships, dangers and privations; hours of loneliness, fear and sorrow; our little babes were born upon those wide, unsheltered prairies; and there, upon the sweeping prairies beneath the cedar trees our hands have planted to mark the sacred place, our little ones lie buried. We toiled in the cabin and in the field; we planted trees and orchards; we helped our loved ones to make the prairie blossom as the rose. The neat cottage took the place of the sod shanty, the log-cabin and the humble dug-out.

Yet, after all our years of toil and privation, dangers and hardships upon the Western frontier, monopoly is taking our homes from us by an infamous system of mortgage foreclosure, the most infamous that has ever disgraced the statutes of a civilized nation. It takes from us at the rate of five hundred a month the homes that represent the best years of our life, our toil, our hopes, our happiness. How did it happen? The government, at the bid of Wall Street, repudiated its contracts with the people; the circulating medium was contracted in the interest of Shylock from $54 per capita to less than $8 per capita; or, as Senator Plumb tells us, "Our debts were increased;" or as grand Senator Stewart puts it, "For twenty years the market value of the dollar has gone down, till to-day the American laborer, in bitterness and wrath, asks which is the worst—the black slavery that has gone or the white slavery that has come?"

Do you wonder the women are joining the Alliance? I wonder if there is a woman in all this broad land who can afford to stay out of the Alliance. Our loyal, white-ribbon women should be heart and hand in this Farmers' Alliance movement, for the men whom we have sent to represent us are the only men in the councils of this nation who have not been elected on a liquor platform; and I want to say here, with exultant pride, that the five farmer Congressmen and the United States Senator we have sent up from Kansas—the liquor traffic, Wall Street "nor the gates of hell shall not prevail against them."

[At this point many women in the audience were severely shocked, and the orator explained that the phrase "gates of hell" was a quotation from the Bible.]

It would sound boastful were I to detail to you the active, earnest part the Kansas women took in the recent campaign. A Republican majority of 82,000 was reduced to less than 8,000 when we elected 97 representatives, 5 out of 7 Congressmen, and a United States Senator, for to the women of Kansas belongs the credit of defeating John J. Ingalls. He is feeling badly about it yet, too; for he said to-day that "women and Indians were the only class that would scalp a dead man." I rejoice that he realizes that he is politically dead.

I might weary you to tell you in detail how the Alliance women found time from cares of home and children to prepare the tempting, generous viands for the Alliance picnic dinners, where hungry thousands and tens of thousands gathered in the forests and groves to listen to the words of impassioned oratory, ofttimes from woman's lips, that nerved the men of Kansas to forget their party prejudice and vote for "Mollie and the babies." And not only did they find their way to the voters' hearts, through their stomachs, but they sang their way as well. I hold here a book of Alliance songs, composed and set to music by an Alliance woman, Mrs. Florence Olmstead of Butler County, Kan., that did much toward moulding public sentiment. Alliance Glee Clubs, composed of women, gave us such stirring melodies as the nation has not heard since the Tippecanoe and Tyler campaign of 1840. And while I am individualizing, let me call your attention to a book written also by an Alliance woman. I wish a copy of it could be placed in the hands of every woman in this land. "The Fate of a Fool" is written by Mrs. Emma G. Curtis of Colorado. This book in the hands of women would teach them to be just and generous toward women, and help them to forgive and condone in each other the sins so sweetly forgiven when committed by men.

[Here the gavel announced that the time was up, but the speaker begged for and received a short extension.]

Let no one for a moment believe that this uprising and federation of the people is but a passing episode in politics. It is a religious as well as a political movement, for we seek to put into practical operation the teachings and precepts of Jesus of Nazareth. We seek to enact justice and equity between man and man. We seek to bring the nation back to the constitutional liberties guaranteed us by our forefathers. The voice that is coming up to-day from the mystic chords of the American heart is the same voice that Lincoln heard blending with the guns of Fort Sumter and the Wilderness, and it is breaking into a clarion cry to-day that will be heard around the world.

Crowns will fall, thrones will tremble, kingdoms will disappear, the divine right of kings and the divine right of capital will fade away like the mists of the morning when the Angel of Liberty shall kindle the fires of justice in the hearts of men. "Exact justice to all, special privileges to none." No more millionaires, and no more paupers; no more gold kings, silver kings and oil kings, and no more little waifs of humanity starving for a crust of bread. No more gaunt-faced, hollow-eyed girls in the factories, and no more little boys reared in poverty and crime for the penitentiaries and the gallows. But we shall have the golden age of which Isaiah sang and the prophets have so long foretold; when the farmers shall be prosperous and happy, dwelling under their own vine and fig tree; when the laborer shall have that for which he toils; when occupancy and use shall be the only title to land, and every one shall obey the divine injunction, "In the sweat of thy face shall thou eat bread." When men shall be just and generous, little less than gods, and women shall be just and charitable toward each other, little less than angels; when we shall have not a government of the people by capitalists, but a government of the people, by the people.

Ladies and gentlemen, I thank you.

TO THE PRESIDENT, IN THE NEGRO'S BEHALF

For decades after the official end of Reconstruction, African Americans in Wilmington, North Carolina, who composed more than half of the city's population, were well represented in political office there, and they gained especially strong political power between 1895 and 1898, when a Republican and Populist majority held sway. In 1898, after a vicious white supremacist campaign in state legislative elections was victorious, a "riot" against black rule in Wilmington broke out. At least ten African Americans died, three whites were wounded, the city's black newspaper was destroyed, and scores of legitimate black office-holders were run out of town. After the riot, white Democrats seized local political office. One African American woman's political and communal involvement took the form of this unusual plea for federal assistance.

Wilmington N.C. Nov. 13, 1898

Wm. McKinley—President of the United States of America

Hon. Sir,

I a Negro woman of this city, appeal to you from the depths of my heart, to do something in the Negro's behalf. The outside world only knows one side of the trouble here, there is no paper to tell the truth about the Negro here in this or any other Southern state. The Negro in this town had no arms (except pistols perhaps in some instances) with which to defend themselves from the attack of lawless whites. On the 10th Thursday morning between eight and nine o'clock when all Negro men had gone to their places of work, the white men led by Col. A. M. Waddell, Jno D. Bellamy, and S. H. Fishblatt marched from the Light Infantry armory on Market st. up to seventh down seventh to Love & Charity Hall (which is owned by a society of Negroes.) And where the Negro daily press was.) and set it afire & burnt it up. And firing Guns Winchesters they also had a Hotchkiss gun & two Colt rapid fire guns. We the negro expected nothing of the kind as they (the whites) had frightened them from the polls saying they would be there with their shotguns, so the few that did vote did so quietly. And we thought after giving up to them and they carried the state it was settled. But they or Jno D. Bellamy told them—in addition to the guns they already had they could keep back federal interference. And he could have the Soldiers at

[Anon.] to President McKinley. November 13, 1898. File 17743–1898. RG R660. Department of Justice. National Archives. The editors are indebted to Glenda Gilmore for locating and providing a copy of this document.

Ft Caswell to take up arms against the United States. After destroying the building they went over in Brooklyn another Negro settlement mostly, and began searching everyone and if you did not submit would be shot down on the spot. They searched all the Negro Churches. And to day (Sunday) we dare not go to our places of worship. They found no guns or ammunition in any of the places for there was none, And to satisfy their Bloodthirsty appetites would Kill unoffending Negro men to or on their way from dinner. Some of our most worthy Negro Men have been made to leave the city. Also some whites, G. J. French, Deputy Sheriff, Chief of Police Jno R. Melton, Dr. S. P. Wright Mayor and R. H. Bunting united states comissioner. We don't know where Mr. Chadbourn the post master is, and two or three others white. I call on you the head of the American nation to help these humble subjects. We are loyal, we go when duty calls us. And are we to die like rats in a trap? With no place to seek redress or to go with our Greivances? Can we call on any other nation for help? Why do you forsake the Negro? who is not to blame for being here. This Grand and noble nation who flies to the help of suffering humanity of another nation? and leave the Secessionists and born Rioters to slay us. Oh, that we had never seen the light of the world. When our parents belonged to them, why the negro was all right[;] now, when they work and accumalate property they are all wrong. The Negroes that have been banished are all property owners to considerable extent, had they been worthless negroes, we would not care.

Will you for God sake in your next message to Congress give us some releif. If you send us all to Africa we will be willing or a number of us will gladly go. Is this the land of the free and the home of the brave? How can the Negro sing my country tis of thee? For Humanity sake help us, for Christ sake do. We the Negro can do nothing but pray. There seems to be no help for us. No paper will tell the truth about the Negro. The men of the 1st North Carolina were home on a furlough and they took a high hand in the nefarious work. Also the companies from every little town came in to kill the negro. There was not any Rioting simply the strong slaying the weak. They speak of special police every white man and boy from 12 years up has a gun or pistol, and the negro had nothing, his soul he could not say was his own. Oh, do see how we are Slaughtered, when our husbands go to work we do not look for their return. The Man who promises the Negro protection now as Mayor is the one who in his speech at the Opera house said the Cape Fear should be strewn with carcasses. Some papers I see say it was right to eject the Negro editor. That is all right but why should a whole city full of negroes suffer for Manly when he was hundred of miles away. And the paper had ceased publication. We were glad it was so for our own safety. But they tried to slay us all. To day we are mourners in a strange land with no protection near. God help us. Do something to alleviate our sorrows if you please. I cannot sign my name and live. But every word of this is true. The laws of our state is no good for the negro anyhow. Yours in much distress, Wilmington NC.

[P.S.] Please send releif as soon as possible, or we perish.

AN INDIAN TEACHER AMONG INDIANS

Born in 1876 on the Yankton Sioux Reservation in Dakota Territory, Gertrude Bonnin chose the pen name Zitkala-Ša after struggling to forge an identity as an educated Indian. Child of a white father, she was raised by her mother speaking only Dakota. At the age of eight she followed the urging of missionaries to leave home to attend a Quaker boarding school for Indians, where she spent seven of the next eleven years. After attending Earlham College, she published numerous stories and autobiographical sketches about the pain of growing up between two worlds. At this point in her autobiographical story, she is a young adult working as a teacher at Carlisle Indian School in Pennsylvania.

One black night mother and I sat alone in the dim starlight, in front of our wigwam. We were facing the river, as we talked about the shrinking limits of the village. She told me about the poverty-stricken white settlers, who lived in caves dug in the long ravines of the high hills across the river.

A whole tribe of broad-footed white beggars had rushed hither to make claims on those wild lands. Even as she was telling this I spied a small glimmering light in the bluffs.

"That is a white man's lodge where you see the burning fire," she said. Then, a short distance from it, only a little lower than the first, was another light. As I became accustomed to the night, I saw more and more twinkling lights, here and there, scattered all along the wide black margin of the river.

Still looking toward the distant firelight, my mother continued: "My daughter, beware of the paleface. It was the cruel paleface who caused the death of your sister and your uncle, my brave brother. It is this same paleface who offers in one palm the holy papers, and with the other gives a holy baptism of firewater. He is the hypocrite who reads with one eye, 'Thou shalt not kill,' and with the other gloats upon the sufferings of the Indian race." Then suddenly discovering a new fire in the bluffs, she exclaimed, "Well, well, my daughter, there is the light of another white rascal!"

She sprang to her feet, and, standing firm beside her wigwam, she sent a curse upon those who sat around the hated white man's light. Raising her right arm forcibly into line with her eye, she threw her whole might

Zitkala-Ša (Gertrude Bonnin), *American Indian Stories* (Washington, D.C.: Hayworth Publishing House, 1921; rept. Lincoln: University of Nebraska Press, 1985), pp. 93–99.

into her double fist as she shot it vehemently at the strangers. Long she held her outstretched fingers toward the settler's lodge, as if an invisible power passed from them to the evil at which she aimed.

Leaving my mother, I returned to the school in the East. As months passed over me, I slowly comprehended that the large army of white teachers in Indian schools had a larger missionary creed than I had suspected.

It was one which included self-preservation quite as much as Indian education. When I saw an opium-eater holding a position as teacher of Indians, I did not understand what good was expected, until a Christian in power replied that this pumpkin-colored creature had a feeble mother to support. An inebriate paleface sat stupid in a doctor's chair, while Indian patients carried their ailments to untimely graves, because his fair wife was dependent upon him for her daily food.

I find it hard to count that white man a teacher who tortured an ambitious Indian youth by frequently reminding the brave changeling that he was nothing but a "government pauper."

Though I burned with indignation upon discovering on every side instances no less shameful than those I have mentioned, there was no present help. Even the few rare ones who have worked nobly for my race were powerless to choose workmen like themselves. To be sure, a man was sent from the Great Father to inspect Indian schools, but what he saw was usually the students' sample work *made* for exhibition. I was nettled by this sly cunning of the workmen who hookwinked the Indian's pale Father at Washington.

My illness, which prevented the conclusion of my college course, together with my mother's stories of the encroaching frontier settlers, left me in no mood to strain my eyes in searching for latent good in my white co-workers.

At this stage of my own evolution, I was ready to curse men of small capacity for being the dwarfs their God had made them. In the process of my education I had lost all consciousness of the nature world about me. Thus, when a hidden rage took me to the small white-walled prison which I then called my room, I unknowingly turned away from my one salvation.

Alone in my room, I sat like the petrified Indian woman of whom my mother used to tell me. I wished my heart's burdens would turn me to unfeeling stone. But alive, in my tomb, I was destitute!

For the white man's papers I had given up my faith in the Great Spirit. For these same papers I had forgotten the healing in trees and brooks. On account of my mother's simple view of life, and my lack of any, I gave her up, also. I made no friends among the race of people I loathed. Like a slender tree, I had been uprooted from my mother, nature, and God. I was shorn of my branches, which had waved in sympathy and love for home and friends. The natural coat of bark which had protected my over-sensitive nature was scraped off to the very quick.

Now a cold bare pole I seemed to be, planted in a strange earth. Still, I seemed to hope a day would come when my mute aching head, reared upward to the sky, would flash a zigzag lightning across the heavens. With this dream of vent for a long-pent consciousness, I walked again amid the crowds.

At last, one weary day in the schoolroom, a new idea presented itself to me. It was a new way of solving the problem of my inner self. I liked it. Thus I resigned my position as teacher; and now I am in an Eastern city, following the long course of study I have set for myself. Now, as I look back upon the recent past, I see it from a distance, as a whole. I remember how, from morning till evening, many specimens of civilized peoples visited the Indian school. The city folks with canes and eye-glasses, the countrymen with sunburnt cheeks and clumsy feet, forgot their relative social ranks in an ignorant curiosity. Both sorts of these Christian palefaces were alike astounded at seeing the children of savage warriors so docile and industrious.

As answers to their shallow inquiries they received the students' sample work to look upon. Examining the neatly figured pages, and gazing upon the Indian girls and boys bending over their books, the white visitors walked out of the schoolhouse well satisfied: they were educating the children of the red man! They were paying a liberal fee to the government employees in whose able hands lay the small forest of Indian timber.

In this fashion many have passed idly through the Indian schools during the last decade, afterward to boast of their charity to the North American Indian. But few there are who have paused to question whether real life or long-lasting death lies beneath this semblance of civilization.

THE STORY OF A SWEATSHOP GIRL

Between 1880 and 1923, three million Jewish immigrants fled the poverty and persecution of eastern Europe and Russia to come to America. Many— men and women—found work in the new ready-to-wear clothing industry, in which both Jewish employers and Jewish laborers played a leading part. Sixteen-year-old New Yorker Sadie Frowne told her story to an editor of a liberal journal, the Independent, *where it was published as one of a series of life stories of ordinary Americans.*

My mother was a tall, handsome, dark complexioned woman with red cheeks, large brown eyes and a great quantity of jet black, wavy hair. She was well educated, being able to talk in Russian, German, Polish and French, and even to read English print, tho, of course, she did not know what it meant. She kept a little grocer's shop in the little village where we lived at first. That was in Poland, somewhere on the frontier, and mother had charge of a gate between the countries, so that everybody who came through the gate had to show her a pass. She was much looked up to by the people, who used to come and ask her for advice. Her word was like law among them.

She had a wagon in which she used to drive about the country, selling her groceries, and sometimes she worked in the fields with my father.

The grocer's shop was only one story high, and had one window, with very small panes of glass. We had two rooms behind it, and were happy while my father lived, altho we had to work very hard. By the time I was six years of age I was able to wash dishes and scrub floors, and by the time I was eight I attended to the shop while my mother was away driving her wagon or working in the fields with my father. She was strong and could work like a man.

When I was a little more than ten years of age my father died. He was a good man and a steady worker, and we never knew what it was to be hungry while he lived. After he died troubles began, for the rent of our shop was about $6 a month and then there were food and clothes to provide. We needed little, it is true, but even soup, black bread and onions we could not always get.

We struggled along till I was nearly thirteen years of age and quite handy at housework and shop keeping, so far as I could learn them there. But we fell behind in the rent and mother kept thinking more and more

Sadie Frowne, "The Story of a Sweatshop Girl," *Independent* 54 (September 25, 1902), pp. 2279–82.

that we should have to leave Poland and go across the sea to America where we heard it was much easier to make money. Mother wrote to Aunt Fanny, who lived in New York, and told her how hard it was to live in Poland, and Aunt Fanny advised her to come and bring me. I was out at service at this time and mother thought she would leave me—as I had a good place—and come to this country alone, sending for me afterward. But Aunt Fanny would not hear of this. She said we should both come at once, and she went around among our relatives in New York and took up a subscription for our passage.

We came by steerage on a steamship in a very dark place that smelt dreadfully. There were hundreds of other people packed in with us, men, women and children, and almost all of them were sick. It took us twelve days to cross the sea, and we thought we should die, but at last the voyage was over, and we came up and saw the beautiful bay and the big woman with the spikes on her head and the lamp that is lighted at night in her hand (Goddess of Liberty).

Aunt Fanny and her husband met us at the gate of this country and were very good to us, and soon I had a place to live out (domestic servant), while my mother got work in a factory making white goods.

I was only a little over thirteen years of age and a greenhorn, so I received $9 a month and board and lodging, which I thought was doing well. Mother, who, as I have said, was very clever, made $9 a week on white goods, which means all sorts of underclothing, and is high class work.

But mother had a very gay disposition. She liked to go around and see everything, and friends took her about New York at night and she caught a bad cold and coughed and coughed. She really had hasty consumption, but she didn't know it, and I didn't know it, and she tried to keep on working, but it was no use. She had not the strength. Two doctors attended her, but they could do nothing, and at last she died and I was left alone. I had saved money while out at service, but mother's sickness and funeral swept it all away and now I had to begin all over again.

Aunt Fanny had always been anxious for me to get an education, as I did not know how to read or write, and she thought that was wrong. Schools are different in Poland from what they are in this country, and I was always too busy to learn to read and write. So when mother died I thought I would try to learn a trade and then I could go to school at night and learn to speak the English language well.

So I went to work in Allen street (Manhattan) in what they call a sweatshop, making skirts by machine. I was new at the work and the foreman scolded me a great deal.

"Now, then," he would say, "this place is not for you to be looking around in. Attend to your work. That is what you have to do."

I did not know at first that you must not look around and talk, and I made many mistakes with the sewing, so that I was often called a "stupid animal." But I made $4 a week by working six days in the week. For there are two Sabbaths here—our own Sabbath, that comes on a Saturday, and the Christian Sabbath that comes on Sunday. It is against our law to work on our own Sabbath, so we work on their Sabbath.

In Poland I and my father and mother used to go to the synagogue on the Sabbath, but here the women don't go to the synagogue much, tho the men do. They are shut up working hard all the week long and when the Sabbath comes they like to sleep long in bed and afterward they must go out where they can breathe the air. The rabbis are strict here, but not so strict as in the old country.

I lived at this time with a girl named Ella, who worked in the same factory and made $5 a week. We had the room all to ourselves, paying $1.50 a week for it, and doing light housekeeping. It was in Allen street, and the window looked out of the back, which was good, because there was an elevated railroad in front, and in summer time a great deal of dust and dirt came in at the front windows. We were on the fourth story and could see all that was going on in the back rooms of the houses behind us, and early in the morning the sun used to come in our window.

We did our cooking on an oil stove, and lived well, as this list of our expenses for one week will show:

ELLA AND SADIE FOR FOOD (ONE WEEK).

Tea	$0.06
Cocoa	.10
Bread and rolls	.40
Canned vegetables	.20
Potatoes	.10
Milk	.21
Fruit	.20
Butter	.15
Meat	.60
Fish	.15
Laundry	.25
Total	$2.42
Add rent	1.50
Grand total	$3.92

Of course, we could have lived cheaper, but we are both fond of good things and felt that we could afford them.

We paid 18 cents for a half pound of tea so as to get it good, and it lasted us three weeks, because we had cocoa for breakfast. We paid 5 cents for six rolls and 5 cents a loaf for bread, which was the best quality. Oatmeal cost us 10 cents for three and one-half pounds, and we often had it in the morning, or Indian meal porridge in the place of it, costing about the same. Half a dozen eggs cost about 13 cents on an average, and we could get all the meat we wanted for a good hearty meal for 20 cents—two pounds of chops, or a steak, or a bit of veal, or a neck of lamb—something like that. Fish included butter fish, porgies, codfish and smelts, averaging about 8 cents a pound.

Some people who buy at the last of the market, when the men with the carts want to go home, can get things very cheap, but they are likely to be stale, and we did not often do that with fish, fresh vegetables, fruit, milk or meat. Things that kept well we did buy that way and got good bargains. I got thirty potatoes for 10 cents one time, tho generally I could not get more than 15 of them for that amount. Tomatoes, onions and cabbages, too, we bought that way and did well, and we found a factory where we could buy the finest broken crackers for 3 cents a pound, and another place where we got broken candy for 10 cents a pound. Our cooking was done on an oil stove, and the oil for the stove and the lamp cost us 10 cents a week.

It cost me $2 a week to live, and I had a dollar a week to spend on clothing and pleasure, and saved the other dollar. I went to night school, but it was hard work learning at first as I did not know much English.

Two years ago I came to this place, Brownsville, where so many of my people are, and where I have friends. I got work in a factory making underskirts—all sorts of cheap underskirts, like cotton and calico for the summer and woolen for the winter, but never the silk, satin or velvet underskirts. I earned $4.50 a week and lived on $2 a week, the same as before.

I got a room in the house of some friends who lived near the factory. I pay $1 a week for the room and am allowed to do light housekeeping—that is, cook my meals in it. I get my own breakfast in the morning, just a cup of coffee and a roll, and at noon time I come home to dinner and take a plate of soup and a slice of bread with the lady of the house. My food for a week costs a dollar, just as it did in Allen street, and I have the rest of my money to do as I like with. I am earning $5.50 a week now, and will probably get another increase soon.

It isn't piecework in our factory, but one is paid by the amount of work done just the same. So it is like piecework. All the hands get different amounts, some as low as $3.60 and some of the men as high as $16 a week. The factory is in the third story of a brick building. It is in a room twenty feet long and fourteen broad. There are fourteen machines in it. I and the daughter of the people with whom I live work two of these machines. The other operators are all men, some young and some old.

At first a few of the young men were rude. When they passed me they would touch my hair and talk about my eyes and my red cheeks, and make jokes. I cried and said that if they did not stop I would leave the place. The boss said that that should not be, that no one must annoy me. Some of the other men stood up for me, too, especially Henry, who said two or three times that he wanted to fight. Now the men all treat me very nicely. It was just that some of them did not know better, not being educated.

Henry is tall and dark, and he has a small mustache. His eyes are brown and large. He is pale and much educated, having been to school. He knows a great many things and has some money saved. I think nearly $400. He is not going to be in a sweatshop all the time, but will soon be in the real estate business, for a lawyer that knows him well has promised to open an office and pay him to manage it.

Henry has seen me home every night for a long time and makes love to me. He wants me to marry him, but I am not seventeen yet, and I think that is too young. He is only nineteen, so we can wait.

I have been to the fortune teller's three or four times, and she always tells me that tho I have had such a lot of trouble I am to be very rich and happy. I believe her because she has told so many things that have come true. So I will keep on working in the factory for a time. Of course it is hard, but I would have to work hard even if I was married.

I get up at half-past five o'clock every morning and make myself a cup of coffee on the oil stove. I eat a bit of bread and perhaps some fruit and then go to work. Often I get there soon after six o'clock so as to be in good time, tho the factory does not open till seven. I have heard that there is a sort of clock that calls you at the very time you want to get up, but I can't believe that because I don't see how the clock would know.

At seven o'clock we all sit down to our machines and the boss brings to each one the pile of work that he or she is to finish during the day, what they call in English their "stint." This pile is put down beside the machine and as soon as a skirt is done it is laid on the other side of the machine. Sometimes the work is not all finished by six o'clock and then the one who is behind must work overtime. Sometimes one is finished ahead of time and gets away at four or five o'clock, but generally we are not done till six o'clock.

The machines go like mad all day, because the faster you work the more money you get. Sometimes in my haste I get my finger caught and the needle goes right through it. It goes so quick, tho, that it does not hurt much. I bind the finger up with a piece of cotton and go on working. We all have accidents like that. Where the needle goes through the nail it makes a sore finger, or where it splinters a bone it does much harm. Sometimes a finger has to come off. Generally, tho, one can be cured by a salve.

All the time we are working the boss walks about examining the finished garments and making us do them over again if they are not just right. So we have to be careful as well as swift. But I am getting so good at the work that within a year I will be making $7 a week, and then I can save at least $3.50 a week. I have over $200 saved now.

The machines are all run by foot power, and at the end of the day one feels so weak that there is a great temptation to lie right down and sleep. But you must go out and get air, and have some pleasure. So instead of lying down I go out, generally with Henry. Sometimes we go to Coney Island, where there are good dancing places, and sometimes we go to Ulmer Park to picnics. I am very fond of dancing, and, in fact, all sorts of pleasure. I go to the theater quite often, and like those plays that make you cry a great deal. "The Two Orphans" is good. Last time I saw it I cried all night because of the hard times that the children had in the play. I am going to see it again when it comes here.

For the last two winters I have been going to night school at Public School 84 on Glenmore avenue. I have learned reading, writing and arithmetic. I can read quite well in English now and I look at the newspapers every day. I read English books, too, sometimes. The last one that I read was "A Mad Marriage," by Charlotte Braeme. She's a grand writer and makes things just like real to you. You feel as if you were the poor girl yourself going to get married to a rich duke.

I am going back to night school again this winter. Plenty of my friends go there. Some of the women in my class are more than forty years of age. Like me, they did not have a chance to learn anything in the old country. It is good to have an education; it makes you feel higher. Ignorant people are all low. People say now that I am clever and fine in conversation.

We have just finished a strike in our business. It spread all over and the United Brotherhood of Garment Workers was in it. That takes in the cloakmakers, coatmakers, and all the others. We struck for shorter hours, and after being out four weeks won the fight. We only have to work nine and a half hours a day and we get the same pay as before. So the union does good after all in spite of what some people say against it—that it just takes our money and does nothing.

I pay 25 cents a month to the union, but I do not begrudge that because it is for our benefit. The next strike is going to be for a raise of wages, which we all ought to have. But tho I belong to the Union I am not a Socialist or an Anarchist. I don't know exactly what those things mean. There is a little expense for charity, too. If any worker is injured or sick we all give money to help.

Some of the women blame me very much because I spend so much money on clothes. They say that instead of a dollar a week I ought not to spend more than twenty-five cents a week on clothes, and that I should save the rest. But a girl must have clothes if she is to go into high society at Ulmer Park or Coney Island or the theatre. Those who blame me are the old country people who have old-fashioned notions, but the people who have been here a long time know better. A girl who does not dress well is stuck in a corner, even if she is pretty, and Aunt Fanny says that I do just right to put on plenty of style.

I have many friends and we often have jolly parties. Many of the young men like to talk to me, but I don't go out with any except Henry.

Lately he has been urging me more and more to get married—but I think I'll wait.

THE TYPEWRITER GIRL

Before the Civil War most office clerks were men. After 1870, as business expansion greatly multiplied low-level office tasks, employers became willing to hire native-born white women, who were prepared for office work by the spread of secondary education. In comparison to factory work, the prestige and respectability of the business world appealed to many women. The term "typewriter" was used at first both for the new machine and for the woman who operated it. We do not know whether Myra Hole worked in an office, but her poems, which present romance as the reward for putting up with the tedium of the "typewriter" job, appeared in Phonographic World, *a magazine for clerical workers.*

THE TYPEWRITER GIRL.

No. 1—Morning.

While the typewriter girl adjusts the last curl,
    And tenderly pats her new tie,
Her thoughts fly away to the work of the day,
    And she starts for her train with a sigh.

"If I only could stay here at home for a day
    How perfectly lovely 'twould be";
But once on the car the "blues" flit afar,
    For there's John, saying, "Come, sit with me."

How pleasant to ride with a friend by one's side
    Seven miles in the fresh morning air.
What though she is late? "Those letters can wait."
    The typewriter girl doesn't care.

But the day's well begun, for a trifle of fun
    Gives her eagerness for the day's work;
To the office she goes, with her cheeks like a rose,
    Resolved not one detail to shirk.

No. 2—Noon.

Among the hungry hordes that throng
The cafés, when the noon-day gong

Myra C. Hole, "The Typewriter Girl," *Phonographic World* 15, no. 2 (October 1899), p. 78; no. 3 (November 1899), p. 149; no. 4 (December 1899), p. 210. The editors are grateful to Ileen DeVault for locating and providing a copy of this document.

Sounds forth its welcome luncheon song,
　　You'll see the typist girl.
You know her by her costume neat,—
Though dainty, not too gay for street,—
Her gloves in hand, her well-shod feet,
　　Her calm air 'midst the whirl.

With stately mien she takes a chair,
And glances down the bill of fare,
Then orders with a reckless air:
　　"Ice-cream on berry pie."
She eats it daintily, of course;
Tries not to think 'twill be the source
Of pangs of hunger and remorse
　　To rack her by and by.

And now she hurries to the store,
There's only twenty minutes more,
And she has purchasing galore
　　That really must be done.
She can't find what she wants; the loss
Of precious time has made her cross,
And she goes back, to meet the boss
　　Eight minutes after one.

No. 3—EVENING.
When blows the loud blast that proclaims "Time at last
　　To put by the work of the day,"
The girl at the keys, with a sinking heart, sees
　　That she'll be requested to stay.

"Just a few letters more. How many? Oh, four;
　　It won't take you long to do those.
At this time of year with the Christmas trade near,
　　It's important that all the mail goes."

Hand and brain work as one—now the letters are done,
　　And she rises in haste to depart.
Outside it is chill, dark and raining; a thrill
　　Of lonely dismay fills her heart.

She's a minute too late for her car, and must wait,
　　The hardest of all things to do.

There's a mist in her eye, and she heaves a big sigh
    That comes pretty near a boo-hoo.

But who on earth's that in the dripping felt hat
    That he lifts with a smile, gay and true?
Tired, hungry, and wet, she can be cheerful yet,
    John had to work late tonight, too.

MURRAY HALL FOOLED MANY SHREWD MEN

In scattered and hard-to-find evidence (like the letters of Julia Underhill in "Union Women in Wartime," part 5) are repeated examples of nineteenth-century women who disguised themselves as men in order to gain opportunities unavailable to women, or to match their own predilections. Most of these remain unknown to history, but occasionally there was a celebrated exposure. The discovery in 1901 that a politician in New York City's Tammany machine was a woman caused a sensation in the press.

Murray H. Hall, the woman who masqueraded as a man for more than a quarter of a century, and the secret of whose sex came out only with her death last Wednesday night at 145 Sixth Avenue, was known to hundreds of people in the Thirteenth Senatorial District, where she figured quite prominently as a politician. In a limited circle she even had a reputation as a "man about town," a bon vivant and all-around "good fellow."

She was a member of the General Committee of Tammany Hall, a member of the Iroquois Club, a personal friend of State Senator "Barney" Martin and other officials, and one of the most active Tammany workers in the district.

She registered and voted at primaries and general elections for many years, and exercised considerable political influence with Tammany Hall, often securing appointments for friends, who have proved their fealty to the organization—never exciting the remotest suspicion as to her real sex.

She played poker at the clubs with city and State officials and politicians who flatter themselves on their cleverness and perspicacity, drank whisky and wine and smoked the regulation "big black cigar"—with the apparent relish and gusto of the real man-about-town.

Furthermore, Murray Hall is known to have been married twice, but the woman to whom she stood before the world in the attitude of a husband kept her secret as guardedly as she did.

The discovery of "Murray Hall's" true sex was not made until she was cold in death and beyond the chance of suffering humiliation from exposure. She had been suffering from a cancer in the left breast for several years . . . but she abjured medical advice for fear of disclosing her sex, and treated herself. When she felt that life was at a low ebb she sent for Dr. [William C.] Gallagher, the awful fear of exposure being supplanted

"Murray Hall Fooled Many Shrewd Men," *New York Times,* January 19, 1901.

by the dread of death. He made an examination and found that the cancer had eaten its way almost to the heart, and that it was a matter of only a few days, when death must ensue.

He kept this information from the patient, fearing the shock might hasten death. He deceived himself for "Murray Hall" knew as well as Dr. Gallagher that the end was near. In years gone by, from time to time, "Murray Hall" had purchased volume after volume of works on surgery and medicine until she possessed a good medical library. Those books were studied, and the knowledge gleaned, no doubt, served to a good purpose in avoiding detection.

Three months ago most of this library was sold to C. S. Pratt, a bookseller. . . . "I knew Hall well, having had many dealings with him, and believed him to be either a native of Ireland or a person of Irish extraction. He was well read and had no use for light literature. What he wanted and what I always sold him was some work on science. . . .

"During the seven years I knew him I never once suspected that he was anything else than what he appeared to be. While he was somewhat effeminate in appearance and talked in a falsetto voice, still his conduct and actions were distinctively masculine. This revelation is a stunner to me and I guess to everybody else who knew him."

"I wouldn't believe it if Dr. Gallagher, whom I know to be a man of undoubted veracity, hadn't said so," said Senator Bernard F. Martin. "Well, truly, it's most wonderful. Why, I knew him well. He was a member of the Tammany district organization, a hard worker for his party, and always had a good argument to put up for any candidate he favored. He used to come to the Iroquois club to see me and pay his dues, and occasionally he would crack a joke with some of the boys. He was a modest little fellow, but had a peppery temper and could say some cutting things when any one displeased him. Suspect he was a woman? Never. He dressed like a man and talked like a very sensible one. The only thing I ever thought eccentric about him was his clothing. Now that they say he's a woman, I can see through that. You see, he also wore a coat a size or two too large, but of good material. That was to conceal his form. He had a bushy head of black hair, which he wore long and parted on the left side. His face was always smooth, just as if he had just come from the barber's.

". . . He was at the polls every election day, voted once any way, as they say, and helped get out the vote. We made him a member of the General Committee, and he was always present and participated in the proceedings until the last two years. His health had been bad as the result of being knocked down on Fifth Avenue by a bicycle, and he had not been very active in politics of late."

Joseph Young, one of Senator Martin's most trusted lieutenants and an officer of the Iroquois Club, was the Tammany Captain of the district when Murray Hall served in the same capacity for the County Democracy.

"I knew him well," said Young, "and I remember that we both worked tooth and nail to get the larger vote. If he's a woman he's the wonder of all the ages, sure's you live, for no man could ever suspect it from his habits and actions.

"Why, we had several run-ins when he and I were opposing Captains. He'd try to influence my friends to vote against the regular organization ticket and he'd spend money and do all sorts of things to get votes. A woman? Why, he'd line up to the bar and take his whisky like any veteran, and didn't make faces over it, either. If he was a woman he ought to have been born a man, for he lived and looked like one."

. . . Hall began the career of a professional bondsman. The singular individual often befriended unfortunates for a consideration, and was doing a profitable business until, on one occasion, he qualified in a sum that aroused the Court's suspicion. . . .

Hall was arrested after attending a meeting at the Iroquois Club one night and locked up in the Macdougal Street Station, but didn't stay long.

On the way to the station the policeman who had the prisoner in charge accepted an invitation to step into Skelly's saloon at Tenth Street and Greenwich Avenue. They had several drinks, for which Hall paid. In the meantime Skelly had sent out for several politicians, who accompanied the officer and his prisoner to the station house. Skelly furnished a bond and Hall was released.

The party returned to Skelly's and had more drinks. Then Hall and several friends went to the Grapevine, Eleventh Street and Sixth Avenue, then to Teddy Ackerman's across from Jefferson Market, drinking wine in both places until they reached a high state of enthusiasm.

Hall was coaxed outside, refused to go home, and started to whip Policeman O'Connor, who tried to arrest him, and succeeded in putting a storm cloud draping under the officer's eye before he was handcuffed. Hall was finally returned to the station house two hours from the time of the first arrest, locked up, and kept over night. Next day his political friends "squared it," and he was released.

Hall's acquaintances, including Senator Martin, say that he appeared to be about fifty years of age. The death certificate places the age at seventy years.

John Bremer, proprietor of the Fifteenth Ward Hotel, Ninth Street and

Sixth Avenue, knew Hall well and had some business dealings with him. "He was a shrewd, bright man . . . ," said Mr. Bremer, "and I wouldn't believe he was a woman if it wasn't for Dr. Gallagher's statement. . . . He'd drink anything from beer up, but I never saw him smoke, though they say he did, and chew, too."

"Yes, 'n play poker or pinochle and was sweet on women," broke in a lawyer who lives at the hotel. "I've known him for a number of years. He could drink his weight in beer and stand up under it.

"Why, I saw him play poker with a party of the Jefferson Market clique one night, and he played the game like a veteran. And for nerve, well, I can't believe that he was a woman, that's all. . . .

"So he's a woman, eh? Well, I've read of such characters in fiction, but, if it's true, Hall's case beats anything in fact or fiction I can recall."

Mrs. Johanna Meyers, who keeps a newsstand and cigar store at 109 West Tenth Street, knew Hall for many years.

"He used to come in here and buy papers and books, but never tobacco," she said yesterday. "His wife used to come in, too. She was a large, good-looking woman, almost twice her husband's weight. She did most of the business in the intelligence office up to the time of her death. She never intimated to me that her husband was a woman, neither did Hall himself nor their adopted daughter, Minnie.

"Last week Wednesday, Mr. Hall sent a servant around here with a message that he was very sick and for me to call without fail between 2 and 3 o'clock next afternoon. My husband was very bad from the grip at the time, and I didn't get a chance to go. He didn't send for me again. He thought a great deal of me and used to come in and sit down and read for hours.

"On my last birthday he gave me a large cake for a present. Not once did I ever suspect from word or action that he was masquerading and was really a woman. I believe that he meant to confide in me and tell me his secret when he sent for me. If I had only suspected I certainly would have gone to see him. His adopted daughter, Minnie, was here this morning.

"The poor girl is terribly shocked over the disclosure. She said she had always believed her foster father was a man, and never heard her foster mother say anything that would lead her to suspect otherwise."

Minnie Hall, the adopted daughter, is the sole heir. She is twenty-two years old. . . .

Where Murray Hall came from, or who she really was, no one seems to know, not even the adopted daughter. It was about twenty-five years ago that "he" first came to public notice in New York. About that time he opened an employment bureau. . . . He had with him a woman known as his wife.

After about three years the wife made complaints to neighbors that her husband was making her life miserable: that he flirted with clients and paid altogether too much attention to other women. This woman suddenly disappeared. Whither she went, when or how, no one knows. The husband never spoke of her after her disappearance, and no one cared enough to make inquiries.

About fifteen years ago Hall moved to a building between Seventeenth and Eighteenth Streets, where he soon after introduced the woman who was known as Mrs. Hall as his second wife. The couple seemed to get along peaceably until seven years ago when they moved to 145 Sixth Avenue. Then, neighbors say, they quarrelled, Mrs. Hall declaring her husband was too attentive to other women. That was the first known of Minnie Hall, the adopted daughter.

Who the child was or where she came from is as much a mystery as the early history of Murray Hall. How a woman could for so many years impersonate a man without detection, deceiving even her physician and some of the cleverest men and women in New York with whom she frequently came in contact, though the secret must have been known to at least two others—the wives—is a mystery quite as inexplicable as the character that accomplished the feat.